Teaching Children to Write

Theory into Practice

Jane B. Hughey
Texas A&M University

Charlotte Slack
College Station, Texas, Public Schools

Merrill
Prentice Hall

Upper Saddle River, New Jersey
Columbus, Ohio

Library of Congress Cataloging-In-Publication Data

Hughey, Jane B.
    Teaching children to write: theory into practice / Jane B. Hughey, Charlotte Slack.
      p. cm.
    Includes bibliographical references and index.
    ISBN 0-13-095194-3
     1. English language—Composition and exercises—Study and teaching. 2. Language arts.
  3. Multiple intelligences. 4. Cognitive styles in children. I. Slack, Charlotte. II. Title.
LB1576 .H7845 2001
372.62'3—dc21   00-039427

Vice President and Publisher: Jeffery W. Johnston
Editor: Linda Ashe Montgomery
Editorial Assistant: Jennifer Day
Production Editor: Mary M. Irvin
Design Coordinator: Karrie Converse-Jones
Project Coordination and Text Design: Carlisle Publishers Services
Cover Design: Rod Harris
Cover Art: Tony Stone
Production Manager: Pamela D. Bennett
Director of Marketing: Kevin Flanagan
Marketing Manager: Amy June
Marketing Services Manager: Krista Groshong

This book was set in New Caledonia by Carlisle Communications, Ltd. and was printed
and bound by R. R. Donnelley & Sons Company. The cover was printed by Phoenix Color Corp.

Photo Credits: All photos by Charlotte Slack

10 9 8 7 6 5 4 3 2 1
ISBN 0-13-095194-3

Preface

Throughout the ages, rhetoric and writing have been significant factors in making and preserving history. Aristotle's logic and his advice about the use of the language around 200 B.C., Gutenberg's creation of the printing press in the 15th century, and the 20th century's gift of technology—all were born of our ability to use and communicate in written language. It is widely recognized that literacy is the mark of an educated person and that a high level of literacy is critical to achieve and maintain a democratic society. How, then, can it be anything but an essential part in our teaching?

Teaching children to write is an awesome responsibility. Since expressing ideas in writing is a basic tenet of literacy, as teachers are obligated to help students become competent, if not accomplished, writers. The purpose of this text is to help teachers successfully accomplish this task.

Other subjects such as reading, mathematics, science, and social studies have relatively standard content and methods along with a plethora of texts, how-to manuals, and directives from state and school district documents. Writing, on the other hand, is often more difficult to teach. Even though curriculum documents identify specific competencies for student success, there are few state-adopted texts, and how-to teaching manuals are almost nonexistent. Teachers are often left on their own to find the necessary resources for teaching writing. Many use trial-and-error methods until they finally settle on some strategies that seem successful, for at least some of their students.

College curricula share some responsibility for the lack of teachers' preparation for teaching writing. In our experience, most preservice and beginning teachers feel far less prepared to teach children to write than they do to teach the other subject areas. Part of this difficulty may come from the widely differing theories about the best strategies for writing instruction. For example, some theorists say that giving children instruction in writing stifles their creativity, while others maintain that students must first learn to develop accurate sentence structures before writing. In one case, children write and write and write without focus on the writing conventions. In the other case, children focus on grammar, sentence diagramming, spelling, and mechanics to the exclusion of developing meaningful thought.

Teaching Children to Write: Theory into Practice blends differing theories into an approach that provides preservice teachers with the solid content and preparation they need to enter the workshop or writing classroom with confidence in their abilities to teach children to write. At the same time, it shows them how to provide children with the freedom they need for creative authorship.

Understanding and Using the Text

Along the margin of each page are quotations from leading researchers and practitioners in the field of writing. These kernels of theory and practice are invaluable to instructors as well as preservice teachers for six reasons.

1. They reinforce the content and practical application of the text.
2. They support the research base and validity of the text.
3. They familiarize preservice teachers with the names of leaders in the field of teaching and writing.
4. They offer topics for discussion among the preservice teachers.
5. They suggest topics and references for further study.
6. They provide a format that makes the text accessible to students.

The multiple intelligences (MIs) theory is introduced in the first chapter. We believe it is a strong factor in successful teaching in the writing workshop. Suggestions for using a multiple intelligences approach are interwoven throughout the book, and a list of possible applications, "Emphasizing the Multiple Intelligences," appears near the end of each chapter. We suggest that the MIs are an essential element of our preservice teachers' evaluation of their own strengths and of the learning strengths of the children they will teach.

A "Theory into Practice" section is the culmination of each chapter and offers discussion questions, topics, and hands-on applications. Activities range from lesson planning to cooperative group work to developing children's literature collections for a teacher's writing workshop. This section is intended for use in the college classroom and in a field-based setting, if one is available.

Several chapters end with a list of children's literature that is applicable to the specific kind of writing presented in the chapter; a bibliography of the professional references in the chapter is also included. This feature facilitates the preservice teacher's search for materials necessary for lesson planning, research papers, and projects.

Each chapter stands alone as a unit for study and discussion. The textbook begins with the basics of teaching that help create a smooth-running writing workshop: student intelligences and learning styles, teaching techniques, strategies to meet individual needs, classroom setting and governance, group work, lesson design, and writing expanded across the curriculum. A chapter on writing assessment methods and their effective applications as teaching tools provides important information for new teachers of writing. An effective approach to integrating grammar into the writing process also appears before preservice teachers delve into the specific strategies for teaching the purposes of writing. Many writing texts skip over these essentials, assuming that they are taught in other courses. We feel strongly that preservice teachers' understanding of these basic essentials largely determines their success in the writing workshop.

Following the essentials presented in the beginning chapters, the text then moves into the deeper content of teaching children to write in a variety of genres and for a variety of purposes, beginning with journal writing and ending with report writing. Since some preservice teachers are preparing for kindergarten and others for eighth grade, we have included topics ranging from helping beginning writers express their thoughts by drawing pictures, to the more sophisticated expression of argument and persuasion. In addition, preservice teachers are encouraged by chapter activities to practice writing in the genres and modes presented so that they are experiencing the writing process that they will be teaching, a habit that the successful teacher of writing must develop.

Since each chapter stands alone, instructors can follow the order that best suits their needs and the needs of their students as they move through the semester. *Teaching Children to Write: Theory into Practice* can be used as a text for undergraduate or graduate writing courses, or as one of a series of texts for language arts courses. Teachers in the field will find it a useful reference in their classrooms.

Acknowledgments

We extend our deep gratitude and thanks to the many colleagues, family, and friends who have supported our efforts and encouraged us along the way. Our special thanks also to those of our students who have taught us what it means to be teachers of writing and "teachers of teachers" of writing. They have been our best teachers. We express our appreciation to the many preservice teachers at Texas A&M University who proved that they could enter a classroom with confidence and enthusiasm for sharing their love of writing with others. We thank the children at Jones Elementary School in Bryan, Texas, and at Southwood Valley Elementary School, in College Station, Texas, who were excited to see the preservice teachers from our Writing Buddy Program arriving to write with them each week. Thanks to dedicated teacher of writing Marisa C. Suhm for sharing her personal journals.

We especially thank those children at Rock Prairie Elementary School and College Station Middle School in College Station, Texas, whose writing samples and photographs appear in our text. Authors whose work appears in the text include: Amie Adams; Ethan Alden; Zachary Baker; Sara Bennett; Sarah Bosse; Ashley Browder; Ellen Bruxvoort; Jessica Campbell; Rebeca Carranza; Daniel Cherbonnier; Deepak Chona; Leyla Choobineh; Nick Commella; Chris Connor; Shannon DuBose; Erick Feng; Thane Fox; Joshua Gantt; Stephen Gehring; Kim Gent; Cole Hanks; Jud Holt; Whitney Holt; Stacey Ingram; Darien Jochen; Vincent Jochen; Ashley Joiner; Georgie Kenney; Paula Kim; Mark Knight; Alex Liu; Brian Liu; Matthew Maddux; Greg Mikeska; Michelle Milburn; Leandra Montoya; Katie Nagyvary; Gavin Norton; Grady Norton; Keegan O'Connell; Sean O'Quinn; Trevor Scott; Katie Seidel; Ellen C. Smith; Zach Smith; Amanda Spaw; Lindsay Speake; Ali Spurgeon; Alex Stephens; Amanda Stone; David Straube; Becky Turner; Hallie Webb; Chris Weldon; and Seth White.

Papers by these students appear in the Instructors' Manual only: Erica Bell; Michael Cifuentes; Marco Miller.

Thanks also to the teachers and parents who shared writing samples with us.

We also thank the reviews of our manuscript for their comments and insights: Tom Bean, The University of Nevada—Las Vegas; Wanda G. Breedlove, The University of South Carolina; Linda Amspaugh-Corson, The University of Cincinnati; Sheila Fitzgerald, Michigan State University; Tanzella J. Gaither, Kershaw County Schools; Sandra R. Hurley, The University of Texas—El Paso; Pose Lamb, Purdue University; Donna J. Merkley, Iowa State University; Ray Ostrander, Andrews University; David G. Perkosh, Cabrini College; and Betty Jo McCarty-Roberts, Florida State University.

Discover the Companion Website Accompanying This Book

The Prentice Hall Companion Website: A Virtual Learning Environment

Technology is a constantly growing and changing aspect of our field that is creating a need for content and resources. To address this emerging need, Prentice Hall has developed an online learning environment for students and professors alike—Companion Websites—to support our textbooks.

In creating a Companion Website, our goal is to build on and enhance what the textbook already offers. For this reason, the content for each user-friendly website is organized by topic and provides the professor and student with a variety of meaningful resources. Common features of a Companion Website include:

For the Professor

Every Companion Website integrates **Syllabus Manager™**, an online syllabus creation and management utility.

- **Syllabus Manager™** provides you, the instructor, with an easy, step-by-step process to create and revise syllabi, with direct links into Companion Website and other online content without having to learn HTML.
- Students may logon to your syllabus during any study session. All they need to know is the web address for the Companion Website and the password you've assigned to your syllabus.
- After you have created a syllabus using **Syllabus Manager™,** students may enter the syllabus for their course section from any point in the Companion Website.
- Clicking on a date, the student is shown the list of activities for the assignment. The activities for each assignment are linked directly to actual content, saving time for students.
- Adding assignments consists of clicking on the desired due date, then filling in the details of the assignment—name of the assignment, instructions, and whether or

not it is a one-time or repeating assignment.

- In addition, links to other activities can be created easily. If the activity is online, a URL can be entered in the space provided, and it will be linked automatically in the final syllabus.
- Your completed syllabus is hosted on our servers, allowing convenient updates from any computer on the Internet. Changes you make to your syllabus are immediately available to your students at their next logon.

For the Student

- **Topic Overviews**—outline key concepts in topics areas
- **Electronic Bluebook**—send homework or essays directly to your instructor's email with this paperless form
- **Message Board**—serves as a virtual bulletin board to post—or respond to—questions or comments to/from a national audience
- **Chat**—real-time chat with anyone who is using the text anywhere in the country—ideal for discussion and study groups, class projects, etc.
- **Web Destinations**—links to www sites that relate to each topic area
- **Professional Organizations**—links to organizations that relate to topic areas
- **Additional Resources**—access to topic-specific content that enhances material found in the text

To take advantage of these and other resources, please visit the *Teaching Children to Write* Companion Website at

www.prenhall.com/hughey

About the Authors

Jane Hughey and her husband, John, live in College Station, Texas, and Oklahoma City, Oklahoma. They have three children and two grandchildren. Jane has been involved with writing research and evaluation and the teaching of writing for several decades. She has authored books and articles about writing. She is the director of Profile Approach to Writing, a National Diffusion Network program in the U.S. Department of Education. Jane has worked with school districts in all parts of the country. She serves on the graduate faculty in the Department of Curriculum and Instruction at Texas A&M University. She has been active in establishing Writing Buddy programs and working with professional development programs for preservice teachers through EDCI. She is currently the director of the English Language Institute at Texas A&M.

Charlotte Slack earned her bachelor's and master's degrees from The Ohio State University. Drawing on her 25 years of experience in the classroom, she is the author of numerous articles and two books on writing. She currently teaches in College Station, Texas, and frequently presents writing workshops at schools and conferences. She and her husband, Doug, have two daughters and one grandson.

Brief Contents

Contents

Teaching Children to Write

Set the Stage for Writing

*In workshops everybody writes. Teachers who compose
along with their students have no choice but to implicate
themselves in the same messy struggle toward meaning.*

Knoblauch and Brannon, 1984

Chapter Outline

3

Children love to communicate. They delight in sharing information about themselves and what they know with those around them. Because of their willingness to share and communicate, teaching children to write is an immensely rewarding experience. While many adults profess to dread writing and find it a difficult and arduous task, most children love to draw, talk, sing, and write about their feelings and experiences. When children are encouraged in their expression, celebrated in their efforts, and shown how to create effective pieces of writing, they are enthusiastic. They write much and they write often. Even those children without a natural "gift for gab" learn how to express themselves by exploring ideas, sharing experiences, and brainstorming with each other. A change in attitude toward self-expression, especially in writing, tends to develop as students progress through their formal education. As they take the risks that personal expression involves, they sometimes meet with criticism and correction rather than encouragement and support.

> My major objectives as a teacher are for students to develop positive attitudes toward writing and to increase their ability to negotiate the entire writing terrain, from conception to completion. Ziegler, 1981

To set the stage for positive teaching and learning, we will share with you what has worked for us in our writing classrooms. Our combined experiences with teaching writing come from several sources, ranging from our own classroom experiences, to teacher training, to study and observations of others' experiences, to our own research. *Teaching Children to Write: Theory into Practice* presents writing theory along with the successful application of that theory in a writing workshop setting. Throughout the book, we have placed theory and practice side-by-side. Kernels of theory from leading researchers in both education and writing appear in the margins alongside more detailed discussion of those theories. One of the precepts we follow in our approach comes from Vygotsky (1962): We begin where our students are in their learning, and we couch their learning in a social setting. The writing workshop experience provides the fertile ground for creative young writers to grow and blossom.

The Writing Workshop Experience

> Crucial to sustaining the atmosphere of intellectual responsibility in a workshop is the teacher's willingness to trust students' abilities to discover their own stances on important questions and willingness to give them time and flexibility for pursuing their own conclusions. Knoblauch and Brannon, 1984

The writing workshop is a unique setting with many special features. Characterized by both freedom and structure, the writing workshop is more like a laboratory or a studio than a regular or traditional classroom. Writers learn, experiment, share, and develop their skills with expert guidance in a safe and supportive environment.

Atwell (1987) says, "Writers need regular chunks of time" (p. 17) for exploration, inquiry, and the writing process: exploration and inquiry through channels such as talking with others, reading, researching, thinking, and scribbling. Most writers need this kind of incubation time. As Knoblauch and Brannon (1984) point out, "useful thought takes time, and workshops make time available" (p. 111). The writing workshop is a special chunk of time set aside for writing each day.

While the workshop is rooted in the *writing process*—prewriting, writing, revising, editing, and publishing—it includes much more. It sets the stage for writing as an ongoing *lifetime skill* with *multiple audiences and multiple purposes*. Children's *creativity* is enriched in both content and style when the *structures* of written communication are clearly presented to them. At the same time, they make choices about their own work. Teachers become facilitators and collaborators while providing children with a *safe environment* in which to produce writing.

Teachers write too. One of the ways we take responsibility for [...]
to be knowledgeable about writing, and to share our writing w[...]
students see that we, too, struggle at times to find just the right [...]
and start over, and that we get feedback when we get stuck. At [...]
our knowledge of writing with our students. Because the work[...]
plicity and structure, there are many other considerations as t[...]
sponsibility for their knowledge and teaching.

Graves (1983) says "the time for writing is set by what the teacher does, not by what the teacher says" (p. 12). To achieve the tone and mood we want in our workshop settings, we follow these guidelines.

Teaching Guidelines: The Writing Workshop

- Teachers wear many hats: writer, guide, collaborator, facilitator, and instructor.
- Writing is an ongoing process of discovery, inquiry, and development.
- Writers are free to explore their thoughts, experiences, and imaginations through the spectrum of their multiple intelligences and various learning styles.
- In collaborative groups, writers brainstorm ideas, share feedback on progress, and respond to finished products throughout the writing process.
- Individual writers have time for the more solitary acts of researching and generating information and creating and revising their own renditions of prose, poetry, letters, or reports.
- A variety of learner-centered writing experiences include peer group interaction, individual production time, and teacher-led instruction.
- Writers receive instruction in and experience with a wide array of writing modes, techniques, and skills.
- Writers frequently choose their own topics and projects.
- Teachers incorporate grammar and mechanics into the context of writing.
- Writers publish their work with peers and wider audiences.

Writing workshop, then, is both free and structured. Students are free to brainstorm, discuss, plan, share, and choose what they want to create. However, as Calkins and Harwayne (1987) note, "In the child-centered workshops . . . we have learned that youngsters need responsibility as well as choice. Choice does not need to be accompanied by chaos"(p. 33). We believe that the right kind of structure leads to higher levels of creativity and production.

Because of the complex and dynamic characteristics of writing, many of its aspects defy the tidy, logical formulas and theories that characterize many other disciplines. However, educational research on learning guides us on a broad path of generally accepted principles that apply to all subjects in the classroom setting and have specific implications for writing. In this section, theories of multiple intelligences, learning styles, teaching modes, group dynamics, and classroom management for the writing workshop set the stage for a successful writing program.

Writing teachers need to take responsibility for their knowledge and teaching. Atwell, 1987

Writing is a craft. It needs to be demonstrated to your students in your classroom . . . from choosing a topic to finishing a final draft. Graves, 1994

Students often need an external spark to ignite writing. Writers use instinct, experience, and talent to take the first step of the creative process: finding potential material. A good assignment is anything that helps students take that first step. Ziegler, 1984

In a writing workshop, the structure is more like that in an artist's studio. Calkins and Harwayne, 1987

Multiple Intelligences in the Writing Workshop

Any rich, nourishing topic—any concept worth teaching—can be approached in at least five different ways that . . . map onto the multiple intelligences. Gardner, 1993

The field of brain research is burgeoning with new information that has strong implications for how children learn and, therefore, how teachers teach. In this area, the work of researchers (Diamond & Hopson, 1998; Jensen, 1998; Caine & Caine, 1997; & Sylwester, 1995) offers knowledge for application to the classroom. Howard Gardner's (1983, 1987, 1993, 1997) work with the multiple intelligences meshes with the latest brain research and offers keen insights for teachers in providing successful writing experiences. When we teach with our students' multiple intelligences in mind, their writing promises higher creativity and excitement, and students increase and sustain their early enthusiasm for writing. We begin here, as we do in the workshop, by focusing on our writers' multiple intelligences (MI).

The Content and Products of Learning

Intelligence refers to the human ability to solve problems or to make something that is valued in one or more cultures. Gardner, 1993

Intelligences defined. What exactly do we mean by multiple intelligences? Everyone is endowed with some measure of the multiple intelligences. Traditional education practices identify and value two kinds of intelligence: linguistic and logical-mathematic. These two intelligences drive academic testing and the assessment of IQ. They are also the basis of many standardized academic tests such as NAEP, ITBS, SAT, ACT, GRE[1], and many statewide tests. While these two intelligences are vitally important to our ability to learn, they are only part of the learning equation.

Just as we look different from one another and have different kinds of personalities, we also have different kinds of minds. Gardner, 1983

Gardner (1997) identifies not two, but eight, different intelligences: linguistic, logical-mathematical, spatial, bodily-kinesthetic, musical, interpersonal, intrapersonal, and naturalist intelligence. He speculates that there may be even more. Gardner defines intelligence as "the ability to solve problems or to fashion products that are of consequence in a particular cultural setting or community" (Gardner, 1983, p. 7). He sees early identification of strengths as "very helpful in indicating what kinds of experiences children might profit from; but early identification of weaknesses can be equally important. If a weakness is identified early, there is a chance to attend to it before it is too late, and to come up with alternative ways of teaching or of covering an important skill area" (1993, p. 11).

We can all get better at each of the intelligences, although some people will improve in an intelligence area more readily than others, either because biology gave them a better brain for that intelligence or because their culture gave them a better teacher. Gardner, 1997

Figure 1–1, on the Multiple Intelligences Theory, defines the core components of each of the eight intelligences. According to Gardner's interpretation of the intelligences, they are inclusive; that is, everyone has all of the intelligences in varying strengths. Some people are stronger in some of the intelligences than in others. No two people are endowed with exactly the same set of intelligences. The varying strengths of our intelligences make a given subject "easy" for one person while causing another to struggle. If a classroom of children represents a potpourri of all the intelligences, then we as teachers need to teach to all of the intelligences so that all children learn. Throughout this text, we offer suggestions as to how to accomplish this goal.

---

[1]National Assessment of Educational Progress, Iowa Test of Basic Skills, Scholastic Aptitude Test, Academic Competency Test, Graduate Record Exam.

FIGURE 1–1
Multiple Intelligences Theory

INTELLIGENCE	DESCRIPTION
Linguistic	Capacity to use language to express what's on your mind and to understand other people. Sensitive to sounds, structure, meanings, and functions of words and language.
Logical-spatial	Capacity to understand the underlying principles of some kind of a causal system or to manipulate numbers, quantities, and operations. Sensitive to logical or numerical patterns; ability to handle long chains of reasoning.
Spatial	Capacity to represent the spatial world internally in your mind. Can perform transformations of initial perceptions.
Bodily-kinesthetic	Capacity to use the whole body or parts of the body—hand, fingers, arms—to solve a problem, make something, or put on some kind of a production. Ability to control body movements and handle objects skillfully.
Musical	Capacity to think in music; hear patterns and recognize, remember, and perhaps manipulate them. Ability to produce and appreciate rhythm and pitch; appreciation of the forms of musical expression.
Interpersonal	Capacity to understand people by discerning and responding appropriately to the moods, temperaments, motivations, and desires of other people.
Intrapersonal	Capacity to understand yourself, knowing who you are, what you can do, what you want to do, how you react to things, which things to avoid, and which things to gravitate toward. Ability to discriminate among emotions; knowledge of your weaknesses and strengths.
Naturalist	Capacity to discriminate among living things (plants, animals) and sensitivity to other features of the natural world (clouds, rock formations). Ability to recognize and classify living things and natural phenomena; ability to recognize cultural artifacts.

Adapted from Checkley, Kathy. The first seven…and the eighth: A conversation with Howard Gardner. *Educational Leadership*, 55 (September 1997), pp. 8–13.

If we can develop ways to teach and learn by engaging all seven [now eight] intelligences, we will increase the possibilities for student success. Campbell, 1995

Identifying teachers' multiple intelligences. We find that by knowing our own personal MI strengths and weaknesses, we become more sensitive to the individual learning needs of our students and to our own teaching styles, modes of presentation, and design of materials. We are a major part of this teaching and learning proposition, too. Most likely, our stronger intelligences will determine how we prefer to learn, how we tend to teach, and how we feel about teaching writing. We recommend that all teachers analyze their personal intelligences with Armstrong's (1994) Adult Multiple Intelligence Inventory in appendix A to develop a greater awareness of personal strengths and a sensitivity to the potential differences in groups of students.

In most areas of the curriculum, materials can be presented in a plethora of ways. Gardner, 1993

The ways in which intelligences combine and blend are as varied as the faces and the personalities of individuals. Blythe and Gardner, 1995

Identifying children's multiple intelligences.   In working with children, Armstrong (1994) suggests that the multiple intelligences be defined as ways of being smart. He tells children, "All of you are intelligent." Using his multiple intelligences "pizza" (Figure 1–2), we ask our children to identify and discuss the slices of the pizza on the chart and the accompanying questions that most closely resemble them.

QUESTIONS FOR DISCUSSING THE MULTIPLE INTELLIGENCE PIZZA

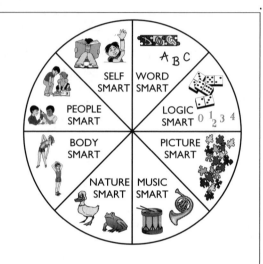

Word Smart:

How many of you can speak?

How many of you can write?

Number or Logic Smart:

How many of you can do math?

How many people here have done a science experiment?

Picture Smart:

How many of you draw?

How many people here can see pictures in their heads when they close their eyes?

How many of you enjoy watching moving pictures on television, in the movies, or in a Nintendo game?

Body Smart:

How many people here like sports?

How many of you enjoy making things with your hands, like models or LEGO structures?

Music Smart:

How many here enjoy listening to music?

How many have ever played a musical instrument or sung a song?

People Smart:

How many people have at least one friend?

How many of you enjoy working in groups at least part of the time here in school?

Self Smart:

How many of you have a secret or special place you go when you want to get away from everybody or everything?

How many of you like to spend at least part of the time working on your own in class?

Nature Smart:

How many of you would like to have class outside at least some of the time?

How many of you like to hike, fish, walk in the woods, or climb a tree?

How many of you like to see what different insects look and act like?

Adapted from Armstrong, Thomas. 1994. *Multiple Intelligences in the Classroom.* Alexandria, VA: Association for Supervision and Curriculum Design.

FIGURE 1–2   The MI Pizza

We celebrate the strengths and preferences of everyone in the class and emphasize that our differences will show us how to help each other. In addition, we use Armstrong's (1994) Checklist for Assessing Students' Multiple Intelligence in appendix B to gain further insights into the students' personal strengths. This information helps us plan effective ways to teach and group our students for writing experiences. We also keep in mind that the MIs are not permanent labels for children. "Children's intelligences, the manner in which they display them, and how successful they are, shift, grow, and vary over time (Hatch, 1997, p. 28).

By focusing on a variety of intelligences in our teaching, we can help students develop weaker intelligences and use the stronger intelligences as "entry points" to learning. When students develop specific ideas for a story, they may employ brainstorming (linguistic and interpersonal), hands-on experiences (kinesthetic), or visuals (spatial) to stimulate their inventive processes. These strategies provide a far more effective approach to teaching content development than the standard instruction teachers often give to children when they tell them to "think about something exciting and write about it." Thus, different intelligences lead to various strategies for addressing specific tasks. For example, when a student with a strong naturalist intelligence has difficulty understanding organizational strategies for various kinds of writing, we use patterns and examples from nature to help make the connection to the writing experience.

Discovering and taking into consideration students' multiple intelligences in the writing classroom have a great impact on student learning and on our teaching. By teaching the concept of descriptive writing in a variety of ways, we illustrate how the multiple intelligences become an integral part of daily lessons.

Teaching Strategies: Learning Description Through the Multiple Intelligences

Linguistic intelligence. Read books such as *Owl Moon* by Jane Yolen or *Chicken Sunday* by Patricia Palacco. Discuss the authors' use of adjectives, adverbs, similes, metaphors, and interesting verbs. A third-grade teacher in one of our schools uses cartoon characters to represent the five senses. Kalieda-Color, Nose Tickler, Sizzling Sound, Fuzzy Feeler, and Tongue Tingler (Landmann, 1990) appearing in appendix C are cartoon characters that stimulate lists of descriptive words to be referenced for later writing.

Spatial intelligence. Compose an oral or written story describing the actions and events in the wordless book *Tuesday* by David Wiesner. Display particularly interesting pictures and show films. Visualize and draw characters and settings that are described in a piece of writing. Draw the setting or characters for stories before writing about them. Construct a three-dimensional representation of a scene or a theme for a story.

Logical-mathematical intelligence. Arrange a student-made puzzle of a scene, a person, an object, describing what appears. Arrange a jumbled written description in its logical order. Read several of Donald Sobol's books from the Encyclopedia Brown series such as *Encyclopedia Brown: Boy Detective* or *Encyclopedia Brown and the Case of the Disgusting Sneakers.* Describe the logic and skills displayed by the main character.

Musical intelligence.   Listen to a variety of music and use description to characterize each piece. Make up songs that describe people, objects, or animals. Match appropriate music to different kinds of description or characters such as those in *Peter and the Wolf* by Sergio Prokofiev. Why does the piccolo represent the bird? How are they alike?

Bodily-kinesthetic intelligence.   Explore touch and feel books written for infants and toddlers such as *Pat the Bunny* and *Pat the Puppy* by Dorothy Kunhardt. Reach inside a mystery box or a bag of items. Without looking, feel and smell the items. Describe the objects with adjectives, similes, or metaphors. Create a diorama, describing it as it develops. Before or after writing, act out descriptions or characters. Play Charades.

Interpersonal intelligence.   Read *The Hundred Dresses* by Eleanor Estes, *My Friends* by Taro Gomi, or *Animal Farm* by George Orwell and discuss the interactions of the characters. In cooperative groups, brainstorm descriptive words that illustrate a scene or object from one of these books. Share feedback with peers in small group sessions.

Intrapersonal intelligence.   Create descriptions of a place or a feeling in your personal journal. Read *Amelia's Notebook* by Marisa Moss or some books from the *Dear America* series by Scholastic Publishers. Write a description of a place or a feeling from one of these books. Write a personal reaction to descriptive passages from literature.

Naturalist intelligence.   Read *Woodsong* by Gary Paulsen, *Ring of Bright Water* by Gavin Maxwell, or any number of books on nature. Walk on a nature trail, visit a garden or explore the playground in the rain. Describe what you see, smell, hear, touch, and feel, how things behave and change, or how things interact with each other.

These activities develop description in writing (linguistic intelligence) and illustrate how the multiple intelligences serve as both content and as a means of experiencing that content. Hatch (1997) cautions, however, that it is unnecessary to organize teaching around the intelligences; it is better, he suggests, to organize teaching around the children's needs. For example, "If a child . . . struggles in math or English, his teacher might give him opportunities to survey his classmates and tabulate the results, or to cowrite biographies of family and friends" (Hatch, 1997, p. 28). In Figure 1–3, the Multiple Intelligences Teaching Strategies offer other examples of teaching practices that address the various intelligences.

Notice that many of the strategies overlap more than one intelligence. Since writing is a linguistic skill, we believe our efforts to tap our students' other intelligences are particularly important to effective teaching in the writing workshop.

Our culture is definitely linguistic. Radio, television, computers, books, magazines, newspapers, catalogs, and billboards all have a linguistic focus. Reading and writing are the basis of education in our schools. Armstrong (1994, p. 7) says the linguistic intelligence "explodes" in early childhood and remains robust until old age. Even so, not all learners possess equally strong linguistic intelligence. This intelligence may be more challenging for some learners and, therefore, writing may not come as easily to them. In the chapters that follow, we will incorporate the multiple intelligences to help develop writing.

FIGURE 1–3
Multiple Intelli-
gence Teaching
Strategies

INTELLIGENCE	TEACHING STRATEGIES
Linguistic	Use storytelling or debate.
	Write a poem, myth, legend, short play, or news article.
	Create the script for a talk show radio program.
	Conduct and write up a personal interview.
Logical-mathematical	Translate a concept into a mathematical formula.
	Make up syllogisms or analogies.
	Experiment with science materials.
	Work a riddle or a puzzle.
	Describe patterns of symmetry or parallel structures.
Bodily-kinesthetic	Dramatize or role play a situation or story you are writing.
	Create a movement or sequence of movements.
	Make task or puzzle cards for a mystery story.
	Build or construct something and describe the process.
	Plan/attend a field trip and take notes.
	Use hands-on materials to demonstrate a writing concept.
Spatial	Chart, map, cluster, or graph.
	Create a three-dimensional model, videotape, or photo album.
	Invent a board or card game.
	Illustrate, draw, paint, sketch, or sculpt.
Musical	Give a presentation with musical accompaniment.
	Sing/create a rap or song.
	Indicate rhythmical patterns.
	Explain how music is similar to other concepts.
	Make an instrument and explain the process.
	Demonstrate a concept with an instrument.
Interpersonal	Conduct a meeting.
	Participate in a group or service project.
	Teach someone a writing concept.
	Practice receiving and giving feedback.
	Debate; have or be a mentor.
Intrapersonal	Describe your strongest qualities.
	Set and pursue a writing goal.
	Describe a personal value.
	Write daily journal entries.

(continued)

FIGURE 1–3
*(Continued from
previous page)*

	Self-assess your written work.
	Use technology in your writing.
Naturalist	Create observation notebooks.
	Describe changes in local/global environment.
	Care for pets, wildlife, gardens, parks; explain the importance.
	Use binoculars, telescopes, microscopes to describe a phenomenon.
	Draw or photograph natural objects and write something important about them.

Adapted from Campbell, Linda. How teachers interpret MI theory. *Educational Leadership*, 55 (September 1997), pp. 14–19.

Learning Styles in the Writing Workshop

Like the multiple intelligences, learning styles personalize education by connecting students' lives to classroom learning (Guild, 1997). Both are catalysts for positive student learning and both are learner-centered theories. However, there are basic differences in that "learning styles are concerned with differences in the *process* of learning, whereas multiple intelligences center on the *content and products* of learning" (Silver, Strong, & Perini, 1997, p. 22). Furthermore, multiple intelligences theory is based in cognitive science, while learning styles theory stems from psychoanalytic research.

The Process of Learning

Most learning style models describe the learning process or how individuals absorb, think about, and evaluate information. Theorists agree that personality, individualized thoughts and feelings, is a major factor in learning. Like the multiple intelligences, Silver, Strong, and Perini (1997) say "learning styles are not fixed throughout life, but develop as a person learns and grows" (p. 23). Most students, we find, possess and practice a mixture of styles, and therefore we recognize that helping writers practice with a variety of different learning styles is more important than labeling individual preferred learning styles.

Learning styles theory identifies personal approaches to learning. For example, while some students learn best through visual experiences, others relate to auditory stimuli, and still others remember best through kinesthetic experiences. Some writers need open-ended discovery approaches to learning, others need structured and symbolic approaches, and yet others need practical hands-on applications. No matter what the subject area, we have a preferred learning style that helps us better comprehend various

Research now documents that teaching students through their individualized learning styles results in: (1) increased academic achievement; (2) improved attitudes toward school; and (3) reduced discipline problems. Dunn, Beaudry, and Klavas, 1989

concepts. Learning style approaches that enhance the writing workshop include (1) sensory learning modalities such as visual, auditory, and kinesthetic and (2) the more abstract classifications of analytical, commonsense, dynamic, and intuitive learners.

Visual, auditory, and kinesthetic learning styles.   When we present lessons or new information about a skill or strategy, we use visual, auditory, and kinesthetic learning styles simultaneously. For example, we first explain orally to the class what we are going to do (auditory). Then, either simultaneously or as a second step, we display a colorful poster, a film, or a transparency on the overhead projector (visual) while continuing to discuss the lesson. Third, we write on the board while students take notes. Students then take on roles in small groups where they practice the concepts (kinesthetic). Later, students practice the activity themselves and act out what they have learned or produced (kinesthetic).

Analytic, commonsense, dynamic, and imaginative learners.   We also recognize the value to our writers of the more abstract levels of teaching wherein learners respond to materials and activities as analytic, commonsense, dynamic, or imaginative learners (McCarthy 1990). This learning style approach shows children's need to ask, "Why? How? What if? How does it feel?" about the material they are absorbing.

During a lesson on mapping as a prewriting strategy, *analytical learners* may wonder *what* purpose mapping serves as a writing strategy. It may help them to know that mapping allows them to capture ideas quickly for later use. They may need to know that their brains work faster than their hands can record and that mapping helps compensate for this phenomenon. Explanations increase interest and help analytic learners develop learning connections.

Commonsense learners, on the other hand, respond more readily to the mapping strategy when they know exactly *how to use* it. They may be more interested in how to capture ideas and the format for doing it—that is, the act of jotting down key words. These learners want to know how they can make the strategy work for them in what they are doing right now. They want to know where the circles and spokes go in relation to each other and how to translate the information from the map into a piece of writing.

Dynamic learners take the strategy of mapping to a new and different level. They experiment with other ways to apply the strategy. *What if* I use pictures instead of words in my mapping? *What if* I used mapping for taking notes in science class in addition to brainstorming for writing? They find new and different ways to think about and apply strategies.

Imaginative learners approach the mapping strategy or concept from the stance of, "*How do I like it? How does it feel to me?*" For example, "does it make me feel like I have more control over my thoughts and ideas? Or do I prefer outlining because mapping seems disjointed and messy?" Figure 1–4 is compiled from McCarthy's (1990) 4 MAT learning styles for the classroom and illustrates characteristics of these four types of learners.

The students . . . were asked to identify the ways in which they would achieve best. Experimental investigations revealed that when they were taught as they had indicated, students did, indeed, achieve better than when they were taught in ways that differed from their preferences. Dunn, 1988

If a teacher teaches and evaluates only in one cognitive mode, he or she is adequately serving only those students who prefer to learn in that mode. Loper, 1986

The choice or mode of presentation can, in many cases, spell the difference between a successful and an unsuccessful educational experience. Gardner, 1993

ABSTRACT	
ANALYTICAL LEARNER	COMMON-SENSE LEARNER
The comprehender.	User of content and skills.
Wants to know *what* about things.	Needs to know *how* things work.
Understands at the conceptual level.	Perceives information abstractly.
Perceives information abstractly.	Processes information actively; practices and
Processes information reflectively.	personalizes.
Devises theories by integrating observations with	Must act on ideas, not just read about them.
what they know.	Learns by testing theories and applying common sense;
Learns by thinking through ideas.	actions inform thoughts.
Needs to know what the experts think.	Must exercise ability.
Values sequential thinking.	Needs hands-on experiences.
Needs details.	Believes if something works, use it.
Finds ideas fascinating.	Resents being given answers (down-to-earth problem
Often enjoys ideas more than people.	solver).
Is sometimes cool and aloof.	Values strategic thinking.
Seeks intellectual competence.	Likes to experiment and tinker to find out how things
Seeks personal effectiveness.	work (skills oriented).
Is highly skilled verbally.	Has a strong need to work on real problems.
Generally, is an avid reader.	Wants to see how what they are learning is of immedi-
Traditional classroom well suited to needs.	ate use to them.
The innovator.	The meaning maker.
Wants to know the *if* of any situation; *if* demands	Wants to know the *why* of things.
synergy.	Vision is critical.
Applies learning in new ways; maximizes uniqueness.	Connects personal life and content.
Perceives information concretely.	Has a compelling need for ideas.
Processes information actively.	Perceives information concretely.
Seeks hidden possibilities.	Processes information reflectively.
Encourages distinct competence.	Integrates experience with the self.
Integrates experience and application.	Learns by listening and sharing ideas.
Learns by trial and error.	Is an imaginative thinker who believes in his or her
Tends to take risks.	own ideas.
Is enthusiastic about new things.	Works for harmony; needs to be personally involved.
Relishes change.	Is interested in people and culture.
Excels when flexibility is needed.	Seeks commitment.
Often reaches accurate conclusions in the absence of	Sometimes has difficulty with decisions because he or
logical justification.	she sees all sides.
Is a risk-taker who is at ease with people.	Seeks meaning and clarity.
Sometimes manipulative and pushy.	Sometimes finds school fragmented and disconnected
Seeks to influence.	from the personal issues they find most interesting.
Sometimes finds school tedious and over-sequential.	Struggles to connect school content with need to grow
Seeks to pursue interests in diverse ways.	and understand the world.
DYNAMIC LEARNER	IMAGINATIVE LEARNER
CONCRETE	

Compiled from McCarthy, Bernice. 1990. Using the 4MAT system to bring learning styles to the classroom. *Educational Leadership, 48* (October), pp. 31–37.

FIGURE 1–4 Types of Learners

Teaching Modes

With attention to the multiple intelligences and learning styles, we also attend to our modes of teaching. How do we deliver instruction and guidance to writers in our workshops? Hillocks (1986) identifies four distinct teaching styles: presentational, natural process, environmental, and individualized. We use all of them at various times in the workshop.

In the presentational mode of teaching, we impart information through lecture, models, and assignments. In this mode, as in the whole group concept, we take control of the whole class in order to give directions, make assignments, and teach new content.

In the natural process mode, we incorporate strategies such as journal writing, brainstorming, mapping, and dialogue. It is a relaxed and free mode that we use for whole group, small group, and individual work. Coaching from the sidelines as students work with heuristics and plan their writing fits well in this mode.

In the environmental mode, we involve students in group sharing, role play, and problem solving. In this mode, students research, experiment, inquire, and explore. We take the role of resource person and facilitator.

In the individualized mode, we use conventional one-on-one interaction. Student-teacher conferences, peer conferences, and working pairs characterize this mode. We work directly with individual writers as either advisor or collaborator.

Each mode has its own appeal for teachers and for students; however, as Hillocks admonishes, using a combination of all four teaching modes helps teachers address the variety of learning styles that exist among students. All four teaching modes, as do the learning styles and the multiple intelligences, work with the writing process.

Most children can master the same content; how they master it is determined by their individual learning styles. Dunn, Beaudry, and Klavas, 1989

Teaching Strategy: Synthesis of Approaches

The bottom line is that learning is a complex process and students learn in various ways. Guild, 1997

The strategies in Figure 1–5 on Teaching(Narrative Sequencing illustrate a variety of ways to reach a maximum number of students with a lesson. Every learner is connected in some way to the writing process. In this series of activities, all multiple intelligences, learning styles, and teaching modes are synthesized in the teaching of story narrative sequencing.

The Learner-Centered Workshop

In the first class meetings of the year, students discuss "how we want to be treated by others," and "what kind of class we want to be." Lewis, Schaps, and Watson, 1996

The learner-centered classroom, discussed in many books on the subject of classroom management, is best equipped to accommodate the growing understanding of these complex intelligences and learning styles. This concept suggests that students be given a degree of autonomy to determine their discipline, their choice of content, their styles of learning, their time lines, their requirements, and their outcomes. The teacher takes a back seat and becomes a facilitator.

Teaching Strategies	Multiple Intelligence	Learning through Senses	Learner Classification
Presentational teaching to the whole group: explain why stories are arranged in certain ways. Use a hamburger to represent the essential parts of the story. The top bun represents the introduction, the filling represents the specific events and details, and the bottom bun is the conclusion. Students practice sequencing these three elements by arranging jumbled paragraphs from a story.	Linguistic Spatial Bodily-kinesthetic	Auditory Visual Kinesthetic	Commonsense Analytical
Environmental teaching: In small groups, students trace the growth from seed to fruit or egg to mature animal. Point out that most things have a beginning, sequential development, and end. Students practice arranging papers written by anonymous students in logical sequence and discuss why the pieces of the story fit together as they do.	Logical-mathematical Bodily-kinesthetic Interpersonal Naturalist	Auditory Visual Kinesthetic	Imaginative Commonsense
Natural process teaching: Students map and discuss how their own story creations should be arranged and experiment with how their stories would change if they were arranged differently.	Linguistic Logical-mathematical Intrapersonal	Visual Kinesthetic	Analytical Dynamic Imaginative
Individualized teaching: Students consult with the teacher or with each other, individually, for feedback on their progress.	Interpersonal	Auditory	Imaginative Analytical
Environmental teaching: Students add music and sets to their stories and act out the sequence of the story for their classmates, either in small groups or for the whole class.	Spatial Bodily-kinesthetic Musical Interpersonal	Auditory Kinesthetic	Dynamic Imaginative

FIGURE 1–5 Teaching Narrative Sequencing

TEACHER-CENTERED WORKSHOP	LEARNER-CENTERED WORKSHOP
Teacher is sole leader	Leadership shared
Management is in the form of guidance	Management is in the form of oversight
Teacher takes responsibility for organization	Students facilitate operations of classroom
Discipline mostly from teacher	Discipline mostly comes from self
A few students help teacher	All students can be part of management
Teacher posts rules	Teacher and students develop rules together
Consequences fixed for all students	Consequences reflect individual differences
Rewards mostly extrinsic	Rewards mostly intrinsic
Students allowed limited responsibilities	Students share responsibilities
Students see only people paid to be in school	Community volunteers are common

Adapted from Frieberg, Jerome H. From tourists to citizens in the classroom. *Educational Leadership 54* (September 1996): pp. 32–36.

FIGURE 1–6   Workshop Management Styles

> In a "working with" environment, the focus is on students' underlying motives in order to help them develop positive values and a love of learning; the preferred methods include the creation of a caring community and a genuinely engaging curriculum. Kohn, 1996

> Developing a system of management that is contrary to the traditional teacher-in-control approach is a difficult and slow process for most of us. . . . However, if the goal of education is independence, then children need to learn to behave and interact without teacher supervision. Routman, 1994

The Role of the Teacher

The role of the teacher in such a learner-centered environment becomes critical and requires extraordinary skill. Learner-centered classrooms don't mean that teachers turn classes over to students. They reflect the fact that the teacher focuses on learner needs versus teacher needs. Rather than an authoritarian style of management wherein the teacher determines the goals, content, procedures, and discipline, an authoritative management style teaches and practices democracy. This democracy enables students to be comfortable with their own learning strengths and needs in order to achieve maximum learning.

A democracy is necessarily laden with rules and expectations that respect the individual. A learner-centered environment requires that the teacher know how to foster optimum learning and make the necessary decisions and arrangements for learning in a democracy. Optimum learning happens when students have meaningful participation in classroom goals, content, codes of conduct, and consequences for misbehavior. A democracy establishes an atmosphere of acceptance of new ideas and of differing opinions. The teacher helps students create a setting where the standards, expectations, and boundaries of this democracy are clear. Compare characteristics of these management styles in Figure 1–6.

Behavioral Standards

A variety of factors facilitate an authoritative teacher in a learner-centered setting. First, behavioral standards are not only desirable but necessary. Learner-centered does not mean "anything goes" because that would not be conducive to learning. When behavioral expectations are clear, students learn the limits and are free to operate within those limits. Even though students may go through antics of rebellion or anger at the limits, they want to know the limits. Will my teacher give in if I make a big fuss or will the teacher adhere to the limits no matter what? Once the students learn that the limits are secure, they can relax and learn.

In a democratic classroom, the teacher and students work together to develop the limits—a necessity in the writing workshop. We begin the year with a class meeting to talk with students about behavioral standards. What do they think will make the best learning environment? What kind of classroom do they want to live in day after day? During discussion, most students express a desire for an orderly classroom. They want a predictable environment, and they want to be able to accomplish their tasks without being bothered by undue distractions.

Our role in this discussion is authoritative in that we guide the students toward a democratic concern for their fellow classmates. What standards of behavior will ensure all students have a right to a safe and comfortable learning environment?

Equal Participation

How can every student be given an equal chance to participate in class discussions? Invariably, students discuss whether raising hands is necessary or desirable. Students usually decide that raising hands before speaking is a simple way to allow all students to participate. It doesn't mean the teacher is always in charge. It means that whether the teacher or a student is leading a class discussion, all participants have an equal right to speak. In adult settings, raising hands is a socially acceptable behavior, and it makes sense in a democratic classroom as well.

If students decide that raising hands is really not necessary, then the authoritative but democratic teacher allows the student decision to stand. After some experience with the system of shouting out in class discussions, the teacher then brings the students back for evaluation and discussion of the expectations. In a democratic classroom, students usually want the issue brought up for discussion before the teacher suggests it. Students are quite good at setting behavioral expectations at the beginning of the year and then practicing democracy as they discuss together how to resolve issues that arise.

Needs of the Writing Workshop

The needs of student writers become important issues in a democratic classroom. Much of the act of writing is a solitary experience as ideas formulate and translate into words. At times, the atmosphere of the writing classroom is one of privacy and quiet. At other times, it is one of excitement as stories are shared. To take full advantage of the multiple intelligences and learning styles in the learner-centered classroom, we help our students determine when and how to work together and when to work alone. They learn how to work in groups with respect for all ideas. Further, they learn how to

When students feel they have a voice, they feel empowered, have increased motivation for participating in instructional activities, and often think of creative support systems that adults may not have identified. Hoyt and Ames, 1997

. . . educators who establish firm boundaries, foster warm, personal relationships in the classroom, and enable students to have an impact on their environment strengthen students' attachment to school, their interest in learning . . . and their positive behaviors. Elias *et al.,* 1997

In a room where I want to demonstrate, conduct conferences, and convene small groups of children, I need a class that knows how to operate without my immediate attention. Graves, 1991

respect others' need for quiet and privacy during individual time. Criteria for establishing the desired atmosphere and working arrangement find a place on the agenda of the student class meetings.

An authoritative teacher creates a democratic environment where the students feel safe and are free to learn and express themselves. Students appreciate an environment where they know what is happening and why and where the activities have meaning for them.

Group Dynamics in the Writing Workshop

> If we want to nurture students who will grow into lifelong learners, into self-directed seekers . . . then we need to give them opportunities to practice making choices and reflecting on the outcomes. Schneider, 1996

> Many teachers use class meetings or sharing circles as tools for building a sense of community. Elias et al., 1997

Teaching writing requires selecting the best teaching strategies and learning environment while also making the best use of precious and limited class time. Effective groups in the writing workshop depend on both the teaching strategies we use and the tasks to be accomplished. Student groups fall into two basic categories: whole class and small groups. While each group has an important place in the writing classroom, the writing task to be completed determines the group size, membership, and duration.

Whole Group Teaching

> The teacher is still the person who must take a major share of the responsibility for a successful classroom. Graves, 1991

Centralized authority.   Teaching to the whole class in the writing workshop is most effective when the objectives serve general purposes that benefit all members of the class. We centralize authority in the classroom to command the full attention of all students at one time. This is the time when we explain writing assignments in detail, model or demonstrate, and present information about concepts. To *centralize* authority, we locate ourselves in the classroom so that all students can see and hear us clearly, where "all eyes and ears are front and center." In addition, the way we conduct whole class activities determines the success of our goals. Whole class teaching requires that we, as teachers, take the authority and hold the leadership role in a convincing manner. Figure 1–7 outlines strategies for whole group teaching.

Small Group Teaching

> A teacher may wish to teach lessons or units cooperatively and others competitively or individualistically. Matching the goal structure and the learning activity is one of the most important steps in structuring your classroom. Johnson and Johnson, 1987

Shared responsibility.   Once we have accomplished our objectives in a whole group meeting, students decentralize—that is, they break into smaller group sessions to work on their writing tasks collaboratively, or they work individually, writing on their own. Small groups offer students opportunities to demonstrate their specific expertise, to bond with other classmates, and to rely on each other for success in their projects. In small groups, because the responsibility is shared, students are more open to writing stories or making changes such as those required by the revision of written work. The old saying, "Two heads are better than one," works here. When members of the writing group perceive the classroom as pleasant and supportive of their needs, they develop trust and respect for each

WHEN TO USE WHOLE GROUP TEACHING	STRATEGIES FOR WHOLE GROUP TEACHING
• State requirements or give directions: making an assignment.	• Take center stage where all students can see and hear. Ask students to rearrange chairs or desks for this purpose.
• Introduce new information. For example, teach a lesson about editing marks or how to use a thesaurus or demonstrate the steps for giving directions.	• Establish eye contact with students to ensure that they are connecting with the message.
• Conduct evaluation. For example, ask students to read individual pieces of writing to the whole class.	• Change body language. Students learn from body movement as much as words.
• Conduct simple problem solving. For example, discuss goals of current or future writing assignments.	• Be knowledgeable, confident, and convincing in delivery.
• Brainstorm for points of view, lists of ideas, extension of basic concepts.	• Use a clear, concise voice that is loud enough for all to hear. Change inflection occasionally. Use pauses to emphasize important points.
• Perform as a group. For example, sing, chant, read poetry, and give choral reviews.	• Respond to comments, questions, and body language. Students' expressions (such as a wrinkled brow) often indicate the need for further explanation or reteaching.
	• Use a checklist or other system to ensure participation of all class members.

FIGURE 1–7   Whole Group Teaching Strategies

other's efforts and expertise and are more willing to take risks with their creativity. They read work in progress for reactions and suggestions from their group. They ask the kinds of natural questions that a truly interested reader would ask of a writer.

Teacher responsibility.   Decentralizing the classroom into small groups does not free us from responsibility. In fact, our job becomes more complex as we not only help establish the tasks to be completed, set the guidelines and duration of the tasks, monitor the groups to see that they are on task and achieving the stated objectives, but we also teach our students the cooperative skills required to work in groups.

Group behavior.   When we first establish collaborative groups, we introduce only one or two behaviors at a time. Students need to know what behaviors are appropriate and desirable. The group allows each participant to carry out his or her responsibility, although all must agree on and approve the final product. This guideline assumes that all have a share in the group work and that all ideas will be treated with respect. The result is reassurance for overly anxious students and energy for unconcerned students. (Davidson and O'Leary, 1990) As young writers collaborate, we monitor the groups' progress toward task completion and their interpersonal skills. Once we have taught our students how to work collaboratively, we then have the task of "getting out of our own way" and letting the process work.

In a cooperative group, [students] may develop higher levels of trust, feel less vulnerable to taking risks, and feel more comfortable than in the class as a whole.

There is now substantial evidence that students working together in small cooperative groups can master material . . . better than can students working on their own. Slavin, 1987

Except among the gifted, many students in grades 3-8 will learn better in small well-organized groups than either alone or with the teacher. Dunn, Beaudry, and Klavas, 1989

FIGURE 1–8
Small Group Seating Arrangements

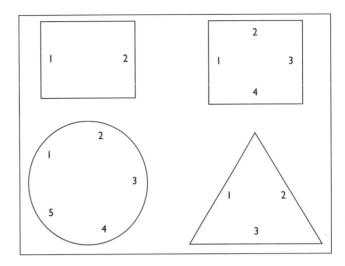

Group seating for maximum effectiveness. We position group members for maximum success in their activities. Eye contact builds high interaction, while side-by-side seating produces low interaction. Therefore, in groups of two, three, or four, we arrange students so that pairs sit directly across from each other, triads sit in equilateral triangles, and four-somes in squares so that all face each other. Foursomes that are seated as two pairs will tend to pair off rather than work as a foursome. Further, any member who is seated in an unequal position is cast as a potential control figure. We ask our students to try out different seating positions in small groups to see that such positioning does, in fact, make a difference. The seating arrangements in Figure 1–8 foster optimum interaction and success in group work. (See seating arrangements in appendix D.)

An effective teacher is an extremely good classroom manager. Wong and Wong, 1991

The teacher's job begins in earnest when the cooperative learning groups start working. Johnson and Johnson, 1987

The way we organize our classrooms affects children's views of themselves as readers and writers and has an impact on their attitudes toward school and learning. Routman, 1994

Individual writing time. Last but not least, we plan a large portion of the writing time for our budding young writers to work on their own. After they have had opportunities to exchange ideas, learn together, and gain confidence from shared responsibility, we provide the solitary time that writers need for creating their own unique expression. During this time, writers respect the need for quiet and privacy for each other as they work.

To use cooperative, small groups in the writing workshop, we recommend these strategies outlined in Figure 1–9 (on page 22) for planning.

Organizing the Writing Workshop

I recommend that writing time be scheduled regularly so that children can anticipate it. Calkins, 1986

The time spent in planning schedules, routines, procedures, and transitions pays dividends when students actively and productively engage in quality writing. Long before the first day of school, we visualize each step of what we plan to do, down to the smallest details.

WHEN TO USE SMALL GROUP TEACHING	STRATEGIES FOR SMALL GROUP TEACHING
• Create high interest, scaffold learning, and stimulate ideas through brainstorming, debate, and discussion.	• Clarify expectations and set objectives. Specify tasks to be completed.
• Provide hands-on practice, experience, and application of concepts; frequent opportunities to participate with support of peers.	• Complexity of tasks varies by age. Young children need one specific goal with a concrete outcome such as making a list or drawing a picture. Older students can accomplish more complex tasks such as analyzing a piece of writing for its organizational qualities.
• Promote morale, build common bonds and trust among students, build confidence and a willingness to take risks.	• Clear directions on charts or lists with specific expectations for tasks facilitate group success.
• Accomplish complex problem-solving such as developing plot, main idea, details, and sequencing.	• In terms of group size, young children focus best in pairs. Older students work in twos, threes, or fours. Groups that are too large lead to subgroups. However, author's circle can function effectively with larger numbers.
• Facilitate efficient use of time by accomplishing simultaneous tasks: one group provides feedback on papers while another group brainstorms new topics.	• Group membership is influenced by the type of task to be accomplished. *Heterogeneous groups* usually optimize benefits of small groups. Multiple intelligences, learning styles, gender, personalities, interests, and skills guide selection. *Random groups* are less conducive to learning and are used sparingly. When they are formed, members are assigned using a system of numbers, objects, or alphabetical order. *Self-selected groups* can have a negative impact on group efficiency. Friends choose friends, often leading to personal conversations, off-task behavior, or someone being left out.
• Motivate students to stay on task.	• Frequent rotation of group membership assignments leads students to develop the expectation that they will work with everyone.
• Evaluate mastery of concepts. With high levels of student participation, teachers can observe and assess mastery.	• Specific jobs for each student—researcher, reporter, recorder, reader, timekeeper, materials organizer, illustrator, or encourager—ensure full participation and the responsibility of each member to the group.
	• Time limits are realistic and are set at the beginning. Tasks for young children match attention spans in one class period. Older students can accomplish tasks over a period of days.
	• Groups monitor their own on-task behavior and achievement of objectives.
	• Groups monitor their own collaborative skills.

FIGURE 1–9   Small Group Teaching Strategies

Regular, frequent time for writing also allows students to write well. When they have sufficient time to consider and reconsider what they've written, they're more likely to achieve clarity, logic, voice, and grace of good writing. Atwell, 1998

Daily Writing

New teachers have the advantage of planning from the very beginning to make writing a priority and to establish the essential components to make it successful. Students need to be engaged in the activity of writing each day. How much time do you give daily to reading and arithmetic? Isn't writing as important a life skill? Frank, 1995

Some days they spend in deep thought as they create and develop their individual compositions. Some days they participate in whole class lessons to learn about organizational strategies or similes. Some days they work in small groups listening to peers share compositions. Writing is more than putting pencil to paper or fingers to computer keys.

The number one problem in the classroom is not discipline; it is the lack of procedures and routines. Wong and Wong, 1991

The Time Factor

As students work on individual writing assignments, they benefit from the structure of a routine, starting and ending at predictable times. There are important advantages to asking students to stop writing on a project even though it is unfinished. Writing benefits perhaps more than other subjects from rest. Because writing is such an introspective activity, it sometimes becomes difficult to self-evaluate what is being written until later, when the words have had a chance to be separated from the original thoughts. Accomplished authors quickly admit that they write and then put the piece away. Later, they return to the piece to evaluate it, to revise, and to continue the line of thought. The intervening rest allows time for new ideas, new words, and new angles to develop so that the writing is more productive. Young students need that rest time, that opportunity for reflection, as much as adults do. Some avid young writers continue writing because they "just want to finish this one little bit." We show them how to capture their ideas with mapping-type strategies, lists, or diagrams so their additional thoughts will not be lost in the interim. They appreciate the opportunity to stop on a note of enthusiasm and return to the work at a later time.

By establishing routines and procedures for writing, we are making the best use of our brain's normal functions. Sylwester, 1995

Setting aside predictable time for writing is important. . . . It allows children to take control of their own writing processes. Calkins, 1986

An appointed end to the writing period is also in keeping with the reality of everyday life. The routine of "start, then stop, start, then stop" is the norm for the daily activities of most adults and children alike. Rarely do adults have long blocks of uninterrupted time to accomplish tasks, and writing is no exception.

Each writer needs a daily writing folder for work in progress and another that stays on file in the classroom to store the whole collection of a students' finished pieces. Atwell, 1987

Organizing Materials

An integral part of preplanning involves the equipment and logistics of the writing classroom. While methods of successfully handling paper, pencils, and portfolios vary widely from classroom to classroom, the importance of strategic preplanning is paramount. We plan routines that maximize the use of class time and promote student responsibility. The first days of school, we discuss and practice procedures so that students take responsibility for their writing experiences. Figure 1–10 lists classroom-tested suggestions we have used in setting up a writing classroom.

- **Paper:** For younger students, assign helpers to pass out paper from a central supply. Or, place supplies of paper at several locations in the classroom so students can obtain their own paper as needed. This limits storage of large amounts of paper in individual desks and gives students a chance to move around. For older students, paper is available in a writing center. Or, each student may maintain a fresh supply of paper in his or her own writing portfolio.

- **Pencils:** Ask students to have two sharp pencils at the beginning of each day. A container for "dull" pencils collects used pencils.

- **Daily writing folders:** Supply students with manila or pocketed folders to hold their daily ongoing writing projects. These can be kept in their desks or designated boxes in the classroom. For intermediate or middle school students', maintain an easily accessible filing cabinet or other storage facility for writing folders in the writing classroom.

- **Portfolios:** Portfolios for final or published copies of writing are best stored in areas separate from daily folders. Manila folders or other special folders work well for this purpose. Plan to photocopy final work. Send home photocopies and keep original work in the portfolios. At the end of the year, the folder of the year's work goes home.

- **Reference materials:** Students need easy access to dictionaries, encyclopedias, almanacs, thesauri, and the Internet as they write, revise, and edit their work.

- **Displays:** Plan bulletin board space to display student work and illustrations.

- **Students who finish early:** When students finish a writing assignment, have them refer to their personal lists of writing topics to begin a new composition or project. The routine of reserving writing time for writing becomes firmly established.

- **Sharing work:** Plan space for students to share their writing with peers. A simple chair for the author with students seated on the floor works well. An adjustable music stand makes an effective podium for young writers.

Figure 1–10   Organizing the Writing Classroom

Summary

Readiness is the primary determinant of teacher success. Wong and Wong, 1991

Children love to communicate, and their communication blossoms in a setting that is alive with students actively involved and excited about their writing. The writing workshop is characterized by both freedom and structure. Teachers are, at the same time, facilitators, collaborators, and instructors. Such a setting requires a teacher who knows how to meet the students' varying needs effectively. Writers in a learner-centered workshop discover the ongoing, lifetime process of writing and the value of making choices. Writers work with their peers to exchange feedback and to take pieces of their work to publication.

Teachers appreciate and work with the wide range of their students' multiple intelligences and learning styles, and they plan lessons and activities with that knowledge in mind. Teachers are also aware of their own MIs and learn to use all modes of teaching to reach their students.

Workshop teachers determine when to use whole group, small group, and individualized activities. They teach the concepts of effective group work by paying special attention to the group goals, objectives, tasks, roles, membership, size, rotation, timing, and seating arrangements that best achieve the stated writing objectives.

The authoritative teacher designs and leads a learner-centered classroom based on democratic principles. Students and teacher work together to establish the organization of the workshop, while students learn to take responsibility for the decision making, limits, and behavioral expectations that make for the success of the workshop.

In an organized workshop, students follow established workshop routines and procedures to optimize learning opportunities. Before student writing begins and throughout its duration, teachers attend to the small details such as pencils, paper, folders, and resources that create a smooth running workshop.

Theory into Practice

Using the information from this chapter and your class discussions, select activities from the following suggestions to put into practice what you have learned about setting the stage for a writing workshop.

1. Think back over your own writing instruction and experiences. In a personal journal, answer the following questions: What is your reaction to your own writing experience? When are you most comfortable writing? What kind of writing do you most enjoy?

2. Discuss with a classmate whether or not you feel prepared to teach writing when you enter the teaching profession. What kinds of knowledge and skills do you think you need to develop to be successful as a writing teacher? Share your thoughts with others in small group discussions.

3. Explore Vygotsky's theory of the "zone of proximal development." Discuss how it fits in with the writing workshop concept?

4. Complete Armstrong's Adult Multiple Intelligence Inventory in appendix A and discuss the results with your instructor and classmates.

5. Administer Armstrong's Checklist for Assessing Students' Multiple Intelligences in appendix B, or use his MI pizza with several K-8 students. Discuss the results and how you would use this information to teach and facilitate writing.

6. Administer a learning styles survey to several students and to yourself. Discuss ways in which this information could affect your teaching.

(continued)

7. List and discuss writing activities conducive to whole group teaching and others conducive to small group work. When do students need individual writing time? Discuss reasons why some activities might appear on more than one list.

8. Develop a list of behavioral expectations for a writing classroom.

9. Design a room plan for desks and writing supplies that is conducive to a writing workshop setting. Seat yourselves in appropriate configurations for groups of two, three, four, and whole class for specific activities you are carrying out in this class. Analyze the effectiveness of different seating arrangements.

10. Discuss the pros and cons of authoritative versus authoritarian classrooms.

11. Discuss the pros and cons of collecting student paper and pencils at the beginning of the year and making the supply available to all students during the year.

CHILDREN'S LITERATURE

Estes, Eleanor. 1988. *The hundred dresses.* New York: Harcourt Brace.

Gomi, Taro. 1995. *My friends.* New York: Chronicle Books.

Kunhardt, Dorothy. 1990. *Pat the bunny.* New York: Golden Books Publishing Company.

———. 1993. *Pat the puppy.* New York: Golden Press.

Maxwell, Gavin. 1996. *Ring of bright water.* New York: Penguin.

Moss, Marisa. 1994. *Amelia's notebook.* Berkeley, CA: Tricycle Press.

Orwell, George. 1946. *Animal farm.* New York: A Signet Classic.

Palacco, Patricia. 1992. *Chicken Sunday.* New York: Philomel Books.

Paulsen, Gary. 1991. *Woodsong.* New York: Puffin Books.

Prokofiev, Sergio. 1986. *Peter and the wolf.* New York: Viking Press.

Sobol, Donald J. 1990. *Encyclopedia Brown and the case of the disgusting sneakers.* New York: William Morrow.

———. 1985. *Encyclopedia Brown: Boy detective.* New York: Bantam Skylark.

Wiesner, David. 1991. *Tuesday.* New York: Clarion Books.

Yolen, Jane. 1987. *Owl moon.* New York: Philomel Books.

BIBLIOGRAPHY

Armstrong, Thomas. 1994. *Multiple intelligences in the classroom.* Alexandria, VA: Association for Supervision and Curriculum Design.

Atwell, Nancie. 1987. *In the middle.* Portsmouth, NH: Boynton Cook Publishers.

Atwell, Nancie. 1998. *In the middle,* 2nd ed. Portsmouth, NH: Heinemann.

Blythe, Tina, and Howard Gardner. 1995. *A school for all intelligences.* Creating the school of the future: The multiple intelligences series. Alexandria, VA: Educational Leadership.

Caine, Geoffrey, and Renate Nummela Caine. 1997. *Education on the edge of possibility.* Alexandria, VA: Association for Supervision and Curriculum Development.

Calkins, Lucy M., and Shelley Harwayne. 1987. *The writing workshop: A world of difference.* Portsmouth, NH: Heinemann.

Calkins, Lucy. 1986. *The art of teaching writing.* Portsmouth, NH: Heinemann.

Campbell, Bruce. 1995. *Multiple intelligences in the classroom.* Classroom applications: The multiple intelligences series. Alexandria, VA: Educational Leadership.

Campbell, Linda. 1997. How teachers interpret MI theory. *Educational Leadership, 55* (September), 14–19.

Davidson, Neil, and Pat Wilson O'Leary. 1990. How cooperative learning can enhance mastery teaching. *Educational Leadership, 47* (February), 30–34.

Diamond, Marion, and Janet Hopson. 1998. *Magic trees of the mind.* New York: Dutton.

Dunn, Rita, Jeffrey S. Beaudry, and Angela Klavas. 1989. Survey of research on learning styles. *Educational Leadership, 46* (March), 50–58.

Dunn, Rita. 1988. Commentary: Teaching students through their perceptual strengths or preferences. *Journal of Reading, 31,* 304–309.

Elias, Maurice J., Joseph E. Zins, Roger P. Weissberg, Karin S. Frey, Mark T. Greenberg, Norris M. Haynes, Rachael Kessler, Mary E. Schwab-Stone, and Timothy P. Shriver. 1997. *Promoting social and emotional learning: Guidelines for educators.* Alexandria, VA: Association for Supervision and Curriculum Development.

Frank, Marjorie. 1995. *If you're trying to teach kids how to write, you've gotta have this book!* Nashville, TN: Incentive Publications.

Frieberg, Jerome H. 1996. From tourists to citizens in the classroom. *Educational Leadership, 54* (September), 32–36.

Gardner, Howard. 1983. *Frames of mind: The theory of multiple intelligences.* New York: Basic Books.

Gardner, Howard. 1987. Beyond IQ: Education and human development. *Harvard Educational Review 57.* (May), 187–193.

Gardner, Howard. 1993. *Multiple intelligences: The theory in practice.* New York: Basic Books.

Gardner, Howard. 1997. Multiple intelligences as a partner in school improvement. *Educational Leadership, 55* (September), 20–21.

Graves, Donald H. 1983. *Writing: Teachers and children at work.* Portsmouth, NH: Heinemann.

Graves, Donald H. 1991. *Build a literate classroom.* Portsmouth, NH: Heinemann.

Graves, Donald H. 1994. *A fresh look at writing.* Portsmouth, NH: Heinemann.

Graves, Donald H., and Virginia Stuart. 1985. *Write from the start.* New York: E. P. Dutton.

Guild, Pat Burke. 1997. Where do the learning theories overlap. *Educational Leadership, 55* (September), 30–31.

Hatch, Thomas. 1997. Getting specific about multiple intelligences. *Educational Leadership, 54* (March), 26–29.

Hillocks, George, Jr. 1986. *Research on written composition.* Urbana, IL: National Council of Teachers of English.

Hoyt, Linda, and Cheryl Ames. 1997. Letting the learner lead the way. *Primary Voices K-6, 5* (August), 16–26.

Jensen, Eric. 1998. *Teaching with the brain in mind.* Alexandria, VA: Association for Supervision and Curriculum Development.

Johnson, David, and Frank Johnson. 1987. *Joining together: Group theory and group skills.* Englewood Cliffs, NJ: Prentice Hall.

Johnson, David, and Roger Johnson. 1987. *Learning together & alone: Cooperative, competitive & individualistic learning,* 2nd ed. Englewood Cliffs, NJ: Prentice Hall.

Knoblauch, C. H., and Lil Brannon. 1984. *Rhetorical traditions and the teaching of writing.* Upper Montclaire, NJ: Boynton/Cook Publishers.

Kohn, Alfie. 1996. What to look for in a classroom. *Educational Leadership, 54* (September), 54–55.

Landman, Rick. 1990. Illustrator. *Sensory Creatures.* College Station, TX. College Hills Elementary.

Lewis, Catherine C., Eric Schaps, and Marilyn S. Watson. 1996. The caring classroom's academic edge. *Educational Leadership, 54* (September), 16–21.

Loper, Sue. 1986. In survey of research on learning styles. *Educational Leadership, 46* (March), 50–58.

McCarthy, Bernice, 1990. Using the 4 MAT System to bring learning styles to the classroom. *Educational Leadership, 48* (October), pp 31-37.

Routman, Regie. 1994. *Invitations: Changing as teachers and learners K-12.* Portsmouth, NH: Heinemann.

Schneider, Evelyn. 1996. Giving students a voice in the classroom. *Educational Leadership, 54* (September), 22–26.

Silver, Harvey, Richard Strong, and Matthew Perini. 1997. Integrating learning styles and multiple intelligences. *Educational Leadership, 55* (September), 22–29.

Slavin, Robert E. 1987. Cooperative learning and the cooperative school. *Educational Leadership, 45* (November), 7–13.

Sylwester, Robert. 1995. *A celebration of neurons: An educator's guide to the brain.* Alexandria, VA: Association for Supervision and Curriculum Development.

Sylwester, Robert. 1996. Brain research: Metaphors of the mind. *For Leaders of learners.* Texas Association for Supervision and Curriculum Development, (August), 1–2.

Vygotsky, Lev S. 1962. *Thought and language* (E. Hanfmann, ed. and trans.). New York: John Wiley and MIT Press.

Wong, Harry K., and Rosemary Tripi Wong. 1991. *The first days of school.* Sunnyvale, CA: Harry Wong Publications.

Ziegler, Alan. 1981. *The writing workshop, Vol. 1.* New York: Teachers & Writers Collaborative.

Ziegler, Alan. 1984. *The writing workshop, Vol. 2.* New York: Teachers & Writers Collaborative.

Thematic Units and Lesson Plans

The Brain Institute at UCLA has demonstrated that anything novel or different elicits an alering reflex in our brains and causes us to attend to the different thing rather than that to which we have been attending. This discovery in brain research comes as no surprise to a teacher who has thought she was teacing a fascinating lesson until a bee flew into the classroom.

Hunter, 1988

Chapter Outline

CONTENT AREA GOALS
Grade Level Goals
Writing Goals

THEMES
Sources for Themes
Development of Themes
Content themes
Project and problem-based themes
Student Choice

LESSON PLANS
Teaching Guidelines: Lesson Plans
Goals and objectives
Materials
Time

Instructional procedures
Motivation
Lessons and activities
Closure
Guided practice
Independent practice
Adaptations and extensions
Student assessment
Teacher self-assessment
Mini-Lessons
Emphasizing the Multiple Intelligences

SUMMARY
Theory into Practice

31

The room is arranged. The supplies are ready. We are aware of the diversity of our students' multiple intelligences and learning styles. We know how to manage various groupings of students. It is time to plan what will happen on a day-to-day basis in the writing workshop. In this chapter, we employ a four-step process to determine where writing fits in the overall scheme of our students' experience. To begin, we establish content area goals. To help our students select their writing topics and projects, we create themes into which we integrate the content of writing. We plan writing strategies and generate activities to support the content within the context of the theme; and then we develop lesson plans.

Content Area Goals

Most teachers begin their planning by asking themselves, What is it that I want my students to take away? What do I pay attention to all of the time, come back to again and again? Perrone, 1994

Perrone (1994) believes that the answers to the questions "What do I want my students to take away?" and "What do I pay attention to all the time?" help form our overarching goals. *Goals* are deep understandings of certain concepts. *Objectives* are the particular skills or habits needed to achieve the goals. Good and Brophy (1997) explain that teachers identify the "capabilities and dispositions that they want to develop in their students throughout the year as a whole and in each of the curriculum units." The desired outcomes translate into broad goals that encompass all subject areas, including writing. Because we measure what we teach, these goals also determine the assessment procedures that we use.

Of course, the ultimate goal is a literate society. Democracy is futile without an informed citizenry. Within that broad goal are developmentally appropriate goals for each grade level established through experience and tradition. This generally accepted set of grade level goals make it possible for a second grader in one state to move to a second-grade classroom in another state and find somewhat similar content being taught. While wide variations in and exceptions to these grade level goals exist, there nonetheless remains a common acceptance of grade level content and expectations. Curriculum materials, textbooks, trade books, teaching methods, and procedures frequently target specific grade levels.

Grade Level Goals

Without a clear conception of the desired outcomes, it is impossible to plan, teach, or assess in powerful ways. Shanahan, 1997

To prepare students to meet increasingly higher expectations as they grow in their education, it is important to teach the essential knowledge, skills, and curriculum required of each grade level. How do new teachers discover what to teach at a particular grade level? Reviewing curriculum documents from state departments of education is a starting place. In addition, many school districts create curriculum documents for each grade level, and curriculum materials are also available from educational publishing companies. Such materials and textbooks may or may not offer the best quality; nonetheless, they serve as reliable references for learning about the necessary content and skills for a grade

A 5ᵗʰ grade math teacher . . . tells me that when she asks her students to write out the process for solving a math problem in sentence form, they understand the new concept far better than before. We teachers need to remember that it is when students formulate ideas clearly enough to put them down on paper that they reach a true understanding. Jennings, 1996

level. Other teachers on the school campus are also valuable sources of information about grade level expectations. Usually experienced teachers willingly share their knowledge and expertise with newcomers to the profession. Based on a variety of these sources, we suggest possible approaches to goal setting and planning for the writing workshop.

Writing Goals

While writing easily lends itself to application in other content areas and enhances learning in those areas, we take care to teach the specific content of writing itself. Writing is a craft requiring basic knowledge and special skills students must know. A strong basis in writing skills strengthens all other content areas. However, learning writing skills and strategies should be more than an "add-on" or a learning support to other subjects.

Themes

It was the transdisciplinary nature of the real world that we wanted our students to grasp—the fact that no problem could be solved with mathematics or science or language arts only. Lauritzen and Jaeger, 1994

Integrated instruction works best when, within the context of meaning, students are still given opportunities for enough instruction, guidance, and practice to allow them to become accomplished. Shanahan, 1997

Finding ways to integrate writing goals into the overall curriculum brings the best results. For optimum motivation and learning, we plan for writing in meaningful settings and contexts. Those meaningful contexts often lead us to thematic/interdisciplinary approaches where writing becomes a natural part of the content students are learning and the experiences they are having both inside and outside of the classroom. Thematic/interdisciplinary teaching is the essence of connected, meaningful learning in a learner-centered environment. The concept is simple: rather than teaching the content of writing through isolated subjects on unrelated topics, the subjects of reading, science, mathematics, social studies, and writing are blended and interrelated with the broad goals of writing.

Those goals guide learning while allowing students' learning styles and strong multiple intelligences to support the development of weaker intelligences. For example, a student with a strong logical-mathematical intelligence strengthens her linguistic intelligence by writing in a meaningful math context. Or, students linguistically strong find they learn math or science more easily through the language medium. Using a thematic approach, students employ writing to support all intelligences and to improve learning. Emig's (1977) hand, eye, brain theory suggests that the act of writing something down causes that information to be imprinted on the brain, thus enhancing memory and knowledge for all content areas.

We design thematic units not only to reflect important content for each subject area and for writing but also to allow for a certain measure of student choice in learning. We act as guides and facilitators in determining themes conducive to our students' learning. These themes can be interesting and motivating to students if we help students see the connections and relevance to their lives. The goal is to optimize motivation and learning for students through meaningful connections and applications to real life and to make writing assignments meaningful within those contexts.

Sources for Themes

How do we determine themes? Two sources guide our decisions. One obvious source of ideas for thematic units is the students themselves. We survey students early in the year to find underlying themes among their interests. We use the results to plan materials as we progress through the year. The interest surveys guide selection of objectives and activities and inherently motivate student learning. See appendix E for a student interest survey that can be adapted for various grade levels. Whatever the interest area, it must lend itself to teaching the basic principles and concepts of both subject matter—science, mathematics, and social studies—and writing.

A second source of themes comes from the required curriculum for the school, such as the activities and related materials for a particular grade level. New teachers confer with experienced teachers on the school campus and examine the textbooks and supplementary materials that are provided by the school district to see what concepts or overall themes seem to emerge.

At times, we select a broad theme that can be adapted to fit most all content and subjects, one that allows wide flexibility as the unit develops, and one that holds strong promise of student interest and involvement. Themes can be very broad in nature, or they can be more focused. Some possibilities for themes include communication, immigrants, growing, sports, technology, community, animals, plants, the environment, earth's resources, cultures, transportation, ecology, change, prehistoric animals, oceans, space, weather, relationships, and health.

Broad themes connect learning over a semester or occasionally an entire school year, with each subject developed into more intense areas of study. For example, a broad weather theme could include units on floods, water, or climates. An animal theme could focus on different animal species such as dinosaurs, mammals, birds, or amphibians. A health theme could be divided into units on diseases, world food supplies, or systems of the body. Each of the broad themes allows options for student choice and in-depth study.

Other themes are more specific, with durations of a week, a month, or a grading period. Themes that would lend themselves to shorter lengths of study might include hunting dogs, early aviation, chocolate, major league baseball, or poisonous snakes.

Development of Themes

While there are many ways to develop a thematic unit, one that has proved successful for us is a mapping procedure. We begin with a circle in the center that identifies the theme. From the theme, we branch out to core subject areas and identify the content goals of each subject. A fully integrated unit may include subjects such as art, music, and physical education as well.

Students participating in a Professional Development School program through the university and working with students in the classroom for a semester developed thematic units and lesson plans for their students. See Figures 2–1 a,b for outlines for both brief and extended themes about dinosaurs and Figure 2–2 for a corresponding lesson plan.

If teachers appear to enjoy learning about school subjects, students are likely to develop similar interests. . . . Enthusiastic teachers are alive in the room; they show surprise, suspense, joy and other feelings in their voices and they make material interesting by relating it to their experiences and showing that they themselves are interested in it. Good and Brophy, 1997

Language Arts

Reading activity: students will read the book, *Dinosaur Valley* in groups of four.

Writing activity: students will write and perform a readers theater skit reenacting events in the book.

Science

Reading activity: read *Dinosaur Cousins* as a class.

Writing activity: take field trip to local zoo. Write a letter as a class zookeeper telling what we learned about animals relating to dinosaurs.

Dinosaurs

Music

Reading activity: read to students as a class the book, *I'm Tyrannosaurus: A Book of Dinosaur Rhymes.*

Writing activity: using either a dinosaur in the book or another we've studied, the students will write a poem that rhymes to present to the class as a rap.

Math

Reading activity: read *Two Dozen Dinosaurs* in groups of three, especially p. 14

Writing activity: In groups, write word problems about the dinosaurs listed on p. 14, Megalosaurus, Apatosaurus, Lambeosaurus, and Baryonyx. With the information about each dinosaur given, if they went to a restaurant and ordered something to eat, what would they eat off of the list given in the book and how much would their meals cost?

FIGURE 2–1A
Preservice Teacher Thematic Units—Brief

> Given the existing research on writing-thinking relations, there is a strong argument for using writing across the curriculum to support learning. Dahl and Farnan, 1998

> Integration does not do away with the need for direct explanation or drill and practice. There is more to learning than just doing, or we could profitably abolish schools and put children to work. Shanahan, 1997

Content themes.   After determining subject content and shaping a thematic map, we combine the content and the theme into meaningful learning experiences and incorporate writing as the tool for learning throughout the unit. We consider and plan the natural or most logical form of writing that grows out of each content area. For example, in the study of a water cycle, the most logical form of writing would perhaps be a process narrative or "how-to" explaining the water cycle or some other weather phenomenon.

In workshop with the students, we brainstorm a list of activities and available resources such as books, guest speakers, videos, experiments, games, art projects, songs, plays, articles, and Internet resources to support our study. As we match the subject area list with the writing content goals, depending on the grade level, we review the writing skills necessary for the assignments or introduce appropriate writing concepts for the first time. We look for meaningful activities that directly support the writing goals and content students need to know. For example, reading the editorial page of the newspaper provides real-life examples of persuasive writing. Such articles become the basis for lessons on the characteristics of persuasive writing and for teaching political processes.

Similarly, in the dinosaur unit, we find that the math goal of finding relative size and ratios for making models fits into the context of a logical writing component that uses the

Social Studies
- find regions where dinosaurs lived
- describe the place (description) where they lived
- find the location (maps) where they lived
- explain they did not live with cave men
- explain extinction
- relate Loch Ness monster (cousin?)
- tell how they relate to each other (citizenship)

Writing:
- describe what it would be like to have a pet dinosaur
- describe what it would be like to live in the time of dinosaurs

Reading:
- *Learn About Texas Dinosaurs* by Elena T. Ivy & Georg Zappler
- *Extinction is Forever* by Donald Silver
- *Where to Look for a Dinosaur* by Bernard Most
- *Tyrone the Horrible* by Hand Wilhelm
- *If the Dinosaurs Came Back* by Bernard Most

Science
- go on a museum tour
- observe fossils
- invite a guest speaker
- go on a dinosaur track field trip
- measure tracks—observing
- learn what they ate
- understand extinction
- construct dinosaur models

Writing:
- journals
- writing observations
- write a lab report
- write stories about carnivores/herbivores
- write a thank-you letter to the curator
- write how a fossil is found and how it was formed
- produce an ad for a fossil hunter

Reading
- *Dinosaur National Monument* by David Petersen
- *Dinosaurs Walked Here: and Other Stories*
- *Fossils Tell* by Patricia Lauber
- *The Dinosaur: A New Discovery* by Janet Stewart
- *Dinosaur Bones* by Aliki Brandenberg

Math
- learn—how big are dinosaurs?
- describe relative size to something we know
- make models of size relative to each other
- count dinosaurs
- outdoor activity—show size with yarn or sketches in a parking lot through estimation

Writing:
- pick a dinosaur and describe how big it is, how many of them there were, or how long ago they lived using similes and metaphors and descriptive words
- what would it be like if you were as big as a dinosaur?

Reading:
- *The Dinosaur Encyclopedia* by Michael Benton
- *Two Dozen Dinosaurs* by Catherine Ripley
- *I am a Big Dinosaur* by Francis Crozat
- *Dinosaur for a Day* by Jim Murphy

Art, Music, PE
- make dinosaur mobiles
- make diorama of a dinosaur in its habitat
- draw favorite dinosaurs
- make plaster footprints
- sing songs about dinosaurs
- walk like a dinosaur
- act like a dinosaur
- make stamp tracks

Writing:
- write a song
- describe how you moved
- title your artwork
- write poems
- from the footprint, describe what the animal is like

Reading:
- *Dinosaurs and How They Lived* ed. Angela Wilkes
- *Tyranosaurus Was a Beast* by Jack Prelutsky
- *Dinosaur Cousins* by Bernard Most

DINOSAURS

Language Arts
- watch movie: Land Before Time, Baby, Jurassic Park
- put on a play about dinosaurs
- read dinosaur poetry
- make up new dinosaur names for people

Writing:
- write a play
- write a poem
- journal-reactions to movies/books
- expository writing—write a report about a dinosaur
- become a dinosaur and tell about a day in your life
- describe a dinosaur from a footprint

Reading:
- *Dinosaur for a Day* by Jim Murphy
- *Dinosaurs Walked Here: and Other Stories Fossils Tell* by Patricia Lauber
- *The Magic School Bus: In the Time of the Dinosaurs* by Joanna Cole
- *The Big Golden Book of Dinosaurs* by Mary Elting
- *Time Train* by Paul Fleischman

FIGURE 2–1b
Preservice Teacher Thematic Units—Extended

FIGURE 2–2
Preservice Teacher—Lesson Plan

SCIENCE—WRITING LESSON PLAN: DINOSAURS

by Janna Hablinski

THEME/SUBJECT:
Dinosaurs/Science

GRADE LEVEL: 4.

GOAL:
Students will learn to write in letter format.
Students will understand that letter writing is a life skill.
Students will learn to address an envelope properly.

OBJECTIVES:
Students will write in letter format.
Students will use past knowledge to elaborate in their letters using detailed descriptions.
Students will address an envelope properly.

MATERIALS/RESOURCES:
Museum's address
paper
pens and pencils
envelopes
stamps
large model of addressed envelope
overhead or chalkboard to model writing a letter

TIME:
1 hour for each of 4 days

INSTRUCTIONAL PROCEDURES:
After visiting the museum, we will need to thank the curator for allowing us to come; this should be explained to the students. The students will brainstorm in small groups. The demonstrations by the teacher should be done as a class. The first day is for brainstorming. On the second and third days, the letters will be written, revised and edited. Writing should be done individually, and revisions and editing should be done with peers. On the fourth day, the envelopes will be addressed. A predetermined checklist based on a rubric should be used to evaluate the finished product. Copies of the finished product will be put in a working portfolio to see progress of the letters.

LESSONS AND ACTIVITIES:
The students should break up into small groups to brainstorm. The students should come up with things they liked the most along with other things for which they want to thank the curator. They should use descriptive words in their explanations of these things.

On the day to teach letter format, the teacher should first demonstrate on the board or overhead how to write a thank-you letter. The teacher should point out the opening of the letter and the closing. Explain that this is the format of a letter and all letters have an opening and a closing. Proper capitalization, punctuation, and indentation should be highlighted also. Models of the format should be left up for visual guidance during the students' writing time. The students will write letters individually. One to two days should be left to write the letters to allow for revising and editing. The revising and editing can be done in small groups for peer help.

The last day should be used for teaching addressing envelopes. The proper format should be demonstrated on the overhead or board and a large model should be displayed as well. The format will be as follows:

Name

street address

City, State ZIP code

The address needs to be on the correct location of the envelope and the return address should also be shown and explained. The students should address an envelope to their family or a friend first to practice. Then they will address one for their letter. Then they can stamp their envelopes to mail.

(continued)

Figure 2–2
Preservice Teacher—Lesson Plan *(continued)*

Adaptations and Extensions:
A form letter can be provided for those who need adaptations to the lesson. Students can fill in the blanks of this letter and then rewrite it on their own paper.

Students who finish early can write another letter to a friend or family member telling about the field trip. These students can also decorate their letters.

Evaluation:
The portfolios will be checked for progress. A copy of the product will be evaluated using a predetermined checklist based on a rubric. The checklist will include proper format of the letter and envelope, elaboration and details, and proper opening and closing.

Self-evaluation of the lesson should include the following:

-Did the students work well in their groups?

-Did students know most of the information? If so, a review could be used next time instead.

-Was there enough variety to keep the children interested? Decorations can be added or the students could make a card along with a group letter.

-Did the students use the correct format? If not, it should be retaught.

---

comparison mode and creates written conclusions based on the comparisons. When we teach reading through nonfiction articles and books related to dinosaurs, a logical composition component is writing articles about changes in the world's environment. When we incorporate social studies content about how dinosaurs coexisted with other life forms, the writing assignment may develop as a piece about what it would be like for man to live in that era. The science content meshes with the social studies in exploring the dinosaurs' extinction. The writing content involves learning to take notes, summarizing the information, and explaining the phenomena. Activities to support the science content and the logical writing components take a variety of forms:

> Problem-based learning is a mechanism for allowing students to come to grips with significant academic subject matter. Savoie and Hughes, 1994

- Describe places where dinosaurs lived—write reports that include materials, methods, results, and conclusions.
- Learn to identify different species of dinosaurs—write to compare and contrast.
- Construct models of different dinosaurs—write how-to papers on the procedures.
- Watch videos on dinosaurs—write "learning log" entries telling the main ideas of the videos.

> Instead of a synthetic unit arranged around a process or topic, exploration of real problems places the focus on application of skills and knowledge. Lauritzen and Jaeger, 1994

Project and problem-based themes.   Some researchers suggest that the best teaching is project-based or problem-based. Using these approaches, our students participate in choosing what they want to explore and produce, and they then apply their knowledge and skills to solve real-life, complex problems (Lauritzen & Jaeger, 1994; Wolk, 1994). We find that such meaningful, hands-on involvement with the curriculum provides strong motivation and student interest in the thematic unit. Project- and problem-based themes also provide an ideal setting for performance or authentic assessment. With any theme, we encourage students to ask questions that might be answered through inquiry and/or projects.

Student Choice

During a weather theme, one of our students wondered how citizens are warned about severe weather. This question led to a research project for him on how warning systems have changed over time or how warnings are different for tornadoes and floods. He investigated how lives in the past might have been saved if current technology had been available. He contacted meteorologists about future plans for improved warnings. Ultimately, he wrote the procedures for and designed an improved warning system of his own. In these student-chosen projects and problems, we maintain a clear sense of basic curriculum goals for the students. Students are held accountable for mathematics, science, social studies, reading, and writing competencies on a level that matches their abilities, the school standards, and requirements for essential literacy. We exercise care to ensure that students do not complete an educational experience with large gaps in knowledge and skills that would hinder progress on future endeavors.

This ideal of student choice in curriculum is combined with realistic expectations that students be exposed to a wide variety of knowledge and experiences. For example, a student with a consuming interest in horses finds a theme based on horses very motivating and may not want to explore ideas in any other area. Authoritative teachers recognize that their job includes exposing students to a wide range of topics and interests. This same student would benefit from and enjoy a study of other cultures but might not explore cultural themes if left completely on her own to choose. To provide new experiences and open new avenues of interest, we use strategies such as popular movies, field trips, unusual activities, or interesting visitors to nudge students toward inquiry in other subject areas. Authoritative teachers use the interests of their students to guide curriculum decisions, but they also strive to expose students to new horizons of learning.

Even though some suggest that research does not necessarily support learning gains through thematic units (Shanahan, 1997), it is apparent that both teachers and students find such instruction rewarding. Shanahan's guidelines in assuring that thematic units promote in-depth learning as opposed to simply providing a "motif" for learning unrelated concepts include: (1) establishing a clear conception of learning outcomes and (2) giving deliberate attention to content in each discipline, including writing.

Dahl and Farnan (1998) conclude that because a natural link exists between writing and thinking, interdisciplinary writing leads to better understandings of ideas and concepts. Therefore, as the theme develops, we look for natural applications for writing in other subject areas. The work of Langer and Applebee (1987) suggests that writing assignments that cause students to manipulate ideas lead to more permanent and more complex learning. This kind of writing includes comparison, evaluation, explanation, and drawing conclusions. Therefore, writing in other subjects needs to be more than response to short answer questions or restatement. Rather we look at areas where writing content becomes a natural outgrowth of other subjects, and we teach the skills for that writing content in the context of the subject areas.

The weather chart in Figure 2–3 suggests the integration of writing into a weather unit for grade levels K–8.

In order to make good decisions about what to teach and how to teach it, teachers need to establish worthwhile goals and keep these goals in sight as they develop and implement their plans. Good and Brophy, 1997

When children are allowed to choose what to explore, they become intrinsically motivated—more than happy to work hard and strive for quality. Wolk, 1994

FIGURE 2–3A
Thematic Weather Chart

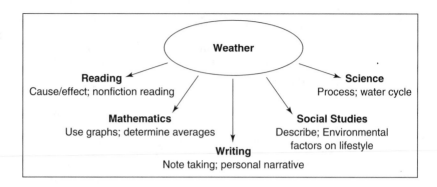

Lesson Plans

Teachers I have worked with have taken at least three to five years to develop a schedule and lesson plan format they feel comfortable with. All of these teachers expect their daily plans to change. Routman, 1994

The next step divides the content/activities into meaningful chunks of learning within the various subject areas. We translate each chunk of learning into learning objectives for the students. Then, we use those objectives to create daily lesson plans.

Lesson plans are the step-by-step instructions for what we do when we come face to face with the students. Consequently, they require careful planning and attention. There is no one perfect lesson plan. In fact, daily lesson plans take many forms, but they typically contain essential components that allow students to build meaning and grow in their learning toward desired goals and objectives. Because they are not yet experienced in the classroom, our preservice teachers write plans that include every detail of the lesson. As with any kind of writing, it is a way for them to think through the processes they will follow in guiding students through the material they are presenting. As they gain in experience they, like most seasoned teachers, include less detail in their lesson plans. At the beginning, we find that more detail is better.

Teaching Guidelines: Lesson Plans

Lesson plans can be designed for one day's class or for several days' duration. Several essential components make lesson plans successful:

- Goals and objectives
- Materials
- Time for lesson
- Instructional procedure
- Motivation
- Lessons and activities
  - Closure
  - Guided practice
  - Independent practice
- Adaptations and extensions
- Assessment (students and teacher)

Grade	Mathematics	Reading	Science	Social Studies
K	Write or dictate sentences that explain information in simple weather graphs.	Illustrate and label pictures of different kinds of clouds.	Dictate descriptive, clarifying words for the weather while on a nature walk.	Create a class journal entry recalling a field trip to a television weather studio.
1	Write story problems that apply number operations such as 1+4 and 6−3 or an adventure story about a windy day.	Read *The Snowy Day*. Write a story telling how you would spend a snowy day.	Using a classroom weather chart, write sentences to record the number of days of rain, sunshine, etc.	Write a story that explains why rainy days are beneficial.
2	Create a weather picture using geometric shapes. Write an adventure story about the picture.	Read *The Cloud Book* and *The Popcorn Book*. Write a paper explaining how the books are alike and different.	Write a "how to" paper on making a tornado in a bottle.	Write a paper explaining how an airline pilot uses weather in his or her job.
3	Write a paper describing activities appropriate for 30 degree weather.	Read *Cloudy with a Chance of Meatballs*. Write a diary entry for a day in that town.	Create a cloud book that illustrates and describes different categories of clouds.	Invite a meteorologist to speak to the class. Write a friendly letter expressing thanks.
4	Write a composition that explains through examples how the ability to round numbers is important to a meteorologist.	Read *Grasshopper Summer*. Use inference to explain what you think the next year will be like for the family.	In a composition, compare and contrast a hurricane and a tornado.	Experiment with ways to keep ice from melting. Write a report comparing the success of various strategies.
5	Write a paper explaining differences in recorded temperatures between light and dark objects placed in the sun.	Read weather reports in newspapers and on the Internet over a period of days. Write a paper explaining which source gave the best information.	Conduct experiments that illustrate the water cycle. Write a "how to" paper that describes the experiments.	Write a description of how the local climate impacts the kinds of jobs in the community.
6	Write a "how to" composition on steps and strategies to use in determining average rainfall for a year.	Search the Internet or other sources for information about weather disasters. Compare and contrast the damage from two events.	Use information about lightning to create an advertisement explaining safety precautions for thunderstorms.	Research the Johnstown, PA, flood. In a report, explain how modern weather equipment could have saved the town.
7	Write a persuasive paper for using the metric system to convey weather information in the United States.	Read a collection of weather poems. Write poems about weather.	Write a paper explaining why weather forecasters are sometimes wrong in their predictions.	Write a composition explaining the impact of weather on immigrants crossing the Great Plains in the 1800s.
8	Write a paper that explains how weather forecasters use percentages to predict rainfall.	Read about El Niño. In a research report, explain the impact of El Niño on the weather of the United States.	Write a persuasive paper on the merits of using sunscreen. Use scientific information about the sun to support your ideas.	Research the jobs and credentials of meteorologists. Write a paper explaining reasons for being a meteorologist.

FIGURE 2–3b

Goals and objectives.   We look at the content goals we have established for our students. Within those content goals, we identify the meaningful chunks of learning that students need. Exactly what skills do the students need to accomplish the goal? Those are the objectives. In most cases, we design a series of lesson plans with specific objectives to accomplish the broader content goals established in the thematic unit. Objectives describe the results we expect from our students, and those expectations guide the lesson plans that we develop. The content of writing in the following chapters will determine writing goals and objectives that will then be translated into daily lesson plans.

As we establish a goal and develop activities and lesson plan objectives, we keep in mind the age of the children and the personality of the class. Small children need smaller chunks of learning in each objective, and their limited attention spans shorten the duration of lesson activities. In the preservice teacher's lesson plan in Figure 2–4 for second graders, the goal was to write a business letter and the writing objectives were to review friendly letter format and relate it to business letter format. The objectives also included consciousness raising about the audience for the letter.

Older students sustain work on more complex goals and objectives that assume broad background knowledge. The pace should remain lively enough to hold student interest over a period of time. For some younger students, a week's unit on a broad goal is adequate, while older students sustain study on a goal over a more prolonged period of time. Following a reading lesson on *An Egyptian Pyramid* by Jacqueline Morley, students discussed Egyptian society, beliefs, and practices. The writing lesson was an outgrowth of the discussion and focused on strengthening elaboration skills in story narrative. The lesson plan in Figure 2–5 was developed by a preservice teacher working with fifth and sixth graders.

While the lesson plans presented in this chapter are quite thorough, several of them could be improved by including more specific verbs in the objectives. In lesson plans, we state objectives in verbs that describe what the students will be able to do as a result of the lesson. Objectives relate to basic knowledge or to higher order thinking skills. According to Bloom's taxonomy (Bloom & Krathwohl, 1984), those levels of thinking, ranked in order from the least to the most complex, are knowledge, comprehension, application, analysis, synthesis, and evaluation. Objectives written for the knowledge level are the least complex, while objectives written for the evaluation level are the most complex.

Appropriate objectives are based on the complexity of the broad thematic goals and the age, knowledge base, needs, and experience of the students. Younger students need to build a knowledge base before they move to higher levels of thinking. For example, young students need to know the components of a story beginning and then apply that basic knowledge to their writing. Older students can learn an array of story introductions and apply them to a range of appropriate papers. Gradually students move from basic knowledge to the higher order thinking skills.

In the chart of Bloom's taxonomy in Figure 2–6, each thinking level is described along with the verbs that define that level. The student-learning examples and sample questions/activities suggest how to structure the lesson.

FIGURE 2–4
Preservice Teacher Lesson Plan

WRITING LESSON PLAN

ACTIVITY: To become familiar with a Texas town, each student will write to a tourist bureau of a Texas town. They will request information about attractions in that town. This lesson will be done after the reading lesson has been completed.

THEME/SUBJECT:
"A Taste of Texas"

GRADE LEVEL: 2ND GRADE

GOAL:
Writing a business letter

OBJECTIVES:
#1.   Awareness of audience
#2.   Determine purpose: to seek information about a Texas town
#3.   Locate addresses of tourist bureaus
#4.   Become familiar with business letter format
      - Return address
      - Inside address
      - Greeting
      - Body
      - Complimentary closing
#5.   Review punctuation and capitalization used in letter format
#6.   Review friendly letter format
#7.   Practice note-taking

MATERIALS:
Texas! Live the Legend book (includes addresses), lined paper, pencil, pen, unlined white paper, envelopes, stamps, overhead projector, transparency sheet, and marker.

TIME:
One hour for 2 days

INSTRUCTIONAL PROCEDURES:
I will begin by letting the students individually brainstorm to decide which town they would like to find out more about. They could refer to a Texas map or discuss it with a friend to decide. After each student has made a decision, I will pick a town that no one has picked. With this town, I will demonstrate to the whole class how to look up its address in the book I have provided them. The addresses are listed in alphabetical order so I will demonstrate to the students how to look at the first letter of the town, then the second, until the town is found. There will be three of the books available to find addresses. The students will divide into three groups and each student will have a chance to find the address of their town.

The students will then meet again as a whole class. At this time the students will review by giving me the parts of a friendly letter format. The students will list these one by one on the board. After reviewing what we already had known about this format, I will tell them how to write a business letter. This will be done on the board beside the friendly letter format. I will show that the return address stays the same, but in the business letter, before the greeting you must put the address of the person you are writing to. I will then show that the body and the complimentary closing are the same. As we establish the business letter format on the board, the students should take notes to refer to when doing the writing. This will give the students a checklist to use when writing to make sure they have all parts.

Next, we will discuss aloud the audience that we will be writing to and the purpose. This will be done as before. Since we have already written friendly letters, we will discuss that we are writing to a different audience so we must use a more formal style of communication. In this letter we will be

(continued)

FIGURE 2–4
Preservice Teacher Lesson Plan (*continued*)

asking them to send us information on their town and we will need to give reasons we want the information. This will all need to be done in a formal way. We will list the closings used in a friendly letter format and we will then come up with closings for a business letter together. This whole process will be done with interaction between me and the students.

I will then demonstrate on the overhead how to write a business letter. I will use a town that no one else has picked because I do not want to do the work for them, I just want to show them how it should be done. I will ask for ideas from the students as I demonstrate. My job is to model how to express their ideas in a formal way. We will stop when we get to a point where a DOL can be done, such as in the case of writing an address. I will put it on the board and we will work together to find capitalization and punctuation in it. As we find where to apply each, we will write the rule for it on the board. The students should also take notes on the rules to refer to when writing. DOL's will be done with each part of the letter as we do the demonstration. This incorporates grammar lessons within writing lessons.

After the demonstration, the students will individually begin brainstorming what they will write. After they have decided, they will then write their own business letter to a tourist bureau of a Texas town to request information.

LESSONS AND ACTIVITIES:
We will do a mini-lesson first on how to find the address of the bureau. After the students have found the addresses of their town, the class will do a mini-lesson on the format of a business letter compared to a friendly letter. A mini-lesson will also be done on the audience we will be writing to and how the letter will reflect this. As the students become ready to write the letter, we will continue our lesson on the parts of a business letter. The students will write the letter on lined paper to begin with. It will be folded in squares like a book. On each section, the students will write a part of the letter. When it comes to the final letter, the students will then write the letter on unlined white paper. They will match each section of their book with the notes they had taken and this will help them become familiar with the parts of the letter that must be included. This will also be used as a checklist for the students to check for all parts. The last mini-lesson will be done when all students have completed their letters and when they are in final form to mail. As a whole class, we will then write the format to address an envelope on the board. As we do this on the board, the students will each address their own envelopes. We will then collect the letters to be mailed.

NOTE: If the students know the letters will be mailed, they will put much more effort in it. They know it is being read by someone other than the teacher for something other than a grade.

ADAPTIONS AND EXTENSIONS:
For the learners who are slower, I will give a sheet of paper that has the letter format marked on it so the students know where to put what. Some students may write slower so I will be sure to have some extra time set aside for these students. During this extra time, the fast writers can go to the reading learning center and read books that will be available about Texas and its many towns. Reading is never considered a waste of time. Some advanced students may choose to write to two towns or to write to the mayor of a town instead of the tourist bureau.

(continued)

EVALUATION AND ASSESSMENT:
The students' letters will be evaluated by using a checklist of the parts of a letter as well as for the DOL's we discuss in class dealing with grammar and punctuation. The checklist will be given to the students before they write so they know what is expected of them. The evaluations and comments will then be given on a comment sheet in the student's writing folder. I will do evaluation of the letter by checking off the things on the checklist that the students know about.

From this same checklist, I will be able to evaluate myself. I will use this after the lesson has been completed to see if I had included a mini-lesson for each part that needed it. I will then be able to see how I got through to the students with this lesson by looking over their checklist as a whole class. If the majority got points taken off in a similar place, I know that I should try a new lesson style here next time or even reteach that skill next class time. The checklist will be the key for both evaluations!

If the content goal is to develop skills in comparative writing in a cloud theme, the following objectives represent chunks of learning that might be appropriate for middle elementary students:

Sample Objectives: Students will be able to

- Read and recognize similarities and differences in *The Cloud Book* by Tomie DePaola.
- Elaborate similarities and differences—of two types of clouds observed in nature.
- Organize in writing a point-by-point or block comparison of two types of clouds.

Materials. In designing the motivation, procedures, practice, and assessment for teaching a lesson, we keep a separate list of each material or piece of equipment needed, no matter how small or inconsequential it may seem. As we develop the lesson plan, we place the list of materials at the top of the plan, much like ingredients are listed at the beginning of a recipe. This list makes preparation efficient and teaching smooth. There is nothing more frustrating for both teacher and students than to begin a lesson and have to stop midstream because one essential element to carry out the lesson is missing.

Time. We consider carefully how much time to spend on each objective and activity. Sometimes we teach one objective and students master it in a day, while another objective stretches over several days. Figure 2–7 features a five-day lesson plan developed by a preservice teacher.

If an objective requires more than a week, especially with younger elementary students, we consider restating that objective to encompass a smaller chunk of learning. Of course, class periods and school schedules directly affect the amount of time devoted to an objective in any one day. Further, in writing workshop, if a student wants to continue working on a piece, that is certainly an option.

Instructional procedures. We find it most important to think about the most effective approach for teaching or guiding the lesson. What are the students' stronger multiple

Pacing is an important consideration in lesson planning and execution. Judging the time needed to present a lesson will get easier as you become familiar with the curriculum and the students. Montgomery, 1994

- Brainstorm as a class, and then write a comparison and contrast of the life of a common Egyptian citizen and a priest or ruler, individually, or in groups of 2–3.

- Read the text and get in groups of 3–4 to make a time line of important events in Ancient Egyptian history. The time line may be made with dates and illustrations.

- Read the book, *Pyramid*. Break into groups and discuss the importance of the afterlife in Ancient Egyptian society.

- Choose one of the gods and do individual or small group research on one of the gods. Compile the entire class's work into a class book on Egyptian gods.

- Look at various maps of the Nile Valley. Discuss the importance of the Nile for Egyptian civilization. Brainstorm contributions of the Nile to Egypt.

Social Studies — Ancient Egypt — Art — Math — Language Arts

- Read in *Ancient Egypt* that Egyptian society did not use money. Brainstorm in groups (2–3) ways life would be different in a society without money.

- Use the pyramids of ancient Egypt as an intro to solid geometry.

- Supply various travel brochures to the class. Have them break into groups. Assign them budgets and have the students write travel itineraries of places in Egypt they would like to visit and how much the various excursions will cost.

- Read book *Into the Mummy's tomb*: prediction strategies, how to, writings, vocabulary.

- Ask students to write about what they would have wanted in their tombs had they lived in Ancient Egypt.

- The Mummy's Message game: Students decode hieroglyphics and read clues to decipher the mummy's message. This would be the culminating activity.

- Cartouche activity: Students elaborate on a description of a ruler given in his cartouche.

- Students write journal as if they lived in Ancient Egypt.

- Watch Video: *Pyramid* and observe art in tombs and pyramids as well as the sculptures, paintings and writing. After watching video read the "news paper" *Pyramid Times* for visual/linguistic reinforcement.

- Read about and look at artifacts that were found in Tut's tomb in *Treasures of Tutankhamen*.

- Try to replicate Egyptian hieroglyphics.

- Make and decorate personal cartouche; use the meanings of Egyptian hieroglyphics to describe oneself, or make up own code pictures (writing activity).

- Make models of the pyramids.

- Make dioramas of tombs, scenes of a pyramid being built, etc.

FIGURE 2–5A
Preserve Teacher Thematic Unit

intelligences? What kind of interest catcher should we use? Should we demonstrate or model? Should we use large group, small group, individual work, or a combination of all? Demonstrations form the basis of nearly all lessons in the workshop. Good and Brophy (1997) recommend a series of procedures to use in demonstration lessons. Their procedure begins with focusing student attention and then telling students exactly what it is that they will learn. Before students can learn, they must be motivated to learn and focus on the task at hand. When we choose objectives that meet students' needs, students have greater intrinsic motivation for learning the objectives.

FIGURE 2–5B
Preservice Teacher Lesson Plan

WRITING LESSON

THEME/SUBJECT: Ancient Egypt

GRADE LEVEL: 5TH-6TH

GOAL: Elaboration

OBJECTIVES:
—students will work cooperatively in groups
—descriptive words
—transitional words
—sequencing of events
—paragraphing
—introductions
—conclusions

MATERIALS:
—books and with pictures of artifacts found in Egyptian tombs (enough for each student to look at)
—pens and pencils for the students
—markers, crayons, map pencils
—plastic bags of vocabulary words (items that would be found in Egyptian tombs)
—generic story starter: When the archaeologist walked into the tomb he saw a coffin and a lot of other things. Suddenly his torch blew out and he was scared.

TIME: 2 hours (2 class periods)

INSTRUCTIONAL PROCEDURES:
First the class should be divided into groups of 2–3. Hand out the generic story starter to the children and put it on the overhead. Ask the students to brainstorm with each other about how the archaeologist got into the tomb, and then what the archaeologist might have seen when he entered the tomb. Allow about 10 minutes. Then ask the students to brainstorm all the things that might have caused the torch to go out. Next have the students brainstorm possible endings to the story. Allow about 15 minutes.

Now tell the groups to choose the ideas they like the most and have them write the framework for their story. Allow about 10 minutes. When it looks like groups are finished, make sure they are, and then begin helping the students add to and elaborate on their stories by asking them questions and brainstorming ideas with the whole class.

Ask the class to tell you some words that could be used to describe objects found in the tomb. Write these words on the board or overhead. Now ask the groups to look at their stories and use some of the descriptive words brainstormed by the class as well as their own words to embellish their stories. Remind students to double space their stories so they will have room to edit them. This will probably be the end of the first hour (class period). This allows the students to have time away from their stories so they can look at them fresh the next day.

The next day, have the groups look at their stories. Do the events in their stories follow a logical sequence? Give them time (10 minutes) to change or add anything they want before they start the next phase of editing their story. Ask the groups if they have any transitions in their story. Brainstorm transition words on the board with the whole class. Tell the students who needed to add transitions to their story to do so, and ask the students to consider changing the transitions they had if they prefer some of the transitions that were brainstormed.

(continued)

FIGURE 2–5B
Preservice Teacher Lesson Plan (*continued*)

Now have the students look at their introductions and conclusions. Ask the students to see if their introductions have all the elements of a good introduction. Tell them to add what they think is necessary. Now ask the students to see if the conclusion has answered the question of what blew out the torch. Give the students time to illustrate their stories if they wish to do so.

Have the students look over their stories one more time to see if there are any changes that they want to make. Finally, ask for volunteers to share their stories with the class. If they want to, allow them to act out their stories, illustrate them, or make dioramas of the tomb.

ADAPTATIONS•/EXTENSIONS*
•place students who have trouble with their writing skills in groups with linguistically gifted students
•do not force students to share their stories
•make story strips for students who have great difficulty writing their own stories
*students can take the story the group made and add to it individually

*students can tell the story from the perspective of an "observer" in the tomb
*students can make up their own story about an Egyptian adventure

EVALUATION AND ASSESSMENT:
1. Evaluation of the students' cooperation in groups can be done by walking around the room during group time and observing the students together. Evaluation of the other objectives will be done when the class brainstorms and when the groups share their stories. If the stories have good introductions and conclusions, have details, follow a logical sequence, and use descriptive words for elaboration, the objectives have been met.

2. I will know if the lesson is a success by observing the groups during group time. I should pay attention to how the groups are working together. The class must also participate during the brainstorming period for the lesson to work. Finally the students must enjoy sharing their stories with the class.

Motivation. Focus, or motivation, involves capturing student attention with some novel concept, activity, idea, or personal connection. We attract and maintain attention by presenting something novel to the students, or we use something that happens in the classroom or is happening in their lives. That novelty is connected to meaning for the students (Hunter, 1988). To determine the motivation for lessons, we review the multiple intelligences menu in Chapter 1 in Figure 1–3 and select strategies that relate to the intelligences, as appropriate for our students.

Knowledge

DESCRIPTION (TO KNOW – TO RECALL)

- remembering previous learned material
- lowest level of learning
- listing learned information
- bringing to mind appropriate material
- recalling information
- bringing to mind stored knowledge
- reciting learned information
- remembering
  - terms
  - methods
  - facts
  - concepts
  - specific items of information
- related to Guilford's Cognition, Convergent and Memory Operations from the Structure of the Intellect

QUESTION/STATEMENT VERBS

arrange	recall
cite	recite
choose	repeat
check	reset
define	reproduce
describe	say
find	select
group	show
hold	sort
identify	spell
label	state
list	tell
locate	tally
match	touch
name	transfer
offer	underline
omit	write
outline	
pick	
point to	
quote	

STUDENT LEARNING EXAMPLES

- remember an idea or fact in somewhat the same form in which it was learned
- question and answer sessions
- workbooks/work sheets
- programmed instruction
- remember things read, heard, seen
- games
- information searches
- reading assignments
- drill and practice
- finding definitions
- memory games
- quizzes
- questions have right and wrong answers

SAMPLE QUESTIONS/ACTIVITIES

- Label the parts of a plant.
- Show the numerals one to ten in Roman numeral form.
- Group together all the four-syllable words.
- List the freedoms included in the Bill of Rights.
- Identify the food group each of these foods belongs to.
- Write definitions to the following words.
- Locate different examples of capitalization in the following story.

FIGURE 2–6A
Bloom's Taxonomy Charts

Comprehension

DESCRIPTION (EXPLAINING AND UNDERSTANDING)	QUESTION/ STATEMENT VERB		STUDENT LEARNING EXAMPLES	SAMPLE QUESTIONS/ ACTIVITIES
ability to grasp the meaning of material	comprehend alter	extrapolate advance calculate	communicate an idea in a new or different form	Give reasons for the energy crisis.
interpreting material	convert change construe	contemplate	forming relationships (analogies, similes)	Explain why we have bus safety rules.
seeing relationships among things		offer	predicting effects of changes	Outline the steps necessary for an idea to become a law.
projecting effects of ideas	expand	project propose	justifying the method used	Restate the reasons for weather changes.
communicating an idea in a new or different way	moderate	scheme submit	debate	Estimate the top priorities facing our government in twenty-five years.
lowest level of understanding	qualify		dramatization	Define the relationships you see between politics today and in the early 1800's.
explaining ideas	transform translate vary		"What if . . . .?"	Interpret the chart showing the rate of inflation over the past ten years.
summarizing material	interpret		giving examples of	Summarize the story.
understanding facts and principles	account for annotate		paraphrasing	What were the underlying factors that contributed to the Revolutionary War?
estimating future trends	define		peer teaching	
predicting consequences	demonstrate explain expound		show and tell	
interpreting charts and graphs	infer		small group projects	
related to Guilford's relationships, systems and implication process and convergent thinking operation	outline spell out		estimating "Just suppose . . ." give reasons for story problems	

FIGURE 2–6B
Bloom's Taxonomy Charts

Application

DESCRIBING (USING IDEAS)	QUESTION/STATEMENT VERBS		STUDENT LEARNING EXAMPLES	SAMPLE QUESTIONS/ ACTIVITIES
applying concepts and principles to new situations	apply adopt avail	relate	using knowledge from various areas to find solutions to problems	Put this information in graph form.
applying laws and theories to practical situations	capitalize consume construct	solve try take up	applying ideas to new or unusual situations	Compare and contrast attitudes toward space exploration today and in the 1940's.
solving of mathematical problems	classify collect		simulation activities	Organize the forms of pollution from most damaging to least damaging.
constructing charts and graphs	devote	use utilize	role playing/role reversal	
demonstrating correct usage of a method or procedure	exercise exert employ exploit	wield	producing a newspaper, stories, etc.	Collect examples of private citizens influencing government.
applying rules, methods, concepts, principles, laws, theories	handle		model building	
	make use of mobilize manipulate		interviewing	You are in charge of a 1970's Hall of Fame. Who would be in it? Why?
requires higher level of understanding than comprehension	organize operate		groups presentation	
making use of the known	ply put in action put to use profit by		conducting experiments	How does the principle of estimation help you outside of school?
			making up classifications	
			experiments	Capitalize on the idea of school spirit. Plan posters, acts, plays, etc., that will promote school spirit.
			solving problems by use of known information	
			practical applications of learned knowledge	Sketch a picture that relates your feelings of recess.
			suggest actual uses of ideas	

FIGURE 2–6C
Bloom's Taxonomy Charts

51

Analysis

DESCRIPTION (BREAKING DOWN)	QUESTION/ STATEMENT VERBS	STUDENT LEARNING EXAMPLES	SAMPLE QUESTIONS/ ACTIVITIES
— breaking material down into component parts	audit take apart test for	— uncovering unique characteristics	— Simplify the ballet to its basic moves.
— understanding the organizational structure	breakdown uncover	— distinguishing between facts and inferences	— Inspect a house for poor workmanship.
— analysis of relationships between parts	check canvass differentiate	— evaluating the relevancy of data	— Search through a painting to uncover as many principles of art as possible.
— recognition of organizational principles involved	dissect divide deduce diagram	— recognizing local fallacies in reasoning — recognizing unstated assumptions	— Read a nonfiction book. Divide the book into its parts. Tell why the parts were placed in the order they were.
— requires understanding of both the content and structural form	examine include inspect infer	— analyzing the organizational structure of a work (of art, music, or writing)	— Look into the forces that might cause pressure for our legislators.
— analyzing the elements	look into reason	— comparing and contrasting — outlining written material	— Inspect two presidential addresses. Compare and contrast them.
— related to CPS - problem finding	separate simplify syllogize section scrutinize	— problem identification — attribute listing	— Think of a problem situation facing our country. Identify several real problems that make up this situation.
— related Guilford's systems and divergent thinking	survey search study screen sift subdivide	— morphological analysis	

FIGURE 2–6D
Bloom's Taxonomy Charts

Synthesis

DESCRIPTION (FORMING NEW WHOLE)	QUESTION/STATEMENT VERBS		STUDENT LEARNING EXAMPLES	SAMPLE QUESTIONS/ACTIVITIES
putting parts together in a new whole	blend build	recorder reorganize rearrange reconstruct	developing an original plan	Create a new song for the melody of "Mary Had a Little Lamb."
formulating new patterns or structures	create combine compile compose construct	revise structure	hypothesizing	Combine elements of drama, music and dance into a stage presentation.
abstract relationships	cause constitute conceive	yield	writing a well-organized theme	
communicating an idea in a unique way	develop design		writing a creative story; poem, or song	Develop a plan for your school to save money.
prosing a set of operations	effect evolve		proposing a plan for an experiment	Create a model of a new game that combines thinking, memory, and chance equally.
creating new or original things	form formulate		integrating the learning from different areas into a plan for solving a problem	
take things - pattern them in a new way	generate		formulating a new scheme for classifying objects	Reorganize a chapter/unit from your textbook the way you think it should be.
related to CPS implementation and planning	make mature make up modify		finding new combinations	Find an unusual way to communicate the story of a book you have read.
related to Guilford's transformation area and divergent operations	originate produce plan		identifying goals and objectives	Formulate positive changes that would improve learning in your classroom.
			showing how an idea or product might be changed	

FIGURE 2–6E
Bloom's Taxonomy Charts

53

Evaluation

DESCRIPTION (JUDGING)	QUESTION/ STATEMENT VERBS		STUDENT LEARNING EXAMPLES	SAMPLE QUESTIONS/ ACTIVITIES
— ability to judge the value of material	appraise assay accept assess adjudge arbitrate award	rule on rate rank reject referee settle summarize	— making judgments about data or ideas based on either internal or external conditions or criteria	— Decide which person would best fill a position.
— use of definite criteria for judgments	classify censure criticize conclude	support umpire	— rating ideas	— Rank the principles of "good sportsmanship" in order of importance to you.
— value judgments based on clearly defined criteria			— accepting or rejecting ideas based on standards	— Decide which proposed plan is the best.
— highest learning outcomes		weigh	— judging the logical consistency of written material	— Read two different accounts of an incident. Decide which story is most logical in its portrayal.
— use of cognitive and affective thinking together	describe decide discriminate decree determine		— judging the adequacy with which conclusions are supported with data	— Judge the posters or murals your class has just constructed.
— related to CPS - solution finding and decision making	evaluate explain		— judging the value of a work (of art, music, writing) by using internal criteria or external standards of excellence	— Justify the actions of your favorite historical figure.
— related to Guilford's evaluation area	grade interpret		— generating criteria for evaluation	— Determine the necessary criteria for a good resource.
	justify judge prioritize		— making evaluations of peer projects and presentations — evaluating one's own products and ideas	— Summarize the involvements you have had with your class this year.

Taylor, T. Roger. 1994. Workshop for College Station Independent School District, College Station, TX.

FIGURE 2–6F
Bloom's Taxonomy Charts

FIGURE 2–7
Preservice Teacher Lesson Plan

WRITING LESSON

THEME/SUBJECT: Texas
GRADE LEVEL: 3

GOAL: To create a time line of their own life and write a story using the time line as an outline.

OBJECTIVE: The students will make time lines of their own lives to use in ordering their lives' events for writing their own stories. They will understand outlines, time lines, story order, and the revision process using mini-lessons.

MATERIALS/RESOURCES:
The Tree that Would Not Die by Ellen Levine

TIME: The lesson will be taught in five days—forty-five minute segments each.

INSTRUCTIONAL PROCEDURES:
The whole class will read *The Tree that Would Not Die* together on the rug to introduce the lesson. We will discuss the story as an entire class first and then discuss the sequence of events in pairs. The pair discussions will lead to a whole class discussion about sequence and order. I will introduce and create a time line from the story we just read asking for student participation. I will ask the students questions such as, "What came next? Then what?" I will then demonstrate a time line of my own life. The students will begin to create a time line of their own lives individually. They will be allowed to take the time line home for clarification and parent suggestions. I will attach a note to the paper explaining the assignment. After completing the time lines, the students will discuss their time line in a whole class setting. I will then present a story of my own life written in sentence form using my time line as an example. The students will be

given this assignment and asked to do it individually. They will edit and revise in pairs, and after a final copy has been produced, will read their stories to the class.

LESSONS AND ACTIVITIES:
DAY 1: To warm everyone up and get their brains going we will sing "Texas Our Texas." The students will then read *The Tree that Would Not Die* and discuss the events in Texas's history. We will discuss what "sequence of events" means and how the history of Texas has a sequence. They will break into pairs and do further discussion about sequence of events and try to jot down the sequence of this story. I will show the class several time lines and how they progress in time (sequence order). A mini-lesson on time lines and what to include will be done in whole class instruction (lecture). I will also discuss in this mini-lesson what to include and not to include in the time line—similar to a main idea mini-lesson. The whole class will participate in creating a time line of Texas history using only the story. I will make the time line horizontally using the entire marker board at the front of the classroom to make the time line. I will ask them to make the time line without using dates because the story does not contain dates, just a sequence of events.

DAY 2: I will open with asking for volunteers in refreshing our memory about the story we read and the history of Texas the day before and ask someone to explain sequence to the class. I will then introduce a time line of my life on the overhead; it will be horizontal just like the one from *The Tree that Would Not Die* that the class created yesterday. My time line will have pictures and drawings that go with the time or event. A refresher mini-lesson

(continued)

FIGURE 2–7
Preservice Teacher Lesson Plan (*continued*)

on making time lines will be done again by asking the students to tell me how we make time lines in whole class discussion. The students will then go to their individual work spaces and make a time line of their own lives just as the one from the life of Texas on a large piece of manilla paper. They will work on the paper for the majority of the period. They can take these home to complete with parental assistance. The students need to bring photos to paste on their time lines for day 4.

DAY 3: We will open by discussing our time lines and how we are going to use it as a framework for writing a story about our history (life). A mini-lesson on outlining will be refreshed—I am assuming they have written a story using an outline previously. I will read my life history and point to my time line and show where I got the information for what I say in my story. The students will then receive another mini-lesson on story structure (introduction, body, conclusion). They will be asked to work individually on their stories. They may finish at home if necessary. The students need to bring pictures depicting events in their lives to school the next day.

DAY 4: The students will get their stories and break up into revision groups of four. They will hear a mini-lesson on revision (I am assuming they have revised one another's papers before). I will just have polite reminders for the students when reading another student's paper. The students can begin to make their final copy when they are finished with their revising in their groups. They will be asked to bring pictures and draw to add to their time lines once their stories are finished.

DAY 5: Time lines and stories are to be presented by every student in the class.

ADAPTATIONS: Those students who are not able to write or finish their story can "tell" their story using their time line as they go. A written form does not have to be used in giving the presentation. They can use the time line as notes in "telling" their life stories.

EXTENSIONS: The students who finish early can help those who are not finished revise and they can add more pictures and details to their outlines. I do not want those who are done early to be punished by having to do "extra" work so they never finish early. I want to provide fun activities for them. They can help make the back drop for the "Our Time Lines" bulletin board, or help set up the video equipment for the presentations. There will be an educational games center where the students can go if they are done early any time they wish.

EVALUATION: I will evaluate the students' work on whether or not the time line is in sequential order and if their stories somewhat follow their time lines in sequential order. Since I am stressing sequence in writing in the lesson, I want the students to be assessed on sequence in writing. I will evaluate my lesson and make adjustments considering the time allotted, the difficulty, and the meaningfulness. I want the students to have enough time to complete the assignment and I will add extra time or extend the days as seems necessary throughout the week. If the students are having a difficult time, I will just ask them to make the time line and use it to tell their history. Finally, if the students understand sequence in a story and in writing then I will continue to use this lesson. If the students have a clearer meaning of sequence and order, then it was successful! If the students are confused about sequence and order and do not understand, I will attempt to create another lesson to teach these concepts. If the students are having a good time and feel supported in their writing, then I will know they enjoy learning about Texas and writing.

Strategies for focusing student attention range from the elaborate to the simple. Sometimes we use an elaborate strategy that stages a "puppet" enactment of a concept related to the objective. For example, we arouse interest in compare/contrast writing with elaborate puppets representing cirrus clouds and cumulus clouds. A simpler focus to introduce compare and contrast writing consists of marking a white paper with a black crayon and then with a white crayon. Whether elaborate or simple, the focus draws student attention to the lesson being taught.

In lesson planning, we advise that a teacher explain in detail exactly how to present the focus. If the focus is a science experiment, for example, we explain how to demonstrate cloud formation, outline the steps of the experiment, and list how it relates to the students' prior knowledge. We always strive to construct a meaningful context for the students. Some motivational ideas appear in Appendix E.

Once we have captured student attention, we tell students what will happen in the lesson and what they will learn. This step allows students to organize their thinking in preparation for the lesson.

Lessons and activities. After we identify effective procedures for our lesson, we turn our attention to learning activities, which are the core of the lesson plan. Exactly what will we do and what will the students do to master the objective? What activities are most effective in helping students learn the objective? This is the point at which imagination, creativity, and resourcefulness come in to full play. Fortunately, a wealth of resources available for teachers on a wide variety of subjects and topics make this task manageable, but we are responsible for determining what resources and procedures are the best for our students.

First, we consider students' prior knowledge so that our teaching procedures can build on what students already know. We determine the activities that will support the objective and involve the students in the learning experience. The lesson plan provides student interaction with their peers, the teacher, and the content being presented. It breaks the lesson into small parts and presents those parts in a logical sequence. We reflect on and visualize what we will say and do and write those procedures into the plan in explicit detail. Using a step-by-step approach while writing the procedures, we build meaning and connections during teaching.

With our students, we describe and discuss in detail each part of the lesson, review labels and vocabulary words, and thoroughly explain exactly what they need to know and be able to do. The more details included in the procedures, the better the plans will be. The details require us to think through our lesson and avert problems before they occur. By using detailed plans in our teaching, we have confidence in our lesson and can be enthusiastic in our presentation.

We are constantly mindful of the students' multiple intelligences and learning styles in making decisions about the teaching procedures.

Closure. Closure is a simple yet effective component of the lesson plan. During closure, we complete the lesson by reviewing and summarizing the main ideas of the objective. Closure provides a time for the students to clarify concepts and ask questions that still lurk. After closure, students should be able to say, "Now I understand. I can do this."

Lessons begin with a review of previous work or prerequisite concepts and an overview of what is to be learned. Demonstration procedures are of an appropriate length for the students, and, because of the careful lesson explanation, reduces the incidence of student errors. Ysseldyke, Christenson, and Thurlow, 1997

Unless you verbalize the thinking processes that guide what you do and how you do it, some students may learn no more from watching your demonstration than they would from watching a magician perform a baffling trick. Good and Brophy, 1997

A lesson is thought to be clearly presented if students not only understand what they have to do but how to do it. Ysseldyke, Christenson, and Thurlow, 1997

As a neophyte teacher I made the mistake of . . . essentially asking children to produce a product . . . rather than first showing children how to write. May, 1998

Depending on the lesson, closure follows the specific procedures, the guided practice, the independent practice, and the assessment. We provide several opportunities during lessons to review and summarize concepts in closure activities.

Guided practice.   After being presented with a concept, students need time to practice the new concept while the teacher monitors and supports their efforts. Extensive support during guided practice is essential. If students practice incorrect methods or skills, they must then unlearn the mistakes before learning the correct information.

Cooperative groups and learning centers enhance guided practice. Students help and learn from each other while practicing with the support of peers and the teacher. While creating guided practice materials and activities, we continually assess how they support the specific objective and how the practice will make the students more proficient in the objective. Caution: Practice materials should provide specific practice on the particular skill to be learned rather than "busy work" or work that does not support mastery of the skill. Activities for guided practice in cooperative groups range from written responses to brainstorming to sharing writing to completing worksheets to role playing. Again, we use the multiple intelligences and learning styles to guide practice activities. The multiple intelligences also serve as a method for determining group membership, and they are sometimes the focus of a series of learning centers.

Independent practice.   As with the other components, this section of the lesson plan ties directly to the lesson objective. Exactly what is it that the students must learn and be able to do? During independent practice, students move toward autonomy and mastery of the objective. Materials are very similar to those used in guided practice, but now they focus on the individual success of each student rather than group interactions and successes. We carefully check the independent practice materials to be sure that students perform successfully. Then we reteach any students who exhibit difficulty and provide more support for their work.

Adaptations and extensions.   Adaptations to the lesson plan are the adjustments we make for students who need different approaches or materials from those that we present to the workshop group as a whole. These adaptations may take the form of individualized lessons for students who are mainstreamed in the school system but who are unable to accomplish the same tasks as their classmates. We teach the basic principles and information, but we present it in a form that is more understandable to those students.

Extensions are the additional plans we make for those students who work faster than others or who need enrichment to help maintain their interest in the assignment or project. Extensions may be generalized for a number of students or individualized for specific ones. The idea is not to simply add more but rather to broaden and deepen the area of study. Well planned extensions are a must for the gifted students in the class.

There needs to be a sufficient amount of practice . . . to increase fluency and automaticity of skills as well as exposure to various activities to increase generalizations and application of skills. Ysseldyke, Christenson, and Tharlow, 1997

Practice periods should be the shortest amount of time in which it is possible to really work on the task. Hunter, 1988

Massing practice at the initial stages of learning makes for fast learning. Hunter, 1988

Success and self-esteem go hand in hand. Wolk, 1994

Student assessment.   During assessment, students demonstrate independent mastery of the objective. Design of the assessment relates directly to the objective: Exactly what is it that the students are learning to do? Assessment checks for progress toward the objective and the goal. For authentic or performance assessment, we evaluate the process and the quality of writing incorporated in a final thematic project designed and carried out by the students.

We keep in mind that not all lesson objectives require mastery of a concept or a skill. Some concepts are introduced at one point and then revisited later in the year. Not every student masters each lesson objective each time, particularly if higher order skills are required.

Teacher self-assessment.   After each lesson, we reflect on the successes of the lesson in terms of student learning and response. We make notes on timing, procedures, activities, and interactions, and we record observations about how to improve the same lesson in the future.

Many open-education teachers, in their enthusiasm for process and for student input in the curriculum, seem to reject formal instruction entirely. Yet when students are deeply absorbed in their subject matter, formal instruction can bring students to new levels of understanding, and teacher-intervention can lead them to probe, test, and learn. Calkins, 1986

Mini-Lessons

A common concept in writing instruction is the *mini-lesson.* The idea of a mini-lesson is to teach a quick 5- or 10-minute lesson on a skill or a concept based on the teacher's observation of students' performance. Sometimes our students need a short lesson on a convention such as quotation marks, or they may need to understand a literary device such as alliteration. Observation of the students' work and behavior allows us to know what mini-lessons are needed at a particular time. By definition, mini-lessons are short, informal and unstructured and may be taught to small groups or to the whole class.

The mini-lesson concept is further explained by the fact that not all students need the same lesson at the same time. The approach assumes that those who don't need the lesson at the time it is taught will remember it later and apply it correctly to their work as the need arises. That doesn't always happen, however, so there are occasions for teaching to small groups.

If it's worth teaching at all, it's worth teaching so it is really learned and not forgotten tomorrow or next week. Hunter, 1988

Mini-lessons can play a valuable role in the classroom. After we teach a particular concept, some students may still have trouble applying the concept to their writing. They may not be sure how to apply it to a new genre of writing, or they may have simply forgotten it. A quick 5- or 10-minute mini-lesson can serve as a powerful technique for retrieving and connecting past knowledge to new situations.

The brain is attracted to novelty and soon stops paying attention to things that are routine; however, excess stimulus, as well as extreme lack of stimulus, block learning. Oelklaus, 1998

However, most content in writing and other subjects is best taught with the full lesson approach. If students need to learn something, they deserve thorough instruction and an opportunity to practice the concept. Few students master skills from a short lesson, particularly if they can't apply the skills immediately.

We recommend that teachers analyze the content of writing as it is presented in the following chapters along with the ages and needs of the students, and then consider

Student success rates . . . are enhanced when teachers explain the work and go over practice examples with students before releasing them to work independently. Good and Brophy, 1997

what to teach to help students grow as writers. Above all, begin where the students are. Design lessons to help students succeed at each step of the writing process. Carefully planned teaching allows writers to practice and "play" with the information and skills as they write; at the same time they learn the basic content of the craft of writing. Anything worth learning is worth teaching so that students understand it. Using a full lesson plan approach similar to that described earlier in this chapter helps teachers accomplish this goal.

EMPHASIZING THE MULTIPLE INTELLIGENCES

Linguistic: Provide the group with several weather-related books that have similes and ask students to skim the books looking for examples. When they find similes, ask them to create new similes that would fit into the same sentences.

Logical: Students conduct a weather experiment to make clouds and take notes on what they observe.

Musical: Students create a song about clouds.

Spatial: Using art paper, cotton balls, glue, crayons or markers, students create cloud mobiles and explain the process they used.

Bodily-kinesthetic: Students take turns dramatizing a weather phenomenon and describe them in writing.

Intrapersonal: Provide a set of photographs or magazine pictures of people with different facial expressions and ask students to write similes that express the feelings of the people in terms of the clouds that seem to match those feelings.

Interpersonal: Interview others—a student, family member, or a weather person—about their experiences or attitudes toward clouds. Summarize their responses in writing.

Naturalist: Students observe the current day's clouds and write predictions about the weather for the day.

SUMMARY

Thematic units provide students with meaningful connections for optimum motivation and learning. Thematic units are interdisciplinary approaches to content and writing among broad subject areas that integrate the multiple intelligences and allow students many choices.

Thematic units contain the essential content students need to learn, both in other subject areas and in writing. A mapping technique is an effective means for developing a theme that ties all of the subjects together. Content goals are meshed with the theme, and student activities are created that teach the content. Content and activities are divided into meaningful chunks of learning that relate to the age and background level of the students. Measurable objectives are designed to teach those meaningful chunks of learning within the focus of the theme. The specific objectives become the content of lesson plans.

Writing fits into any theme. When we integrate writing into the overall theme, we teach the content of writing in many and varied, yet meaningful, contexts.

Lesson plans include the following components: goal/objective, materials, motivation, teaching procedure, closure, guided practice, independent practice, evaluation, and time for the lesson. Objectives are stated with verbs that describe what the students will be able to do as a result of the lesson and should strive to incorporate higher order thinking skills. Mini-lessons offer valuable reteaching opportunities to reinforce and review students' writing skills.

Theory into Practice

Using the information from this chapter and class discussions, select activities from the following suggestions to put into practice what you have learned about thematic units and planning lessons.

1. Think back to your elementary school years. Discuss some thematic units that you remember. What made those units particularly memorable?

2. Discuss with your classmates the benefits of a thematic unit approach. Discuss the obstacles to implementing a thematic unit in your first year of teaching.

3. Brainstorm list of themes, and then suggest writing genres or a set of writing skills that might support the subject matter of the themes.

4. Using a state or school district curriculum document, list the knowledge and essential skills for written language for three consecutive grade levels.

5. Select a thematic unit topic. Use a webbing procedure to develop and limit the theme.

6. Select a goal for writing content. Using the charts in Figure 2–6, develop a sequential set of objectives for lesson plans that would help students achieve that goal. Include higher order thinking skills in the objectives. Use the multiple intelligences and learning styles for motivation activities.

7. Brainstorm some other ways to teach similes using two or three multiple intelligences approaches.

8. Discuss other means of assessing student performance for a lesson.

(continued)

9. Create a detailed lesson plan for one of the objectives. Include materials, focus, specific procedures, closure, guided practice, independent practice, and evaluation. Estimate the duration of the lesson. Teach the lesson plan to a group of students. Write an evaluation of your lesson in which you explain how the lesson was received by the students, how well they learned it, and how you felt about the lesson. Include changes you would make in the lesson as a result of the experience that you had in teaching it.

BIBLIOGRAPHY

Bloom, Benjamin S., and David R. Krathwohl. 1984. *Taxonomy of educational objectives, handbook 1: Cognitive domain.* New York: Addison-Wesley.

Calkins, Lucy. 1986. *The art of teaching writing.* Portsmouth, NH: Heinemann.

Dahl, Karin L., and Nancy Farnan, 1998. *Children's writing: Perspectives from research.* Literature Studies Series. Newark, DE: International Reading Association; and Chicago: National Reading Conference.

Emig, Janet. 1977. Writing as a mode of learning. *College Composition of Communication 28* (May): 122–8.

Emig, Janet. 1983. *The web of meaning.* Upper Montclair, NJ: Boynton/Cook Publishers.

Good, T. L., and J. E. Brophy. 1997. *Looking in classrooms.* New York: Longman.

Hunter, Madeline. 1988. *Teach more—faster!* El Segundo, CA: TIP Publications.

Jennings, D. 1996. Why write? *English in Texas* (Winter): 8.

Langer, Judith, and Arthur Applebee. 1987. *How writing shapes thinking: A study of teaching and learning.* Urbana, IL: National Council of Teachers of English, Research Report No. 22.

Lauritzen, Carol, and Michael Jaeger. 1994. Language arts teacher education within a transdisciplinary curriculum. *Language Arts, 71* (December): 581–587.

May, Frank B. 1998. *Reading as communication to help children write and read.* Upper Saddle River, NJ: Prentice Hall.

Montgomery, Susan D. 1994. *Beginning educator handbook.* Boise: Idaho Department of Education.

Oelklaus, Nancy. 1998 Conversations about learner characteristics. *For Leaders of Learners.* Texas Association for Supervision and Curriculum Development (January): 1.

Perrone, Vito. 1994. How to engage students in learning. *Educational Leadership, 51* (February): 11–13.

Routman, Reggie. 1994. *Invitations: Changing as teachers and learners K–12.* Portsmouth, NH: Heinemann.

Savoie, Joan M., and Andrew S. Hughes. 1994. Problem-based learning as a classroom solution. *Educational Leadership, 52* (November): 54–57.

Shanahan, Timothy. 1997. Reading-writing relationships, thematic units, inquiry learning . . . in pursuit of effective integrated literacy instruction. *Reading Teacher, 51* (September): 12–19.

Taylor, Roger. 1994. Workshop for College Station Independent School District in College Station, TX.

Wolk, Steven. 1994. Project-based learning: Pursuits with a purpose. *Educational Leadership, 52* (November): 42–45.

Ysseldyke, James E., Sandra L. Christenson, and Martha L. Thurlow. 1987. *Instructional factors that influence student achievement: An integrative review.* Minneapolis: University of Minnesota Instructional Alternatives Project.

Writing Assessment

From the viewpoint of educators, the primary purpose of assessment is to help students by providing information about how instruction can be improved.

International Reading Association, 1999

Chapter Outline

How good a job are you doing? For today's educators, this question looms large. . . . In about half of the United States, accountability is centrally controlled; in the other states, control is more local. Willis, 1999

With local assessment the most critical level of the education system is teachers. Willis, 1999

Testing is a form of assessment that involves the systematic sampling of behavior under controlled conditions. "High stakes assessment in reading," 1999

When decisions about students must be made that involve high-stakes outcomes . . ., rely on multiple measures rather than just performance on a single test. "High stakes assessment in reading," 1999

Accountability underlies almost everything we do in our educational system, and writing assessment is no exception. We assess to find out what students have learned, what they need to learn, and how teachers are teaching. ". . . . Assessment is the process of gathering information to meet a variety of evaluation needs. As a process, it is built around multiple indicators and sources of evidence, and in this sense, it is distinguished from testing" (Chittenden, 1991, p. 24). When children's writing samples are the assessment texts, the assessments constitute direct accountability for the school, the teachers, and the students.

Centrally controlled assessment is usually thought of as formal assessment or large-scale testing. It brings to mind a single test administered by someone from outside the classroom setting, and it is conducted under tightly controlled conditions. When control is local, we think of assessment as informal. It is conducted over time by teachers and students, often casually or unobtrusively in the classroom or writing workshop.

When and how we use various assessment procedures affects student attitude, motivation, grades, promotion, and placement. Most stakeholders in the process (students, teachers, parents, administrators, and community members) mistakenly equate assessment with testing or grading. A student exclaims, "I hate writing assignments when the only grade I get is a B or a C and red marks all over my paper! I wonder why the teacher wrote 'good job!' on my paper. What was 'good' about it?" Or a teacher sighs, "It is the weekend again, and I am loaded with stacks of papers to grade while my family is out having fun. Why didn't I choose to teach math?" However, assessments encompass far more than simply testing and assigning grades. In this chapter, we address two different types of assessment: one is the formal, single high-stakes test and the other is the more informal ongoing assessment within the workshop.

Formal assessment.   At one end of the spectrum is assessment involving formal testing. With formal assessment, the test and scoring are standardized and a specific performance standard is set. Test administrators maintain tightly controlled conditions using standardized test questions, an established rubric, and multiple independent evaluators. They keep writing prompts secure for the test, assign seats to the examinees, monitor time limits, and evaluate the test results with highly trained raters who score the writing samples under controlled conditions. Student performance is often reported with a single number and little or no feedback on the performance. Examples of formal assessment include the periodic nationwide *Writing Report Card* from the National Assessment of Educational Progress (NAEP) and a growing number of annual statewide and local tests of writing. In many school districts, these high-stakes tests determine a school district's rating as well as students' promotion and graduation. Willis (1999) says that some argue for the value of this kind of assessment "because the test measures student achievement relative to the state's content standards" (p. 6). The results and reporting guide decisions about staffing, student placement, curriculum, and instruction. In many schools, the stakes are so high that teachers are expected to "teach to the test." Indeed, in some cases, teachers' continued employment rests on the test results. Because the stakes for this kind of assessment are high, it is important that teachers understand how it works and its long-range effects.

In their preparation programs, teachers should be provided with a range of approaches that place testing in a proper balance with observation, interviewing, and performance samples. Ragin, 1987

Informal assessment. At the other end of the spectrum are those who ascribe to the idea that accountability rests on teachers' adjusting their practices to maximize the likelihood of student success and to minimize student failure. Proponents of informal assessment realize that since we use multiple methods for teaching, we must use multiple methods of assessment, methods that are compatible with our teaching. Thus, informal assessment techniques include daily workshop observations, student performance samples of writing over extended periods of time, peer and teacher response and individual conferences, projects, self-reflection, and also test-like measures such as writing on demand. Teachers hold the key to this kind of assessment. They teach it, they guide it, and they encourage it. These measures combine to provide broad evaluative feedback to writers and parents, the assignment of grades, and data for curriculum and instruction planning and design.

While formal large-scale testing provides valuable information about students' writing, the multifaceted measures of informal evaluation on the local level provide a wealth of information that is even more important to students' growth and development as writers.

Terminology. Because of the specialized terminology used in assessment and testing, we rely on Wheeler and Haertel's (1993) *Resource Handbook on Performance Assessment and Measurement* to define the terms that refer to writing assessment: assessment, performance assessment, criteria, standard, evaluation, scoring rubric, scoring scale, consistency, prompts, and portfolios. A table of these terms and their definitions appears in appendix F.

New directions in school or district assessment should, whenever possible, build on classroom practices. Chittenden, 1991

Performance assessment. Today most writing assessments, both formal and informal, are performance assessments measured with criterion-referenced scales; that is, they include tasks that reflect what people really do, and they are judged according to a predetermined standard. According to Marzano, Pickering, and McTighe (1993), these performance tasks require an extended period of time to complete, and they require students to construct new knowledge. They are accompanied by the following characteristics:

- identification of content standards
- use of complex reasoning processes
- creation
- analysis of the task
- reflection of the standards,
- explicit communication of the standards

Make assessment measures resemble learning tasks . . . some of the best examples of more learning-like tests are writing assessments. Shepard, 1989

Hughes (1991) suggests that "the best way to test people's writing is to get them to write" (p. 75). In both formal and informal assessments, that is generally what we do. However, this simple statement raises many questions about assessing writing. How often should we assess? Should we assess all or selected products? What kinds of assessment should we use? How should we use each kind and when? How should we use the results?

Purposes for Assessment

To address issues related to assessment, we examine the purposes for assessment, the various types of assessment, writing tasks and assessment conditions, interpretation of assessment results, and reporting issues. Since we teachers are encouraged to use multiple forms of assessment, we need to know the purpose of each. We need to know when each of the purposes is appropriate and beneficial to the students and to the writing program. Even if we don't use all assessment forms, we need to clearly understand them because of the far-reaching effects they can have on students' attitudes, motivation, and development as writers. Several of the most valid and frequent reasons for examining writing in our schools are to:

- design and plan curriculum and instruction
- encourage growth through revision and meaningful feedback
- determine ability
- place students in appropriate courses
- assign grades
- promote students to another grade
- measure proficiency
- identify errors for correction
- conduct research

Types of Assessment

The type of assessment we use depends on the purpose for the assessment. Some assessments help answer research questions, some lend themselves to large-scale testing, and some promote growth and improvement in writers and writing instruction. Some of the most widely used types of assessment are *discrete-point, frequency-count marking, holistic impressionistic, primary-trait,* and *analytic.* Examples of rubrics and scales for some of these assessment types appear along with the descriptions.

Discrete-point assessment.   Discrete-point assessment measures students' *recognition* of writing skills with objective tests such as multiple choice or cloze tests or the correction of a writing sample. It is often used as a segment of a formal standardized test battery. This kind of measurement may also be used informally in a more traditional writing class as a worksheet, quiz, or test. Discrete-point assessment measures editing skills rather than effective communication, skills quite different from a student's ability to *produce* writing. For example, students may be asked to recognize surface features of writing, such as correct spelling and placement of punctuation marks in a short passage, but recognition of the features of writing does not mean that those students can communicate through the effective production of writing.

Frequency-count marking.   Frequency-count marking provides detailed information about a student's actual writing sample and is valuable for formal research or informal error correction. It involves analyses of subject-verb agreement; comma faults or fragments; and the numbers of syllables in a word, words in a sentence, sentences in a paragraph, and words in a piece of writing. It assesses writers' mechanical sophistication or grade level use of language, but it, too, indicates little about writers' ability to reason or communicate a message.

Holistic assessment. Holistic assessment is traditionally and effectively used for formal proficiency testing such as the large-scale testing of writing objectives or minimal values, or for components of standardized test batteries. It measures a student's ability to produce a writing sample. A general criteria or specific standard is established, determined by the purpose for the test and the population being tested. Raters practice evaluating compositions with the criteria/scale and sample papers before they read students' tests; however, the readers often do not have the rubric before them as they rate the papers. Therefore, their scores are often referred to as impressionistic. In other words, raters mark each paper by the whole impression it makes on them.

The traditional ABCs of writing classrooms also illustrate holistic impressionistic assessment. Teachers have a set of criteria in mind that supports their grading, but too often the writers are not privy to those criteria. Too often the teacher's criteria shift and change from one paper to the next or from one grading session to the next. Holistic impressionistic assessments report only a single numerical score (1, 2, 3 . . .) or letter (A, B, C . . .), which represents an overall description of a piece of writing. For example, on a four-point holistic scale, a score of 3 for one student may indicate a technically perfect paper that lacks inspiration, creativity, or substantial organization. For another student, a score of 3 may indicate exceptional creativity and sophistication in the treatment of subject matter but a lack of mastery in grammar and mechanics. Both writers receive the same score but for different reasons. Additional feedback, if given, usually consists of descriptive comments about the students' performance—sometimes an overwhelmingly time-consuming task and sometimes, depending on the commentary, highly ineffective, as we will discuss later in the chapter. While it works quite well for large-scale assessment, this kind of assessment tends to give neither teachers nor students specific information as to students' strengths or weaknesses and little or no direction in the writing process. The scale in Figure 3–1 represents the type of rubric used for many large-scale tests.

Primary-trait assessment. Primary-trait assessment uses a focused holistic scale. It, too, is used for large-scale testing such as in the writing assessment by the NAEP. The scale is similar in many ways to the holistic impressionistic scale, but with one exception. Each set of criteria emphasizes a specific kind of writing such as descriptive, informative, or persuasive. "Primary Trait Scoring is more difficult than other methods" because each writing task requires a separate scoring guide that "defines precisely what segment of discourse is to be evaluated" (Lloyd-Jones, 1977, p. 37). Again, in testing situations, a "whole" score is the only measure communicated to the student. The primary trait score is a single number representing the quality of the paper according to the scoring guide for that trait. The scale in Figure 3–2 from Lloyd Jones (1977, pp. 52–53) illustrates a primary-trait scoring guide developed specifically to assess writers' use of *dialogue.*

Holistic evaluation is obviously to be preferred where the primary concern is with evaluating the communicative effectiveness of . . . writing. . . . The application of clear, appropriate criteria was felt to be important. Weir, 1990

A great danger of impression marking a piece of writing is that impression of the quality as a whole will be influenced by just one or two aspects of the work. Weir, 1990

Score of 0: Papers in the 0 range fail to respond to the assignment. This range includes papers that
- do not address the assigned task or that are blank
- contain only a word or brief phrase in response to the task
- simply copy or paraphrase the assignment
- are incoherent
- reply, "I don't want to take this test" or "I don't know"
- are illegible
- are written in a language other than English

Score of 1: Papers in the 1 range attempt to address the topic; they are responses that lack elaboration. This range includes papers that
- do not address the audience
- address the topic, but only briefly
- do not stay on the topic
- do not address the type of writing requested
- lack organization
- are laden with syntactic and mechanical errors, impeding understanding

Score of 2: Papers in the 2 range address the purpose and audience but contain minimal responses. This range includes papers that
- show audience awareness
- are somewhat elaborated
- are organized but are repetitive or lack information
- demonstrate some control of diction, syntax, and mechanics, but it is limited

Score of 3: Papers in the 3 range respond well to the writing task. The writer's meaning is clear. This range includes papers that
- show an apparent awareness of audience
- are moderately well-elaborated
- show a clear organizational pattern, but include some unnecessary information
- demonstrate clear control of language structures

Score of 4: Papers in the 4 range are consistently outstanding in all features and show an overall fluency in written communication. This range includes papers that
- show a clear awareness of audience throughout the paper
- are highly elaborated with specific details to develop ideas
- show a consistent and complete organizational pattern
- demonstrate appropriate and sophisticated diction, syntax, and mechanics

A three-point holistic scale by Sager (2000) appears in Appendix G.

FIGURE 3–1　Holistic Impressionistic Scale for Scoring Written Composition

Use of Dialogue

0 Does not use dialogue in the story

1 Direct quote from one person in the story. One person may talk more than once. When in doubt whether two statements are made by the same person or different people, code 1. A direct quote of a thought also counts. Can be in hypothetical tense.

2 Direct quote from two or more persons in the story.

Point of View

0 Point of view cannot be determined or does not control point of view.

1 Point of view is consistently one of the children. Includes "If I were one of the five children . . ." and recalls participation as one of the children.

2 Point of view is consistently one of an observer. When an observer joins the children in the play, the point of view is still 2 because the observer makes a sixth person playing. Include papers with minimal evidence even when difficult to tell which point of view is being taken.

Tense

0 Cannot determine time or does not control tense (one wrong tense places the paper in this category, except drowned in the present).

1 Present tense—past tense may also be present if not part of the "main line" of the story.

2 Past tense—If a past tense description is acceptably brought up to present, code as "past." Sometimes the present is used to create a frame for past events. Code this as past, since the actual description is in the past.

3 Hypothetical time—Papers written entirely in the "If I were on the boat" or "If I were there, I would." These papers often include future references such as "when I get on the boat I will." If part is hypothetical and the rest past or present and tense is controlled, code present and past. If the introduction, up to two sentences, is only part in past or present then code hypothetical.

From "Primary Trait Scoring" by Richard Lloyd-Jones in (Eds. C. R. Cooper and L. O'Dell) *Evaluating Writing,* 1977. National Council of Teachers of English, pp. 33–66.

FIGURE 3–2 Primary-Trait Scale for "Children in a Boat": Dialogue

The topic directs students to write a story about a picture of children on a boat. The assessment addresses three categories: writers' use of dialogue, point of view, and tense. The final scoring guide for the entire exercise follows.

Entire Exercise

0 No response, sentence fragment
1 Scorable
2 Illegible or illiterate
3 Does not refer to the picture at all
4 I don't know

For example, the following sample responses for two nine-year-olds (p. 55) were scored this way:

| Dialogue | 0 | Point of View | 1 | Tense | 3 |

> I would tip the Boat over and push it in the water. And then
> I would go for a Ride.
> I would jump in the water.
> I would Push it in the water while evey Bosy.
> I would push evey Body off the boat.

| Dialogue | 0 | Point of View | 2 | Tense | 0 |

> Well, five children are standing on an over-turned boat. All of
> them are having fun jumping and hopping on it. It was a pretty
> windy day and the girl could have fallen in the lake. I thought
> one of them was going to hurt themselves by jumping and
> sprane their ankle. Three boats are tied to a booy in the lake.

Analytic assessment.   Analytic assessment is defined by Diederich (1974) as looking at the various qualities of a piece of writing: qualities such as the richness, soundness, clarity, and development of ideas and their relevance to the topic and purpose; usage, sentence structure, punctuation, and spelling; organization and analysis; wording and phrasing; and finally style, originality, interest, sincerity, and individuality. While analytic scales are occasionally used for large-scale testing, they are more often used in the workshop or classroom for profiling strengths and weaknesses or for obtaining an overall summary of students' writing. These qualities are similar to those of the impressionistic or primary trait assessment, but not so focused on specific genre as the primary-trait. Qualities of the assessment are spelled out in a rubric—a weighted set of criteria—used by the readers. An analytic scale, or checklist, describes in detail the readers' intuitive responses to writing. "Scores may be recorded as check marks for presence or absence of an attribute, marked on a numerical or descriptive rating scale, or put in the form of a brief comment" (Wheeler and Haertel, 1993, p. 17). Further, the scale provides a common vocabulary for discussing writing and a means of communication between reader and writer. A well-known bare-bones analytical scale (Diederich, 1974), developed from an analysis of teachers and community members, illustrates this approach in Figure 3–3.

More elaborated analytical checklists and scales appear later in the chapter.

Regardless of the scale that is being used for assessment, writers should know on what standard they are being judged. In other words, they should have an opportunity to become acquainted with the scale prior to the assessment. Even more, the scale should be part and parcel of the teaching and learning process in writing.

The analytic approach to grading and teaching considers writing to be made up of various features, such as creativity or punctuation, each of which is to be scored separately; an analytic score is made up of a sum of the separate scores, often a weighted sum. White, 1985

	Low		Middle		High	
General Merit						
Ideas	2	4	6	8	10	
Organization	2	4	6	8	10	
Wording	1	2	3	4	5	_____
Mechanics						
Usage	1	2	3	4	5	
Punctuation	1	2	3	4	5	
Spelling	1	2	3	4	5	
Handwriting	1	2	3	4	5	_____
					Total	_____

From Holistic Evaluation of Writing by Charles R. Cooper in *Evaluating Writing*, 1977, 3–31. National Council of Teachers of English.

FIGURE 3–3 Diederich's Analytic Scale

Writing Tasks and Assessment Conditions

Different modes, audiences and purposes require writers to use various "registers," to choose different organizational strategies, and even to provide different types and amounts of information. Odell, 1977

Teachers have been known to come into the teachers' lounge bemoaning the fact that their students have "bombed" on a writing assignment. It has happened to all of us. What we realize as we try to discover the cause of such disasters is this: The problem isn't with the students but with the writing tasks. Writing tasks vary widely and are determined by the purpose for the assessment.

Formal Assessment

Structured, preset writing tasks are used for formal assessments. These formal writing tasks are traditionally administered within a strict time frame and in a highly regulated, secured, and structured setting. Students see the writing task for the first time when they are asked to respond to it; in addition, writers are asked for an immediate response. An administrator or teacher distributes the writing topic and instructions to the students and then monitors the assessment. Students sit in assigned seats and work individually. They read the topic, plan, write, revise, and edit in a single sitting, usually within a time frame ranging from 30 minutes to several hours.

In some schools, this formal assessment more closely reflects the writing process. For example, after students receive the assigned topic, they may have several class periods or the entire school day to think, brainstorm, gather information, plan, draft, revise, and produce a finished piece of writing.

In formal assessments, usually two or more readers, trained with specific criteria, evaluate written responses and assign a score to each paper. "Because they offer a standard, systematic means for assessing writing, traditional methods of writing assessment are especially useful for comparing groups of students' writing performance beyond the classroom level" (*NAEP's 1990 Portfolio Study*, 1992).

Informal Assessment

Back in the workshop, writing tasks and conditions are different from those of the formal assessment. At the beginning, end, and often throughout the semester in the workshop, students produce more formal writing samples for diagnostic purposes or to measure mastery. Similar to the formal assessment, all students write on the same topic and under the same conditions. In addition, specific writing genres are occasionally assessed in the same way.

Like the more formal assessment, it is a healthy practice for teachers to assess sample papers with the criteria for the assessment. For the fairest assessment, two teachers read each paper. This practice also helps teachers discover whether or not they are in agreement with the school's writing standard and with each other. Rater reliability, or consistency in rating, is desirable in any setting, formal or informal. A student should be able to take his or her paper to any rater and receive approximately the same rating and feedback from each one.

Creating Writing Tasks

When all of our writers write on the same topic, we follow some basic principles for developing the writing tasks. For example, the topic includes a situation (a letter), a purpose (explain, persuade, narrate), an audience (the real reading audience), and a request that students develop their writing with specific reasons, examples, and/or details. To ensure that writers have the best possible advantage, we use writing tasks that follow a set of universal criteria (Jacobs et al., 1981).

Universals for Determining a Topic

The universal criteria for developing a topic for the purpose of assessing writing are that the topic be *realistic, appropriate, understandable, personal, reliable, feasible,* and *fair*
The most effective and enabling topic or assignment for all writers is

- Realistic: The content of the task is real and reflects the kinds of writing that students are likely to encounter in the real world. Especially in formal assessment, because of the time limitations for developing content, it is best to avoid tasks that require children to imagine or guess at a situation.
- Appropriate: The content of writing tasks is general enough that any student given the task will have some knowledge of it or be able to find out about it within the pa-

---

As soon as a teacher or school wants to compare the achievements of students from one classroom with those of another, the need for a standard method of assessment arises. *NAEP's 1990 Portfolio Study*, 1992

Four important questions for assessors: What are our purposes in evaluating student writing? What do we hope to learn as a result of our evaluation? What do we mean by *competence* in writing? What kind of tasks does *writing* entail? Odell, 1977

The construction of appropriate topics remains more an art than a science, however, and it is therefore crucial when judgments are made about how well students have done in a writing assessment to examine the particular topics that have been given. Applebee, Langer, and Mullis, 1989

rameters of the assessment. On the other hand, parameters of the task are focused in such a way that students can address it succinctly within the time frame. In addition, it is important to question whether or not the task is appropriate for the grade level and the population.

- Understandable: Concise and clear wording of the task creates a context in which the writer is not likely to misread or misunderstand the topic. For example, when asked to give "concrete" examples, several middle school writers taking a large-scale test wrote a discussion of concrete (as in sidewalks).
- Personal: The task appeals to a wide variety of interests, with special attention to the experiences and interests of the group being assessed. Can students with strengths in different multiple intelligences find a sufficient number of ways to approach the topic? Can children in Wisconsin easily write about armadillos? Conversely, can children in Texas easily write about porcupines? Are these the types of tasks that children might care about?
- Reliable: The task elicits the intended type of writing. For example, if we are assessing writers' progress in informative writing, the task is specific enough that the writers don't produce narrative writing instead.
- Feasible: Formal assessment often includes specified time limits for the writing. Writing tasks lend themselves to development within the time allotted for completion. One way to determine the feasibility of a writing task is to write in response to the topic ourselves and then double or triple the time, depending on the age and stage of the writers.
- Fair: Most readers, even teachers, have biases. Tasks that ask writers for opinions that might be unpopular with readers lead to bias in evaluation. Topics give writers a variety of acceptable approaches, and readers are open to several accurate interpretations. When we develop topics, we apply these universals.

Task analysis. Let's say we plan to administer an hour-long diagnostic test of children's writing skills near the end of the school year. Assuming that we want to assess third-grade writers' ability to use a descriptive narrative genre, would the following topic meet the universal criteria? Is it realistic, appropriate, understandable, reliable, personal, feasible, and fair? Have purpose, audience, and specific instruction been included?

> In the stories you have read this semester, you have met many interesting characters. To guide other readers to the books that you like best, we will compose a booklet of our favorite characters and some of their adventures. *Briefly describe one of your favorite characters so that your readers can know what he (she, it) is like and tell a story about one of his (her, its) adventures. Be sure to use specific details in your story.*

For a fair assessment, audience and purpose must be explicit. Odell, 1977

The task calls for information that writers already possess, giving them a range of choice in content. It specifics situation (booklet), purpose (descriptive story), and audience (teacher/peers). Further, it meets the universal criteria. This topic would be acceptable for an assessment.

Now consider the possibility of the following topic for sixth-grade writers at the end of the year.

New students will be coming in to the sixth grade in the fall. Write a chapter for the Student Handbook. *In this chapter, explain to new students how to become a member of one of the school's sports activities or clubs. Be sure to include the steps they must take and use examples and specific details.*

The task specifies situation (chapter in a handbook), purpose (how-to informational), and audience (new students). Content is based on personal experience or information that can be researched. It allows students with strengths in any of the multiple intelligences to provide information for the chapter. While this task meets most of the criteria for a time-restricted assessment, it falls short on one very important criterion—feasibility. Writers would need more than an hour to complete such an assignment. They might draft a plan for this writing task in an hour, but they would need workshop time to research, discuss, and develop the specifics of the chapter. We would not use this topic for a time-restricted assessment. This writing task would lend itself more readily to a more informal extended writing workshop project.

When a more formal assessment is required or when we want to know how well our writers can respond to spontaneous requests to write, we work with other writing teachers to brainstorm the best possible writing tasks and examine them to be sure they meet the universal criteria. By structuring writing tasks with care, we provide models for our students as they learn to create their own writing tasks. These writing tasks are assessed with criteria appropriate to the specific writing task.

Student-selected writing tasks.   Contrary to the more formal assessment of teacher-made topics, writers also develop their own writing tasks with a high level of student input as to the topics and a large measure of student-to-student and student-to-teacher interaction. In other words, writers use extended processes to develop their products. In both formal and informal situations, writing tasks that are developed and designed with care result in more effective products. Some writing tasks grow out of students' own special interests. In the writing workshop, students write and produce papers on a regular basis, experimenting with the genres and modes that we present in the workshop. As soon as they can, students choose the content that goes into the framework. We model the development of topics in workshop, and with practice, our students learn to recognize the kinds of questions they want to pose and answer. They use the features of the formal writing task that include situation, audience, and purpose; but since they choose the content, we serve as guides in helping them develop topics they can realistically address. In this way, students learn how to create and develop their own writing tasks.

Criteria, scales, and rubrics.   Without a structured setting and time restraints, students write freely in writing workshop. Many write great quantities. They often share their ideas with each other in pairs, in small writing groups, or as a whole class. Along with all this activity, we introduce and model the development of criteria, scales, or rubrics for various kinds of writing. Rather than the quick assessment of impressionistic scoring, we more often use analytic checklists, scales, and criteria. Another primary difference is that the criteria are no longer used strictly for measurement and grading. Now they are used for evaluation and feedback as an integral part of learning. In workshop, the scales and criteria become aids to teaching and learning as writers incorporate them into the writing process. Students use the criteria during the process, *as they write*, to self-monitor and to give feedback to each other. The criteria furnish the vocabulary for discussing writing in the workshop. When it is time for a grade, writers know and understand the standard they are striving to reach.

Results and Reporting

Formal assessment.   In formal assessment, the single test score is most often the deciding factor. Results or grades from formal testing typically report proficiency or general progress. Rightly or wrongly, accurately or inaccurately, these scores sometimes become the sole measure used to make high-stakes decisions about students' futures in terms of promotion and placement. Test scores placed in permanent folders follow students as they progress through the grade levels. Results may be reported in a school newsletter to parents and in the local newspapers as the school's report card to the community. To make the important decisions about students' progress, promotion, and placement, we believe that a combination of formal and informal assessments is best.

Informal assessment.   In the informal setting of the writing workshop, the evaluation of students' writing and their writing processes is reported in a number of ways: in student-teacher conferences, student-teacher-parent conferences, and on report cards. Report cards frequently list single letter or numerical grades, while conferences, teacher feedback, and student reflections in the portfolio provide rich description of students' writing progress and verbalization of goals for future improvement.

Diagnostic writing.   In the workshop setting, especially at the beginning of the school year when we assess writing samples for diagnosing writers' strengths and weaknesses, we return the samples to the writers with feedback for revision, but we do not return a fully scored evaluation to the students. Instead we use the diagnostic results to make instructional decisions. Results lead to individualized instruction for some writers or to whole class mini-lessons when it is obvious that many writers lack knowledge of a specific skill or concept.

Later in the year, after students have made significant improvement in their writing skills, a comparison of the early and later results may serve as an effective way to show writers how much improvement they have made.

> I think we need to recognize that the fallibility of human judgment will always be with us and we should temper our claims about the findings of writing . . . assessment. Purves, 1992

> We provide activities and assessments in different learning styles and MIs that allow students to learn through manipulatives, writing, oral presentations, and self-reflection. . . . Upon reflection, we realized that our testing practices were incongruent with our instructional beliefs. Geocaris and Gardner, 1991

> The assessment practices of effective teachers are closely interwoven with instructional decisions. Calfee, Henry, and Funder, 1988

Writing Workshop Assessment

Attitude and Motivation

Students' attitudes toward writing determine their enthusiasm for the writing process. Our classroom experiences and a body of research show that writers respond favorably to understanding the material and knowing what is expected of them. They like making choices and having time to think, create, and share. They want feedback from their teachers, family, and peers. They want to know what to fix and how to fix it, and they want the opportunity to fix the parts of their writing that need changing. Most writers don't usually respond well to the traditional approach to assessing writing. In the traditional classroom, the teacher often starts with a lesson on a mode of writing, uses a standard teacher-made assignment, and requests a finished product. When the product is turned in, it may receive an impressionistic grade with copious comments written on the face of the paper about what to do on the next paper. Or it may be marked up with little or no commentary. Negative feelings often abound on both sides of the desk when writing is regularly taught, tested, and graded with little attention to what students have created or little collegial feedback during the process.

We ask the teachers who participate in our writing workshops, "Do you grade every piece of writing that your students write?" and "How do you grade your students' work?" Many teachers who teach writing rooted in the way they were taught when they were in school say it is their "duty" to grade everything. They say that the children won't write unless they know it is for a grade. This is often true. They also say that parents are unhappy when they don't mark all of the errors in the child's papers. This, too, is often true. They say they use *ABC* grades, write comments on the students' papers, and correct grammatical errors and word choices. They sometimes ask students to revise. The results—neatly recopied papers with exactly, and only, the changes or corrections that the teacher wrote on the papers. Figure 3–4 illustrates a student paper marked by the teacher without evaluation or feedback, but with a request to revise.

The Best Christmas

My best Christmas I ever had was last year. My family went to see my aunt and my cousins for Christmas. While we were there my aunt cooked a big turkey and we also had ham, gravy, and potatoes. For desert we had rhubarb pie, cherry pie and chocolate cake.

After dinner my aunt played Santa Claus. It was very funny because she was going around passing out presents and saying HO, HO, HO. My cousin got a motorcycle. And I got a jambox and a telefone. After supper we were finished unwrapping the presents. We watched Daisy and Geoffrey on television until it was over. We went a outside and rode on the motorcycle til all night dark. Finally, Christmas was over and it was time for us to go back home. I will never forget that Christmas not just because i fun, its because i got to see my family on the best time of year.

Scratched out marks are the writer's, but lined out sentences and circles are the sole measure of the teacher's response to this writer.

FIGURE 3–4   Student Writing Sample, Marked with No Feedback on Evaluation

Others who teach writing as a process are hesitant to talk about grades at all. They ask students to write often and to keep their creations in their writing folders. Teachers and peers provide feedback and offer suggestions about work in progress. Periodically, writers select specific pieces to revise for finished products. These pieces eventually receive grades after they have gone through the writing process, but numerical or letter grades are few and far between. It is a fact of life that most of our school systems require testing, grading, and evaluation. Teachers held accountable for their teaching and for the progress of their students learn when to use each kind of assessment for the maximum benefit of students' growth in writing and for the improvement of instruction and curriculum.

Teaching Guidelines: Grading Versus Evaluation

While every piece of writing is *evaluated* by someone, even if that someone is the writer, only selected pieces of writing need to be *graded,* and then with specific criteria known to the writers from the beginning of the assignment.

Self-evaluation occurs when we write in journals and then read the entry to see if we have said what we intended to say. We ask someone to listen to a sentence as we search for more effective wording. We apply a rubric or checklist to a draft to find the gaps and missing pieces. All of this is evaluation, but without a grade. In writing workshop, grading occurs after writers take time to work through the writing process. We encourage teachers to think about the difference between grading and evaluating as they guide students in the writing workshops and classrooms that they manage.

To grade, according to *The American Heritage Dictionary,* means to arrange in a series or according to a scale or to determine the absolute quality of something. For example, grades of eggs and meat indicate relative levels of quality. A grade in writing is "a mark" indicating a student's level of accomplishment, progress, or proficiency. Statewide and national writing tests grade students' writing performance. To take away the mystery and fear of grading, we provide students with sufficient information about a writing topic, sample papers, and appropriate rubrics. We then ask them to discuss and grade anonymous papers. Many become quite fascinated with the analytic process.

To evaluate, on the other hand, means to find the value or amount of something or to appraise it by indicating areas in need of improvement. Evaluation leaves room for change in that value. For example, when a homeowner sells a house, a Realtor provides an appraisal of its value, with one list of the attractive qualities and another list of the needed repairs. The seller has an opportunity to fix those negative features before the final value is established. Like the appraisal of a house, "evaluating in teaching is most effective if it is flexible enough to allow for change and improvement on the part of the student. Such flexibility is best achieved if evaluation is accompanied by positive, yet well-defined, directional feedback" (Hughey and Hartfiel, 1989, p. 3).

Feedback is defined as the "reciprocal effect of one person or thing upon another, especially as a reaction that affects the behavior of whatever produced the reaction" (*The American Heritage Dictionary*). Positive, focused, and facilitative feedback in writing becomes the means by which teachers guide students. Students learn what is valued and what needs to be changed. Teachers and students, as thoughtful evaluators, become collaborators in the writing classroom. With testing and grading, the focus is on product. With evaluation and feedback, the focus is on both process and product.

Evaluation and feedback are essential keys to revision and the recursive nature of writing. As such, they fit well in the writing workshop where students learn to inquire, to explore subjects and genre, and to develop and grow as writers. As assessment tools, evaluation and feedback are crucial to the writing process. Our experiences with evaluation and feedback in the writing workshop lead us to a portfolio assessment approach that includes evaluation, feedback, revision, and grades.

Portfolios

Many teachers find themselves caught between the requirements of the mandated curriculum on the one side and the requirements of authentic assessment practices on the other. Zessoules and Gardner, 1991

Not all schools use a portfolio approach. Many schools have their own standard assessment practices that are determined by the faculty or by the administration, and teachers are obligated to follow the school's guidelines for that particular assessment. More than a specific method of evaluation, what really matters is that teachers and students communicate and collaborate to improve the teaching and learning of writing. That goal can be accomplished in many different ways. However, we do use a portfolio system that is quite effective; and because there is so much available information about portfolio systems, we will share with you what works for us.

Teaching Guidelines: Portfolios

Portfolios allow assessors to examine a body, rather than a sample of students' work in order to judge the quality of that work. Stock, 1991

The idea of portfolios is not new. Camp and Levine (1991) point out that artists and student artists have long used portfolios to demonstrate the range and quality of their work. We are aware that portfolios serve different purposes at different times and that there are as many different portfolio approaches as there are teachers. We have found that for our developing writers, the benefits of portfolios are many. Portfolios allow writers to:

- select the contents
- collect a variety of genre
- evaluate writing process and product
- track progress over time
- develop independence through self-reflection

Portfolios allow teachers to

Portfolios are performance-based tasks. These measures are often referred to as authentic assessment, and they are designed to present a broader, more genuine picture of student learning. Zessoules and Gardner, 1991

- model best practice
- improve teaching
- inform instruction
- take the role of facilitator or coach

Select the contents.   We mentioned in Chapter 1 that our students keep writing folders and portfolios in the classroom. The writing folder holds a student's complete set of writing for the year from prewriting activities to drafts with evaluation and feedback to polished products. Separate and different from the cumulative folders are students' portfolios. Portfolios contain only selected works, the pieces that the writers have identified as those they want to take back into the writing process for revision and publication. While our writers participate in the selection of pieces to include in the portfolio, we offer help and guidance in their selections, especially with our younger writers.

Collect a variety of genres. It is not uncommon for our students to perform at different levels when they write in different genres. As a result, we don't make direct comparisons of different genre such as narrative and persuasive writing or poetry and reporting. For a measure of progress in a specific genre, students need to develop multiple pieces of writing in that genre, which can then be compared for growth. In addition, it often takes more than one or two pieces of writing to get a realistic picture of a writer's ability in a particular genre. Johnny may be a superlative narrator yet have trouble with writing informatively, while Judy may write research reports easily and have trouble with narration. Portfolios give both student and teacher a clear picture of these differences, and thus a clear picture of where instruction and encouragement need to be focused. A portfolio approach enhances the writing process by encouraging the inclusion of different genres of writing for a variety of audiences.

Evaluate process and product. Because of the recursive nature of the pieces that go into portfolios, we find this approach, in a writing workshop setting, to be extremely valuable for observing writers' strategies and activities during the writing process. As collaborators in this setting, the writers' peers, too, can evaluate and give feedback on both the process and product. Through effective evaluation and feedback, students see their continuous progress both in the strategies they use to develop writing and in the products they produce. For our writers, portfolios become personal anthologies that show their progress toward instructional goals. Based on writers' goals or the portfolio standard, students include work that demonstrates they have met the goals. Geocaris and Ross (1999) note, "if students truly understand the content, they will be able to explain it, predict it, apply it, demonstrate its importance, justify or critique it, make connections with other facts, and avoid common misconceptions" (p. 30).

Track progress over time. In tracking progress over time, we track both writing processes and writing products. How our students arrive at the product is an important part of their growth. Without collections of writers' work, it is difficult to track changes in writing strategies. Camp and Levine (1991), looking for a way to track writing development, wrote "through the use of the portfolios, we hoped students would become aware of, and demonstrate, the ways in which they used writing as a tool for learning, as well as the ways in which the writing strategies they used had changed over the year" (p. 201). We find that by using checklists and rubrics, in conjunction with writing tallies, writers themselves participate in tracking their own development. One of the greatest joys in the writing workshop is to be able to celebrate students' progress with them. One student, comparing his work from the beginning and the end of the year, yelped in an astonished tone, "Did I write that?"

Sidebar quotations:

If we want to assess a student's ability to perform more than one kind of writing task, we must have at least two samples of the student's writing *for each kind of writing.* Odell, 1977

Students collect more than a diverse body of finished work. In fact they gather what we have come to call biographies of works, a range of works, and reflections. Wolf, 1989

Portfolios give us the chance to have more and better conversations about students' writing and our own role in the classroom. Harrington and Molinder-Hogue, 1997

Keeping a writing portfolio gives students the opportunity to judge their work and their growth over time. *School Talk,* 1999

Checklists.   With our younger children, we use checklists such as the ones in Figure 3–5, presented later in this chapter, to track their progress. These checklists become a part of the writing folder and are used as ready references when writers begin their revision process. Our older students often use somewhat more sophisticated scales and extended criteria such as the ones in Figure 3–6. Generally, we develop these scales with student participation so they have a vested interest in the criteria used for evaluation. Most writers appreciate being a part of this assessment and enjoy seeing their improvement and growth.

[Portfolios] are the sort of assessment . . . designed primarily to give feedback to educators working directly with students and planning local programs. Brandt, 1989

Writing developed over time allows the writing process to work. Referring to the process, Wolf (1989) notes that "Any writer's work unfolds over time . . . knowing how to pursue the work of writing is as much a part of what is learned as is the sense of where a semicolon goes or how dialogue ought to sound" (p. 38). Writing tracked and encouraged over time engenders independence and reflection. It allows for more thoughtful development, time to think and incubate ideas, time to put a piece away and return to it with fresh eyes, time to explore and experiment, time to start over with a different topic, time to gather information, time to develop a piece that is of interest to the writer, time to discover the audience, and time to review and reflect on the writing already attempted. It allows writers to view where they have been and where they want to go with their development. They learn enough about the process that they are able to set their own goals for future development. We learn from their efforts where we need to set our future goals for improving our curriculum and our teaching.

Scales and Criteria

Instructional rubrics make teachers' expectations very clear. . . . Instructional rubrics provide students with more informative feedback about their strengths and areas in need of improvement. Andrade, 2000

One of the most effective strategies for assessing and tracking progress in student writing is the use of scales and criteria. Hillocks' (1987) research shows that "scales, criteria, and specific questions that students apply to their own and others' writing have a powerful effect on enhancing quality. Through using the criteria systematically, students appear to internalize them and bring them to bear in generating new material even when they do not have the criteria in front of them" (p. 74). Our students are proof of this theory for we have used scales and criteria with great success.

Peer Evaluation

Teachers in a school or at a particular grade level could cooperatively develop a scale . . . a separate scale for each of the major types of writing. . . . Still another use for an essay scale is to set a standard, to draw a line for adequacy. Cooper, 1977

Others agree that as a class begins to engage in peer evaluation, various rating scales can provide useful structure. In fact, the whole class often begins peer evaluation by working through a rating scale and sample papers representative of different levels of writing to illustrate specific writing features. We use this practice with anonymous pieces of writing so that students are comfortable with the process and no one is placed "at risk" by having his or her writing examined publicly. We rate the papers together, discussing the various features of each. We discuss why one paper is easier to read or more interesting than another. We discuss the kinds of comments or questions we use to give feedback from the evaluation—and we talk about what kind of grade each paper might receive without further revision. Once students are comfortable with this process, they are ready to work in smaller groups with peer evaluation.

Group dynamics.   In Chapter 1, we discussed the importance of working in both large and small groups and the necessary procedures for assuring the success of group interaction in the workshop. Those strategies are crucial to the success of peer evaluation where writers meet in small support groups to respond to each other's writing. Before evaluation can begin, a climate of sharing and trust must be established. Beaven (1977) suggests that students first work in pairs and that the pairs are students who don't know each other well. Later, writers work as groups of four for brief periods of time. Peer groups may have assigned roles (recorder, organizer, questioner) and the roles may rotate throughout the session. Membership in the groups changes often.

To be effective peer evaluators, students need to know the writing criteria they are using, but just as importantly they need to know how to respond effectively in a small groups or writers' circle. Before we establish and use peer evaluation in the workshop, we model comments and questions for them to show them how to respond.

Building criteria.   Criteria and scales seem to be especially successful when our students participate in building sets of criteria with us. We begin, as we do so often in the writing process, by reading literature in the specific genre. As Cooper (1977) suggests, we teach mini-lessons in which we read both printed material in the genre we are studying and student papers, listing the important features of the writing. Our writers find that some of these features are recurrent in many genres and others are specific to a particular genre. They notice that for prose pieces audience and purpose, beginning, middle, and ending, specific patterns of development, appropriate word choices, effective sentence structures, and spelling and punctuation that aid the readers' understanding appear again and again. When the list is established, we apply the criteria to samples of varying quality levels, encouraging writers to discuss which features are effective and which ones are not. Along with this discussion, we model appropriate and effective comments and questions. Finally, writers use the scale and sets of questions to guide their peer evaluation sessions.

In the rubrics for the writing process, students find recurrent demands for prewriting heuristics, drafting, sharing, responding, and rewriting. By building these criteria together, writers are better equipped to use them in peer and self-evaluations.

Process criteria.   We use both process and product criteria to assess writing. Assessing the process helps us to know whether or not writers are using the full range of strategies available to them. When we find growth and improvement, or areas in need of improvement, we look to the writers' processes to inform ourselves and our students about what they are doing effectively or what they might try next. We use a set of criteria, along with the writers' materials, as evidence of the process.

In our own classrooms, we have begun to see that a day spent on analysis of responses, both peers' and teachers', is a day well spent. Harrington and Molinder-Hogue, 1997

We must constantly remind ourselves that the ultimate purpose of evaluation is to enable students to evaluate themselves. Costa, 1989

By teaching students how to use the objective responses of peers to judge the effectiveness of their writing and by using grading rubrics that emphasize audience response . . . teachers can authentically teach students about the role of audience. Wyngaard and Gehrke, 1996

Teaching Strategies: Writing Process Criteria

A list of criteria for the writing process often includes questions for the writer:

- How did you determine a writing purpose?
- Who is your audience? What do you know about them?
- What kind of prewriting strategies have you used?
- Who evaluated for you? A writing buddy, teacher, writing group?
- What kinds of feedback did you get?
- Have you used the suggestions? Why? Why not?
- Have you written a second, third, or fourth draft?
- Do you plan to revise and publish this piece? Why? Why not?
- What do you think you can do to improve in this piece?
- How do you feel about this piece of writing? Why?

I recommend that researchers, teachers, and students construct analytical scales for use with the major kinds of writing commonly required or encouraged in schools. Cooper, 1977

In rubrics, less is more . . . each evaluative criteria must represent a key attribute of the skill being assessed. Each criterion must be teachable. Popham, 1997

Product criteria.   For assessing both process and product, *a combination of primary-trait* and *analytic assessment* methods seems to work best. We use *checklists* from both to guide our whole class discussion, peer groups, and individual conferences; taped responses; written comments and observations; and reflection and self-evaluation. Thus, our holistic or intuitive responses are guided by the criteria and questions underlying that intuition and based on what we are teaching and learning. For example, as we teach the how-to of informational writing, we create a rubric that includes the features we want to find in that kind of writing. As we teach the genre and work together with students to develop writing in this mode, we list its features, beginning with those of greatest importance.

The profile criteria for writing is an example of the rudimentary features for prose—narrative, informative, and persuasive writing. These criteria can be used with students at any grade level in which these writing strategies have been discussed and used. As students become more expert writers, they add more sophisticated features to the set of criteria. An expanded, weighted version of these criteria appears in the accompanying box, and a checklist version appears in Appendix H.

Teaching Strategies

PROSE CRITERIA

Content: suits audience/purpose—one idea expressed—specific details and elaboration—relates to topic—creative

Organization: effective lead-in/topic sentence—logical order (time, space, importance)—effective connecting/transitional words—conclusion

Vocabulary: correct word forms—meaning clear—effective word choice—descriptive/figurative language

Language Use: sentence variety—complete sentences—correct verb tenses, word order, agreement (subject-predicate, noun-pronoun)—articles—negatives

Mechanics: mastery of spelling—capital letters—punctuation—first sentence indented—neat

From Hughey, J. B. and Hartfiel, V. F. 1987. *The profile guide*. College Station, TX: Writing Evaluation Systems.

Odell (1977) reminds us that competence is "discovering what one wishes to say. . . . Before students can proofread their work to eliminate errors in spelling and grammar, they have to have something to say" (p. 98). We usually focus only on the development of message for the first round of evaluation, saving grammar and mechanics for a later evaluation.

Teaching Guidelines: Focused Checklists

The samples in Figure 3–4 are primary-trait type checklists developed by Slack for grades two through four (2000).

FIGURE 3–4A Examples of Checklists

Name
_____

Descriptions
In your composition, you have:
_____ followed directions
_____ correct order
_____ sequence words—blue
_____ three sentences about each item
_____ expanded, complex sentences
_____ long composition
_____ location words—red
_____ similes using *as*—green
_____ similes using *like*—yellow
_____ star writer words—stars
_____ purposes for objects/actions
_____ sensory details—purple
_____ interesting words—orange
_____ most words spelled correctly
_____ correct punctuation
_____ complete sentences
_____ correct tense
_____ neat handwriting

Name
_____

Stories
In your composition, you have:
_____ followed directions
_____ a clear beginning
_____ a clear conclusion
_____ correct order
_____ sequence words—blue
_____ expanded, complex sentences
_____ fully developed ideas
_____ long composition
_____ location words—red
_____ similes (*as* and *like*)—green, yellow
_____ star writer words—stars
_____ sensory details—purple
_____ interesting verbs—orange
_____ most words spelled correctly
_____ correct punctuation
_____ complete sentences
_____ correct tense
_____ neat handwriting

Slack, Charlotte, 2000. *Foundations for Writing.* San Antonio: ©ECS Learning Systems, Inc.

FIGURE 3–4B   continued

Name	Name
Directions	Compare/Contrast
In your composition, you have:	In your composition you have:
_____ followed directions	_____ followed directions
_____ a clear introduction	_____ a clear introduction
_____ a clear conclusion	_____ a clear conclusion
_____ correct order	_____ correct order
_____ sequence words—blue	_____ sequence words—blue
_____ expanded, complex sentences	_____ expanded, complex sentences
_____ long composition	_____ long composition
_____ location words—red	_____ location words—red
_____ star writer words—stars	_____ star writer words—stars
_____ elaboration with details	_____ elaboration with details
_____ elaboration with examples	_____ elaboration with examples
_____ elaboration with reasons	_____ elaboration with reasons
_____ interesting words—orange	_____ interesting words—orange
_____ most words spelled correctly	_____ most words spelled correctly
_____ correct punctuation	_____ correct punctuation
_____ complete sentences	_____ complete sentences
_____ correct tense	_____ correct tense
_____ neat handwriting	_____ neat handwriting

Slack, Charlotte, 2000. *Foundations for Writing.* San Antonio: ©ECS Learning Systems, Inc.

Teacher response is a key factor in the ultimate success of portfolio assessment. Harrington and Molinder-Hogue, 1997

Teaching Guidelines: Analytical Scale

With older students, *analytic scales* may include several levels of mastery for each of the descriptors and numerical weighting that show students what grades would be given if they were being graded. During the creation and drafting of a piece of writing, we use no number or letter scores of any kind—only responses to the work in progress. We find that to assign numbers and grades before the piece is ready for assessment tends to "ring down the curtain" for the writer and indicate that the process is completed. Having numerical values on the scale serves an important purpose, however, even though they are

FIGURE 3–4C   continued

Name
_____

                          Persuasion
In your composition, you have:
_____ followed directions
_____ a clear introduction
_____ a clear conclusion
_____ correct order
_____ sequence words—blue
_____ expanded, complex sentences
_____ long composition
_____ star writer words—stars
_____ elaboration with facts
_____ elaboration with reasons
_____ elaboration with comparisons
_____ elaboration with examples
_____ interesting words—orange
_____ most words spelled correctly
_____ correct punctuation
_____ complete sentences
_____ correct tense
_____ neat handwriting

Slack, Charlotte, 2000. *Foundations for Writing.* San Antonio: ©ECS Learning Systems, Inc.

not yet used. Students see what grade range would be assigned without revision of the piece, and they see how their grades will improve if they do make changes. They also see specific features designated as *strong* or *in need of improvement.* These features are aligned with the numerical weighting that will eventually be used for the grade. The corresponding numerical scale is applied only when the writer declares the work finished and ready for grading. In this way, when a grade is required, there are no earthshaking surprises; and students have every opportunity to improve their work before it is submitted for a grade. See the sample profile materials developed by Hughey and Hartfiel (1985) in Figures 3–5 and 3–6.

FIGURE 3–5A   Profile Rubric

LEVEL I	COMPOSITION PROFILE		
STUDENT		DATE	TOPIC

	SCORE LEVEL	CRITERIA	COMMENTS
CONTENT	30-27	**EXCELLENT TO VERY GOOD:** suits audience/purpose • one idea expressed • specific development • relevant to topic • creative	
	26-22	**GOOD TO AVERAGE:** one idea expressed but some unnecessary information • some specific development • mostly relevant	
	21-17	**FAIR TO POOR:** nonspecific statement • incomplete development • little relevance	
	16-13	**VERY POOR:** not related • no development	
ORGANIZATION	20-18	**EXCELLENT TO VERY GOOD:** effective lead/topic sentence • logical order (time-space-importance) • effective connecting/transitional words • conclusion	
	17-14	**GOOD TO AVERAGE:** adequate lead/topic sentence • logical but incomplete order • adequate connecting/transitional words • adequate conclusion	
	13-10	**FAIR TO POOR:** weak or no lead topic sentence • illogical order • lacks connecting/transitional words • weak or no conclusion	
	9-7	**VERY POOR:** no main idea • no organization • not enough to evaluate	
VOCABULARY	20-18	**EXCELLENT TO VERY GOOD:** correct word forms • meaning clear • effective word choice/description/figurative language	
	17-14	**GOOD TO AVERAGE:** mostly correct word forms • meaning not hidden • adequate word choice • some description/figurative language	
	13-10	**FAIR TO POOR:** many incorrect word forms • slang • meaning unclear • limited word choice • little description/figurative language	
	9-7	**VERY POOR:** inadequate vocabulary • not enough to evaluate	
LANGUAGE USE	25-22	**EXCELLENT TO VERY GOOD:** sentence variety • complete sentences • correct verb tenses, word order, agreement (subj-pred, noun-pron), articles, negatives	
	21-18	**GOOD TO AVERAGE:** simple sentences • mostly complete sentences • several errors in verb tense (past-present-future), word order, agreement (subj-pred, noun-pron), articles, negatives, run-ons	
	17-11	**FAIR TO POOR:** few complete sentences • frequent errors in verb tense, word order, agreement, articles, negatives, run-ons	
	10-5	**VERY POOR:** unable to use sentence rules • many sentence errors in verb tense, word order, agreement, articles, negatives, run-ons	
MECHANICS	5	**EXCELLENT TO VERY GOOD:** mastery of spelling, capital letters, punctuation • first sentence indented • neat	
	4	**GOOD TO AVERAGE:** occasional errors in spelling, capital letters, commas, periods, question marks, indention	
	3	**FAIR TO POOR:** frequent errors in spelling, capital letters, commas, periods, questions • difficult to read	
	2	**VERY POOR:** dominated by errors in spelling, capital letters, commas, periods, questions • illegible handwriting	

TOTAL SCORE   READER   COMMENTS

Hughey, Jane B. and V. Faye Hartfiel. 1989. *The profile guide.* College Station, TX: Writing Evaluation Systems.

FIGURE 3–5B Extended Criteria

LEVEL I		EXTENDED PROFILE CRITERIA

The PROFILE represents the essential elements of writing that you use to write successfully. This card contains a detailed description of the principles at the EXCELLENT TO VERY GOOD level. The descriptors of the PROFILE are only reminders of these principles.

Check your writing with the PROFILE to be sure your meaning is clear to the reader. Refer to this card if you need to be reminded of the descriptor meaning.

Excellent to Very Good indicates successful and complete communication. *Good to Average* means good communication, but your readers may still have some questions. *Fair to Poor* and *Very Poor* suggests a communication breakdown of some kind. Your meaning is not clear. Review the questions to find the breakdown; then revise your papers for clearer communication.

	DESCRIPTOR	CRITERIA
CONTENT	Audience/purpose	Is your writing suited to the specific audience you are writing for? Is it written for a specific purpose? What is your purpose? Who is your audience?
	One idea	Are all the sentences in the paragraph about the same main idea? Does each sentence add (1) new information about the main idea or (2) a different view of the main idea? Is there enough information?
	Development	Is the paragraph written with a specific method of development such as personal experience? description? facts? examples? comparison and contrast (how one thing or idea is like or different from another)?
	Relevance	Does the information in your paragraph fit the assignment?
ORGANIZATION	Topic sentence	Is the topic sentence strong? Is it complete enough for all the other sentences to relate to it? Is the topic sentence limited enough so that it can be fully developed by the other sentences in the paragraph? Does the topic sentence tell clearly what the rest of the paragraph is about?
	Logical order	Are you ideas written in a reasonable order to reflect your purpose? **Time** - Are you writing about something that happened? or how to do something? Tell things in the order that they happened or in the order that they should be done. **Space** - Are you describing something? Describe a thing or a place with a definite order such as from beginning to end, top to bottom, bottom to top, right to left. **Importance** - Are you telling about how important something is? Write the least important ideas first and the most important ideas last.
	Connecting words	Are there words in the paragraph that connect two or more ideas - words such as - *and, but, or, nor, if, so,* and *because*?
	Transitional words	Are there words in the paragraph that connect two or more ideas - words such as - *first, second, next, after that, last*?

(continued)

FIGURE 3–5c   Sample Tally

VOCABULARY	Word forms	Are the correct forms of words used? noun, verb, adjective, or adverb?
	Meaning clear	Are your words clear enough to make your reader understand *exactly* what you mean?
	Description	Does the paragraph contain words that make your reader see, hear, smell, taste, and feel what the subject is about?
	Figurative language	Is there effective use of similes and metaphors?
LANGUAGE USE	Complete sentences	Does each sentence have a subject and a verb?
	Tense	Are verb tenses correct for what you are writing about? Do the helping verbs say what you mean for them to say?
	Word order	Is normal word order used, except for emphasis?
	Subject/predicate	Do subjects agree with their verbs? If the subject is plural, is the verb also plural?
	Pronouns	Do pronouns agree with the nouns they replace? Gender (1) John - he; Mary - she; bicycle - it Number (2) boys - they; you and I - we; desk - it Function (3) Mary and *I* are going to the movie. (subj.) Please give the cokes to John and *me*. (obj.)
	Articles	Are - *a, an, and the* - used correctly?
	Negative	Are negative words such as *no, none, not,* and *nothing* used correctly?
	Run-on sentences	Are sentences separated with the correct end punctuation?
MECHANICS	Spelling	Are words spelled correctly?
	Capital letters	Are capital letters used where necessary?
	Punctuation	Are commas, periods, question marks, exclamation points, and quotation marks used correctly?
	Handwriting	Is handwriting easy to read?

Hughey, Jane B. and V. Faye Hartfiel. 1989. *The profile guide.* College Station, TX: Writing Evaluation Systems.

Tally.   Our upper level elementary and middle school students keep a tally attached to the inside of the writing folder. The tally lists the major criteria for both process and product, along with spaces for students to record their progress for the writing they have submitted for evaluation. Writers maintain their tallies to show an ongoing picture of progress and growth. See the example in Figure 3–6.

PROGRESS TALLY FOR THE COMPOSITION PROFILE

STUDENT _____

CONTENT

PAPER	AUDIENCE/PURPOSE	SUPPORT	RELEVANCE	DEVELOPMENT	CREATIVITY

ORGANIZATION

PAPER	MAIN IDEA	TOPIC SENTENCES	ORGANIZATION	LOGICAL ORDER	TRANSITIONS

VOCABULARY

PAPER	CONTEXT	WORD FORM	PRECISE MEANING	EFFECTIVE	FIGURATIVE LANGUAGE

LANGUAGE USE

PAPER	SENTENCES				TENSE	AGR	#	WO/F	PRO	PREP	NEG
	VARIETY	CF	FRAG	R-O							

MECHANICS

PAPER	SPELLING	PUNCTUATION	CAPITALIZATION	PARAGRAPHING	HANDWRITING

Hughey, Jane B. and V. Faye Hartfiel. 1989. *The profile guide.* College Station, TX: Writing Evaluation Systems.

FIGURE 3–6 Sample Tally

Strategies for Feedback

When students exhibit the need for approval and want feedback for validation by an audience, they have such a strong personal identification with their writing that they are extremely vulnerable in their efforts to communicate in writing, especially when the effort is open to evaluation. Golub, 1982

Teacher feedback.   Far more important than numbers on a scale are the kinds of comments that teachers give to writers about their work in progress. When Conners and Lunsford (1993) studied rhetorical comments on students' papers, they found the interchange "one in which overworked teachers dash down a few words which very often tell students little about how or why their papers succeed or fail" (p. 211). In a study of the effects of school experiences on sixth- and seventh-grade students, Hoge, Smith, and Hanson (1990) found that school climate and feedback from teachers had the greatest effect on academic self-esteem. What we do in responding to our writers affects their motivation to write and becomes the model they will use. As Atwell (1987) so aptly observes, "Writers need response. Helpful response comes during—not after—the composing. It comes from the writers' peers and from the teacher, who consistently models the kinds of restatements and questions that help writers reflect on the content of their writing" (p. 17).

From us, writers learn how to be effective peer evaluators, that is, how to comment and how to question. The *Standards for the Assessment of Reading and Writing* (1994) maintain that "a teacher who knows a great deal about the range of techniques readers and writers use will be able to provide students (and parents) with specific, focused assessments. . . . If teachers' comments are specific, providing a clear picture of each student's special strengths and weaknesses, rather than comparing students to each other, these characteristics will be reflected in students' self-evaluations" (p. 28). Consequently, it is crucial that we model *best practice* in teaching our writers how to become effective peer evaluators and effective self-monitors. We show them how to include the following features in their responses (Hughey and Hartfiel, 1989):

Noticing and praising whatever a student does well improves writing more than any kind or amount of correction of what he does badly, and that is especially important for the less able writers who need all the encouragement they can get. Diederich, 1974

Teaching Strategies: Responding to Writing

- Comment during and after the process
- An understanding of the writing concepts
- Substantive questions
- Facilitative comments
- Limited or focused response
- Hierarchy of importance
- Positive and specific responses
- "You" versus "the paper"
- Few or no written comments on the paper

Comment during and after the process.   Writers need feedback during the writing process. When they are struggling to communicate an idea, they need to know whether or not the potential audience will understand what they are trying to say. What better place to try out their ideas than with their teachers and their classmates. Sommers (1982) says when "teachers fail to tell students how to make the paper better. . . . Without comments from readers, students assume that their writing has communicated their meaning and perceive no need for revising the substance of their text" (p. 149).

An understanding of the writing concepts.   We often use a variety of feedback strategies, many of which are listed in Chapter 5 on revision. These strategies contain the specific writing features from the scales and criteria we are using. Students question or comment on the writing based on these criteria. They practice using substantive and helpful comments and questions. They learn to respond from a knowledge base of writing concepts, and they respond with interest, respect, and courtesy.

Substantive questions.   Questions that ask for more information about the writing further the process and stimulate thought. For example, "What do you do after you carve the face in the pumpkin?" may help the writer fill in missing steps in a process. We avoid questions that can be answered with a "yes" or a "no" such as, "Did you carve your pumpkin with a knife?" Answers to this kind of question fail to produce new information, and they fail to stimulate creative or critical thinking. Further, comments and questions should pertain to the writers' content and intent. To do otherwise takes ownership away from the writer.

Facilitative comments.   Comments that suggest what might be done about a writing problem are more helpful than comments that simply identify a problem. Terminology on the rubric can serve the purpose of identifying writers' strengths and weaknesses, leaving the evaluator free to facilitate improvement. Markings on the rubric may show a weakness in the use of certain vocabulary in a piece of writing. A facilitative comment guides or directs the writer; for example, "Use the thesaurus to find synonyms for *thing* and *guy*," is more helpful than the comment, "Avoid vague word choices."

Limited or focused response.   Since we want our feedback to serve writers, we avoid an overload of response. Collins (1990) recommends the use of "focus correction areas" to avoid more feedback on a single draft than anyone can possibly use. Yet we must take care not to overrespond in the focus areas. O'Neill (1990) documented an actual decrease in mechanical skills when writers were exposed to frequent focus corrections in mechanics. Focusing on only a few areas of development at a time allows writers to gain mastery before they move on to another facet of the process. Depending on the age and the maturity of each individual writer, we determine the appropriate amount of response. For example, we limit comments and questions to one or two features for weak writers or for younger writers, while we may use several comments and questions for older or more advanced writers. Numerous suggestions, especially for changes in many different features, often overwhelm writers and tend to turn them away from the effort instead of encouraging them to continue. We follow Hillocks' (1984) advice and "direct comments to a few key elements of our students' composition, rather than providing more diffuse and often meaningless, evaluative remarks" (p 165).

Teaching Strategies

EXAMPLES OF FACILITATIVE FEEDBACK TO WRITERS

Content: To convince Mrs. Wolf to make this change, what else do you think she needs to know about it? Include some additional reasons about why it is important to you.

What is the main idea for your writing? Put it into one sentence in the first paragraph.

Use the **who, what, when, where** questions to fill out the information in the story.

Which of these ideas fit together logically? Group sentences about the same idea.

How does the idea about _____ fit with your main idea? Write an extra sentence or two to show the connection.

Which of these ideas do you think is more important? Tell me more about the one *most important idea.*

What are some other reasons for _____?

What else do you do in _____?

What do you think the arguments on the other side of the question might be?

Use some examples from the story to illustrate your idea in paragraph 2.

Organization: Which sentence in each of your paragraphs tells what the paragraph is about? Add an unusual twist to the sentence that tells what your paper is about.

Write a second topic sentence and ask your peer group which one they think fits your paper best.

Use the Pyramid Poster to organize the ideas in the paper; then fill in the gaps with additional information.

Add connecting words such as—*and, but, or*—between ideas.

Add transitional words such as—*because, as a result, since*—to show connections between ideas.

Which sentence is meant to be the concluding sentence in the paper? Underline it.

Add information to it that ties it to your introductory sentence.

Write a sentence that summarizes what you said in your paper.

Vocabulary: Check the use of the word _____.

What other words describe _____?

Put the nouns _____ and _____ in a mapping circle and write all of the adjectives you can think of to describe them. Then rewrite the paragraph using some of the words you mapped.

Language Use: In paragraph 1, combine sentences 2 and 3 with a connecting word.

Which two ideas in paragraph 1 are most closely connected? Write them into one sentence.

Check sentence 4 to be sure it has a subject and a verb. Underline the subject once and the verb twice—or if one is missing, add it to the sentence.

Run a computer check for punctuation.

Mechanics: Check the spelling of "disiplan." Or check the spelling of highlighted words.

What is the capitalization rule for names of people?

Look up the rule for "commas in a series" in Chapter 2 of your grammar book, then check paragraph 3 to be sure you are using the comma rules correctly.

Adapted from Hughey, Jane B. and V. Faye Hartfiel. 1989. The profile guide. College Station, TX: Writing Evaluation Systems.

Hierarchy of importance. When responding to a piece of writing that has many problems, we focus on suggestions for improvement in this order of importance: content, organization, vocabulary, sentence structures, and mechanics. Content comes first because we find that writers cannot organize what is not there. Once writers have developed a message that says what they want it to, then they are ready to put organization and order to it. At this point, they can also go back into the message to find just the right word or phrase they want to communicate a tone or a concept. Many researchers have found that sentence level corrections before content is developed are futile.

Positive and specific responses. At least one positive, specific response to any piece of writing is mandatory in our writing workshop. For example, "Your description of the 'fuzzy puppy with the cotton puff tail' was so effective that it made me want a dog just like her," as opposed to, "Good description." The writer wonders what part was good and what "good" means.

When readers are not specific in their responses, commentary is not facilitative and writers are confused about readers' understanding of their work. Even facilitative responses need this kind of specificity. Rather than commenting, "Organize your paper," a more specific directive (that still leaves ownership of the paper with the writer) might be, "To make the organization of this paper stronger, lay your ideas out on a Pyramid Board and gather points about the same idea together. Make separate paragraphs for each group of ideas."

We also discourage the use of "right" and "wrong" in our responses. Instead we use word such as "strong" and "effective" to describe writing.

'You' versus 'the paper.' A small but important factor in feedback affects self-esteem. We use "you" or "your" to compliment writers' successful efforts. For example, "Your main idea about the different kinds of weather in this region is excellent and sets the organization for the entire paper." At the same time, we refer to the "paper," "story," or "piece of writing" when we make suggestions for improvement. For example, "To make the story read more smoothly, combine sentences three and four in paragraph two."

Few or no written comments on students' papers. As an artist once pointed out to us, artists don't paint on other artists' pictures. We don't write on our students' papers. Rather we record our comments on sticky notes attached to the papers or we respond on the rubrics that accompany the writing. With very young students who may not be able to find the spot where the punctuation should be changed in the paper, we sometimes use a check mark in the margin to help guide them, but we don't make the corrections for them. The sooner they become responsible for their own corrections, they sooner they really learn. In addition, making our remarks on a sticky note or on the rubric protects the students' pride and integrity in the paper. At the end of the year, students take home compositions with few or no teacher "scribbles" on any papers.

Because we model these evaluative strategies in our feedback to writers and actively teach writers how to use them in peer evaluation sessions, they begin to internalize them and use them for self-evaluation as well. To date, research and our own classroom experience show us that this means of assessment for improving writing works with students

---

Criteria for evaluative commentary, from the most to the least important elements in a piece of writing are central idea/focus, organization/coherence, support/explanation/detail, diction/sentence structure, and grammar/punctuation/spelling. Rubin, 1983.

The student must learn to internalize the qualities of good writing. In the past, I found that sometimes I spent more time correcting the paper than the student did writing it. I have since thrown away my red pen and given up scrawled comments in the margin that only I can decipher. Bertisch, 1993

Criteria for evaluative commentary should 1) facilitate rather than judge, 2) focus on performance rather than on the finished product, 3) give feedback before and after revision, and 4) require immediate revision. Knoblauch and Brannon, 1984

at third grade and up. Coleman (1983) found scales to be effective tools for third-and fourth-grade students. In a three-year study of evaluation and feedback with sixth-, seventh-, and eighth-grade writers, Hughey (1994) found that students need and want evaluative feedback during the writing process and that the use of scales and criteria helps students internalize the principles of writing for continuous use. She cautions, however, that the type, amount, and use of feedback often determine its positive or negative effects on learning.

Grading

Now grading is a funny thing: most of us do it, most of us hate it, and most of our students rely on those grades to "tell them how they are doing," despite our best efforts to foster awareness of the importance of the comment . . . we lavish our time on. Harrington and Molinder-Hogue, 1997

Over and over we read comments like "Why did I have to wait until after the semester was over to find out how I was doing?" "I learned a lot from a great teacher but didn't like not getting any grades." Harrington and Molinder-Hogue, 1997

While using the portfolio focuses our attention on a different kind of assessment during much of the writing process, we do not let it interfere with the necessary communication we must have with our students—grading. As Harrington and Molinder-Hogue (1997) point out, "teachers talk very little together about grading (except for protested grades). Grading gets done in the frantic silence to which we retreat at the ends of semesters" (p. 52). They further observe that when we grade portfolios, "we turn to the portfolio as a *product.*" Students, meanwhile, don't like the grading system that goes along with portfolio approaches that delay grading until the portfolio is completed. "They don't get grades during the semester and thus have difficulty gauging the level of their success" (p. 55).

Expectations.   In the interest of fairness to students, parents, and teachers, we establish at the beginning of the school year how writing will be assessed, both during the workshop and when the finished pieces are graded. They know that we expect a certain number of pieces in their portfolios; that of those pieces, we expect representation of the genre we have studied and practiced in workshop. They know that the criteria will be the standard by which their writing will be evaluated. They also know that their writing won't be graded until they have had ample opportunities to take their writing through the writing process.

Although Strzepek and Figgins (1993) advocate deferring grading until a substantial portfolio has accumulated, we find that students want grades as the semester goes along. They want to know how they are doing and where they stand. Carbone (1995) suggests that a grade is a text and, as such, should be discussed and produced by both teacher and student with care. Following this argument, Harrington and Molinder-Hogue (1997) write "we'd suggest that grades need to be drafted all through the semester. Grades do not need to be assigned to each draft, but students and teachers need to become comfortable with a shared language of assessment" (p. 57).

In our writing workshop, we grade completed pieces every couple of weeks, or more often if students submit work that they consider ready for publication. For grading, periodically throughout the marking period, we direct students to choose pieces of writing for evaluation based on the criteria that we have developed together for each genre. It is wise to guide students in their selections until they are mature enough to make the selections alone (*School Talk,* 1999). It is then that our students revisit, revise, and submit their writing for grades.

In Figure 3–7, a seventh grader's draft, feedback, and revision show how individual pieces of writing are taken to the grading stage.

As students receive feedback on the pieces they are developing for their portfolios, they keep the checklists or rubric responses with the piece of writing. When the finished piece is submitted for a grade, we have the history of the piece in hand, which guides us in our evaluation.

We can see where the writers' efforts have affected changes, additions, and deletions in the finished product. On individual pieces of writing that are to be included in the portfolio, students submit prewriting, drafts, and finished pieces for the more formal assessment. Using the rubrics, checklists and scales that accompany each kind

Grades should grow out of a clearer understanding of texts, roles, and responses.
Hunt, 1989

FIGURE 3–7A
Seventh Grader's Draft

The Cluster

"The best thing about seventh grade is the Cluster". One thing is that there aren't hardly ever any tests unless they are on disiplan. That saves me time for the studying I have to do at home. Also all jve do are small thing like Origamies in Art and puzzles in Home Ec. And things like that and when we do those we do about 4 or 5 at a time and we get 100 for then whether we do them right or not and we can also throw them away if we don't like them. And the last and best all of my friends are in there to. Encourage me even if I do it wrong. That is why the Cluster is the best thing I liked in seventh grade.

FIGURE 3–7B Assessment of First Draft

LEVEL II **COMPOSITION PROFILE**

TOPIC *Cluster*   DATE   STUDENT *Kim*

SCORE	LEVEL	CRITERIA	COMMENTS

CONTENT

30-27 EXCELLENT TO VERY GOOD: (appropriate to audience/purpose) • strong main idea/supporting ideas • ideas related • specific development • effective combination of outside information • creative

26-22 GOOD TO AVERAGE: (adequate reasoning) • main idea partly developed • (lacks detail) • occasionally unrelated ideas • some combination of outside information

21-17 FAIR TO POOR: poor reasoning • unnecessary information • very little development • no combination of outside information

16-13 VERY POOR: irrelevant • no development • (or) not enough to evaluate

Comments: Tell what the Cluster is in the revision. Please add specific information about art and home ec classes. What is origamy? What else do you do in art class?

ORGANIZATION

20-18 EXCELLENT TO VERY GOOD: effective main idea/topic sentences • organized (beginning, middle, end) • logical order • effective transitions

17-14 GOOD TO AVERAGE: (clear topic sentences) • adequate introduction/conclusion • logical but incomplete sequencing • adequate transitions

13-10 FAIR TO POOR: no topic sentence • no introduction/conclusion • illogical order • limited sequencing/organization/transitions

9-7 VERY POOR: does not communicate one idea • no evidence of organization • (or) not enough to evaluate

VOCABULARY

20-18 EXCELLENT TO VERY GOOD: language suits context • correct word forms • word meanings precise • effective word choice/figurative language

17-14 GOOD TO AVERAGE: adequate to context • mostly effective and correct word forms/choice (somewhat redundant) • meaning clear • some figurative language

13-10 FAIR TO POOR: frequent (errors in idioms/word forms/word choice) cliches/slang/redundancies • meaning confused • no figurative language

9-7 VERY POOR: inadequate vocabulary for topic • (or) not enough to evaluate

LANGUAGE USE

25-22 EXCELLENT TO VERY GOOD: sentence variety • correct sentence structure, (verb tenses), (agreement), number, word order/use, pronouns, prepositions, negatives, articles

21-18 GOOD TO AVERAGE: simple constructions • (minor problems in sentence structure) • few errors in verb tense, agreement, number, word order/use, pronouns, prepositions, negatives, articles

17-11 FAIR TO POOR: ineffective sentence constructions • several errors in verb tense, subject-verb agreement, number, word order/use, pronouns, prepositions, negatives, articles, run-ons, fragments

10-5 VERY POOR: limited mastery of sentence rules • many errors in verb tense, subject-verb agreement, number, word order/use, pronouns, prepositions, negatives, articles, run-ons, fragments

Comments: Make 2 or 3 separate sentences out of sentence 4.

MECHANICS

5 EXCELLENT TO VERY GOOD: mastery of spelling, punctuation, capitalization, paragraphing • neat

4 GOOD TO AVERAGE: occasional errors in (spelling,) punctuation, capitalization, paragraphing

3 FAIR TO POOR: frequent errors in spelling, punctuation, capitalization, paragraphing • handwriting unclear

2 VERY POOR: dominated by errors in spelling, punctuation, capitalization, paragraphing, illegible handwriting

Comments: Check the spelling of
– disiplan
– origamies

TOTAL SCORE   READER   COMMENTS
I am interested in knowing more about the Cluster. It sounds like fun.

FIGURE 3–7C
Seventh Grader's
Revised Writing
Sample

THE CLUSTER

The Cluster was my favorite class in 7th grade because it was lots of fun and not much work. The Cluster is a class that lasts for one semester. It is divided into different subjects every six weeks so it gives us a chance to see if we like different things like art and home ec. In art we learn how to do Origamy. That is the way the Japanese people fold colored paper into shapes of birds, flowers, and other things like that. And sometimes we finger paint or watercolor. In Home Ec., we work puzzles and learn how to bake cookies that we get to eat in class. Besides it being fun we always make good grades in Cluster. One thing is that there are hardly ever any tests unless they are on discipline. That saves me time for the studying I have to do at home for other classes. Even if we do four or five projects at a time the teacher gives us 100 for them whether we do them right or not. We can also throw away the things we make if we don't like them. And the last and best all of my friends are in there to encourage me even if I do a project wrong. That is why the Cluster is the thing I liked best about seventh grade.

We must set up structures and communication lines that allow students to see the connections between grading and assessment. Harrington and Molinder-Hogue, 1997

We must expand the range and variety of assessment techniques we use; and we should include teachers' assessment. Other authentic assessments include direct observations of behavior, portfolios of student work, long-term projects, logs and journals, student interviews . . . and writing samples. Costa, 1989

Central to [portfolios] are two aims . . . to design ways of evaluating student learning that . . . will also model personal responsibility in questioning and reflecting one's own work . . . to find ways of capturing growth over time so that students can become informed and thoughtful assessors of their own histories as learners. Wolf, 1989

of writing and that were used during the process for feedback, we arrive at a grade for the paper. Writers record the feedback and the grade on the tallies in their folders so we can follow their progress on the various genres. However, we assign an overall portfolio grade according to the students' progress from beginning to end of the semester.

While each paper in the portfolio may receive a specific grade, the portfolio as a whole will be evaluated and graded based on grades for the products, writers' reflective statements about their learning and progress, and the process checklist showing the breadth and depth of strategies they have used. Other factors that determine writers' overall grades include our observations of their ongoing efforts and individual conferences with students about their writing.

Observation.   While it is somewhat time consuming and not always easy to do, we keep notes on student participation, interaction, and use of the process during workshop. These observations prove especially helpful when we meet with our students in conferences about their writing and also when we meet jointly with parents and students.

Conferences.   Conferences are the valuable times when we sit down one on one with our writers and evaluate their progress with them. Observations, rubrics, tallies, portfolios, and writing folders serve as useful tools for such conferences because we have a body of work and a number of varied sources for discussing growth and setting goals. We prefer to go to the students' work area for conferences. By going to them, we gauge the effectiveness of the conference and move on when we feel that we have maximized communication.

Self-reflection.   Although self-reflection could be accomplished under any circumstances, it is a natural outgrowth of the portfolio system that we use. Students' work is gathered in one place, so it is easy for them to look through it and analyze the changes that have taken place. Being able to verbalize what they see happening to themselves as

FIGURE 3–7D Assessment of Revision

LEVEL II — **COMPOSITION PROFILE**

TOPIC *Cluster-revised*   DATE   STUDENT *Kim*

	SCORE	LEVEL	CRITERIA	COMMENTS
CONTENT	27	30-27	EXCELLENT TO VERY GOOD: (appropriate to audience/purpose) • strong (main idea/supporting ideas) (ideas related) (specific development) • effective combination of outside information • creative	
		26-22	GOOD TO AVERAGE: adequate reasoning • main idea partly developed • lacks detail • occasionally unrelated ideas • some combination of outside information	
		21-17	FAIR TO POOR: poor reasoning • unnecessary information • very little development • no combination of outside information	
		16-13	VERY POOR: irrelevant • no development • (or) not enough to evaluate	
ORGANIZATION	18	20-18	EXCELLENT TO VERY GOOD: effective main idea/topic sentences (organized) (beginning, middle, end) (logical order) • effective transitions	
		17-14	GOOD TO AVERAGE: (clear topic sentences) • adequate introduction/conclusion • logical but incomplete sequencing • adequate transitions	
		13-10	FAIR TO POOR: no topic sentence • no introduction/conclusion • illogical order • (limited) sequencing/organization (transitions)	
		9-7	VERY POOR: does not communicate one idea • no evidence of organization • (or) not enough to evaluate	
VOCABULARY	16	20-18	EXCELLENT TO VERY GOOD: language suits context • correct word forms • word meanings precise • effective word choice/figurative language	
		17-14	GOOD TO AVERAGE: (adequate to context) • mostly effective and correct word forms/choice • somewhat redundant • (meaning clear) some figurative language	
		13-10	FAIR TO POOR: frequent errors in idioms/word forms/word choice • cliches/slang/redundancies • meaning confused • no figurative language	
		9-7	VERY POOR: inadequate vocabulary for topic • (or) not enough to evaluate	
LANGUAGE USE	21	25-22	EXCELLENT TO VERY GOOD: sentence variety • correct sentence structure, verb tenses, agreement, number, word order/use, pronouns, prepositions, negatives, articles	
		21-18	GOOD TO AVERAGE: (simple constructions) (minor problems in sentence structure) • few errors in verb tense, agreement, number, word order/use, pronouns, prepositions, negatives, articles	*Let's work together on punctuation in complex sentences.*
		17-11	FAIR TO POOR: ineffective sentence constructions • several errors in verb tense, subject-verb agreement, number, word order/use, pronouns, prepositions, negatives, articles, run-ons, fragments	
		10-5	VERY POOR: limited mastery of sentence rules • many errors in verb tense, subject-verb agreement, number, word order/use, pronouns, prepositions, negatives, articles, run-ons, fragments	
MECHANICS	4	5	EXCELLENT TO VERY GOOD: mastery of spelling, punctuation, capitalization, paragraphing • neat	
		4	GOOD TO AVERAGE: occasional errors in spelling, punctuation, capitalization, paragraphing	*Spelling is improved.*
		3	FAIR TO POOR: frequent errors in spelling, punctuation, capitalization, paragraphing • handwriting unclear	
		2	VERY POOR: dominated by errors in spelling, punctuation, capitalization, paragraphing, illegible handwriting	

TOTAL SCORE **86**   READER **SL**   COMMENTS *Your revision shows definite improvement in content development!*

100

Students, teachers, researchers, and evaluators . . . agreed: the reflective student letters were the most significant entries in many of the portfolios. Camp and Levine, 1991

writers heightens their sense of accomplishment and engenders pride in their work. They become authors in the true sense of the word. In verbalizing analyses of their work, they begin to see how and why they progress. They see which strategies work for them and which ones do not. Ownership in the process is deepened.

When we consider how assessment affects the interests and talents of all of our students, we make an effort to vary the assessment process so that all students more easily understand it. To appeal to a broad range of the multiple intelligences in our writing workshops, we use a variety of strategies. (See the accompanying box.)

EMPHASIZING THE MULTIPLE INTELLIGENCES

Literary: Students read and respond. They compare literary characteristics of high-quality writing samples with characteristics of their current writing project to determine areas where the paper can be improved.

Logical/mathematical: Students systematically evaluate in an organized way. They use base ten blocks to represent the "weights" of importance of various components of the paper. For example, they use three 100-unit "flats" to represent content and two flats to represent each of the following: organization, vocabulary, and language use and one flat to represent mechanics. In self-assessment, students use the unit representations as guides to the importance of the various components. When added together, the flats equal the completed 1000-unit cube.

Spatial: Students see patterns in their own and others' development. They use a two-dimensional pyramid to represent the relative importance of various components of quality writing. With horizontal divisions, the bottom foundation of the pyramid represents content, the next section organization, the next vocabulary, and so on to the pinnacle, which represents mechanics.

Musical: Assign musical instruments according to size to the various aspects of the paper to make it "harmonious." For example, the tuba represents the content while the piccolo represents the mechanics. Attention to components of the paper should be relative to the size of the instrument.

Bodily-kinesthetic: Students demonstrate evaluation and feedback. They place a piece of tape on the floor. As they read their papers aloud, students follow these directions: (1) If the sentence adds information to the paper, take one step forward. (2) If the sentence is repetitive, take one step back. (3) If the sentence is off topic, take one step sideways.

Interpersonal: Students engage in peer evaluation and feedback using small group peer conferences.

Intrapersonal: Students monitor their own work by using self-reflection to determine whether the paper communicates the personal beliefs of the writer.

Naturalist: Students relate components of a paper to examples in nature. For example, younger students enjoy using a bug to represent their papers. The body of the bug stands for the content, the head stands for organization, three legs stand for vocabulary, the other three legs stand for language use, and the antennae stand for mechanics.

Perhaps one of the most effective ways to summarize the concepts intertwined with the assessment of writing is to review the *Standards for the Assessment of Reading and Writing* that were established by the International Reading Association (1994). With assessment viewed as an interpretive process and the texts for assessment coming in the form of students' writing, teachers assess students' writing and make evaluative comments about writers' work. Eleven standards guide our local assessments (see accompanying box).

Teaching Guidelines

STANDARDS FOR THE ASSESSMENT OF READING AND WRITING

1. The interests of the student are paramount in assessment.

2. The primary purpose of assessment is to improve teaching and learning.

3. Assessment must reflect and allow for critical inquiry into curriculum and instruction.

4. Assessment must reflect the intellectually and socially complex nature of reading and writing and the important roles of school, home, and society in literacy development.

5. Assessment must be fair and equitable.

6. The consequences of an assessment procedure are the first, and the most important, consideration in establishing the validity of the assessment.

7. The teacher is the most important agent of assessment.

8. The assessment process should involve multiple perspectives and sources of data.

9. Assessment must be based in the school community.

10. All members of the educational community—students, parents, teachers, administrators, policy makers, and the public—must have a voice in the development, interpretation, and reporting of assessment.

11. Parents must be involved as active, essential participants in the assessment process.

International Reading Association, 1994

SUMMARY

Assessment plays a crucial role in the writing classroom both as a powerful tool for teaching and as a method of accountability for schools, teachers, and students. Assessment ranges from formal, large-scale testing conducted in tightly controlled conditions to more informal classroom measures that include student-student and teacher-student collaborative feedback. In both cases, the assessment is based on performance tasks, which are measured with criterion-referenced rubrics.

The purposes for assessment dictate the types of assessment used. Classroom teachers typically use a variety of assessment tools to provide feedback and measure student growth and to design curriculum and instruction based on student needs. While types of assessment include discrete-point, frequency-count marking, impressionistic, primary-trait, and analytic, the more important assessment types for the workshop or classroom are probably primary-trait and analytic. Writing topics for assessment allow optimal student performance by including considerations of audience and purpose and by being realistic, appropriate, understandable, personal, reliable, feasible, and fair.

Student and teacher attitudes and motivation relate directly to the methods of assessment and the kind of feedback employed with the assessment. Writing workshop assessment differs from more formal assessment in that evaluation comes in the form of feedback on the qualities of a piece of work, while grading occurs after students have had the opportunity to carry a piece of writing through the writing process.

Portfolios containing selected pieces offer a valuable tool for documenting students' strengths and weaknesses and for showing growth over time. Teachers use a variety of different scales and criteria to evaluate students' writing and they model strategies and techniques for evaluation and feedback for their writers. Writers, in turn, use the criteria and feedback techniques for peer evaluation and self-monitoring.

Scales and criteria are used to assess formal and informal writing tasks. They are an integral part of portfolio evaluation and are also used to measure both process and products. With teacher modeling and instruction in their use, scales and criteria are effective tools in peer and self-evaluation. Students practice evaluating with anonymous sample papers and by building rubrics.

Teachers base writers' grades on individual pieces of writing and on writers' use of the process. Grades on writing products are derived from the criteria developed in class, while grades on the process are based on classroom observations, peer interaction, individual conferences, and students' self-reflections.

Theory into Practice

1. List occasions on which you would use each of the types of assessment.

2. Divide into groups of three or four and discuss the values of both formal and informal assessment. Share your views with other groups in a whole class discussion.

3. Write a brief analysis of norm-referenced and criterion-referenced assessment. Which one would you choose to use? In whole class discussion, explain your choice.

4. Brainstorm and debate the advantages and disadvantages of the portfolio approach to assessment.

5. Analyze the two prompts suggested in this chapter with the universal criteria. Apply each of the criteria and discuss why the prompt would or would not be acceptable for a writing assessment task.

6. In groups of three or four, develop two or three writing topics using the universal criteria. Identify your writers' grade level and interests. Establish an audience, a purpose, and a situation. When you have completed your topics, share them with the class on an overhead and critique them with the universal criteria.

(continued)

7. Develop two comparable writing tasks for one genre. Critique them with the criteria.

8. Develop the framework for a writing topic so that students with any one of the multiple intelligences could fill it in with content representative of one of their stronger intelligences.

9. Use a set of three or four sample papers. With an appropriate set of criteria, use the strategies for feedback outlined in this chapter to practice responding to the writers. Use both questions and comments.

10. Build a rubric for literary writing (narrative) for fourth-grade students.

11. Using the set of papers from question 9, determine a grade for each paper based on its writing features. Compare your scores with those of others in the class. Where did you agree? Where did you disagree? Why?

12. Write a lesson plan for teaching students how to be peer evaluators.

BIBLIOGRAPHY

Andrade, Heidi G. 2000. Using rubrics to promote thinking and learning. *Educational Leadership, 57* (February), 13–18.

Applebee, Arthur N., Judith A. Langer, Ina V. S. Mullis, Andrew S. Latham, and Claudia A. Gentile. 1994. *NAEP 1992 Writing Report Card.* Washington, DC: Office of Educational Research and Improvement.

Applebee, Arthur N., Judith A. Langer, and Ina V. S. Mullis. 1989. *Understanding direct writing assessment.* Princeton, NJ: Educational Testing Service.

Atwell, Nancie. 1987. *In the middle.* Portsmouth, NH: Heinemann.

Beaven, Mary A. 1977. Individualized goal setting, self-evaluation, and peer evaluation. In *Evaluating writing* (Charles R. Cooper and Lee Odell, Eds.). SUNY at Buffalo: National Council of Teachers of English, pp. 135–156

Bertisch, Carole A. 1993. The portfolio as an assessment tool. In *Process and portfolios in writing instruction, vol. 29* (Kent Gill, Ed.). Urbana, IL: National Council of Teachers of English, pp. 54–62

Brandt, Ron. 1989. On misuse of testing: A conversation with George Madaus. *Educational Leadership, 46* (April), 26–29.

Calfee, R. C., M. K. Henry, and J. A. Funder. 1988. A model for school change. In *Changing school reading programs* (S. J. Samuels and P. D. Pearson, Eds.) Newark, DE: International Reading Association.

Camp, Roberta, and Denise Levine. 1991. Portfolios evolving, background and variations in sixth- through twelfth-grade classrooms. In *Portfolios: Process and product* (Pat Belanoff and Marcia Dickson, Eds.). Portsmouth, NH: Heinemann, pp. 194–205.

Carbone, Nick. 1995. *Grades as text.* Paper. Conference on College Composition and Communication. Washington, DC (March).

Chittenden, Edward. 1991. Authentic assessment, evaluation, and documentation of student performance. In *Expanding student assessment* (Vito Perrone, Ed.). Alexandria, VA: Association for Supervision and Curriculum Development, pp. 22–31.

Coleman, D. R. 1983. Effects of using a writing scale by gifted primary students. *Gifted Child Quarterly, 27,* 114–121.

Collins, John. 1988. *Implementing the cumulative writing folder program: A comprehensive guide with answers to the most frequently asked questions.* Andover, MA: The Network, Inc.

Conners, Robert J., and Andrea Lunsford. 1993. Teachers' rhetorical comments on student papers. *College composition and communication, 44* (May), 200–223.

Cooper, C. R. 1986. Studying writing: Linguistic approaches. *Written Communication, 1,* 108–123.

Cooper, Charles R. 1977. Holistic evaluation of writing. In *Evaluating writing* (Charles R. Cooper and Lee Odell, Eds.). SUNY at Buffalo: National Council of Teachers of English.

Cooper, Charles R., and Lee Odell. 1977. *Evaluating writing: Describing, measuring, judging.* SUNY at Buffalo: National Council of Teachers of English.

Corbett, William D. (1989). Let's tell the good news about reading and writing. *Educational Leadership, 46* (April), 53.

Costa, Arthur L. 1989. Re-assessing assessment. *Educational Leadership, 46* (April), 2.

Diederich, Paul B. 1974. *Measuring growth in writing.* Urbana, IL: National Council of Teachers of English.

Geocaris, Claudia, and Maria Ross. 1999. A test worth taking. *Educational Leadership, 57* (September), 29–33.

Golub, J. N. 1982. *Characteristics of students' classroom talk surrounding the assignment, production, and evaluation of a writing task.* (Technical Research Report-Document 229 757) Washington, DC: ERIC.

Harrington, Susanmarie, and Tere Molinder-Hogue. 1995. The role of product in process: An approach to grading and teacher response. *English in Texas, 28,* 52–60.

Hartfiel, V. Faye, Jane B. Hughey, Deanna R. Wormuth, and Holly L. Jacobs. 1985. *Learning & SL Composition.* Rowley, MA: Newbury House.

Haswell, R. H. 1983. Minimal marking. *College English, 45,* 600–604.

Hiebert, Elfieda H., and Robert C. Calfee. 1989. Advancing academic literacy through teachers' assessment. *Educational Leadership, 46* (April), 50–54

High stakes assessment in reading. 1999. *The Reading Teacher, 53* (November), 257–263.

Hill, Margaret H. 1997. National and state standards for English. *English in Texas, 28* (Fall), 10–18.

Hillocks, George, Jr. 1984. What works in teaching composition: A meta-analysis of experimental treatment studies. *American Journal of Education, 93,* 107–132.

Hillocks, George, Jr. 1986. *Research on written composition.* Urbana, IL: National Council of Teachers of English.

Hillocks, George, Jr. 1987. Synthesis of research on teaching writing. *Educational Leadership 44.* (May), 177–186.

Hoge, D. R., E. K. Smith, and S. L. Hanson. 1990. School experiences predicting changes in self-esteem of sixth and seventh grade students. *Journal of Educational Psychology, 82,* 117–127.

Hughes, Arthur. 1991. *Testing for language teachers.* New York: Cambridge University Press.

Hughey, Jane B. 1994. *The effects of facilitative teacher response and revision strategies on adolescent writing achievement.* Unpublished dissertation. Texas A&M University.

Hughey, Jane B., and V. Faye Hartfiel. 1989. *The profile guide.* College Station, TX: Writing Evaluation Systems.

Jacobs, Holly L, Stephen A. Zinkgraf, Deanna R. Wormuth, V. Faye Hartfiel, and Jane B. Hughey. 1981. *Testing ESL composition: A practical approach.* Rowley, MA: Newbury House Publishers.

Joint Task Force on Assessment. 1994. *Standards for the assessment of reading and writing.* Newark, DE: International Reading Association, and Urbana, IL: National Council of Teachers of English.

Knoblach, C., and L. Brannon. 1984. *Rhetorical traditions and the teaching of writing.* Upper Montclair, NJ: Boynton Cook Publishers.

La Fontana, Virginia. 1996. Throw away that correcting pen. *English Journal, 85* (October), 71–73.

Lloyd-Jones, Richard. 1977. Primary trait scoring. In *Evaluating writing* (Charles R. Cooper and Lee Odell, Eds.). SUNY at Buffalo, NY: National Council of Teachers of English, pp. 33–66.

Marzano, Robert J., Debra Pickering, and Jay McTighe. 1993. *Assessing student outcomes: Performance assessment using the dimensions of learning model.* Alexandria, VA: Association for Supervision and Curriculum Development

Meier, Deborah. 1996. Supposing that . . . *Phi Delta Kappan* (December), 271–284.

Munk, Dennis, and William D. Bursuch. 1998. Can grades be helpful and fair? *Educational Leadership, 55* (December/January), 44–47.

Odell, Lee. 1977. Measuring changes in intellectual processes as one dimension of growth in writing. In *Evaluating writing* (Charles R. Cooper and Lee Odell, Eds.). SUNY at Buffalo, NY: National Council of Teachers of English, pp. 107–132.

O'Neill, Mary G. 1990. *The effects of focus correction on the writing of urban seventh-grade students using the cumulative writing folder program across the curriculum.* Ann Arbor, MI: VMI Dissertation Services.

Podis, L. A., and J. M. Podis. 1986. Improving our responses to student writing: A process-oriented approach. *Rhetoric Review, 5,* 90–98.

Popham, W. James. 1997. What's wrong—and what's right—with rubrics. *Educational Leadership, 55* (October), 72–75.

Purves, Alan C. 1992. Reflections on research and assessment in written composition. *Research in the Teaching of English, 26,* 108–122.

Ragin, C. C. 1987. *The comparative method: Moving beyond qualitative and quantitative strategies.* Berkeley: University of California Press.

Rubin, D. 1993. Evaluating freshman writers: What do students really learn? *College English, 45,* 373–379.

Sager, Carol. 2000. The Sager scale: Components of excellence. Chestnut Hills, MA: Sager Educational Enterprises.

School Talk, 4, July 1999 (Cora Lee Five and Marie Dionisio, Eds.). Urbana, IL: National Council of Teachers of English.

Shepard, Lorrie A. 1989. Why we need better assessments. *Educational Leadership, 46* (April), 4–9.

Slack, Charlotte. 2000. *Foundations for writing, book I.* 2nd ed. ed. San Antonio, TX: ECS Learning Systems.

Soltis, J. M., and H. J. Walberg. 1989. Thirteen-year-old's writing achievements: A secondary analysis of the four national assessment of writing. *Journal of Educational Research, 83,* 22–29.

Sommers, Nancy. 1982. Responding to student writing. *College Composition and Communication, 33,*148–156.

Stock, Pat L. 1991. The rhetoric of writing assessment. In *Expanding Student Assessment* (Vito Perrone, Ed.). Alexandria, VA: Association for Supervision and Curriculum Development, pp. 72–105.

Strzepek, Joseph E., and Margo A. Figgins. 1993. A polemic on evaluating writing. In *Process and portfolios in writing instruction,* vol. 29 (Kent Gill, Ed.). Urbana, IL: National Council of Teachers of English, pp. 47–53.

Weir, Cyril J. 1990. *Communicative language testing.* New York: Prentice Hall.

Wheeler, Patricia, and Geneva D. Haertel. 1993. *Resource Handbook on Performance Assessment and Measurement.* Berkeley, CA: The Owl Press.

White, Edward M. 1985. *Teaching and assessing writing.* San Francisco, CA: Jossey-Bass.

Wiggins, Grant P. 1993. *Assessing student performance.* San Fransisco, CA: Jossey-Bass.

Willis, Scott. 1999. The accountability question. *Education Update, 41* (November), 1–8.

Wolf, Dennie Palmer. (1989). Portfolio assessment: Sampling student work. *Educational Leadership, 46* (April), 35–39.

Wyngaard, Sandra, and Rachel Gehrke. 1996. Responding to audience: Using rubrics to teach and assess writing. *English Journal, 85* (October), 67–73

Zessoules, Rieneke, and Howard Gardner. 1991. Authentic assessment: Beyond the buzzword and into the classroom. In *Expanding student assessment.* (Vito Perrone, Ed.). Alexandria, VA: Association for Supervision and Curriculum Development, pp. 47–71.

Grammar Through Writing

*What all students need . . . is guidance in understanding
and applying those aspects of grammar that are most relevant to writing.*

Weaver, 1998

Chapter Outline

The Writing/Grammar Relationship

In a university class of preservice teachers, moans and groans rose spontaneously from the group when we reached the point in the class syllabus that dealt with grammar. "I hate diagramming," volunteered one student. "It helps me see the sentence structures," chimed in another. "I never could remember the parts of speech," another added. A quick survey of the class revealed that most had studied grammar in isolation and few felt confident enough of their knowledge of grammar to teach it. Most associated grammar with the red marks on their compositions. Even though grammar had been a major percentage of their writing grades throughout their elementary and secondary experiences, it was always taught as a separate subject.

Traditional Grammar Approach

Evidence suggests that when assessment of writing focuses primarily on grammar and mechanics, students' writing development is not served. Dahl and Farnan, 1998

Imagine the reaction of these preservice teachers when we suggest that they change their approach to grammar as they experienced it; that is, we recommend eliminating grammar class. "What! No grammar class?" they exclaim. "Not exactly," we respond as we propose that grammar become an integrated part of the writing workshop. We believe that grammar must be taught; however, as Hillocks' (1987, p. 74) research shows, "The study of traditional school grammar (i.e., the definition of parts of speech, the parsing of sentences, etc.) has no effect on raising the quality of student writing." In fact, Hillocks shows that a heavy emphasis on mechanics and usage actually results in significant losses in overall writing quality. We agree. We have seen it in our own classrooms at the elementary, middle school, high school, and university levels.

When children learn the rules of grammar in isolation, they lack the connection to apply the rules to their writing. When their understanding of grammar is "highly developed, a state of automation occurs which allows writers the freedom to cease constant monitoring of the basic rules and conventions and to concentrate instead on developing the content and message of the written communication to accomplish specific purposes . . ." (Hughey, 1994, p. 29).

Most children believe they can write. . . . Children who are encouraged to draw and scribble at an early age later read and write more readily and effectively than children who are denied these important formative experiences. Cramer, 1998

Shaughnessy (1977) points out that students' papers that seem to be nothing but chaos, when examined more carefully, actually reveal "little that is random or illogical." "The keys to their development as writers," she notes, "often lie hidden in the very features of their writing that English teachers have been trained to brush aside with a . . . scribbled injunction to 'Proofread!' " (p. 5). Teaching grammatical structures and teaching writing are not usually interwoven. However, students' grammatical difficulties in writing are too often signs of their unfamiliarity with certain features of the grammatical code that "governs formal written English" (p. 45). So how do our writers most effectively learn a functional grammatical schema, one that strengthens their writing?

Excerpts from Chad's paper (Figure 4–1) illustrate Shaughnessy's point that there is often something hidden in the chaos. Although unfamiliar with the conventions of language, his concept of storytelling is evident. Because we initially encouraged Chad to create his story without regard for the rules of grammar and spelling, he was able to

FIGURE 4–1
Student Writing
Sample

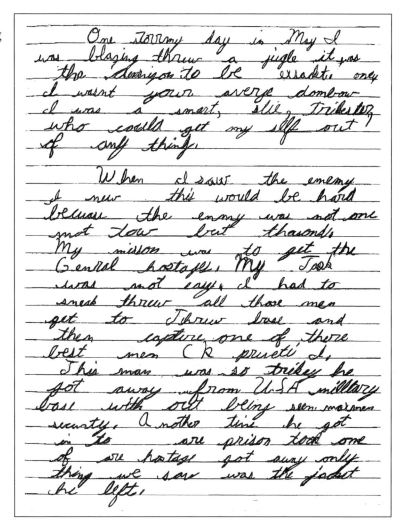

Certainly, no one
consciously lays out
the grammatical
scheme for a sen-
tence: "Let's see, sub-
ject with modifier,
verb, object, plus re-
strictive clause. Now,
how will I fill that
in?" Hillocks, 1987

freely express his ideas and develop his story. Later, during editing activities, he attended to the issues of grammar and spelling.

We may have won-
derful ideas and in-
teresting ways of ex-
pressing things that
have nothing to do
with apostrophes, hy-
phens, or proper
handwriting slant.
Wilcox, 1996

We believe all writers need the freedom to develop ideas without regard to conventions
in the beginning phases of writing. Templeton and Morris (1999) report that this procedure of initial writing without regard to conventions is a lifelong phenomenon practiced
by children and adults alike. We believe that children like Chad would quickly, and perhaps permanently, balk at writing if we emphasized grammar and spelling issues while he
worked to develop his ideas. Wilcox (1996) draws a clear line between composing and
transcribing. He defines composing as "discovering, shaping, and expressing what is inside
you. Transcribing is putting it on paper . . . too many of us tend to mix the acts together"

grammar with the little g refers to the rules of preferred or prescribed usage associated with standard language. . . . It is the art of being correct. Baron, 1989

(p. 13). Barnitz (1998) agrees that too much instruction in conventions is counterproductive during the composing process. We see instruction of the conventions in a meaningful and balanced way as an important part of the composing process.

Grammar in Context

Even though writers need the freedom to generate ideas without regard to grammar, we believe that there is a place for grammar in the process and that the concepts are best taught within the context of writing. Writing and grammar become integral parts of the same process. Grammar taught in a meaningful writing context results in retention and understanding of grammar functions rather than memorization of rules in isolation. Writers learn when and why to use certain structures instead of simply how to use them. Students need practice using grammar in writing because, like other aspects of the language, grammar is best learned in actual use. The lifelong benefits of knowing how to use grammar correctly and effectively reflect an educated person.

Teaching selected aspects of grammar in the context of their use promises to be more effective than teaching grammar more thoroughly, but in isolation. Weaver, 1998

Farr and Daniels (1986, p. 46) find that of 15 key factors associated with effective writing, four apply to the issue of the incorporation of grammar and mechanics:

- Direct instruction in specific strategies and techniques for writing
- Reduced instruction in grammatical terminology and related drills, with increased use of sentence combining
- Teaching of writing mechanics and grammar in the context of the students' actual compositions, rather than in separate drills and exercises
- Moderate marking of surface structure errors, focusing on sets or patterns of related errors

To their last point, we add that this marking only comes at the editing stage in the process.

Conventions

Grammar . . . can offer a great deal to those who are learning to write. . . . Writers at all levels need to know what options are available to them. Shuman, 1995

Incorporating Grammar and Writing.   We teach the development of writing content and organization as primary skills, but such skills are incomplete without attention to grammar and mechanics. As we develop the different purposes and modes of writing, we focus on particular sentence structures, sentence variety, punctuation rules, word choices, spelling, and other conventions that speed the writers' messages along to their readers. We engage in direct teaching of the skills in lessons that fit into our writing content objectives. For example, as students work to develop story narrative, we teach the use of dialogue and the associated mechanics of punctuation and capitalization related to quotations. We recommend that readers of this text return to this chapter to review associated grammar points as the purposes and modes of writing are discussed in later chapters.

Grammar concepts function as building blocks much like concepts in mathematics that build on previous learning. Bad habits begun in early stages of learning are hard to break later on, just as good grammar habits stay with writers for a lifetime.

Grammar References. To begin the process of incorporating grammar into writing, we recommend that every writing teacher have a comprehensive reference collection for grammar, mechanics, and spelling. We do, and we use the references often. Basic references include an unabridged dictionary, a thesaurus, and a basic reference for mechanics and punctuation issues of style. Classic references for writers include *Elements of Style* by Strunk and White, *The Chicago Manual of Style* by the University of Chicago Press, and *On Writing Well: The Classic Guide to Writing Nonfiction* by Zinsser. In addition, the Internet provides a wealth of writing reference support. The National Writing Centers Association, a National Council of Teachers of English Assembly, maintains an extensive online list, "Resources for Writers," that includes links to major universities (often called OWLs or Online Writing Laboratories) and other valuable resources. In the classroom, when students have grammar, mechanics, and spelling questions, we show them how to find the answers and explain concepts to them. We also bookmark Internet links to multiple sources for our writers at the upper grade levels so they can search for their own answers.

> Writers need a thorough knowledge of conventions. They need to put markers to help the text flow like speech, so that readers feel that the writer is present and talking directly to them as they read. Graves, 1991

We caution our writers that the spell check and grammar programs on their word processing packages are not always accurate. Writers need to know the rules and conventions so they can judge for themselves whether a change needs to be made or not.

Published Work. To stimulate interest in grammar, our students regularly publish their work. The most powerful motivation for correcting grammar and spelling is knowing that authentic audiences will see the finished work.

> Publish writing— there is nothing like performance to make us try to make ourselves and our writing presentable. Bishop, 1995

Figure 4–2 gives an overview of the points of grammar that we emphasize with our students in the various purposes and modes. In the following discussion, we demonstrate how to integrate grammar points in the writing workshop. While we focus on some of the common problems faced by young writers and new teachers, this section is not intended as a comprehensive grammar curriculum.

Development of Strategies

> If we take the view that conventions are there to help me and that each one offers an opportunity to better understand what I am trying to say then I want them in my repertoire of tools for writing. Graves, 1994

With beginning writers, we look at the literature that they are learning to read. We discuss the author's use of capital letters and periods. We point out the importance of these marks and conventions in helping us make sense of the story. We discuss what would happen if the marks were missing. As Graves (1994, p. 192) remarks, "If we focus on conventions as aids to understanding what we mean and conveying that to our readers, then we set out on an alternative road to helping our students learn. Conventions now become useful tools." When our youngest writers adopt this concept of grammar as a helpful tool, then we motivate them to incorporate correct grammar at the earliest stages. After exploring literature for its grammar components, then we model and discuss the correct grammar of a sentence at teachable moments during the day, making the grammar an integral part of the writing process. For example, while writing a sentence on the board or a transparency, we say:

> I begin my sentence with a capital letter because all sentences begin with a capital letter. The capital letter tells the reader that I am starting a new idea, and my new idea will be in this new sentence. I leave a finger space between each word in the

PURPOSES	VOCABULARY	GRAMMAR	MECHANICS
Expressive: To explore one's feelings, ideas, beliefs	Adjectives Vivid verbs Connecting words (conjunctions)	Simple declarative sentences Questions Past/present tense Person Pronouns Dates Friendly letter format	Periods Question marks Exclamation marks Indenting Capital letters Commas Spelling
Literary: To entertain one's self or others	Adverbs Similes Metaphors Onomatopoeia Synonyms	Dialogue First and third person Gerunds Exclamations Past/present/future tenses Poetry patterns, rhythms, stanzas, lines	Quotation marks Commas Paragraphing
Informative: To explain to or instruct others	Transitional words Comparatives Causals	Commands Second person Negatives Compound sentences Parallel structures Complex sentences Sentence combining Subjunctive Understood you Words in a series Introductory phrases Subordinate clauses Sequential order in clauses Coordinating conjunctions Independent clauses Conjunctive adverbs	Semicolon Colon Dash Parentheses
Persuasive: To convince, persuade, or change others	Synthesis of all	Compound sentences Complex sentences Compound/complex sentences Parallel sentence structures Subjunctive sentence structures Sentence variety Word choice	

Adapted from Hughey, Jane and Faye Hartfiel. 1989. *The profile guide.* College Station, TX: Writing Evaluation Systems.

FIGURE 4–2   Grammar Points Related to Purposes of Writing

sentence. The space makes it easy for the reader to tell one word from another. I put a period at the end of the sentence. The period is a sign telling the reader that I have finished the idea of the sentence.

After students have mastered the basics, new concepts are added very gradually in the same manner. We look for grammar lessons that fit the writing context and model them for students' writing. If questions become a part of their writing, we discuss the structure of questions and the correct punctuation. With constant references to literature, teacher modeling, and oral explanation of writing followed by practice in writing sentences, beginning writers learn that the appearance of words on paper is important to the message they send to the reader.

They learn that missing capital letters and periods, for example, cause confusion for the reader. Grammar becomes a helpful tool for expressing ideas.

Teaching Guidelines for Sentence Structures

Daily Language Mini-Lessons. Daily oral language mini-lessons (also called DOLs), developed by Wisconsin teachers in the classroom, consist of short, specific grammar lessons that students practice each day. These mini-lessons find their way to many classrooms as a strategy to teach grammar without the long, often uninteresting exercises offered in many English textbooks. The language mini-lesson is intended to give students practice on a particular grammar point each day. While we use the concept of the original DOL to present a daily grammar point, we adapt it to fit our needs and our philosophy of teaching grammar within the context of writing. We determine which grammar points are pertinent to the writing we are doing in the classroom and present those points in 5- to-10-minute lessons at the beginning of our writing classes. We review the literature our students are reading, and we watch our students' writing for indications of particular grammar and punctuation needs. We follow Shuman's advice in selecting only those obvious common conventions rather than "arcane uses writers seldom have occasion to use" (1995, p. 119). In this manner, the grammar points blend into the context of the subject matter and the appropriate writing modes. Evaluation of mastery is reflected in the students' writing.

Brosnahan and Neuleib (1995) found that interactive tasks stimulate interest in learning and promote retention of skills. Our classroom experiences support this research. An example of this integrated approach follows.

Strategy for daily language mini-lessons. Before class, we write a sentence that illustrates the grammar point for the day on the board or on a transparency. No punctuation or capitalization is included in the sentence, but mistakes are included as in the sentence that follows.

first he arrange string glue paint construction paper and scissors on a drop cloth

Next, we divide students into teams. In a small group cooperative effort, each team takes a turn contributing suggestions for completing the sentence. If the suggestion is correct, the team wins a point. If the suggestion is wrong, other teams have the opportunity

Certain aspects of the constructivist theory of learning . . . is that the learner must form hypotheses about concepts, in the process of coming to understand them. Weaver, 1998

to win the point. The team with the most points at the end of the activity wins—first in line for lunch or some other privilege. As students answer correctly, a member of the team makes the changes to the sentence on the board. After the sentence is completed, all students write the correct sentence in their spiral grammar notebooks. They then work together in groups of two or three to identify and write their own rules for the changes made to the sentence. From the corrected sentence,

First, arrange string, glue, paint, construction paper, and scissors on a drop cloth.

Students develop grammar rules:

1. Capitalize *first* because it is the first word in the sentence.
2. Use a comma after *first* since it is an introductory (transitional) word in the sentence.
3. Use commas after string, glue, paint, construction paper as words in a series.
4. Remove *he. You* is the understood subject because the sentence is a command form used to give directions.

Through an understanding of grammar, as opposed to rote memorization of forms, students can begin to see the connections between grammatical choice and audience, and, more important, they can begin to understand what these choices say about themselves as writers and human beings. Glover and Stay, 1995

When students participate in the analysis of the sentence and the creation of the rules, we find that they more often remember the grammar point and apply it as they write. Working in teams helps shy or hesitant students interact, and they learn by observation and listening to others. Keeping a grammar notebook with correct examples and rules makes a handy reference for the students when they write on their own.

Jingles and Rap.   Incorporating rhythm and rhyme in grammar content makes it easier to remember. The CD album *School House Rock* (1996) from American Broadcasting Companies, Inc., puts lively learning to music. Students love songs from the "Grammar Rock" CD such as "Conjunction Junction," "Interjections," and "A Noun is a Person, Place, or Thing" in the grammar portion of the album. By singing the rules, internalization comes more easily than it does through rote memorization. Writers of all ages join in the fun of creating their own songs for the grammar points.

Jingles such as " *i* before *e* except after *c* and sometimes *w* and *y*" or "when two vowels go walking, the first one does the talking" also help children internalize rules that may be difficult to process otherwise. Both strategies appeal to the students with a musical intelligence.

Grammar instruction need not be totally discarded as long as there is ample time for authentic literacy lessons. Barnitz, 1998

Sentence combining.   Sentence combining is one of the most effective strategies to help students develop sentence structures for the various writing modes. It is a simple matter of joining related ideas that have a logical connection, an appeal to students with logical-mathematical intelligence. Mastering this strategy adds fluency to writers' work. Hillocks (1987) reports that instruction in sentence combining results in significant gains in syntactic maturity and sentence quality for students on all levels. When students possess a repertoire of sentence structures, they more easily select appropriate styles for their writing. Repeatedly filling out worksheets that ask for recall of information is not the same as being challenged to write pieces of discourse that express ideas and arguments in clear and concise written language (Farr & Daniel, 1986).

Students need not only to practice ways of combining sentences but to discuss which ways are more effective and why. Weaver, 1979

Strategy for sentence combining. Practice with combining exercises allows students to play with ideas, sentence structure, word choices, and the creation of mental images. In our classrooms, we see students move from simplistic sentences to fully elaborated ideas after they practice with sentence combining skills. For example, students move from an elementary level of expression such as:

My cat is furry. He has brown and white spots. He is very playful.

to the more fluent sentence that follows. Students practice combining these three related simple sentences by looking at the logical placement of the information into one sentence that uses the information from all three.

Subject = cat

Description of cat = furry, brown and white spotted

Action = is playful

My furry, brown and white spotted cat is very playful.

Students who can handle a higher level of abstraction practice combining sentences such as the following:

It rained hard for a week. The house flooded. Everything in the house washed away.

The relationship of the ideas is cause and effect, which can be expressed in a compound/complex sentence instead of three simple sentences.

Because it rained hard for a week, the house flooded and everything washed away.

Many sentence-combining books are available on the market; however, we believe that this strategy is most effective when students practice with sentences from their own papers. When they practice with their own writing, they address their own specific needs rather than working exercises that may be meaningless to them and that are out of context. We believe that children learn the language of grammar and writing when they are active participants in their learning and when their learning is presented in a meaningful context. Sentences in the second grader's paper presented in Figure 4–3 improved after sentence combining.

Sentence Variety. Sentence variety has great impact on writers' style and effectiveness. Learning when to use a long sentence, when to be repetitious, when to get right to the point, and when to emphasize with parallel structures add fluency and sophistication to a writer's voice. Sentences of explanation are often relatively long, since they communicate detailed information. Explanation often requires compound and complex sentences with prepositional phrases and embedded definitions. On the other hand, sentences that make a strong point or call for action are shorter and more direct. They call for the reader's attention to drive home the point.

Strategy for checking sentence variety. To consider sentence length in the revision stage, we teach students to make a simple tally of the number of words in each sentence on draft copies. On the computer, students enter a return after each sentence in their

FIGURE 4–3   Student Writing Sample for Sentence Combining

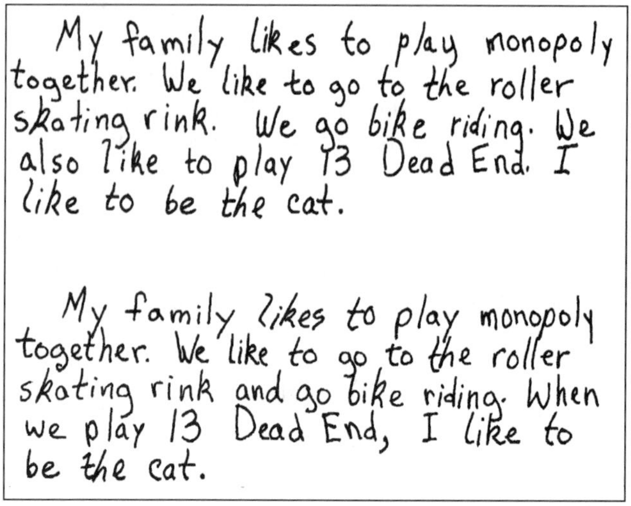

My family likes to play monopoly together. We like to go to the roller skating rink. We go bike riding. We also like to play 13 Dead End. I like to be the cat.

My family likes to play monopoly together. We like to go to the roller skating rink and go bike riding. When we play 13 Dead End, I like to be the cat.

A minimum of grammar for maximum benefits means teaching: 1) concepts of subject, verb, sentence, clause, phrase, and related concepts for editing; 2) style through sentence combining and sentence generating; 3) sentence sense and style through the manipulation of syntactic elements; 4) the power of dialects; 5) punctuation and mechanics for convention, clarity, and style. Weaver, 1996

piece of writing to create a list of sentences down the page. One look at the list shows sentence lengths. This exercise says nothing about the quality of the sentences, but it does show variety in length. Many short sentences probably indicate the need for some sentence combining. Long sentences might be run-ons. If all the sentences are approximately the same length, the presentation needs variety.

Third-grader Gavin made an attempt at using variety in sentence length in his introductory letter to his teacher.

GAVIN'S LETTER

I love sports. One of my strengths is playing baseball. One of my weaknesses is writing, as you can see. I don't hate it. I'm just not good at it. My family consists of my mother, my dad, my brother, and my dog. My hobbies are baseball, football, and work.

Eighth grader David wrote a parody of Edgar Allan Poe's *The Tell-Tale Heart* in which variety in sentence length contributed to the successful style of the piece. Below is an excerpt from his story.

THE TELL-TALE MONKEY

It is impossible to say how first the idea entered my brain, but once conceived, it haunted me night and day. Object, there was none. Passion, there was none. I loved the old Captain. I even liked his pet monkey. He had never wronged me (except once or twice), and he had never given me insult. For his gold I had no desire. I think it was his leg. Yes, it was this! One of his legs was made out of the finest woods in all the land, and whenever it trod near me, my blood ran cold (you see, I am extremely afraid of quality wood). And so by degree, I made

In the elementary grades, students internalize the structure of language through immersion and guidance in authentic daily reading and writing experiences. Routman, 1994

up my mind to take the life of the old sea captain and thus rid myself of his wooden leg forever.

The harmony of all of the sentences together makes the writing a pleasure for the reader. The variety of expression and selecting just the right sentence for just the right context keeps readers interested and encourages them to continue reading.

A Potpourri of Common Grammar Issues.   Other issues addressed in our grammar instruction are highlighted in the chart in Figure 4–4. This list is not intended to be a complete list of pesky problems but rather a reminder of some of the common misuses of the language in writing.

The sole purpose of punctuation and capitalization is to clarify the meaning of written words. At the proofreading stage, our writers focus on the conventions and rules for punctuation and spelling. As they work in groups and read for each other, they become aware of the effects that the presence or absence of these markers have on an audience. When a misspelling or errors in punctuation lead to confusion for their readers, they realize the

PURPOSES FOR WRITING	COMMON USAGE FOR STUDY
Expressive	• **Pronoun agreement.** *He went by himself.* *They went by themselves.* *Bob and I went home.* • **Verb tense consistency.** *The frog was slimy. The frog leaped high.*
Literary	• **Dialogue.** *Something strange is going on here," observed Meg.* *"Tell me more!" Dennis demanded.* *"When he came back," Tara mused, "he went straight to bed."* *"Did you see the dark clouds coming this way?" asked Julia.* • **Introductory modifying phrases.** The introductory phrases must be followed by a comma and refer to the subject in the main clause. *Hopping down from the swing, Mandy swooped up her cat.*
Informative	• **Understood "you."** *First, [you] assemble all materials.* • **Words in a series.** *Arrange string, glue, paint, and paper on a drop cloth.* • **Introductory phrases.** *To wash a dog, use soap designed for dogs.* • **Colons.** *Try the following exercises: walking, biking, tennis, and swimming.* • **Negatives:** *Don't open the package before you are ready to use it.* • **Coordinating conjuncitons.** *Dogs bark, and cats meow.* *Dogs bark; cats meow.* *Not only do dogs bark, but they also growl and sometimes bite.*
Persuasive	• **Synthesis.** Emphasize integration of all other purposes

FIGURE 4–4   Common Grammar Use Problems

Adapted from Hughey, Jane B. and V. Faye Hartfiel, 1989. *The profile guide.* College Station, TX. Writing Evaluation Systems, Inc.

importance of attention to these details. Our writers learn punctuation and capitalization as an integral part of the grammar of sentence structure. Through group work and daily oral language activities that include these skills, writers build their own reference charts and keep them in their writing folders. This approach helps assure that they learn the rules because they have an active role in creating them. We also post punctuation and capitalization charts for ready reference in the classroom. Figures 4–5 and 4–6 present simple but effective rules for punctuation and capitalization.

PUNCTUATION	USES AND EXAMPLES
Period	• At end of sentence making statement or request. *My dog had puppies last night. Please pass the mustard.* • After abbreviations. *U.S.A. Dec. Mr. Mrs. Dr. Ms.* (Miss does not need a period because it is not an abbreviation. • After initials. *Chris M. Noack*
Question mark	• At the end of a sentence that asks a question. *What time is it?*
Commas	• Items in a series. *We played cards, charades, and basketball at the party.* • To separate numbers in dates. *November 20,1914* • To separate cities and states. *Sioux City, Iowa.* • Between two independent clauses when joined by coordinating conjunctions. *We tried our best, and we won the prize.* • To set off long clauses. *In spite of the drenching rain, the game went on.* • In quotations. *"I love to write stories," said Mary. "I always knew," said Joe, "that we would finish the job." Anna said, "It's time to go home."* • To set off appositives. *My, what a great cook you are!* • After the greeting of a friendly letter. *Dear Aunt Alma,* • After the closing of a letter. *Your good friend, Eric.*
Apostrophe	• In contractions. *Can't won't I'll they're* • To show possession. *My dog's bowl is missing. The boys' team lost the game.*
Exclamation point	• At the end of a sentence or word that expresses strong feeling. *I love the zoo! Wow!*
Quotation marks	• To set off the exact words of a speaker in a sentence. (See examples from 'commas' above.)
Colon	• To introduce a list. *To wash a car you need the following: sponge, soap, towel, and tire scrub brush.* • Between numbers in time. *10:30*
Semicolon	• Between independent clauses; sometimes used in place of a period. *We love the beach; we could stay all day.* • To separate phrases which already contain commas. *We need to record the phases of the moon; star names, constellations, and locations; and the rising and setting times of the sun.*

FIGURE 4–5   Punctuation Chart

Adapted from Hughey, Jane B. and V. Faye Hartfiel, 1989. *The profile guide.* College Station, TX. Writing Evaluation Systems, Inc.

FIGURE 4–6
Capitalization
Rules

- At the beginning of a sentence. *The school is two miles from my house.*
- Proper nouns.
   Names of people. *Mary Smith*
   Titles. *Mr.   Mrs.   Dr.   Miss   Ms.   Major*
   Cities and states.   *Greensboro   New Mexico*
   Countries and nationalities. *Italy   Italians*
   Book and magazine titles. Capitalize the first and last words and all important words in the title. *The Summer of the Swan.   Sports Illustrated for Kids.*
   Days and months. *Friday   May*
   Holidays. *Fourth of July   Memorial Day   Thanksgiving*
   Names of places. *Museum of Art.   Lake Placid.   Pressman Ranch.*
   Names of streets. *Bush Boulevard.   Lee Avenue.*

Teaching Guidelines for Spelling

Problems in Word Use.   In addition to a focus on the vocabulary for transitions in writing, we encourage both teachers and developing writers to attend to specific words that seem to cause problems for writers of all ages. Figure 4–7 was compiled from errors made by preservice teachers in a university writing class. Correct use of these common words signals the mark of an educated writer. As informed writing teachers and models for our students, we believe it is important to use the words on this list correctly. The on-line writing references mentioned earlier in the chapter offer clear guidance on these pesky problems.

Spelling begins in the
extended period of
emergent literacy
during which children learn much
about the forms and
functions of print.
Templeton and Morris, 1999

Development of Spelling and Word Use.   Spelling and word use, like the syntactical and rhetorical aspects of writing, are developmental. They are part and parcel of fluency in written expression. Both vocabulary and spelling skills expand with experience. A number of language researchers identify developmental stages of children's verbal expression, among them Calkins (1983), Manning and Manning (1986), Henderson (1990), and Cramer (1998). Calkins's work is worth studying to see the examples of children's development through these stages. Cramer echoes the theories of Henderson, Calkins, and the Mannings in discussing five developmental stages of children's spelling, as shown in Figure 4–8.

Written words and their spellings are the vehicles writers use to record thought. When we understand the developmental patterns that children experience as they grow in reading and writing skills, we see the benefits of encouraging transitional (also called invented) spelling and the benefits of incorporating direct instruction.

"The understanding of the . . . spelling system develops over time and depends upon considerable experience with meaningful reading and writing" (Templeton and Morris, 1999, p. 105). Cramer's (1998) research over a 30-year period supports this concept. He

FIGURE 4–7
Pesky Word
Use Problems
in Writing

- *Lie* (to recline or rest) and *lay* (to put or place something)
  - *Lay* (past)   *laid* (past)
- *Amount* (noncountable) and *number* (countable)
  - Money   dollars
  - Love   hugs and kisses
- *Less* (noncountable) and *few/fewer* (countable)
  - time   hours
  - money   dollars
- Different from (correct use) and *different than* (incorrect use)
- *If* and *whether or not*
- *There, their, they're*
- *To, two, too*
- *Affect* (verb) and *effect* (noun)
- *Like* (for comparison) and *such as* (for enumeration) ·
- *Quite* and *quiet*
- *ei* and *ie* in spelling
- *Since* and *sense*
- *aloud* and *allowed*
- *accept* and *except*
- *a* child, person, etc.—*he* or *she* (not they)
- each student—*he* or *she* (not they) and *his* or *her* (not their)
- There *are* some good ideas (not There is)
- *Not only* is accompanied by *but also*
- *Suppose* (present tense) and *supposed* (past tense)

Understanding spelling development can help guide spelling assessment and instruction. Knowing what ought to happen at each stage can help you understand why children spell words in ways that may seem bizarre but that are reasonable linguistic approximations and developmentally appropriate. Cramer, 1998

finds that "first-grade children who had extensive experience in early reading and writing using invented spelling quickly became superior spellers. . . . The same children also performed better in reading and writing . . . [and] they maintained their superior achievement across the six years in which their performance was tracked" (p. 84). Gentry (1987, p. 31) maintains that, "By second grade, many children spell at the phonetic and transitional developmental levels and do profit from formal study. But children at lower developmental levels may experience frustration if they are pushed too soon into formal spelling." He advises using small groups and individualization for best results.

Strategies for improving spelling.   Spelling researchers advocate the following strategies to improve spelling skills:

- reading extensively
- taking risks with words through transitional spelling
- individualizing spelling lists

FIGURE 4–8
Stages of Developmental Spelling

STAGE	CHARACTERISTICS
Prephonetic	Children scribble; draw; make wavy, cursive-like lines; write letters. *DuvQevy*
Phonetic	Children make systematic connections between letters and sounds that represent true alphabetic writing; marks the beginning of writing that can be read by the writer and the audience. *sm some*
Patterns with words	Children learn the patterns to which letters and sounds correspond within single-syllable words; add sight words. *rane rain*
Syllable juncture	Children learn the structural principles of syllabication; includes suffixes; inflected endings; dropping, doubling, and changing words that accompany word modifications. *crys cries*
Meaning deviation	Children learn that words related in meaning are often related in spelling. *nashunal national*

Adapted from Cramer, Ronald L. 1998. *The Spelling Connection.* New York: Guilford Press.

- individualizing or pairing study and testing
- practicing with words in context
- using word games and puzzles that promote inquiry and experimentation
- teaching word patterns
- teaching limited spelling rules
- giving explicit instruction in brief, interesting spelling lessons (about 60 minutes a week)
- using phonograms and puzzles

At the middle grades, the Mannings (1986) observed that the range of spelling ability seems to widen as students progress through the grade levels. As a result, they advocate a more individualized approach to spelling with their students and incorporate reading and writing on a regular basis. Their philosophy supports ours in that they believe that "spelling must be kept in that context; that is spelling is for writing." Teachers can help students improve their spelling by working with them in the context of students' own daily writing. Further, they encourage teaching of spelling in both intermediate and middle school through the content areas. While Gentry (1987) recommends spelling throughout all the subject areas for elementary age writers as well, Routman (1994) recommends an integrated approach to spelling whereby students' needs for words form the basis of instruction and practice.

We encourage students to guess at spelling during the composing process. Later, corrections come during the editing phase. Teaching of spelling rules is kept to a minimum and includes only those that have no or few exceptions. Aside from the need for individualization for varying levels of ability at the middle level, the recommendations for spelling remain essentially the same throughout the grade levels.

Spelling is . . . contextual. Contexts in which we write shape the way we spell. In some contexts standard spelling is important; in others it is less so. We use standard spelling if we have the need to use it. Bean & Bouffler, 1991

[Invented spelling] is a way of quickly getting your ideas down. Without invented spelling, writers would have to either limit what they say or distract themselves from the thinking process by taking the time to look words up. Wilde, 1996

Transitional spelling.   Transitional or invented spelling allows young writers to write freely. They know the words they want to use but have not yet learned the spelling patterns. Even adults adopt this same approach during the composing process, ignoring worries about spelling in an effort to "get on" with the ideas. "When kids invent spellings, they think about words and generate new knowledge. Emerging spellers need to invent, because inventing makes them think and learn"(Gentry, 1987, p. 17). Our writers from elementary through middle school demonstrate that they are more willing to write when they are allowed to experiment. We prompt them to sound out words and make guesses at how to spell during the generating process of their writing. A child who writes *krokadahl* is developing ideas with specific detail and description that would be suppressed were he to worry over how to spell the word *as he is writing.* Since we want our writers to describe, add detail, and be specific in the development of their ideas, we see transitional spelling as a success. In the editing stage, writers attend to the correct spellings. While we encourage our writers to experiment, we also encourage them to find the correct spelling or best word during the editing process.

In general, during the composing process, we respond to content, description, and organizational matters and leave grammar, mechanics, and spelling alone. They receive attention later in the process, after the ideas are developed.

Spelling and assessment.   When it is time to evaluate students' writing for revision and editing, we highlight or refer to misspelled words. We do not correct students' spelling for them but rather put the responsibility for the correct spelling on the writers themselves. In our classrooms, we find that when children correct their own errors, they are far more likely to remember the corrections than when they simply recopy corrections we make for them.

We allow for risk taking in spelling and composing during the process, but we do not ignore spelling altogether. We teach spelling lessons, conference with our students about persistent spelling problems, encourage some use of spell check when writers compose on the computer, and provide and encourage the use of dictionaries and thesauri.

In the early grades we focus on the correct spelling of basic words and at the same time encourage risk taking with the spelling of more complex words.

As students progress through the grade levels, increased development expands their spelling abilities and expectations for greater accuracy.

Educating parents.   Children are willing, but parents sometimes wonder about the acceptability of transitional spelling. Templeton and Morris (1999, p. 102) agree that, "Parents . . . are concerned about invented or temporary spelling, fearful this will lead to a lifetime of poor spelling. They wish to see spelling books tucked under children's arms and brought home, a reflection of what they perceive to be the foundation of tried and true traditional values education." Therefore, we use current research to educate the parents about the role of transitional spelling as a normal progression in writing and explain that we also teach the spelling conventions. We reassure them that we teach proofreading and editing at the appropriate times and that student's spelling will improve with practice and experience. Routman (1994, p. 250) relates that, "It has been my experience that if the teacher is knowledgeable about spelling development and current research . . . parents respond positively."

Direct Instruction.   Research demonstrates that, "To read and write words appropriately and fluently and to appreciate fully how words work in context, instruction must balance

The problem of teaching spelling, as we see it, is largely one of helping children to know what is standard. Bean & Bouffler, 1991

[Spelling] enables the writer to record meaning and the reader to construct meaning. To do this, spelling must be systematic. Bean & Bouffler, 1991

Word study becomes useful and instructive when it is based on students' levels of development and when appropriate words and patterns are explored through interesting and engaging activities. Bear and Templeton, 1998

To read and write words appropriately and fluently and to appreciate fully how words work in context, instruction must balance authentic reading and writing with purposeful word study. Bear and Templeton, 1998

authentic reading and writing with purposeful word study" (Bear and Templeton, 1998, p. 223). While we spend only the amount of time necessary to cover the spelling that we think will be helpful to our students, the lessons are systematic and include core spelling principles. This instruction takes approximately 10 to 15 minutes a day, long enough to convey a spelling principle, but short enough to keep students' attention. We prepare spelling lists for study, we offer instruction on spelling patterns, we teach the few rules that do not have exceptions, we explore the systematic changes that occur through what Cramer (1998) terms the *syllable juncture,* and we work with word families.

Spelling lists.   Word lists used for spelling come from a variety of sources. At the middle school level, the Mannings (1986) maintain that the first source, and probably the most beneficial, is a list of misspelled words from an individual student's work. The second source, they say, is high frequency words from spelling series. Perhaps, ultimately, the best source consists of a combination of the two. Our students use both.

Many commercial sources exist for basic spelling lists. Probably the best way to determine which of these lists is most appropriate is to give spelling pretests to discover how well the students have mastered the words included on the lists. When we create our own lists, we take words from the literature we are reading and from misspelled words in students' writing. A spelling list generated by the students themselves is highly popular and tailored to the students' ability levels. We ask, "What words do you want to know how to spell?" When students have a choice in at least some of the words, they take greater interest in the list and are motivated to learn the spellings. In addition, we choose groups of words according to spelling patterns or we use words related to a theme or concept. For example, a pattern list might contain words such as:

fun sun run bun gun dun pun

feature creature structure overture

To teach the change in a word that ends in *y* when a suffix ending is added, we might use:

cried   pried   dried   studied   buried   tried

Spelling rules.   We teach rules (Gentry, 1987) that apply to large numbers of words:

- Use periods in abbreviations.
- Use apostrophes to show possession and in contractions.
- Capitalize proper nouns.
- Add suffixes (*i.e.,* change *y* to *i,* drop the final silent *e,* double the final consonant).
- English words don't end in *v.*
- *Q* is followed by *u* in English spelling.

Spelling games.   Endless numbers of games and interactive class activities available in teacher supply stores and catalogs spark student interest in spelling. Rather than using a preset spelling drill book, these resources show how to create meaningful lessons with a wide selection of activities to meet varying needs. Some activities that we find effective with our younger writers include the following:

- Spray shaving cream onto the desk tops and ask children to spell words in the foam. The foam "erases" easily so children can try new words. This tactile and visual activity appeals to both spatial and bodily-kinesthetic learners.
- Read rhyming books and poems. The chanting reinforces words for those with musical intelligence.
- Use rhyming words in "Hinky Pinkies" for older writers to incorporate fun interaction and involve problem solving. Once children learn how to do Hinky Pinkies, they love creating their own. This kind of exploration and problem solving appeals to the logical and interpersonal intelligences. For example:
  - *What do you call an old football? Weathered leather*
  - *What do you call a worn-out bedroll? A rag bag*
- Create words from word parts or from one long word. Individually or in groups, students try to create as many words as they can within a given amount of time. For example:

  -ice: nice lice rice vice splice mice
  fantastic: fan fact fat sat saint cast

- Create word walls in the classroom. Large sheets of bulletin board paper or chart paper hold student-generated words. The presence of the word wall provides the visual stimulus that many of our writers need in order to learn the spelling of words. Word walls change as the group moves on to new vocabulary.
- Use "Hang Ten" for student feedback. With Hang Ten, students who need help with spelling, or ideas for overused words, clip their problem word to a clothes hanger that resides in a corner of the writing classroom. Other writers in the class contribute suggestions on the remaining nine clips to help the struggling writer out.
- Play Scrabble games for upper grade students. To play Scrabble at this level does not mean that students have to be competitive; they can adapt the rules of the game to make it a joint effort or to eliminate winners and losers. Our students love to team up and play with several equally balanced teams.

The accompanying box summarizes suggestions to put multiple intelligences to work while teaching grammar and spelling.

SUMMARY

Research reveals that a heavy emphasis on teaching grammar results in loss of writing quality. In contrast, presenting grammar, mechanics, and spelling through writing works. Writing and grammar are not separate functions but work together to produce writing that communicates clearly. Good grammar habits have lifelong benefits for young writers and deserve careful attention within the writing process.

EMPHASIZING THE MULTIPLE INTELLIGENCES

Linguistic: Play Hang Ten to find synonyms for overused words.

Logical/mathematical: Create as many words as possible, from one word, within a set amount of time.

Spatial: Diagram sentences to see the relationships of clauses.

Musical: Use songs and raps to learn the grammar rules; rhyme.

Bodily-kinesthetic: Spell new words in shaving cream or with sidewalk chalk.

Interpersonal: Play Scrabble.

Intrapersonal: Individually list as many words as possible with common endings (*-ice, -ate*).

Naturalist: Find parallel structures in nature.

Beginning writers learn to apply grammar conventions as a necessary part of communicating their ideas. Daily oral language activities allow teachers to present necessary grammar instruction at the point that students need particular skills to apply to their writing. During these short, daily activities, students work in groups to solve grammar issues related to incorrect sentences and record associated rules for later reference. Daily language mini-lessons address sentence combining, punctuation, capitalization, sentence structure, and word usage.

Language mini-lessons complement the modes of writing. While all grammar is used for almost all writing, the mini-lesson topics focus on specific uses of language that are appropriate to the various genres. For example, expressive writing includes friendly letter format, pronoun agreement, and verb tense. Literary writing topics include dialogue, introductory modifying phrases, and poetry. Informative writing topics include the command form of the verb, words in a series, introductory phrases, the colon, negatives, subordinate clauses, sequential order, compound sentences, and complex sentences.

Variety in sentence length and word use have a strong impact on style or voice in writing, and some language instruction focuses on these issues. Particular attention is given to pesky problems that plague student and adult writing alike.

Spelling skills develop through predictable stages as young writers grow in their abilities. Transitional spelling describes progress through these stages as students attempt to apply their incomplete knowledge to words they want for compositions. Children learn to spell most effectively through interaction with writing rather than through isolated word lists. Spelling improves when students study words selected for their individual needs and for connections with content areas. A variety of games and interactive strategies spark student interest in spelling.

As students generate ideas, they write without concern for spelling or grammar rules. During the revision and editing phases of writing, students attend to the pertinent spelling and grammar concerns so that compositions become integrated writing-grammar communications.

Theory into Practice

1. Examine and discuss Strunk and White's Elements of Style and Zinsser's On Writing Well: The Classic Guide to Writing Nonfiction. What parts of the books seem most applicable to the elementary or middle school writing workshop? How could these books be used in workshop?

2. Compare *The Chicago Manual of Style* to another grammar reference book. Determine which book would be the best choice for a teacher's classroom reference materials.

3. Visit several Internet sites that provide grammar reference information. Determine which sites offer the best information for classroom use.

4. Design lesson plans for teaching a grammar point related to each of the four purposes of writing. Use a literature-based format for beginning writers and a language mini-lesson strategy for older students. Share the lesson with classmates.

5. Develop a list of CDs and other music references that teach grammar skills. Develop a list of "jingles" or other mnemonics to teach grammar points.

6. Write a lesson plan for a particular grade level on basic sentence combining skills.

7. Write a mini-lesson to address at least one of the items in Figure 4–4.

8. Write sentences with each of the commonly misused words in Figure 4–7. Share sentences with classmates to ensure accuracy.

9. Ask a group of beginning writers to write a story. Compare their writing to the Stages of Developmental Spelling Chart in Figure 4–8 to determine their spelling needs.

10. Write a letter to parents about the stages of spelling and the value of transitional spelling.

11. Develop some new spelling games in addition to those listed in the chapter to stimulate interest in correct spelling.

BIBLIOGRAPHY

Barnitz, John G. (Ed.) 1998. Revising grammar instruction for authentic composing and comprehending. *Reading Teacher, 51* (April): 608–610.

Baron, Dennis. 1989. *Declining grammar.* Urbana, IL: National Council of Teachers of English.

Bean, Wendy, and Chrystine Bouffler. 1991. *Spell by writing.* Portsmouth, NH: Heinemann.

Bear, Donald R., and Shane Templeton. 1998. Explorations in developmental spelling: Foundations for learning and teaching phonics, spelling, and vocabulary. *Reading Teacher, 52* (November), 222–242.

Bishop, Wendy. 1995. Teaching grammar for writers in a process workshop classroom, chap. 12 in *The place of grammar in writing instruction,* Susan Hunter and Ray Wallace (Eds.). Portsmouth, NH: Boynton/Cook Publishers.

Brosnahan, Irene, and Janice Neuleib. 1995. Teaching grammar affectively: Learning to like grammar, chap. 14 in *The place of grammar in writing instruction,* Susan Hunter and Ray Wallace (Eds.). Portsmouth, NH: Boynton/Cook Publishers.

Calkins, Lucy McCormick. 1983. *Lessons from a child on the teaching and learning of writing.* Exeter, NH: Heinemann Educational Books.

Cramer, Ronald L. 1998. *The spelling connection.* New York: Guilford Press.

Dahl, Karin L., and Nancy Farnan. 1998. *Children's writing: Perspectives from research.* Literature Studies Series. Newark, DE: International Reading Association, and Chicago: National Reading Conference.

Farr, Marcia, and Harvey Daniels. 1986. *Language diversity and writing instruction.* Urbana, IL: National Council of Teachers of English.

Gentry, J. Richard. 1987. *Spel . . . is a four-letter word.* Portsmouth, NH: Heinemann.

Glover, Carl W., and Byron Stay. 1995. Grammar in the writing center: Opportunities for discovery and change, chap. 9 in *The place of grammar in writing instruction,* Susan Hunter and Ray Wallace. (Eds.) Portsmouth, NH: Boynton/Cook Publishers.

Graves, Donald H. 1991. *Build a literate classroom.* Portsmouth, NH: Heinemann.

Graves, Donald H. 1994. *A fresh look at writing.* Portsmouth, NH: Heinemann.

Henderson, E. H. 1990. *Teaching spelling,* 2nd ed. Boston: Houghton Mifflin.

Hillocks, George Jr. 1987. Synthesis of research on written composition. *Educational Leadership 44* (May), 71–82.

Hughey, Jane and Faye Hartfiel. 1989. *The profile guide.* College Station, TX: Writing Evaluation Systems.

Hughey, Jane B. 1994. *The effects of facilitative teacher response and revision strategies on adolescent writing achievement.* Unpublished Dissertation, Texas A&M University.

Manning, Maryann M., and Gary Manning. 1986. *Improving spelling in the middle grades.* 2nd ed. Washington, DC: National Education Association.

Routman, Regie. 1994. *Invitations: Changing as teachers and learners K-12.* Portsmouth, NH: Heinemann.

School House Rock, 1996.

Shaughnessy, Mina P. 1977. *Errors & expectations.* New York: Oxford University Press.

Shuman, R. Baird. 1995. Grammar for writers: How much is enough? chap. 8 in *The place of grammar in writing instruction,* Susan Hunter and Ray Wallace (Eds.). Portsmouth, NH: Boynton/Cook Publishers.

Strunk, William, and E.B. White. 1995. *Elements of style.* New York: Allyn and Bacon.

Templeton, Shane, and Darrell Morris. 1999. Questions teachers ask about spelling. *Reading Research Quarterly, 34* (January/February/March) 102–112.

University of Chicago Press. 1993. *The Chicago manual of style: The essential guide for writers, editors, and publishers,* 14th ed. Chicago: University of Chicago Press.

Weaver, Constance (Ed.) 1998. *Lessons to share: On teaching grammar in context.* Portsmouth, NH: Boynton/Cook Publishers.

Weaver, Constance. 1996. *Teaching grammar in context.* Portsmouth, NH: Boynton/Cook Publishers.

Weaver, Constance. 1979. *Grammar for teachers: Perspectives and definitions.* Urbana, IL: National Council of Teachers of English.

Wilcox, Brad. 1996. Separating composition and transcription. *Writing Teacher, 9* (January), 13–14.

Wilde, Sandra. 1996. A speller's bill of rights. *Primary Voices, 4* (November), 7–10.

Zinsser, William Knowlton. 1998. *On writing well: The classic guide to writing nonfiction.* New York: Harper Reference.

chapter

5

Revise and Publish

Initial instruction in revision is best done on a group basis
and can begin as early as second grade, if not in first. Use a
good example about which many positive comments can be
made. Pick one major point that is common in the class as a
suggestion for improvement. . . .

Hillerich, 1985

Chapter Outline

"How do I get my kids to revise? My kids will write, but they just refuse to revise!" lamented a conscientious new teacher. The answer to his question lies in a clear view of the role of revision in the writing workshop. The *NAEP 1992 Writing Report Card* reports that revisions are rare, with only 1 percent of the students indicating that they write successive drafts or outlines or make significant changes. To make significant changes requires knowledge of criteria against which writers can evaluate their efforts. The evaluation and feedback that we discussed in chapter 3 lead to revision—a natural part of the writing process. Revision requires a positive attitude and definite expectations set at the beginning of a writing workshop along with techniques that facilitate teacher and peer feedback and support student revision.

"Why do we need to revise?" our analytic learners ask. The point of revision is to clarify what we write in order to communicate with peak effectiveness to the audience. In other words, the purpose is to prepare our writing for some form of publication. Thus, in the writing process, we explore, generate, incubate, write, and read, and in some cases we revise, edit, and publish.

> The more work-intensive aspect of getting published is perseverance, hard work, and revision. Anthony, student author, 1996

Some teachers lump revision and editing together in the process of improving or polishing a written piece. While both revision and editing may improve writing, they do so in different ways. Revision involves deep change; editing involves surface change. Students benefit from knowing the difference between these two functions of the writing process.

Revision Is Different from Editing

> The writer's attitude when revising should be; I revise to discover what I have to say; I revise to find out how to say it; I edit to make what I have to say clear. Murray, 1994

Editing is proofreading for and correcting surface errors such as capitalization, punctuation, spelling, indenting, grammar usage, and formatting. Editing requires knowledge of commonly recognized rules that govern our language and the ability to apply those rules to a written piece. Such rules define "acceptable" and "unacceptable" uses of standard English. Editing requires students to scrutinize their work for the correct application of the rules. It is not a fluid process, but rather an effort to find the most acceptable and effective way to communicate. Strategies that we proposed in chapter 4, "Grammar Through Writing," deal with editing concerns. While we often save our major editing for the final phases of our writing, in fact, we frequently edit as we write.

Revision, on the other hand, deals with revisiting ideas and refers to the content and organization of the paper, the choice of words, and the communicative value of the composition. There are no definitive "right" or "wrong" ways to express ideas; therefore, revision is a fluid process that attempts to improve the effective communication of ideas. Students need to know that during revision, the goal is to develop and define ideas as clearly and succinctly as possible. Many changes in draft copies become the norm as students learn to express themselves ever more effectively.

Factors that require attention during the revision process often include:

- introductions and conclusions
- organizational structure and logical sequencing of ideas
- content, including main ideas, supporting details, and elaboration
- word choice for clarity, interest, and variation

Revision involves words, phrases, sentences, paragraphs, and themes. The tasks of revision include changing, deleting, substituting, adding, and reordering. Beginning writers usually need feedback from a supportive group or reader to help revision along. Even with the helpful questions of an interested reader, Calkins (1986) finds that younger writers "add on" as a form of revision. These revisions seem somewhat disjointed because answers to readers' questions or extra information writers decide to add is usually added to the end to their writing. As writers mature, however, they become more adept at making their own revisions after letting a piece of writing rest for a while. As they mature, they learn to reread to find appropriate places within their writing to revise. Thus, they are able to achieve greater cohesion in revision, seeing connections and developing internal order.

Revision Is Ongoing

Very young children are likely to resist revision, particularly if they see it simply as copying a piece. Writers benefit from prompts about revising—a series of questions for the writer to consider both during and after writing. Dahl and Farnan, 1998

In writing workshop, revision is a constant. We begin our writing knowing that some of what we write will change and grow. As a result, we revise constantly as we write. Even the chapters in this book have been through many revisions before coming to this finished form.

Since formal revision is a part of the writing process that best serves those writers who have grasped the basic concepts of developing a piece of writing, it is probably inadvisable to stress formal revision from kindergarten through second grade. In these grades, we can prompt children to tell us more, to add more, about what they have to say by friendly, gentle, and interested questioning. By third grade, however, most students who have been writing and receiving instruction in a workshop setting are probably cognitively ready to revise their work on a wider scale.

Some revision takes place in the planning stage, some during drafting. Students need to understand that the first draft is just that . . . a useful 'sloppy copy' with insertions, arrows, cross-outs, rewritten lines, and different word choices. Attention at this stage is always on clarity and organization, not on 'correctness.' Hillerich, 1985

Getting Started.   When speaking to groups of teachers, we often use a gimmick to illustrate our philosophy on giving feedback and guiding revision on written pieces. We ask teachers to begin writing about any topic of their choice. We set a timer for 10 minutes, commenting that they will later share their writing with the group.

The body language from the audience is vivid: knitted brows, sideways glances, rolled eyes, chins set in frustration. Some fumble for paper and pencil. Some tap the desk, checking to see if we notice that they have not yet started to write. Some eventually begin to write with breath exhaled, raised brows, and bugged eyes that say, "Well, here goes nothing!"

We fast-forward the timer to ring after only a few minutes, announcing that they will not need to share their work with the group after all. Sighs and comments of relief fill the room. Then we ask the teachers how they felt about the directions to "write about anything you want and be prepared to share." One participant wrote the following comment during this short time of free writing. She was ready to share it with the group had we called on her:

"I have a very hard time writing when a teacher says, 'Write about anything you want.' What kind of prompt is that? I hate that! I can't remember how many times we were told that in school. For the longest time I hated writing because of that!"

If we as teachers give no directions, provide no criteria for the evaluation of a piece of written work, then there can be no valid feedback to guide revision. With no standards, there is no reason or rationale for change or improvement. Revision requires assessment. If there are no standards, no assessment of the work in relation to those standards can be made.

Therefore, the basis of revision lies in the direct instruction of writing skills and in developing specific criteria and techniques with students so they can evaluate their own and other's writing. Criteria such as those we refer to here are presented in chapter 3 on "Writing Assessment." Teaching students to revise is an ongoing process that begins on the first day of the school year. Students learn revision techniques that become a natural part of the composing process.

Set the Stage for Revision

Often, in middle childhood, children become more self-critical, taking their failures seriously. In addition, they are highly sensitive to the opinions of others. School climate, feedback from teachers, grades, and students' ratings have a great effect on self-esteem. Hoge, Smith, and Hanson, 1990

Since revision is an integral part of the composing process, students need to be aware of the vital role revision plays in quality writing, before they begin to write. Following are some specific guidelines we use to help students in the revision of their work.

Teaching Guidelines: Revision

Keep It Comfortable.   Classroom atmosphere makes all the difference. As we have discussed throughout the early chapters of this book, a key to student attitudes and abilities to write involves the classroom atmosphere. Students must feel it is safe to write, to take risks, to put words on paper that may not necessarily be the best—at first. As teachers, we remain:

- calm about students' seeming inadequacies,
- accepting of their writing as a developmental skill,
- positive in our belief that they can learn and improve, and
- supportive of their attempts.

Student interest in writing begins to fall off rapidly in the upper elementary grades . . . this is when the typically detailed criticism of writing generally appears. Hogan, 1985

In a typical classroom with a crowd of children and a long list of "things to do," we may easily become frustrated and impatient with the student who just won't write or won't follow what we consider to be clear directions. We work to keep a calm, accepting tone of voice. A tone of frustration from the teacher causes students to fear and be apprehensive about writing. Regardless of inner feelings and circumstances, it is important that we keep our voices calm and present ourselves as eager to help.

In the early stages of a writing project, I may encourage students to be sloppy, to cross out, or to invent spellings. When students edit and revise, they begin to take charge of their own education. Clark, 1987

Without this safety net of acceptance, students will learn to fear writing. No one judges the final story by what happened in the formative stages. If our standards are too high during the early stages of the work, students become paralyzed in the face of them. But students know that as a piece gets closer to publication, they must improve and correct it. . . . The audience simply reads the end product. We let our students know that we expect them to play around with words, make mistakes, rethink ideas, and make changes accordingly. "Teachers who only give students one shot at writing a story, one chance to get it right, do not understand how writers work" (Clark, 1987, p. 67).

Writing Is Never Finished.   "I'm through!" our students quickly declare. We teach students the concept that writing is never finished. Even after a piece of writing is finished and published, it can still be improved. The best authors would find places in

We want to help children learn how to reread or "resee" their work. Above all, we want them to have a growing sense of the options available to them during composing. Graves and Stuart, 1985

Good writing is, in fact, the result of extensive revision. Pinker, 1994

I'm a rewriter. That's the part I like best. I despise and am terrified by a first draft. But once I have a pile of paper to work with, it's like having the pieces of a puzzle. I just have to put the pieces of the puzzle together to make a picture. Blume, 1991

their favorite published works that they wish they had written differently (Clark, 1987). Because writing involves choices at every step, there are always better choices to make. The key is understanding that writing is a fluid, changing process that is never finished.

We remind our students that writing is like any other task. Practice improves the skill. Star basketball and baseball players, musicians, and singers all practice daily. Good writers know that "the way to successful writing is through steady practice, sympathetic feedback and rewriting" (Daniel, 1996, p. 52). Writing as a fluid, changing process is a new and difficult concept for students to learn. Writing is never finished because there is never a perfect, correct answer. Writing requires constant reevaluation and consideration.

Student Ownership.   What students write belongs to them. We have no right to take possession of their pieces. What we do have a right to do is give them interested reader responses and ask them questions about what we don't understand or what needs further elaboration. Students easily conclude that they are not good writers if they are asked to change their writing. They think that their writing is "wrong" when, in fact, revision is the effort to make it more effective, not necessarily "right." Therefore, we show them that there are always many ways of expressing ideas and that professional writers expect to revise before they begin to write a piece.

One of the best ways to demonstrate this point is with our own writing. Very early in the year, we write simple pieces, perhaps a letter to a friend or to the class if we do not have other examples available. While computers allow for instant revision, our demonstration works best with a transparency so all can see a visual record of the process. As we write and after we have finished, we revise our work. We draw lines from one idea to another, cross out, insert arrows, make additions, delete, and scribble notes in the margins. As we revise, we talk through this process with the students. We demonstrate that adult writers also revise. Revision is not just a "school" thing that only students do because they don't know how to write. Revision is a valuable part of the process that enables writers to produce quality writing. Most authors don't consider a work finished until it has been revised, sometimes many, many times. Even when they have finished, authors know that more changes could always be made.

We invite local authors to speak to our classes about the revision that they do, so we continually reinforce the idea that all writers, young and old, revise.

The End!   Along with the concept that writing is never finished, we help younger students eliminate "The End" from their papers by teaching them that the conclusion of a story will be part of their writing. The words "the end" will not be needed in their writing. This is another difficult concept for young students to learn, since they have been taught through cartoons and some children's books that stories end with the words "the end." When they are intent on using artfully decorated letters to conclude their pieces, we encourage them to use their spatial intelligence to illustrate a scene in the story instead. In chapter 6 we discuss teaching children how to write conclusions. When this mini-lesson is covered early in the year, students quickly learn how to write conclusions, and then "the end" as a finale to the story is superfluous.

Connecting the ordinary traffic light with teaching composition may seem a bit far-fetched at first. Nevertheless, it's an idea that's working for us. Parker, 1995

Green, Yellow, and Red Developmental Stages.   To help students see the clear distinction and the importance of the revision process in their writing, we suggest a "traffic light approach" using an array of colored folders (Parker, 1995). We issue one green, one yellow, and one red folder to each student. In the green folders, students keep their rough drafts, or sloppy copies. They have a "go" light to write their first thoughts. When the first draft is completed, students move their work to a yellow "caution" folder for revision and editing. Students learn this is a major part of their work as writers, not just a hurry-up-and-finish part of the writing process.

When all changes are made and final copies are prepared, the compositions are then moved to the red "stop" folder. These red folders store the copies of work completed by students during the year. When we teach students how to use the folder system through several writing projects, they handle the folders successfully and at the same time recognize the importance of the revision of their work. The use of the yellow folder helps students spend more time on this aspect of their writing as well. A further benefit to us as teachers is our ability to see, at a glance, where in the process each student is working at any particular time. A red folder means a project is completed; a green folder means a student is still in the first draft stage.

Skip It!   We show students how to skip lines as they write their first draft so that there is space for revision while they write and later in the writing process. Revision is necessary and inevitable because there are always choices to make and we don't always make the best choices the first time we try. When students plan for changes and revision before they begin writing, they are more accepting of revision as it happens. They learn that revision is important not because the writing is wrong, but because it is a natural part of writing. There is always more to add, to say, to change, to show.

When students compose on computers, we also recommend that they double space as they write. The extra space simply lets the writer see words and ideas more easily and facilitates finding the location for changes. When a hard copy is printed out, it is easier for writers to fill in information during revision. Later reformatting can polish the piece for publication.

Stop rewriting for a while. It's the most frightening part of the process for many. Try dropping it until expression loosens up. Just concentrate on getting them to write—anything! Frank, 1995

Give Writing a Break.   Writers and writing need time to rest, time to incubate. Rarely do we expect students to finish a piece of writing in one day or one lesson. Through example, we model how writing is typically started at one time, put away, and then revisited and revised at a later time. The intervening time allows the writer to read the work with a fresh mind, almost from the eyes of a stranger who is reading it for the first time. Teachers who expect students to spend an afternoon writing with the goal of a finished product are denying those students the opportunity to make meaningful revisions. Just as adults benefit from a rest in writing, so do students. Students need to learn that writing changes and improves when writers have an opportunity to step away from the work, incubate ideas, and come back to it with a fresh perspective.

Teaching Strategies: Whole Class Revision

All revision takes place in reference to the criteria students have been taught. Without criteria, revision is impossible. With criteria, revision makes sense. In the classroom where students have been taught to revise during their first draft, and where revision is an expected

There is a need for a shared language, a common vocabulary, a means for teachers and students to address writing concepts in conference, class discussion or by means of written marks. Wall and Hull, 1987

Children write briefly, not for lack of knowledge, but for lack of adequate means for tapping the knowledge they do have. . . . When writers learn the requirements or criteria governing written prose, they activate more extensive and appropriate memory searches which, in turn, result in higher quality writing. Hillocks, 1987

Although [adolescents] readily express an evaluation of their [own] writing, they appear to be only vaguely aware of the criterion they use as a basis for judgment. Golub, 1982

part of writing, the actual methods of revision can be successfully taught. The criteria we use depend on the writing purpose, audience, occasion, and intent. Examples of criteria are presented in Chapter 3. In every workshop, students and teachers will develop the criteria that they need for specific pieces of writing. Based on the criteria, students make decisions about what to revise and how to make changes in their writing.

Revision takes place when a student decides to change a piece of writing. In the workshop, that decision can be influenced by feedback from any or all of three sources: the teacher, peers, and the student's self-assessment.

We're In This Together.   How do students learn the techniques of revision? They learn from example and demonstration. The "writing aloud" lessons that we do with the students in Chapter 6 on how to organize and develop a piece of writing are extended with direct instruction on how to revise as well.

As we write a whole class story, there are always opportunities to revise. We take those opportunities to make improvements and weave them into the work as we write. We cross out, insert, and move ideas. Students see immediately that revision is not saved for later, but is an ongoing part of the process and an avenue for immediate change.

When we have finished composing a whole class story with our students on transparencies, we demonstrate how to revise the work. This demonstration is best done the day after the story is composed so that students have the opportunity to think about and simmer their ideas. First, students use their checklists or rubrics to review the criteria established for the writing. What features characterize quality work?

Next, we reread the composition with the students and encourage them to pick out its effective points. Then we look for inconsistencies, loss of meaning, vague passages, ineffective words, organizational problems, and repetition. Using the checklists, we ask students to suggest changes that would make the story more effective. As they generate ideas, we revise on the transparency and discuss the rationale for the changes. As each change is demonstrated, we discuss in detail how and why the change is made. We also feel free to suggest changes if students do not recognize revision opportunities. They learn from their own participation and from our suggestions. As the class revises the paper, we comment frequently about the improvements being made, pointing out that the first draft is dramatically improved with revision.

Checklists can be coordinated with a color code that helps writers "see" what they have created. We demonstrate on the transparency how colors help highlight qualities of the work. For example, sequence words may be highlighted in blue. Similes may be highlighted in yellow. When students find and highlight in color various aspects of the writing, they take satisfaction in their progress. If some of the criteria cannot be located for color highlighting, we demonstrate how to insert those features in the paper.

Later as students write independently, they take responsibility for color highlighting their own papers since the technique was specifically demonstrated in the whole class story. First drafts become a rainbow of colors as students learn to evaluate and revise their work.

Whose Paper Is That? Evaluate Anonymous Writing.   Another way to lead students toward their own revision is to demonstrate revision techniques on anonymous student compositions from other classes, other teachers, or previous years. We never use compositions from students currently in the class since embarrassment may be overwhelming. On a transparency, we use the same methods of revision that we demonstrated for the whole class story. Using the checklist of criteria, we ask students to evaluate and suggest revisions of the student paper.

We use the specific steps listed in Figure 5–1 for evaluating anonymous student work.

To demonstrate revision using one or more anonymous papers with the whole class is a general and comprehensive approach to revision. The following strategies involve more focused revision of specific problems that writers often have.

FIGURE 5–1
Steps for Evaluating Anonymous Writing

1. Choose papers that illustrate the problem we want to focus on, for example, elaboration, word choice, or organization. Focus on only one problem at a time.

2. Do not choose papers that appear hopeless. Often choose papers from better writers so students understand once again that there is always room for improvement.

3. Focus on content and organization by expressing an interest in the writer's ideas. Avoid focus on the conventions of mechanics, such as spelling, capitalization, punctuation, or penmanship by typing the papers or rewriting them in an easily readable format.

4. Discuss what has been done well in the paper. Pick out the most effective part. It might be just a phrase or word. Model to the class how to respond to a paper. For example, "As I was reading, this part made me stop and think. . . . I could picture what happened."

5. Follow the positive response by asking content questions that pertain to the problem on which you are focusing. For instance, if you are working on elaboration, you might say, "I was wondering about this part. What was the specific time when her father helped her make ice cream?" After modeling and discussing the problem, students ask questions.

6. If you are using more than one paper, move to the next paper and repeat the process. As the papers become more effective, help children recognize passages that explain or illustrate. Point out transitions that guide the organization. Note extraneous, unrelated details that detract from focus.

7. Refer to necessary revision or editing in the context of helping the reader understand the author's message or point. Avoid words like *error, wrong, bad,* or *mistake.*

8. Be respectful of each writing effort.

Cudd, Evelyn. 2000. "Group Revision/Editing Lessons." Unpublished paper, College Station, Texas.

Teaching Strategies: Small Group or Individual Revision

Green Martian Monster: Elaboration.　　We use this interactive technique developed by Sager's (1973) research in environmental education for teaching elaboration with success. Writers of all ages love to take this simple story and apply inquiry to it to produce extended tales of the "Green Martian Monster." This technique helps writers develop a story by adding important detail. It provides a novel, hands-on, interpersonal approach that engages students in focused revision. The results provide a dramatic example of the power of adding elaboration during revision. We begin by reading the following story to our students.

> *The green Martian monster descended on the USA. He didn't have a mouth. "Who goes?" they said. There was no answer. So they shot him and he died.*

After reading this story, we establish groups of three or four students and ask students to do the following tasks:

- Quickly list all of the reasons why a mouthless, green Martian monster might land in the USA.
- List all the places the Martian could have landed.
- Who could "they" have been? List all the possibilities.
- List all the thoughts "they" could have been thinking when they saw a Martian.
- What could have happened between the time the Martian was shot and the time he died?
- Look at your lists. To be interesting and easy to understand, a story needs details such as you have written. Add some of these details to the story and take turns reading the story the way you would have written it.

Writers share their revised tales in the authors' circle with great delight. They see that there are many ways to develop the story, all of which are effective and interesting. They also see that even though each of the stories they create is different, each has its own audience appeal. The important factor, however, is to get students to transfer use of this technique to their own papers after they have used it with the "Green Martian Monster."

What Did You Say? Create Dialogue.　　This focused revision technique helps writers elaborate character and plot through the addition of characters' spoken thoughts. This elaboration brings out more specific interaction between and among the characters in their stories.

Using photographs, pictures from newspapers or magazines, or artwork, we display one picture for the entire class and ask them to brainstorm the conversation that may be taking place between the people in the picture. They discuss what is happening in terms of the action or situation depicted by the picture. Then we demonstrate how this dialogue fits into a class story we are writing.

FIGURE 5–2
Create Dialogue

"Oh, Peter, your buccaneer's hat is so neat! I want one just like yours!" exclaimed Mandy. "How did you do that?" she asked.

"It's easy," replied Peter. "You just fold the paper in half and then in half again."

"Is that all?" questioned Mandy.

"Well, the last thing you do is fold the edges back to make the brim," added Peter. "Then you just put it on and wear it."

"Wow! Thanks for helping me, Peter!"

Daily mini-lesson: oh peter your buccaneers hat is so neat i want one just like yours exclaimed mandy how did you do that she asked

After students have learned how to use dialogue to expand the content of a story, they clip interesting and appropriate pictures of people or animals from magazines, newspapers, or calendars for use in their own stories. They write dialogue for the characters in the picture and share their creations with the class. This dialogue adds valuable elaboration to their stories. The artists in our classes sometimes prefer to create their own illustrations for the dialogue they want to add. Figure 5-2 shows an example of a picture that we used.

Cut-Up Caper: Organization and Sequencing.   This organizational, problem-solving technique is best used with small groups of two or three students. It works like this. We retype and print out a newspaper article or a reading passage, double-spacing between each sentence. We cut the sentences apart and arrange and paste the main idea sentences on an organizational sheet, leaving plenty of space under each sentence. We scramble the remaining supporting detail sentences in random order on a separate sheet. Students then cut out the supporting detail sentences and work together to arrange them logically under the appropriate main idea sentences. Not only is this activity an aid to the logical mathematical intelligence in the writing workshop, but it also appeals to spatial and bodily-kinesthetic intelligences as well.

This hands-on technique demonstrates an organizational strategy for relating main ideas and their supporting details. In other words, it helps students develop the concept of grouping ideas into paragraphs. Students learn that main ideas have little meaning without the supporting details. They understand how to write main ideas and elaborate them with supporting details in their own writing. Most of all, we find it is important to help the students transfer this strategy to their own writing.

One Plus One Equals One: Sentence Combining.   An effective technique for improving a written piece is the process of combining two simple sentences into one complex sentence as we discussed in chapter 4. Students can learn to write complex sentences similar to the ones they are reading. The following excerpt from a piece of student writing is

The practice of building complex sentences from simpler ones has been shown to have a powerful effect on the quality of writing. Hillocks, 1987

a good candidate for a sentence combining exercise. In fact, it can be used for a daily language exercise such as the one described in Chapter 4.

> Next I'll tell you why a solar car is more for your
> every day town car. A solar car can't go that far. This
> can be good or bad. I'm going to tell you why it's good.
> Kids won't get hurt as bad if you have a drugged driver
> or a crazy teen. This is why a solar car is better.

Using literature as a model.   By locating complex sentence structures in books appropriate to the grade level and reading them to students, we model the structures for them. We write one of the complex sentences on the board for display. For example, for young children we might use this sentence from *Not This Bear!* by Bernice Myers: "When Mama Bear served the soup, all the bears lapped it up with their tongues." Discussion of the sentence components shows how the complex structure makes the sentence more interesting. Students trade the words in the sentence with new ones to create new meanings. Later, students practice using the structure in their own writing.

Older students create a list of "star" words, so named because they turn ordinary sentences into stars, particularly when placed at the beginning of a sentence. Some star words include *although, because, in order to, unless, until, since, even though, so that, when.*

Teacher Feedback

Without writing instruction and teacher response, students were less likely to write more than one draft. Schebell, 1988

Obviously the teacher plays a major role in providing feedback to students about their writing. Freedman (1987) finds that "several necessary conditions underlie successful response. . . . First, it leaves the ownership of the writing in the hands of the student writer. . . . Second, it communicates high expectations for *all* students. . . . Third, accompanying their high expectations, teachers give students sufficient help during the writing process to allow them to write better than the students themselves thought possible" (p. 160). Researchers Cooper (1986), Atwell (1998), Graves (1991), and others also agree that, along with responding fully, teachers should respond during the process rather than waiting to comment on the finished product. The manner in which we give feedback is also critical to the attitudes of the writers and the success of the final written copies.

Teaching Guidelines: Teacher Response

The purpose of the feedback should be to increase the effectiveness of the writing during the writing process. Sommers, 1982

What we model, our students learn to use. Therefore, it is important in both oral and written feedback that we observe basic guidelines, outlined in Figure 5–3, for responding to students' writing.

Verbal feedback on work in progress is a valuable tool for improving written work. As students write, we provide specific feedback related to the current work. Several considerations guide teacher feedback to students and students' feedback to each other.

Figure 5–3
Teacher Response
for Revision

- Establish a reasonable set of criteria, based on what you have taught.
- Be sure the students know what those criteria are.
- Make every effort to keep marks and comments off of the students' papers.
- Always give some kind of positive feedback.
- Always give specific feedback.
- Identify the most important areas for improvement and comment only on those.
- Make your comments facilitative; in other words, show the student how to fix the writing problem.
- Limit the number of comments or questions so that the writer will be able to succeed in the revision.
- Provide classroom revision activities that match the feedback you have given.
- Teach your students how to be good peer evaluators.

Teachers need to model responding techniques and terminology for writers. When the teacher's questions to students about their writing were vague and general, so were their answers; when questions were more specific, so were their answers. Atwell, 1987

Teachers should respond fully in a way that leads to substantial revision. Cooper, 1986

A Writing Vocabulary for Discussion. First, all comments should relate to the specific criteria developed with the students during previous writing lessons. Because of those lessons and the criteria established, both teacher and students have a common set of expectations and vocabulary for comments and discussion about the writing. For example, when we have taught students to write introductions to adventure stories that include a kind of day, time, site, and action, we look at students' introductions to check for those specific items. If some are missing, we may ask, "What kind of day are you planning to use in your introduction?" Such comments have significant meaning for students and become specific, helpful guidance as they evaluate and revise their work.

Specific feedback aids revision while vague comments have no positive effect. For example, when a teacher says, "You need more elaboration," the student has no way to apply that general comment to his/her writing. However, notice the difference in this teacher feedback: "In paragraph three, you write about your main character; help me get to know more about her. For example, what does she like to do? Where does she live? How old is she? Who are her friends? What are her hobbies?"

Content information was elicited from fourth and sixth graders through specific questioning, indicating that they needed to learn how to conduct memory searches necessary to develop their ideas more fully. Bereiter and Scardamalia, 1982

Probing Questions and Comments. We use the following kinds of questions and comments to help our students search for additional information. Questions that can be answered *yes* or *no* clearly offer little opportunity for elaboration. Hughey (1986) suggests that probing questions help students evaluate and elaborate their current work and show them techniques to apply to future work as well.

- What are some reasons this event is important to you?
- What is the main idea of this section? What else can you tell about this main idea?
- What does the word *origami* mean?

The majority of sixth graders are at the point of transactional writing and interactive revision. . . . They benefit from questioning and other kinds of feedback in revising their work. Calkins, 1986

- Use a personal example to illustrate this idea.
- Compare this idea to something else.
- Add facts to support the main idea in paragraph two: who, what, when, where, why, how.
- Show connections between ideas with transition words.
- Give some background information for the ideas of your paper.
- Explain the importance of this idea. Why does it matter?
- Describe this idea (or person) in more detail. What does it (he) look like? What does it feel like? What is its shape? What is its size? What is its color?
- Add an unusual "twist" to the sentence that tells what your paragraph is about.
- Write a second topic sentence and ask your writing group which one they think fits your paper best.
- Find the ending sentence. Add information that ties it to your topic sentence.
- Use the thesaurus to substitute different words for _____ (thing, friend, etc.).
- Vary the structure of sentences. Use some short sentences and some longer ones.

When giving feedback, we often find it helpful to use "you" when complimenting the students' writing and to refer to "the paper" when making corrections—a little technique that protects fragile self-esteem.

Too rigid a prior specification can interfere with creativity, causing an idea to be rejected too soon because it doesn't conform to expectations. Smith, 1982

Caveats.   It is wise to use caution in providing verbal feedback. With some students, our comments can be interpreted as the most important guide to their writing. Very quickly, students learn to depend on the teacher for ideas rather than to rely on their own resources. A third-grade teacher reported that one of her reluctant writers would not write unless she was sitting right beside the child to give her guidance. As we discussed the situation, it became clear that the child had come to depend on the teacher to give her ideas and was unable to write without her help. The child could write only after the teacher told her what to say. The teacher, trying to be helpful, hadn't realized what a dependent relationship she had inadvertently fostered with this writer.

When students learn that the teacher will provide help at every opportunity, they take the "easy way out." We must be cognizant of our powerful role as a resource and guard against the possibility that our students become dependent on us. Thus, we keep a balanced schedule of individual teacher/student conferences about works in progress. We guard against taking ownership of the writers' efforts and against wasting valuable class time as students wait for their turn with the teacher.

We keep in mind that initial direct instruction on how to write and how to revise are the best guides for feedback to students. We teach the skills and strategies, then encourage students to practice the skills as they progress through the curriculum. Just as in other areas of learning, writing is developmental. As we guide our students in the development of their skills, we offer frequent and specific feedback to assure that the skills are being mastered. Then, when students are ready to choose and develop their own pieces, they should have the opportunity to write independently without undue teacher intervention in their work. When a student is really stuck and asks for help, or when we determine that an area needs strengthening for a specific student, then we reteach or review small segments during the revising phase.

Of course students can, and do, ask for help with writing problems. We work with them in a facilitative mode and, at the same time, kindly and gently encourage those students to write independently. We assure them that we, or their peers, will read their work again when it is further along, and that we look forward to enjoying their creative ideas. We are mindful that most writers, novice and experienced, have taken risks to express themselves and that their egos may be fragile with regard to their work. Calm and supportive feedback, demonstrating a firm belief that we trust them to produce ideas on their own, seems to be most helpful.

Do I Write On Their Papers?   Students shudder when they see the "bloody pen" marks covering their work. Teachers traditionally and typically read papers with an eye to catch each and every error, scribbling margin notes, underlining, noting mistakes so that students wonder if there is anything worth reading left in their papers.

Research and common sense tell us that such an approach to feedback has little positive effect and, in fact, causes negative attitudes about writing. Feelings of frustration and despair are common responses. With a constant emphasis on what is wrong, students have little enthusiasm or incentive to improve their work the next time. Spandel's (1997) research indicates that student interpretation of our comments may be very different from what we expect. For example, advice to "be specific" causes bewilderment in students. Their reactions to this comment are uniformly negative. They wonder what specific means and their reactions resemble these.

> How can I know what to do if you don't tell me?
>
> Please tell me what you mean.
>
> As a general comment, this is useless. If you can point to a sentence or phrase or word, maybe that is something I can fix.

Even the comment "good job" can bring mixed reactions from students. They consider it too vague to be helpful and think the teacher probably makes the comment to everyone. They wonder, "*What* was good about it and *why?*" In a survey conducted by Land and Evans (1987), students agreed about the importance of meaningful feedback. "Eighty-three percent of the students surveyed said that a grade without comments or marks was 'no help.' Seventy percent said the following assessment practices 'usually help' or 'help a lot': explaining how to fix a mistake, being allowed to revise to make my paper better, having an example of how to make my paper better, individual student-teacher conferences about my paper, being told how to add new ideas, and receiving specific suggestions for improvement" (p. 115).

What Does Help Writers?   Students appreciate comments that are focused, facilitative, specific, and tied to content and organization. Such comments not only show the student how and where to revise, but provide evidence that the teacher has read the text carefully. The following comments are examples of specific feedback:

> Your image of the old woman in her garden was so vivid I could almost hear her voice.
>
> Consider including a sentence or two that show how the rain forest discussion is connected to the paragraph on whales.

Margin notes:

We are learning to direct our comments to a few key elements of our students' compositions, rather than providing more diffuse, and often less meaningful, evaluative remarks. Hillocks, 1986

In addition to the quality of comment, reducing the amount of teacher comment on the page . . . helps to avoid the mental dazzle of information overload. Haswell, 1983

Beneficial commentary is . . . feedback before and after revision, and requires immediate revision. Knoblauch and Brannon, 1984

Evaluative commentary from the most to the least important elements in a piece of writing are Central Idea/Focus, Organization/Coherence, Support/Explanation/Detail, Diction/Sentence Structure, and Grammar/Punctuation/Spelling. Rubin, 1983

So, how do we manage to give written feedback to students that will be helpful rather than harmful, and how do we do it efficiently so that we accomplish the task in a reasonable amount of time? There are no simple answers to those questions; however, we offer these techniques.

Focused Feedback. After students have had perhaps a class period or two to begin writing on a project, we read their drafts and comment or question on sticky notes or separate criteria checklists. Our questions and comments indicate whether or not they have caught the main idea of the assignment and are heading in the right direction. Encouragement that they are on the right track gives them incentive to complete the paper. We keep comments simple and encouraging, and our questions are oriented toward further development of content and organization. Most importantly, we direct students to revision activities that match the feedback we have given.

We give students the opportunity to complete the assignment without further comment. The goal is to develop autonomous writers. When we have provided clear and thorough modeling and practice on the writing skills they need, it is time for them to enjoy the luxury of uninterrupted writing.

Numbering Paragraphs. When papers are put into the yellow folder and are ready for evaluation, we ask students to lightly number their paragraphs in pencil along the left margin. This numbering allows easy referral to a specific part of the paper as it is assessed. Comments then are made on the criteria rubric that we developed with the students. On a rubric, we star those features that are strong and effective and check those that are present but perhaps not as strong as they could be. For missing features, we use focused and facilitative commentary. The students then have direction in how to revise for the next round of writing. We also include comments on portions that the writer has improved from drafting to finished version. The use of the rubric keeps our comments separate from the actual paper, and students retain control and ownership of their writing.

Respecting Ownership. Notice that there is no mention of making corrections on the actual paper. There is little need to write on the paper. Keep comments on the rubric rather than on the paper. The student's dignity is at stake. Regardless of the quality, written work is an introspective product of the student's ability to communicate. A paper rife with red pen marks is analogous to a stab to the heart. It is unnecessary and hurtful. One of our colleagues compared feedback to a piece of writing with feedback to an artist's work. "If you were painting a picture," she said, "how would you feel if someone came along and said to you, 'Your sky isn't quite right. Here, let me paint it in for you,' and then proceeded to paint your picture?"

One day Will came to class with a story he had written the previous night. He wanted his teacher to read it and evaluate it for him. This third grader wanted a "professional opinion" on his work. As he headed to his desk, he turned around and came back. He said, "Oh, by the way, please don't write on my paper." His teacher had never written on any of his papers, but he wanted to be sure that he did not write on this one either. He had put his heart and soul into the story, not to mention the fact that he had spent a lot of time hand writing a nice final copy. He did not want her to spoil it by writing on it.

Josh, a fourth grader, had made progress in developing his organization and content skills. The following text is a typed copy of his self-selected topic for a compare/contrast paper. Figure 5–4 is a portion of Josh's original handwritten copy of the same paper. Had the teacher used a red pen to mark the numerous errors in mechanics and spelling on Josh's handwritten paper, he would have been overwhelmed with the mistakes and felt like a failure. Imagine his strong resistance to future writing. Instead, the comments about his paper appeared on a separate rubric, preserving the dignity of his efforts and recognizing the value of what he had accomplished. Suggestions for revision were clearly noted on the rubric, but Josh was also praised for the successful features of the paper and he was encouraged to continue his efforts.

Hi. I'm going to tell you the benefits and handicaps of a solar car. First I'll tell you the benefits.

Pollution is a big problem with gas powered cars, something solar cars don't give off. Pollution is bad because it makes lungs black and dirty and hurts the ozone. The ozone and lungs are both necessary to live. The ozone blanks us from the sun. Our lungs help us breathe. If either one of these were to not work, we would be wiped out.

Next I'll tell you why a solar car is more for your every day town car. A solar car can't go that far. This can be good or bad. I'm going to tell you why it's good. Kids won't get hurt as bad if you have a drugged driver or a crazy teen. This is why a solar car is better.

Now I'm going to tell my last benefit. A solar car is cheaper in most cases because of how it is built. A solar car is built with two main things that make it cost less. The two are a motor that make it go with batteries and solar panels which charge by the sun.

Now I'm going to tell you the handicaps of a solar car. In the wintertime, it's cold because the sun is not up. Well, you normally go visit family, but this year you can't. A solar car runs off batteries. The panels charge the car by using sunlight. In the winter there is hardly any sunlight. So, how would you go on your usual two-hour trip?

The fact is, you wouldn't.

Now I'm going to tell you the second handicap. Solar cars aren't safe for the driver but are safe for people on the street. The reason being is that a solar car is not made of steel but of fiberglass. Fiberglass is a light covering. A solar car needs a light covering because it does not have much torque. Torque is not speed but pulling power. So, if a solar car falls off of a bridge, it is more likely to get hurt than a gas powered car.

Last but not least, a solar car can't go as fast. For most people, this is good. For me, it is not. It can't go as fast because all power comes from heat. A gas powered car runs on a lot of heat which makes it go faster.

I hope you learned some things from my story.

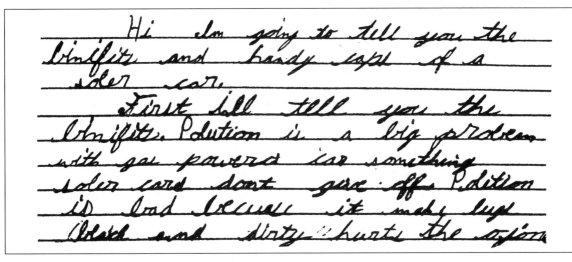

FIGURE 5–4   Portion of Student's Handwritten Paper

Peer Feedback

The ultimate conference is when the student reads the draft, then asks and answers the questions you would ask . . . All you're trying to do is get the student weaned and able to function on his/her own; to read papers with constructive criticism, and make each draft better. Murray, 1994

Perhaps the most powerful feedback to students is from peers. However, some teachers have misused the concept of peer feedback so that it becomes not only unhelpful and even downright hurtful, but it is also a waste of class time. Peer feedback is not simply grouping students together to conference. It is, rather, a collection of techniques in which students have been trained to apply criteria to peers' papers in a supportive, structured, nonthreatening setting. Peer feedback requires that (1) students know and can apply specific criteria to papers, and (2) students know how to make positive, helpful comments.

Teaching Strategies: Peer Response

Author's Circle.   Effective peer feedback is not always based in small conference groups, or in merely trading papers. Peer feedback is also highly effective during the time when writers participate in Author's Circle. Author's Circle is a sharing time in the workshop when writers read their work either to the whole class or to smaller groups. Before student audiences in Author's Circle engage in feedback, we first model how to use positive comments and probing questions that will be respectful and helpful—just as we did in the whole class feedback or the verbal or written teacher feedback. Suggestions for improvement are modeled in a positive manner. Some of the following techniques have proven to be quite effective for us.

Peer critiquing is important, but peers can't critique as well as the teacher does; therefore the teacher is obliged to give students guidance in how to be a good reader. Cooper, 1986

Checking Main Idea.   In Author's Circle, each student in the audience receives a card or small piece of paper. After authors read their work in progress to the class, each student writes a one-sentence comment or question about what he/she thought the paper was about. The comments and questions are given to the author so he or she can determine whether or not the main idea was clear to the audience.

Compliment and Question: Content.   After authors read their written selections to the class, the audience makes three verbal comments to the author. In this adaptation from McGrath (1997), students learn to compliment a specific point in the paper. The second response is a question about the paper. The third comment is a suggestion for improvement. The author listens and thanks the audience for its input. Lengthy discussions are avoided. This activity encourages the audience to listen and supplies the author with valuable feedback that can be applied to the next draft or to future compositions.

Swap Papers: Audience Awareness.   To measure audience understanding, ask students to swap papers. On an attached card or paper, the reader writes comments or questions about the content of the writing.

This Hit Me! Audience Reaction.   In small groups, authors read aloud something they have written. The reader reads the piece again while the listeners jot down words, phrases, sentences, or ideas that have the most meaning for them. Listeners tell why they wrote down the parts they did.

One Part at a Time: Elaboration.   In groups of two, three, or four, writers share a specific part of a written piece. The part may be description of a person or an event, a part for which the writer needs help, the story problem, an elaborated idea, the introduction, the main idea, or the conclusion. Listeners respond with suggestions.

Hang Ten: Vocabulary.   When vocabulary is the focus for revision, students use Hang Ten when they are stumped by word choices. Although this is not a group activity, this technique allows writers to get help from their fellow classmates. One writer, for example, may have used the noun *friend* eight or nine times in the same paper. Using Hang Ten, the writer puts the overused word on the center clip of the Hang Ten hanger (see Figure 5–5) to signal classmates that he needs help thinking of synonyms for *friend.* Classmates write out options and put other word choices on the remaining clips for the writer to consider. The same activity can be used when a writer needs help with descriptive words.

A Deck of Cards: Cohesion.   After students have worked through strengthening the content of their papers, they can often use some help with the fine-tuning of their writing. In this exercise, each student in the Author's Circle receives a card with a writing term printed on it. Words for the cards come from the rubrics we have developed for the particular kind of writing we are working on. Some of the terms include *transitional words or phrases, clear introduction and conclusion, supporting details, sequence words, sentence variety, effective word choices,* and *subject/verb agreement.*

As the writer reads, students listen for the feature listed on the card assigned to them. Members of the audience give the writer quick comments about those features. For example, if a student holds an "introduction" card, then that student comments on the writer's introductory technique. Students can exchange cards after each author's reading

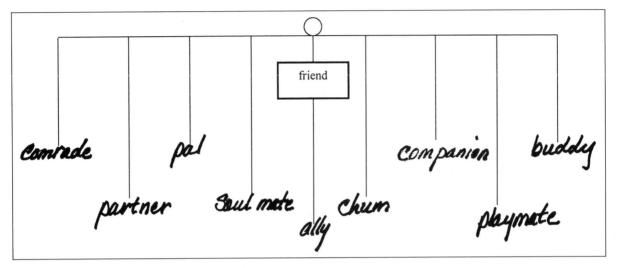

FIGURE 5–5 Hang Ten

so they have different features to listen for in the next piece. Benefits of this activity are that each member of the audience has a specific purpose for listening and that comments and questions provide specific feedback to the writer. Because of the exchange required for these activities, they appeal to those with interpersonal intelligences.

Self-Assessment

Children like to say, "I'm through!" They rarely say, "Sure, I'd like to do this composition all over again!" The key to successful self-assessment and revision lies in the classroom atmosphere that promotes and even celebrates revision. Along with instruction on revision techniques and teacher and peer response, we want students ultimately to take responsibility for the content of their written work and for the revision of that work. When students learn that revision is a natural part of writing and that it is their responsibility to initiate their own revision, they will assume that responsibility far more willingly than if they develop the attitude that it is someone else's job to tell them exactly what to revise.

How Much Revision Is Enough?

Teaching students to revise is an ongoing process in all phases of writing instruction. In the workshop, where the stage has already been set for revision, students see many opportunities to make changes as they write. They understand that words change and ideas develop as the writing progresses. They are not tied to the words written on the paper, feeling that they must be "right" the first time. They accept, and appreciate, that the first words and ideas do not have to be polished. They know that continued work on a piece can eventually produce improvements.

We also remind ourselves that students can be "crushed" with revision if it is carried to an extreme. In fact, we are aware that sometimes a revision does not improve a piece of writing. No piece of writing is perfect, so we don't expect students to revise the same paper again and again—unless they choose to. At some point, students need the satisfaction of bringing a paper to a close, even knowing that it could be better. Even accomplished authors know that their own published work could still be revised.

A teacher, new to the workshop setting, was concerned about the number of revisions her students required. She kept sending papers back to students for more revision because they were not yet good enough, not perfect in all respects. She was reading multiple revisions of many papers, overwhelming herself and her students alike. Embracing the concept that not every single student paper needs to be perfect before being finished was "life changing" for her. No longer did she need to deal with seemingly endless revisions of one writing project, and her students were relieved that they did not have to keep working on the same compositions until they were so tired of them that they no longer cared.

This is a decision that varies with the goals of our writing instruction and with individual students. For example, if the purpose of the writing instruction for a particular day is to practice elaboration techniques, there is little need for revision. This kind of writing is not intended for a final paper. However, if the current writing project involves a finished product that will be carried through to the publishing stage, then revision is an essential part of the process and an admirable goal.

How much revision is enough? The answer can vary from student to student. We are sensitive to the individual needs and personalities of our students. While the writing workshop allows for open-ended revision, there are still time lines and deadlines to meet. That's the way with "real-life" writing. In business, science, the media, and the many other areas in which writing is required, writers must meet deadlines for reports, manuscripts, scripts, and proposals.

Within any specified amount of time, students will achieve different goals in revision, depending on their individual needs and abilities. But all of them need a stopping point. To allow for the needs of each student, we help them improve as much as possible within that time limit. Of course, students may choose to continue working on their own outside this allotted time frame. We let our students know that we expect improvement. We have exposed them to many skills and strategies to help them make that improvement, but there is a time to move on to publication.

Since different revision strategies appeal to different MI's, we vary the revision techniques as often as needed to maintain student interest in the process.

> A reader, however, is not always available. Therefore, feedback must ultimately come from the student's own analysis, with the aid of practice and a comprehensive set of writing principles as guidelines. Students must become their own evaluators. . . . Teachers must . . . transfer that power to the students. Probst, 1990

Teaching Strategies: Individual Revision

Read Aloud.   Perhaps the simplest and yet most effective method of self-evaluation is appropriate for very young, intermediate, and adult writers alike. After a draft is completed, we ask students to find a quiet corner and read their papers aloud to themselves.

When you read
aloud, you can hear
what doesn't work.
Blume, 1991

Reading aloud brings to light many opportunities for improvement that silent reading does not detect. Because of the rhythm and tonal qualities used in reading aloud, this strategy works for writers with musical intelligence. In silent reading, our eyes have a tendency to skim and read ideas that were "meant" to be but are not actually in the paper. Reading aloud highlights those missing elements and is a powerful tool for revision.

Use Criteria: Scales and Checklists. Use the criteria to revise papers. These are the criteria the students have helped develop and are expected to use as their guide to writing. When students have finished writing their drafts, these criteria are the logical basis for their self-evaluation and revision. Sometimes, especially with younger writers, we suggest that students use colors to highlight various parts of their papers, based on the checklist terms. For example, similes are highlighted with green. A main idea sentence is highlighted with yellow. If students fail to locate these features in their papers, they can then revise to include them, if they are appropriate to the subject matter.

Organize with the Pyramid. Using copies of their papers, students cut the individual sentences into strips. They arrange these sentences on the pyramid chart with the following organizational strategy:

Main idea

Main support #1	Main support #2	Main Support #3	etc.
Details	Details	Details	etc.

Conclusion

Students, especially those with spatial or bodily-kinesthetic intelligences, more clearly see whether their main ideas are adequately supported by details, whether transitions connect ideas, and whether introductions and conclusion have been included.

S.O.S. for Fluency. The "Save Our Story" technique adapted from Johnson (1995) is particularly effective with fourth-grade and older students. While it is a linguistic activity, it also appeals to logical and spatial intelligences. Before the students use this strategy independently, we model the revision technique. For example, we ask students to fold a paper into four boxes and label each box with the revision features that we want to emphasize. Students number sentences in their compositions so that teacher and students can refer to specific sentences as the revision proceeds. Some examples of box titles and revision techniques are listed in Figure 5–6.

Words per sentence. Students count the number of words per sentence and record those numbers for each sentence in the box. If all the sentences are similar in length, some variety is needed. If all sentences are quite short, then some can be combined for variety and sophistication in the paper. Long sentences are checked to be sure that they are not run-ons.

Beginning words. Students copy the first four words of each sentence (or as many as will conveniently fit) into the box. These lead words are analyzed for structure and variety. Students quickly recognize repetition and dull beginnings.

FIGURE 5–6
Example of
S.O.S.

NUMBER OF WORDS IN A SENTENCE:		FIRST FOUR WORDS IN A SENTENCE:
#1	13	I'm going to tell
#2	6	First, I'll tell you
#3	15	Pollution is a big
#4	14	Pollution is bad because
ADJECTIVES:		**TRANSITIONAL WORDS:**
Solar		First,
Gas powered		Now
Solar		Last but not least
Black and dirty		

Adapted from Johnson, Jan. 1995. "SOAR" to the stars through revising. *English in Texas,* Fall, 28–29.

Adjectives.   Students check adjectives and analyze them for interest and repetition.

Adverbs.   Students copy adverbs and analyze them for interest and repetition.

Transitional words.   Often a signal of smooth transitions, sequence words can be inserted where appropriate. Repetitive words such as *then* can be replaced for variety.

Verbs.   Students copy verbs and analyze them for variety and interest. Students substitute new verbs for words such as *went, was, said, saw, did, have.*

Similes.   Similes that are unique add to the writer's visual scene.

Paragraphs.   Students count the number of paragraphs. Too few suggest that students forgot to indent or that ideas need to be separated into paragraphs. Too many paragraphs suggest that ideas are not fully developed or that some sentences can be grouped together. (Johnson, 1995)

In a classroom that functions as a community of writers, readers, and editors, they can shape these pieces of their heart into fiction, poetry, and essays that travel far beyond the classroom walls and into the world of published writing.
Rubenstein, 1995

Use a Thesaurus.   As soon as students have some dictionary skills, they can be taught to use an appropriate level student thesaurus to improve their choice of words. The ideal would be to have one thesaurus per student. We demonstrate how to use a thesaurus and allow for ample practice. This practice appeals to both linguistic and intrapersonal intelligences.

When time limits demand that we stop revision or when we deem a piece of writing ready for consumption by others, we move on to publication—the final stage of the process.

Publish Student Writing

"They called me a writer!!!!" Katie wrote to her teacher via e-mail after she won Honorable Mention in a large newspaper's youth writing contest. The recognition of her talents

She said she knew I was going to be a writer when I was a kid because most kids start every sentence with "I," and she said that I always started my sentences differently and wrote in a very distinctive, creative way. She always held the vision for me about what I was going to do, even before I knew what I was going to do. Marston, 1995

as a writer not only boosted her ego and self-confidence, but it may well be the spark of encouragement that will guide her to a profession in writing. Jane Bluestein's (1995) *Mentors, Masters and Mrs. MacGregor,* a collection of memories about influential teachers, touches the heart as we realize the powerful impact we have on the lives of children. Our comments of encouragement and willingness to support the early creative efforts of our young writers have lifelong effects. Publishing student work is a particularly effective way to let children know their work is valued, a way that promises long-term impact on their lives.

Publishing children's writing has several levels of meaning. In general, publishing refers to presenting a story, an article, or a poem so that it can be shared with a larger audience. The format can range from neatly handwritten stories that are read to or by classmates to computer-generated manuscripts that are sent to book companies for publication on the mass market. Between the two ends of this spectrum, teachers find many ways to celebrate writing by helping students publish their work. The underlying goal is to reinforce the idea that writing reaches other people, and as it does, it influences and changes them. There are many ways to make that connection with an audience.

The basic concept of publication is that children learn to write for an audience. In writing workshop, they have the opportunity to share their work with that audience. Work that is written for an audience but that never reaches that audience can be discouraging to children. Some lose interest in writing if no one but the teacher sees their work. At a minimum, children need frequent opportunities to read their stories to their classroom peers. We find that the form of the finished product, or how it is published, is not as important as sharing written work with peers or other audiences. However, we also find that when writers know that their work will be published or shared in some form, they take greater pride in the finished product and spend more time to fine-tune it for that audience. Reaching an audience is the key to recognition for writing efforts.

In this section, we offer suggestions for publishing student writing for audiences ranging from peers and parents to the school campus environment. Then we discuss publication for larger audiences within the community, the state, and the country.

Workshop Publishing

In our writing workshops, we have found the following ideas for publishing writers' work to be most successful.

No effective writing instruction can take place without the publication of student work. Clark, 1987

Dictated Stories. The very youngest writers dictate stories that are recorded by adults. Preservice teachers assigned to one of the kindergarten classes at a local elementary school work with their eager writers to create "big books." Children draw series of pictures about stories that they want to write. After the pictures are completed, the children relate their stories to their preservice teachers, who in turn record the children's own words under the pictures. The preservice teachers then bind the books, title them with the children's titles, and add authors' names. Each author is then recognized by reading or having his or her book read to the class and then placed in the class library.

These stories are read and reread as they become selections in the workshop library. First graders see the importance of making their work neat and presentable to an audience through careful erasures and placements of illustrations.

The Published Copy.   By second grade, we encourage children to rewrite their compositions in their best handwriting on specially lined paper rather than notebook paper. Final copies on notebook paper never seem to look presentable and "finished." For publishing, we keep stacks of lined paper, created on the computer with one-inch margins on all edges. The line spacing is adjusted as appropriate for various grade levels. Easily reproduced in the teacher's workroom, the paper helps students create a polished final copy, one that can be bound later on.

For those younger students who are adept at keyboarding, computers dramatically enhance student efforts to publish pieces of writing. When they move from sloppy copy to final copy, they type their piece of writing into the computer for a professionally printed copy. When computers are readily accessible, some older students do much of their writing on the computer, from prewriting to finished product.

Publication Formats.   Several teacher activity books on the market include easy directions for student-created books. *Read! Write! Publish!* by Fairfax and Garcia (1992) has instructions and simple diagrams for making 20 different books for students to use for publishing their work. Shape books are especially popular with very young writers. Teacher supply stores sell activity books that include shapes such as robots, cars, or various animals that can be traced or reproduced and cut out. Student-created pop-up books are guaranteed to stimulate interest and excitement in publishing. *Pop-O-Mania* by Valenta (1997) and *How to Make Holiday Pop-Ups* (1996) and *How to Make Super Pop-Ups* (1992) by Irvine are jammed with clever ideas.

In the Writing Buddy classes that our preservice teachers conduct with children in the local schools, the preservice teachers and the children make books by cutting out shapes that relate to the main theme of the children's stories, using colored construction paper for the cover. Children love to add illustrations to the cover and to extra pages in their books.

Character dolls.   A popular book format with third, fourth, and fifth graders, especially for storytelling, is the character doll. In their character doll books (see Figure 5–7), authors use a different page for each character, drawing an image of the character' face on the head of the doll and writing about that character on the body of the doll.

Other techniques for putting writing into a published form include the following ideas.

Step books.   Booklets made from plain or horizontally-lined paper folded in half and stapled with card-stock or wallpaper covers are ideal for mini-journals, alphabet books, or other student creations. Step books are clever, attractive to students, and easy to assemble. To assemble, evenly align the side edges of three sheets of plain paper with top edges $1\frac{1}{2}$ inches down on each page (See Figure 5-8A).

FIGURE 5–7
Character Doll

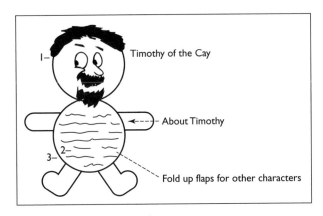

Timothy of the Cay

About Timothy

Fold up flaps for other characters

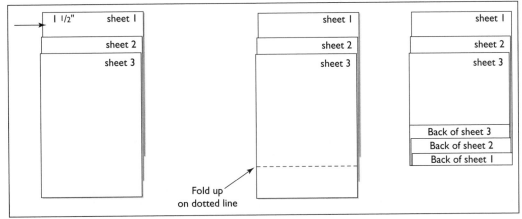

FIGURE 5–8A   Starting the Step Book

Fold up the bottom edges so that six pages result, each page offset $1\frac{1}{2}$ inches from the others.

Now rotate the book so that the fold is at the top or on the side and secure the book with staples at the fold as shown in Figure 5-8B. The exposed edges make space for titles, main ideas, or important concepts from a story or from a cause/effect activity. The space under each page can be used for further text or illustrations.

FIGURE 5–8B
Finishing the Step
Book

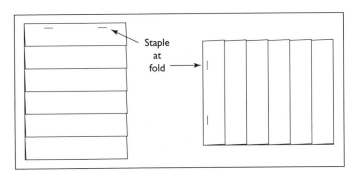

Staple
at
fold

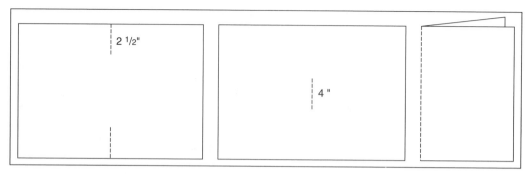

FIGURE 5–9   Slit Book

Slit books.   The folded slit book is particularly attractive to young writers because the pages lie flat, and it has a magical way of staying together without staples or other fasteners:

1. Fold two sheets of $8\frac{1}{2}$ -by-11-inch plain paper in half.
2. On one sheet, cut $2\frac{1}{2}$ -inch slits at the top and bottom of the fold.
3. On the other sheet, cut a 4-inch slit in the center of the fold.
4. Slide the first sheet into the center slit of the second sheet (rolling the paper a bit helps accomplish this step) until the slits on both sheets match.
5. To help students write neatly on this unlined paper, slide a sheet of lined paper underneath each page to provide a faint guide for writing.
6. These books can be attached inside a wallpaper or other decorative cover.
7. For longer books, more sheets can be slit and assembled as one unit in the same manner. However, all sheets must be assembled before writing, as the page arrangement makes it difficult to add pages later. See Figure 5–9.

Graffiti publications.   Frank (1995) has simpler publishing ideas that can be carried out in the classroom. For example, she suggests writing on tee-shirts with permanent pens, writing on a classroom "doodlecloth," decorating a box or a jar with a story or poem, framing a composition in an inexpensive frame, creating a story poster for display, or designing a story mural.

The How-To of Publishing.   Melton's (1985) book *Written and Illustrated by* . . . makes a valuable contribution to every writing classroom, beginning with grade four or so. Using a clearly described, workshop-tested procedure, Melton shows teachers how to turn every student into a self-published author. Melton explains how to help students organize a publishing company, lay out pages, plan and write a story, illustrate the story, edit and type the story, assemble and bind the book, design covers, and host an author/illustrator party. Cleverly encouraging use of the multiple intelligences and learning styles, Melton's directions help each student create a book that is worthy of the designation "published." Younger students benefit from the same procedures but require extensive adult assistance.

Packaging the Finished Product.   Several suggestions for creating and binding student books are presented here. In addition to the format that the finished work takes, we have found that a plastic spiral binding machine is perhaps the easiest and most popular way to bind and publish students' work. It is well worth the investment for a school campus. Children take immense pride in having their stories bound in a manner that presents a professional image.

The Lintor Children's Publishing Center in Phoenix, Arizona, sells classroom and/or schoolwide packages of preassembled book covers and accompanying software templates for publishing student compositions. They can be reached at *childpub@aol.com* or 602-264-7994.

Getting Outside Help with Workshop Publishing

> Once parent volunteers feel comfortable and confident with their role in the [publishing] process, many say it is the most gratifying work they have ever done in their child's school.
> Routman, 1994

Parent Volunteers.   Because publishing classroom compositions is time consuming, Routman (1994) suggests enlisting the help of parent volunteers to operate a schoolwide publication center. In her school, all students have six to eight books published in the center each year. Parents type student stories, if appropriate, and assemble them in wallpaper covers or other bindings. At Valley View Elementary School in McKinney, Texas, all students publish a book each year with the help of parent volunteers who use commercial, preassembled covers and accompanying computer software templates (see source at end of chapter). These student books have a place of honor in the library, and the librarian reports they are among the most popular books checked out by students.

Preservice Teachers.   In the Jones Elementary Writing Buddy program, in Bryan, Texas, preservice teachers devote one day at the end of each semester to helping students publish their anthologies. The preservice teachers act as editors and publishers for their Writing Buddies. Using wallpaper books donated from a local store, cardboard, glue, and the binding machine, they put students' work into finished form. These published books also included introductory pages with a brief author's biographical sketch and photograph, author's name, date of publication, publishing company (Jones Elementary Press), and a pocket for a library checkout card.

Submitting Work to an Audience

Author's Circle.   After writing has been published, sharing compositions can be as simple as using the Author's Circle, where writers sit in the author's chair and read their work to classmates assembled on the floor. A student-sized podium adds an air of importance to the occasion. At Rock Prairie Elementary in College Station, Texas, a simple, adjustable-height music stand serves as a popular podium in the classroom. We also find outside audiences in adjacent classrooms and in other grade levels. Younger children are in awe of older children who come to read their stories and look forward to being able to do the same thing in coming years.

Public Displays.   We send children's writing to doctor offices or other office waiting rooms, banks, store and restaurant windows, and local public offices. Our local banks, post office, and McDonalds are among those establishments that are always willing to display children's writing.

An Authors' Reception.   An end-of-year authors' party for family and friends is an ideal way to celebrate writing and show off student work to a wider audience. Students create invitations and help provide simple refreshments. We find that scheduling two parties allows parents to attend. One party is held during the school day and includes all authors whose parents responded to that party, along with any others who may have parents unable to attend. The second party is held after school or early evening for the convenience of working parents. Students read their compositions at one of the two parties. We ask parents to send reservations for one of the parties, and then we design programs that list students in the party their parents can attend.

Our preservice teachers participating with local elementary schools have firsthand experience with throwing author's receptions for their Writing Buddies. At the end of each semester, in the classrooms where they have participated, the preservice teachers plan an occasion that involves all students in that class and features the writing they have produced. Preservice teachers publish a book for each of their Writing Buddies and put them on display in the classroom. They then plan a reading/writing scavenger hunt by preparing a list of questions that includes information from each of the writers' books. As the reception begins, students get a list of the questions and move around the classroom reading other students' books to find the answers. There are prizes for those who find and answer the most questions correctly, but there are also prizes for all of the students, such as colorful pens or bookmarks. Next, time is carved out for any of the authors who want to read something from their books to the rest of the class. Many children eagerly wave their hands in the air waiting for a chance to share. The reception is an excellent culminating experience for both students and the preservice teachers who have worked with them all semester.

Identifying Wider Audiences

Marion Dane Bauer says, "Most writers, even most adult writers, will not be published . . . ever." (1992, p. 119). Her discouraging attitude about the chances of getting student work published in magazines or books on the mass market is intended to be realistic, and yet it should not overshadow our role as teachers in encouraging children to seek publication in books, magazines, newspapers, and contests. On the other hand, Henderson (1996) maintains that "writers who are determined to publish usually succeed." Teacher Suzanne Rubenstein (1995) tells about a chance meeting with a former student 12 years after graduation. Because Rubenstein had sparked an idea and made her believe in herself, the young woman was writing children's books and hoped to send them to publishers. We never know which of our students will grow up to be published authors. They may not blossom until long after they leave our classes, but we can light the flame that lets them know the possibility is there. The following ideas help writers publishing to wider audiences.

School Literary Magazine.   This type of publication inspires many students to publish for wider audiences. Every year at our elementary school, the campus literary magazine accepts two stories and poems from each classroom along with outstanding artwork for publication. Teachers submit selections on computer disks, and parents carry out the details of publication through the school district's printing office. The magazines are sold for a price that covers the costs of printing, and each classroom has a permanent copy for

---

We need to show students how to recognize potential audiences for given pieces of writing, and we need to look for, create, and demonstrate opportunities for writers to be read and heard. Atwell, 1998

Stephen King, now one of the world's most famous and successful writers, has been writing since he was a child. At one time, he and a friend even published their own "magazine," which they wrote, photocopied, stapled together and then sold to kids at school, charging as much as a quarter. Henderson, 1996

The best thing, I think, about writing is getting published. I love seeing something I've written in a magazine. McDougal, student author, 1996

later classes to enjoy. Charging a minimal amount for the magazine seems to add significance to the publication as opposed to giving copies away.

Reflections. We ask all students to write a one-page paper of reflection about their school. These papers are bound into volumes for placement in the school office and the library. In addition, we take selected papers to a local copy store where they are enlarged to poster size and then displayed in the hallways. We frequently find our students stopping in the hall to read what other students have written.

Student Newspapers. Student-written newspapers provide another popular avenue for publishing. Classroom or schoolwide newspapers offer an easy option for students to see their names as bylines to articles in each issue. Computers make this task quite simple, and older students can take complete responsibility for publication and distribution. See chapter 12 on reports for more information on publishing a newspaper.

Getting published takes dedication, persistence, patience, lots of hard work, good writing, plus a willingness to learn who is publishing what. Henderson, 1996

Children's Magazines. A large number of commercial magazines, written for and by children, also provide avenues for publication. School libraries often subscribe to children's magazines such as *Highlights for Children, Boodle, Writer's Slate, Blue Jean, Merlyn's Pen, Read, Cruz, Stone Soup, Kids' Byline, Creative Kids, Writing, Voices from the Middle, American Girl,* and *Boys' Life,* all of which accept student work. In fact, many publications cater to student submissions only.

Henderson (1996) *The Market Guide for Young Writers* contains a wealth of information for students on how to publish their work. Most of her market lists are for student work only, and her emphasis on a professional approach to publication increases students' chances of success. She emphasizes that the two main ingredients for becoming a published author are the same for adults as for students: (1) find out who publishes the kind of writing the student likes to write, and (2) find out how to submit the material. Her book gives the necessary information for both of those ingredients.

With our students, we read *How a Book Is Made* by Aliki (1986) as a realistic introduction to how an author's ideas are transformed in the publishing process into mass-produced books.

That was the first time I had ever won anything. She had taken that essay that she made me rewrite five times and entered it in a city-wide contest, and I won third prize. Futrell, 1995

Writing Contests. We encourage our students to enter writing contests sponsored by local newspapers or service groups, along with state and national writing contests. Henderson's book lists many writing contests including the "National Written and Illustrated by. . ." contest. As with other publications, following the contest rules is important to having work accepted.

Letters to the Editor. Letters from students to the editors of newspapers have a good chance of publication if they are concisely written on timely topics. A good example is the letter to the editor that was published by the writer's local newspaper. That letter appears in Chapter 11, "Argument and Persuasion." Some newspapers periodically include a student page.

Enter your work because you never know who will print it. Henderson, 1996

Teachers' Writing Committee. Because many teachers are unfamiliar with the how-to of publishing on the mass market, we recommend that a committee of teachers from each campus be organized to promote student writing. On our campus, a writing committee is the clearinghouse for helping students publish their work. The principal routes all information related to contests and other publishing opportunities to this committee. Teachers submit outstanding student compositions to the writing committee. The committee then determines which publications best match the student's writing, gets permissions from parents, and then submits the papers according to the specific guidelines for the publications. We have surprising success using this method, with several acceptances on state and national levels each year.

The Internet.   Limitless opportunities for student publication are available online, whether on a family or school-sponsored web site or on a national level. Our school district web site is full of student writing from all ages. Larson and Boon (1999) offer a list of Internet sites for publishing children's writing along with reviews of each one. As we visited these sites, we found them to be exciting and appropriate for children, and many offered further links to numerous other sites that accept student writing. Such opportunities promise to expand dramatically in the future. As with any use of the Internet, we urge caution in giving children's full information to strangers.

EMPHASIZING THE MULTIPLE INTELLIGENCES

Linguistic: Read and reread writing, silently and aloud, before making changes.

Logical/mathematical: Use the cut-up caper activity to arrange ideas in a logical order.

Spatial: Arrange sentences on the pyramid board for organization of ideas. Create illustrations for publication of a piece of writing.

Musical: Use appropriate background music while you are revising.

Bodily-kinesthetic: Act out a dialogue activity to elaborate on a story narrative. Publish a piece of writing in the character doll or step book format.

Interpersonal: Use an inquiry activity, such as the Green Martian exercise, to develop additional content. Read a finished story in Author's Circle.

Intrapersonal: Use a set of criteria to check writing for inclusion of important elements. Prepare a piece of writing for submission to a children's magazine.

Naturalist: Find a quiet place out-of-doors to review a first draft of writing.

SUMMARY

Revision and editing serve different purposes in the writing process. Editing involves putting the final surface touches on a piece of writing. Editing is proofreading for spelling, punctuation, formatting, and the like. Revision, on the other hand, goes on throughout the writing process. Revision includes revisiting the ideas, the message, the content, the organization, and the word choices of a piece of writing. It includes changing, adding to, and deleting until the message is as clear as the writer can make it.

In a positive classroom atmosphere, students not only learn to accept revision as a natural part of writing, but they also see it as the key to successful writing. They learn that feedback from their teachers and peers is helpful to the process and that "writing is never finished." Writers also learn that no matter how much feedback they receive, the writing is theirs, and theirs alone. They claim and retain ownership of their work. Teachers work with writers to show them how to revise. Revision techniques are taught to the whole class and are practiced in small groups and individually.

Teachers guide writers in evaluation, feedback, and revision by demonstrating how to revise stories or papers created by the whole class or with the teacher's own work. Teacher and students also use appropriate sets of criteria to practice giving feedback and revising with anonymous papers at various levels of development.

Further, writers practice revision strategies in small group sessions or individually. Using a variety of techniques to address the various writing problems that call for revision, students work with nonthreatening activities such as the Green Martian and the cut-up caper. They then transfer the concepts to their own pieces of writing.

When writers have been well prepared to work in small groups, they develop audience awareness as they react knowledgeably, positively, and helpfully to each other's work. With the criteria they have developed for their writing, they respond to each other and as they do, they internalize these criteria for self-assessment.

Publishing is the culminating activity of the writing process. It has several levels of meaning from classroom sharing of completed products to submission of work to local, state, or national writing contests and children's magazines. Writers present their work in its best light. Teachers and parents promote and encourage publication by serving as editors and publishers for young writers. Think of Katie's excitement when she wrote her teacher to tell her "They called me a writer!!!!" Writers are thrilled and excited when they realize, that they, too, are published authors. It is at this stage that many begin to realize their potential for the first time.

Theory into Practice

1. Using a piece of your own writing, ask for peer feedback from three of your classmates, and revise your work. After you have revised, edit the piece for publication, and present it to your classmates.

2. Use an anonymous piece of writing to lead your class or a small group through an evaluation and revision process.

3. In small groups, practice using the guidelines for feedback in this chapter. As an interested reader, ask questions and make comments about several pieces of children's writing or your own. Discuss your questions and comments with each other to determine how to strengthen your feedback strategies.

4. Write a lesson plan for teaching students how to be effective peer evaluators.

5. Practice using a set of criteria, either in the form of a checklist or scale, to respond to student writing.

(continued)

6. In small groups, do the Green Martian activity and share your results with the class.

7. Individually, apply the S.O.S. exercise to your own writing for sentence beginnings, main idea, sentence length, and transitions.

8. Plan three different ways to help children publish books. Use approaches that appeal to different multiple intelligences and learning styles.

9. Plan the details of an author's party using classmates as the writers. Design an invitation and a program and plan activities.

10. Write guidelines and plan a literary magazine for your classmates. As a class, publish the magazine. Or if you have a classroom of children, do this with your young writers.

11. Investigate the submission deadline for two magazines that publish children's work. Write to the magazines for copies of their writers' guidelines. Determine the kinds of writing most likely to be accepted by each magazine.

12. Prepare a manuscript for submission to a particular magazine.

13. Collect information about local and state writing contests. Check with the state office of education, the state affiliates of the National Council of Teachers of English (NCTE), and the International Reading Association (IRA). Make a file of submission guidelines and share the information with your class.

14. Visit Internet sites that publish student work. Expand the list by visiting links at each site. Share with the class. Determine the kinds of writing accepted by each site.

15. Assemble a book—a step book, a slit book, or a character doll—as described.

CHILDREN'S LITERATURE

Aliki. 1986. *How a book is made.* New York: Harper Trophy.

Irvine, Joan. 1992. *Make super pop-ups.* New York: Beech Tree Books.

—. 1996. *How to make holiday pop-ups.* New York: Beech Tree Books.

Myers, Bernice. 1967. *Not this bear.* New York: Scholastic.

Valenta, Barbara. 1997. *Pop-O-Mania: How to create your own pop-ups.* New York: Dial Books for Young Readers.

BIBLIOGRAPHY

Anthony, Christy. 1996. Essay. In Kathy Henderson, *The market guide for young writers.* Cincinnati, OH: Writer's Digest Books, pp. 161–164.

Applebee, Arthur N., Judith A. Langer, Ina V. S. Mullis, Andrew S. Latham, and Claudia A. Gentile. 1994. *NAEP 1992 writing report card.* Washington, DC: Office of Educational Research and Improvement.

Atwell, Nancie. 1998. *In the middle*, 2nd ed. Portsmouth, NH: Heinemann.

Bauer, Marion Dane. 1992. *What's your story? A young person's guide to writing fiction.* New York: Clarion Books.

Bereiter, C., and M. Scardamalia. 1982. From conversation to composition: The role of instruction in a developmental process. In R. Glaser (Ed.), *Advances in instructional psychology 2.* Hillsdale, NJ: Lawrence Erlbaum Associates, pp. 1–64.

Bluestein, Jane. 1995. *Mentors, masters and Mrs. MacGregor: Stories of teachers making a difference.* Deerfield Beach, FL: Health Communications.

Blume, Judy. 1991. In *Meet the authors and illustrators,* Vol. 1., Deboral Kovacs and James Preller (Eds.). New York: Scholastic, pp. 82–83.

Buckley, M. H., and O. Boyle. 1983. Mapping and composing. In *Theory and practice in the teaching of composition: Processing, distancing, and modeling,* M. Myers and J. Gray (Eds.). Urbana, IL: National Council of Teachers of English.

Calkins, Lucy. 1986. *The art of teaching writing.* Portsmouth, NH: Heinemann.

Clark, Roy Peter. 1987. *Free to write.* Portsmouth, NH: Heinemann.

Cooper, Charles R. 1986. Studying writing: Linguistic approaches. *Written Communication, 1,* 108–123.

Cramer, Ronald. 1998. *The spelling connection: Integrating reading, writing & spelling instruction.* New York: Guilford Publications.

Cudd, Evelyn. 2000. Group revision/editing lessons. Unpublished paper, College Station, TX.

Dahl, Karin, and Nancy L. Farnin. 1998. *Children's writing: Perspectives from research.* Newark, DE: International Reading Association.

Daniel, Neil. 1996. Writing, editing, and teaching. *English in Texas, 27* (Winter), 50–52.

Fairfax, Barbara, and Adela Garcia. 1992. *Read! Write! Publish!* Cypress, CA: Creative Teaching Press.

Frank, Marjorie. 1995. *If you're trying to teach kids how to write, you've gotta have this book!* Nashville, TN: Incentive Publications.

Freedman, Sarah Warshauer. 1987. *Peer response groups in two ninth-grade classrooms.* Technical Report No. 12. Berkeley, CA: Center for the Study of Writing, School of Education.

Futrell, Mary. 1995. Essay 76. In *Mentors, masters and Mrs. McGregor: Stories of teachers making a difference,* Jane Bluestein (Ed.). Deerfield, FL: Health Communications, pp. 199–122.

Golub, Jeff N. 1982. *Characteristics of students' classroom talk surrounding the assignment, production and evaluation of a writing task.* (Technical Research Report–Document 229 757) Washington, DC: ERIC.

Graves, Donald H. 1991. *Build a literate classroom.* Portsmouth, NH: Heinemann.

Graves, Donald H. 1994. *A fresh look at writing.* Portsmouth, NH: Heinemann.

Graves, Donald H., and Virginia Stuart. 1985. *Write from the start.* New York: E. P. Dutton.

Haswell, R. H. 1983. Minimal marking. *College English, 45,* 600–604.

Henderson, Kathy. 1996. *The market guide for young writers.* Cincinnati, OH: Writer's Digest Books.

Hillerich, Robert L. 1985. *Teaching children to write, K–8.* Englewood Cliffs, NJ: Prentice Hall.

Hillocks, George, Jr. 1987. Synthesis of research on written composition. *Educational Leadership, 44* (May), 71–82.

Hillocks, George, Jr. 1986. *Research on written composition.* Urbana, IL: National Council of Teachers of English.

Hogan, Michael P. 1985. Writing as punishment. *English Journal, 74* (September), 40–42.

Hoge, D. R., E. K. Smith, and S. L. Hanson. 1990. School experiences predicting changes in self-esteem of sixth and seventh grader students. *Journal of Educational Psychology, 82,* 117–127.

Hughey, Jane B. and V. Gaye Hartfiel. 1989. *The profile guide.* College Station, TX: Writing Evaluation Systems, Inc.

Hughey, Jane B. 1994. *The effects of facilitative teacher response and revision strategies on adolescent writing achievement.* Ann Arbor, MI: UMI Dissertation Service.

Johnson, Jan. 1995. "SOAR" to the stars through revising. *English in Texas,* Fall, 28–29.

Knoblauch, C. H., and Lil Brannon. 1984. *Rhetorical traditions and the teaching of writing.* Upper Montclaire, NJ: Boynton/Cook Publishers.

Knudson, Ruth E. 1989. Effects of instructional strategies on children's informational writing. *Journal of Educational Research, 83* (November/December), 91–96.

Land, R. E., Jr. and S. Evans. 1987. What our students taught us about paper marking. *English Journal 76.* 113–116.

Larson, Jeanette and Belinda Boon. 1999. *Reading and writing on the 'Net.* Austin, TX: Texas State Library and Archives Commission.

Marston, Stephanie. 1995. Essay 125. In *Mentors, masters and Mrs. MacGregor: Stories of teachers making a difference,* Jane Bluestein (Ed.). Deerfield Beach, FL: Health Communications, pp. 211–212.

McAuliffe, Christine. 1994. Revisiting revision. *Writing Teacher, 8* (November), 10–13.

McDougal, Mollie. 1996. Essay. In *The market guide for young writers,* Kathy Henderson (Ed.). Cincinnati, OH: Writer's Digest Books, pp. 143–144.

McGrath, Carol. 1997. A big difference: How feedback improves student writing. *Writing Teacher 10* (January) 14–16.

Melton, David. 1985. *Written and illustrated by . . .* Kansas City, MO: Landmark Editions.

Murray, Donald. 1994. Focusing on quality. *Writing Teacher, 8* (November), 6.

Nystrand, Martin, and Deborah Brandt. 1989. Response to writing as a context for learning to write. In *Writing and response,* Chris M. Anson (Ed.). Urbana, IL: National Council of Teachers of English, pp. 209–230.

O'Neill, Mary G. 1990. *The effects of focus correction on the writing of urban seventh-grade students using the cumulative writing folder program across the curriculum.* Ann Arbor, MI: UMI Dissertation Services (#9110202).

Parker, Cheri D. 1995. Stop-and-go writing. *Teaching Pre K–8, 27* (September), 68.

Pinker, Steven. 1994. *The language instinct.* New York: HarperPerennial.

Probst, Robert E. 1994. Reader-response theory and the English curriculum. *English Journal, 83* (March), 37–44.

Routman, Regie. 1994. *Invitations: Changing as teachers and learners K–12.* Portsmouth, NH: Heinemann.

Rubenstein, Suzanne. 1995. Going public. *Teacher Magazine,* (February), 45–46.

Rubin, D. 1983. Evaluating freshman writers, what do students really learn? *College English, 45,* 373–379.

Sager, Carol. 1973. *Improving the quality of written composition through pupil use of rating scale.* DAI34. Boston University School of Education.

Schebell, Rayma Ann. 1988. *Influences of writing instruction and teacher response on the revising practices of seventh-grade writers.* Ann Arbor, MI: UMI Dissertation Services (#8812381).

Smith, Frank. 1982. *Writing and the writer.* New York: Holt, Rinehart and Winston.

Soltis, J. M., and H. J. Walberg. 1989. Thirteen-year-olds writing achievements: A secondary analysis of the fourth national assessment of writing. *The Journal of Educational Research, 83* (September/October), 22–29.

Sommers, Nancy. 1982. Responding to student writing. *College Composition and Communication, 33,* 148–156.

Spandel, Vicki. 1997. *Dear parent: A handbook for parents of 6-trait writing students.* Portland, OR: Northwest Regional Educational Lab.

Wall, S. V., and G. A. Hull. 1987. The semantics of error: What do teachers know? In *Writing and response,* Chris M. Anson (Ed.). Urbana, IL: National Council of Teachers of English, pp. 261–292.

Welchel, Sandy. 1996. Essay. In *The market guide for young writers,* Kathy Henderson (Ed.). Cincinnati, OH: Writer's Digest Books, pp. 186–188.

Willis, Meredith Sue. 1993. *Deep revision.* New York: Teachers & Writers Collaborative.

chapter

6

Ideas into Words

Brainstorm your arguments, quickly listing all the reasons you can think of to support your point of view. . . . Organize your brainstormed list by numbering arguments in the order you want to present them.

Atwell, 1998

Chapter Outline

At Atkinson Elementary School, the teachers there had learned to tap children's natural desire to write—and that makes everything else in the teaching of writing seem possible. Calkins, 1986

"What can I write about today?" muses one of our workshop writers. Getting started with writing is easy for most young children and continues to be for students who grow up with writing as a natural activity. Young children eagerly tell about what they have seen or experienced. They engage in the concrete exploration of ideas; they talk, draw pictures, read, retell stories, respond to stories, ask questions, make up songs, and act out scenes or events. When they operate in a warm, creative, and responsive atmosphere, children continue to write expansive, creative, thoughtful papers as they grow older. When they learn techniques that tap their imaginations and when they discover new information, their writing matures and becomes more sophisticated. As students put words on paper, we help them create, develop, organize, focus, expand, stir, and refine ideas. The quality, quantity, and character of ideas that children generate depend on several factors: purpose, audience, and message. Successful delivery of their ideas depends on the use of writing conventions that readers expect.

Purpose

Occasions for writing determine purpose, that is, *why* we are writing. Why we write, in turn, influences how ideas are generated and ultimately the final form for the expression of those ideas. Writing a letter to Grandma and creating a short story, for example, have different purposes and forms, and the manner in which ideas are generated is different for each of those purposes. Kinneavy (1971) identifies four purposes for writing: expressive, literary, referential, and persuasive.

Guidelines for Writing Purposes and Modes

What moves us to write obviously must come from our own experience. Koch and Brazil, 1978

Expressive. Letters, diaries, journals, and personal opinion essays focus on the writer and what the writer feels and thinks. Beginning and mature writers alike often explore their own experiences, feelings, and observations to clarify thought, recall sequences of events, or record descriptions. Such self-exploration gives writers access to their personal experiences and adds depth to their writing. In one of his many comic strips about writing, *Peanuts* cartoonist Charles Schulz shows Sally making a show-and-tell presentation (Figure 6–1). She announces to the class that she is going to tell them about something that is endlessly fascinating—*herself.*

Young writers communicate easily about themselves because they have more knowledge about themselves than they do about any other subject.

Literary. Short stories, poetry, novels, drama, songs, and jokes focus on entertainment, yet they can be quite different in form and internal ordering. Literary content frequently stems from writers' personal experiences, research, or others' experiences and attitudes. For example, middle school children in a creative writing program gather information for short stories by visiting cemeteries, historical buildings, and sites of historical events. They view films of the area's history, interview long-time residents about the area, and

FIGURE 6–1 Peanuts

Peanuts reprinted by permission of United Feature Syndicate.

read diaries written by residents from earlier time periods. Their characters develop from their research and from their observations of people in everyday life.

Referential.   Expository or informative articles, texts, histories, analyses, theories, essays, and reports focus on content or subject matter. Referential writing explains a concept or procedure, makes a judgment or recommendation, analyzes, solves a problem, or reports on an event or situation. Writers organize information in specific modal patterns.

Persuasive.   Editorials, political oratory, sermons, advertising, and propaganda focus on audience. Persuasive writing and argument are a culmination of all other genre. To convince or persuade an audience, writers frequently include vignettes in the form of narration or referential reasoning in combination with the moral, ethical, or emotional appeals of persuasion. The writer's primary aim is to convince the audience to change an opinion, make a choice, or take an action.

Modes

One of the many teaching tasks is that of moving students beyond expressive writing to the transactional terms of both audience and subject distance. Hillerich, 1985

Modes are ways to organize writing within the four purposes (see Figure 6–2). For example, classification, analysis, cause and effect, process narrative, comparison, and definition are referential modes. These referential modes appear in a variety of forms such as reports or essays. For example, a comparison mode is an appropriate organizational strategy to use when the purpose is to write a recommendation, say of one book, one movie, one computer, or one team over another. The narrative mode, on the other hand, takes the form of novels or short stories, while poetry may take forms such as sonnets, blank verse, or haiku.

Although the purposes and modes are separate and distinct, they often overlap or are used in tandem in a given piece of writing.

FIGURE 6–2
Purposes, Modes, and Forms

PURPOSES:	SELF-EXPRESSION	LITERARY	REFERENTIAL	PERSUASIVE
Modes of development	Diary Journal Personal narrative	Story Narrative Poetry	Process Narrative Comparison Cause/effect Classification Analysis	Argument Persuasion
Forms	Response to literature, learning journals	Short stories, novels, vignettes, blank verse, sonnets	Reports, essays, articles, letters, recommendations	Editorials, political oratory, sermons, advertising

Audience

The primary audience is always the writer. Then the writing is available to others. Smith, 1982

The generation of ideas is further influenced by the writer's concept of audience. For the youngest writers, the primary audience is "self." Children in the earliest stages of writing are egocentric. They are concerned with what *they* know and what *they* have to say. An outside audience is incidental to them. They may be pleased when someone listens and responds to their creations, but awareness of another audience is undeveloped.

Teachers are only a tryout audience. McDonald, 1975

For all writers, the primary audience is self, but gradually writers move beyond self to additional audiences. The opinions of friends, family, or teachers become important. However, Elbow (1981) notes that teachers alone cannot serve as the real audience. Next, students learn to consider larger audiences such as other classes in the school or acquaintances outside the school setting. Finally, mature writers understand the concept of the unknown reader—the distant reader for whom the writer must hypothesize interest and knowledge. They learn to use the conventions of writing that help readers understand the purpose and the message, recognize the main idea, follow logically from one point to the next, and appreciate the significance of the writing. Audience awareness develops in a pattern of concentric circles that begin with the writer and expands outward to readers who are less and less personally involved with the writer (Figure 6–3). Mature writers begin to consider how readers might react to the substance and style of their writing (Figure 6–4).

Message

After the writer establishes the purpose for a piece of writing and considers the audience, the issue remains, "What do I have to say?" "How do I want to develop my message?"

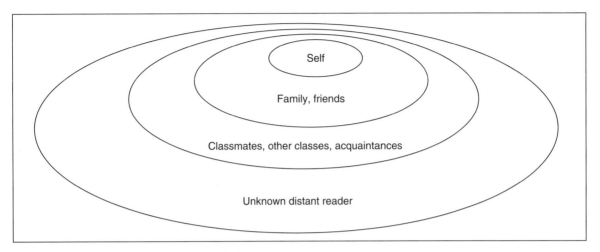

FIGURE 6–3   Concentric Circles for Audience Awareness

FIGURE 6–4
Strategy for Identifying Audience

| |
| Mature writers ask pertinent questions regarding the audience: |
| • Who will read my writing? What do I know about them? |
| • What is my relationship to my readers? |
| • What is my purpose for writing to them? |
| • What might they already know about my subject? |
| • How do I feel about my subject? Will they agree, disagree, or not care? |
| • What do I want them to know or feel? |
| • What questions might they want to ask me? |

When we speak of identifying a topic, we are describing a much bigger task than most students imagine. A student may wish to write an attack on the school administration, but if she has no supporting material, the writer has not sufficiently identified a writeable topic. . . . The student must collect data, examples, reasons, and facts in order to really comprehend the topic. Koch and Brazil, 1978

Heuristics: Guidelines for Developing a Message

Features of Heuristics.   Heuristics aid writing; they are strategies such as brainstorming, mapping, interview, and a myriad of others that help writers develop and organize content. As techniques that set the mind in motion, stimulate thinking, stir memory, coax imagination, and solve problems, heuristics help writers collect relevant information, focus on relationships among ideas, organize thoughts, and draw attention to needed information. They help writers elaborate and create a logical order. Heuristics are ways to "search the mind" and seek information from a variety of other sources. Heuristics also help writers develop the message as it applies to the purpose and the audience.

In writing workshop, we emphasize that heuristics are a private matter and that messiness and informality are acceptable. Heuristics are simply to help writers; thus,

The writer cannot build a good strong piece of writing unless he has gathered an abundance of fine raw material. Murray, 1968

If teachers expect students to become capable writers, they must help them develop prewriting skills . . . for the truly inexperienced writers, teachers must not only motivate them to write . . . but also show them ways of discovering concepts, experiences, and ideas and gathering materials for their writing. Koch & Brazil, 1978

they must be flexible and should be revised often to make writing tasks easier and less time consuming. Just as writers have different learning styles and multiple intelligences, they have preferences for different heuristics. Writers often use more than one heuristic to develop their ideas.

Criteria for Heuristics.   An effective heuristic is broad enough to cover all subjects; therefore, it can be internalized and used repeatedly. Writers should be able to move freely within the heuristic, and it should be flexible enough for the rhetorical situation in general. It should be highly generative, triggering new insights and synthesis of information. Above all, it should be simple and clear enough to support rather than hinder writing (Lauer, 1979). With heuristics, writers learn to generate a wealth of ideas and materials before they begin to create a formal draft. Many authors advise that it is easier to generate lots and then eliminate information that doesn't fit than it is to expand a piece that is struggling for elaboration.

The heuristics we use with our writers build from concrete strategies for younger children to more complex and abstract activities for older students. Later chapters discuss applications of particular heuristics to the various genres of writing. In workshop, we model the heuristics and encourage students to practice them so they understand the processes and possible outcomes. However, we focus on generating information rather than use of the technique itself.

Types of Heuristics

Discussion of Literature.   We find that discussion of quality literature and genres of writing are powerful heuristics for both beginning and experienced writers. As our students study authors' styles and literary techniques, they try out and eventually internalize those writing styles and techniques in their own work. For example, the popular children's book *Alexander and the Terrible, Horrible, No Good, Very Bad Day* by Judith Viorst inspires our students to create their own versions of "bad days" or switch to the positive concept of "good days." Its features of parallel structures, descriptive words, and humorous theme help writers develop and organize their ideas as they write.

Additional reading is as beneficial as additional instruction in writing for improving writing skills . . . when the two are tied together, they mutually stimulate each other. Hillerich, 1985

I try to help writers narrow the focus of their writing . . . and I try to channel their story telling from an oral medium to a written one. Atwell, 1998

Drawing and Oral Narration.   In the *Art of Teaching Writing*, Calkins (1986) demonstrates how very young children begin generating stories through drawings. Children write stories using letter representations for words to label drawings and, thus, to tell the story. Children easily read their stories for the teacher and the class. Even without the drawings, very young children often narrate stories orally while teachers transcribe them. Calkins points out that as children's written language grows stronger, there is less dependence on drawing as a means to communicate the message. At this point, in fact, a reversal may actually occur. Writers may write first and then use drawings to illustrate high points in the writing. When children use a combination of drawing and narrating, the linguistic and spatial multiple intelligences reinforce each other. In this case, the spatial intelligence is an aid to the linguistic. See Figure 6–5 for an example of narrated drawing.

FIGURE 6–5
Example of Nar-
rated Drawing

My favorite part of the school
is the "butterfly garden"
Ashley Browder Age 5

Discourse is a
process; one idea
generates another in
an ongoing progres-
sion. Berke, 1976

Role Play and Dramatization.   When our students act out situations or stories in their
writing, they combine interpersonal and bodily-kinesthetic intelligences to aid in the development of linguistic skills. As they perform their stories for each other, fresh ideas
splash into the script and thus into the data bank of ideas for writing. "Oh, let's have the
main character wake up in the dog house," comes spontaneously from one student; while
another student volunteers that she thinks the character should giggle and have freckles
on her nose. As students write out character descriptions for someone else to role-play,
they learn to develop characters more fully. When our classes act out scenes, they experience a spontaneous richness of detail that is then expressed in written accounts of the
activity. We find that dramatization and role play help writers shed preconceived ideas
and inhibitions and take on the actions, reactions, and ideas of other people. Writers develop perspective, audience awareness, point of view, and persuasive skills.

Strategy for dramatization and role play.   First, we establish the situation clearly. The situation can be a real-life example or make-believe. We use a real-life situation for a persuasive paper such as: "You are going to represent your fourth-grade class in asking the principal for a special favor—an extra day of vacation at Thanksgiving." For make-believe situations, we involve imaginary casts of characters such as Nervous Ned and Brave Bonnie who find themselves in a predicament that needs to be resolved. Secondly, so students can participate fully, we use familiar situations. Students decide who will assume each character, and we provide enough background so that each actor can develop his or her role. Third, we emphasize that students must stay in character, no matter how much he or she may disagree with what the character says or does. Further, we encourage students to talk like the characters, using language and even accents the characters would use. Others in the group are responsible for taking notes. The note takers record the events and the attitudes of each character. When the role play is finished, students discuss the notes, add details, and establish the characteristics important to the purpose, the audience, and the message for the piece of writing.

Journal Writing.   Journals are particularly valuable heuristics for students with strong intrapersonal intelligences. They allow students to write privately about their understandings of things, their feelings and attitudes, and their personal experiences and observations.

Personal journals are much like a diary. Students write in journals about their interests and feelings, and over time, the journal becomes a record of how those interests, feelings, and ideas evolve. These ideas, in turn, become the material for their stories, letters, poems, and other kinds of writing. Some students find personal journals a valuable tool for self-expression and a place to rehearse ideas and evaluate alternatives for action. As students write, they sort out feelings, relationships, problems, and successes.

Strategy for journal writing.   For personal journals to be effective heuristics, students write briefly each day with the "self" as the primary audience. We never grade journals because students need the journal as a place to record anything they want, in the form and fashion they want, without outside judgment on what they write. Furthermore, since a journal is a personal record, there is no established criteria for performance. The goal is to capture ideas, attitudes, and feelings rather than to write at a certain level of competence. It is often helpful for the teacher to respond briefly to journal messages with affirming comments or questions that encourage further development of ideas—but with no corrections or grades. Chapter 7 on expressive writing contains an extensive section on journal writing.

The children's books *Amelia's Notebook, Amelia Writes Again,* and *Amelia Takes a Trip* by Marissa Moss are examples of personal journals that spark the imagination of children. Amelia's real-life feelings, comic antics, and saucy comments stimulate students to create their own journals, share personal views of life, and gain insight on personal problems. The simple but lively illustrations encourage children to augment personal journals with pictures as Amelia did.

The content of the writing workshop is the content of real life, for the workshop begins with what each student thinks, feels, and experiences, and with the human urge to articulate and understand experience. Calkins, 1986

Students know they can write anything in any form in their journals. Berke, 1976

The journal is a starting point, not a destination. Clark, 1987

Learning journals are responses to subject content and, as such, also become data banks of ideas. Such journals include responses to literature, responses to concepts or ideas, or learning logs in which writers record what they are learning and understanding in other subject area classes. Content area learning journals convey to teachers levels of understanding and competence in subject areas and provide an avenue for communicating questions. Learning journals uncover gaps in information and extend the content to broad applications, thus facilitating understanding. As Bennet Serf says, "If you can't write it, you don't know it." Learning journals become an idea bank for written compositions, most often for referential writing such as reports.

Personal Narrative.   This heuristic helps writers generate personal information to use in building self-esteem, creating story characters, or in establishing relationships with specific audiences. Although personal narrative is particularly suited to students with strong intrapersonal intelligences, most students make strong connections with this heuristic. Like the Peanuts characters, writers know the most about themselves, their personal histories or family histories allowing them to tap their own experiences as the basis for their writing. Sharing personal histories with the class also establishes bonds among writers in the workshop setting; informs the teacher about interests, strengths, and capabilities; and gives each student his or her special identification and worth in the eyes of peers. Illustrations or photographs that supplement the personal narratives or decorate the covers spark interest in the writers and the audience, and these student autobiographies become treasured keepsakes.

Dear Diary.   Writers of all ages enjoy this heuristic immensely. Dear Diary, is a pictorial story starter, similar to role play, that asks writers to take on the character of a person, animal, or object in a magazine, photograph, painting, drawing, or newspaper picture. Writers choose to become one of the people or objects in the picture. They then write a descriptive entry about what is happening to them and around them and how they feel about it. For a reticent writer, or one who isn't comfortable writing about personal experiences, Dear Diary serves as a substitute for the personal history in generating descriptions, feelings, and reactions in writing. This heuristic furthers understanding and appreciation of a character's point of view.

Strategy for Dear Diary.   When we use this heuristic in the workshop, we provide students with a selection of pictures that include several characters and interesting action. Students choose a picture and attach it to the inner left side of a manila folder. On the opposite side, they attach a piece of notebook paper. Students adopt the role of someone or something in the picture and write a Dear Diary entry about the character they have chosen in that setting. They include time, place, feelings, and perceptions. Students use descriptive words, details, and background information relating to the experience.

Poems.   Poetry provides another way for students to express personal feelings and thoughts. Like the personal history, this heuristic helps writers learn to know themselves and become aware of their interests. For some writers, there is safety in writing in an

---

Learning requires an act of initiative on [the student's] part. We can only create the conditions in which learning can happen. . . . Learning logs can help create those conditions by encouraging students to ask questions. Calkins, 1986

Students can build their creative confidence through positive autobiographical experiences. Flack, 1999

Our children have rich lives. In our classrooms, we can tap the human urge to write if we help them realize that their lives are worth writing about, and if we help them choose their topics, their genre and their audience. Calkins, 1986

Everyone has a story to tell. Rosen, 1983

FIGURE 6–6
Strategy for De-
scriptive Poetry

MY FAVORITE PLACE

1. Where do you most like to be—of all the places in the world?
2. When do you most like to be there (time and kind of day)?
3. What do you see when you are there?
4. What do you hear when you are there?
5. What do you smell when you are there?
6. What do you do when you are there?
7. Who is there with you?
8. How do you feel when you are there?
9. When will you go there again?

Children can learn to be conscious of the powers of their own minds and decide when and how they will use them. However, they cannot do it without our help. Donaldson, 1978

established poetic form such as haiku, sonnet, or blank verse. The musical rhythm of some forms of poetry is appealing to those writers strong in the musical intelligence.

An especially successful heuristic to help writers develop personal ideas in a poetic form is "My Favorite Place." Writers think of one of their favorite places in the world, a place where they would most like to be, and answer the questions listed in Figure 6–6 with descriptive words or phrases, not complete sentences. Writers use as many descriptive words as possible to help others see, hear, feel, and experience the places they describe. The resulting poems come from the writers' personal experiences with their favorite places and help students see the value of thinking deeply about an idea or subject as the topic of a written piece.

Fourth grader Brian wrote descriptively about parks he visits during his summer vacation in Taiwan.

PARKS IN TAIWAN

Frogs, flooded waters, scooter motorcycles
Wind, rippling water, croaking frogs, popping engines
Chinese food, flowers, aromas
Ride motorcycles, play on playground
Catch minnows and frogs
My father, my uncle
Relaxed, excited, happy
On summer vacation

Chapter 9 offers a more extensive treatment of poetry.

Brainstorming. This powerful heuristic can jumpstart the writing process. Several or many people brainstorming a topic generate a myriad of ideas that one person alone can not.

Brainstorming occurs when a group of people volunteer and record ideas about a topic in a rapid, random fashion. The rapid exchange of ideas required by brainstorming stimulates insights into other opinions and thought processes. This kind of sharing is carried out in an uncritical setting in which all students participate. A recorder, either teacher or student, captures all ideas on a chart, transparency, or board to make them available to all members of the group for possible use in their writing. This heuristic appeals to those writers who are strong in the interpersonal intelligence.

Strategy for brainstorming.   For a successful brainstorming activity, first we establish the focus for the discussion—the subject—and then we establish a reasonable time limit. Students exchange ideas in an open, uncritical manner. A moderator keeps the discussion on track. We assure that all class members have an opportunity to participate. A designated recorder records all ideas as equally worthy. At the end of the brainstorming session, we discuss and analyze the ideas we have produced.

Listing.   This exercise holds appeal for those strong in the linguistic intelligence. Writers attempt to discover personal interests by listing key words that represent their thoughts. This strategy is linear and structured. Writers add, delete, or change items on the list to reflect developing ideas and priorities. Since most people *think* more rapidly than they can *record* complete thoughts, this heuristic allows writers to list key words that represent their ideas, thus capturing thoughts before they escape. Listing is as simple as students keeping an accounting of "Things I Know" stapled to the inside covers of their working portfolios or as involved as making judgements or classifying ideas for later use in a written piece. For example, before beginning a persuasive paper, students list many reasons for supporting a particular issue. They group reasons according to their pro and con positions, and then they rank the points according to importance.

Strategy for listing.   To help students develop lists for generating ideas, we ask them to write the topic at the top of a page and then list quickly and briefly approximately 10 items related to the topic. Writers identify similar ideas by grouping key words on the list and then marking or color coding them. They evaluate the list and select a favorite item or several related items as the basis for further development. Additional heuristics such as brainstorming or drawings further expand these ideas. Following is an example of a listing activity that one student developed into a preliminary outline for a composition.

LIST AND GROUP: THINGS I LIKE

1. music	2. *sports	3. reading	4. draw	5. paint
6. eat	7. walk	8. *soccer	9. family	

Limit and Develop

Subject: Sports/Soccer

Mapping.   Also called webbing or clustering, this heuristic is a less structured way of quickly capturing key words for thoughts and ideas. It has strong appeal for the intrapersonal, linguistic, and spatial intelligences. Writers generate information for writing as they record, organize, and limit ideas. Mapping promotes organizational strategies, helps define and limit

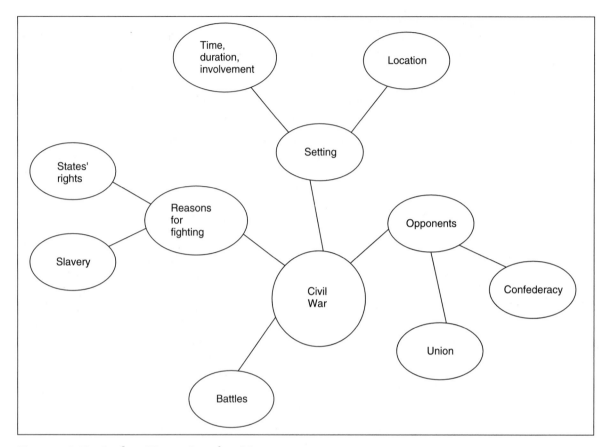

FIGURE 6–7   Student Writing Sample—Mapping

> . . . I want to show kids . . . that above all, writing is an act of thinking and considering. There is no great mystique about coming up with topics; ideas come because I anticipate I'll be writing and look for them. Atwell, 1998

topics, and points out areas for further development. This heuristic allows writers to use lots of imagination in recording ideas. Depending on individual preferences, writers use key words in their word maps, color code related chunks of information, or illustrate ideas.

Strategy for mapping.   A successful mapping strategy begins with the subject printed in the center of the page with a circle drawn around it. Students print key words related to the subject on lines with each line connecting to the center circle or to another line in the map. When finished, they connect related ideas with dotted lines, decide which ideas lend themselves to further development, and note what additional information is needed. Figure 6–7 demonstrates mapping.

Venn Diagram.   This heuristic appeals to logical/mathematical and spatial writers. Venn diagrams help writers focus on similarities and differences in objects, situations, education, stories, characters, or events, and they help writers practice critical analysis. The overlapping sections of the circles show similarities while the outside sections show differences. Figure 6–8 uses a Venn diagram to compare and contrast the traditional *Little Red Riding Hood* with the Chinese tale of *Lon Po Po.*

FIGURE 6–8
Student Writing
Sample—Venn
Diagram

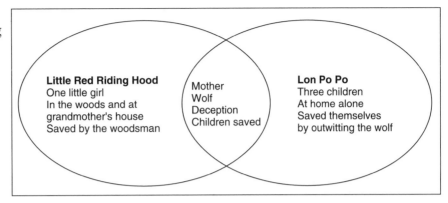

Outlines. These exercises appeal to logical/mathematical and spatially oriented writers. Pyramid outlines are graphic outlines that organize the information a writer may have gathered with some of the other heuristics. Some writers prefer the traditional outline format (I. A. 1. 2. B. II. A.), although the pyramid outline is more flexible for others and easily allows for changes during the generating and planning process.

Strategy for a pyramid outline. To create a pyramid outline, students identify the audience and write a tentative purpose statement at the top of the page. They use key words or phrases to record a main idea in a box at the top of the page. Below this top box, they make a row of middle boxes that hold the major supporting ideas, which later become separate paragraphs. Then they arrange these supporting ideas in order according to importance, time order, or spatial order. Next, they list related details in a set of lines below each supporting idea. Finally, they write a tentative ending or conclusion in a bottom box. In small groups, writers check the relevance of ideas to each other and to the main idea and check to be sure that the conclusion is logically related to the purpose statement. See Figure 6–9 for an example of a pyramid outline.

Students are given very little opportunity in our schools to organize information on their own, and yet this is a crucial part of both writing and learning. Calkins, 1986

For beginning writers, a simplified form of the pyramid outline is developed into a paragraph with a main idea, three or four supporting ideas, and a conclusion. This format supports the initial teaching of sequence of events or other kinds of order. This example demonstrates a simple form of a pyramid outline:

Main idea: Reasons for the Civil War

Support 1: economy
Support 2: states' rights
Support 3: slavery

Conclusion: These three factors created massive internal conflict in our history.

Spread-It-Out. A heuristic that we use quite successfully to help writers of all ages focus on paragraph development and topic sentence development is called *Spread-it-out.*

Strategy for spread-it-out. With a single sheet of paper cut into quarters and stapled together at one corner, students write their main ideas on the first piece of paper. On the

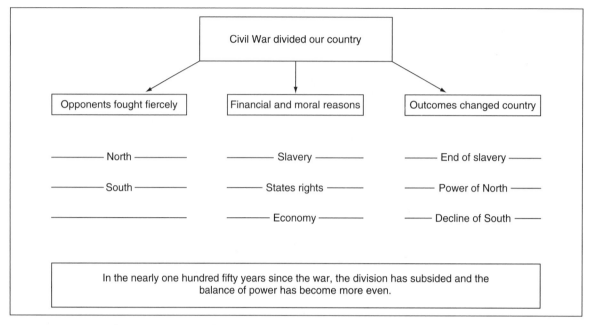

FIGURE 6–9   Student Writing Sample—Pyramid Outline

second sheet, each writer writes only one supporting idea at the top of the sheet. On the third sheet, a second supporting idea is written at the top of the sheet. The fourth sheet is for either a third supporting idea or a concluding idea. Now the writers go back to the second and third sheets to fill the sheet with specific details, description, facts, examples, or other information related to that specific supporting idea. When the specifics have been filled in, then writers work on a sentence that summarizes what they have written, and that is written in on the last page of the booklet (see example in Figure 6–10). Each sheet of the booklet serves as a paragraph in the final draft of the paper.

The major support statement at the top of each page of the booklet then becomes a topic sentence for the paragraph. Naturally, developing these skills may take more than the quarters of a sheet of paper; however, this is a graphic way to help those students who are more oriented to the logical, spatial, and bodily-kinesthetic intelligences learn the concepts of organization in writing.

Looping.   This highly linguistic heuristic focuses writers on the generation and development of a main idea. It is often used as a follow-up to one or more of the previous heuristics.

Strategy for looping.   Our writers begin with a specific subject and write it at the top of the page. They write three loops without stopping to correct or change anything. Writing a loop means writing on the chosen topic for a few minutes without stopping. At the end of each loop, writers stop to read what they have written, underline the kernel or main idea in the loop, and begin the second loop with that specific idea as the heading.

> By writing we find out what we know, what we think. Writing is an extremely efficient way of gaining access to that knowledge that we cannot explore directly. . . . By writing what I think I know, I develop what I potentially knew.
> Smith, 1982

Dogs as pets	Kind of dog	Care	Training	Conclusion
_____ _____ _____ _____ (main idea)	_____ _____ _____ (supporting idea)	_____ _____ _____ (supporting idea)	_____ _____ _____ (supporting idea)	_____ _____ _____ (summary)

FIGURE 6–10   Spread-It-Out Heuristic

This exercise is repeated a third time. The goal is to write "lots" rather than "well." Reasonable time limits facilitate this strategy. For younger children, 3 to 5 minutes per loop is usually sufficient, while older or more mature writers may be able to sustain a loop for 5 to 10 minutes.

Experiment and Observation.   These heuristics have special appeal to the naturalist and logical/mathematical intelligences. They emphasize situational contexts in that writers learn about how they identify with various situations and the objects or actors in those situations. When students don't possess all of the information they need in their internal data banks, they go outside themselves to generate information and material. One of the ways to do this is to conduct personal experiments or make firsthand observations. This heuristic is particularly helpful as students write across the subject areas. We encourage students to perform or observe experiments or processes and record exactly what they see using specific names, places, dates, times, sequences, detailed descriptions, and all other important information. Subjects of experiments or processes can be as simple as squeezing oranges for juice or as complex as observing butterfly larvae hatch, plants grow, magnetism, chemical reactions, condensation, weaving, or electricity. This heuristic emphasizes the difference between fact and opinion and the importance of careful observation and measurement. Note taking is essential to this heuristic, as the notes become the basis for finished reports or other written works.

Strategy for experiment and observation.   Students record information related to all five senses and include drawings to supplement the notes. They discuss findings with other observers or experimenters and add relevant and delete irrelevant information. When writers compare notes with each other, they become aware of bits of information or steps they have left out.

Interviewing.   This interpersonal heuristic aids writers in two ways. First, writers identify experts or people who are knowledgeable about specific areas and seek out the information they need for writing. The interview also gives writers valuable knowledge

Even young children are good at observing a person and writing down as many physical characteristics as possible. Clark, 1987

My best friend is my notebook. When I hold it in my hand, it reminds me to collect details through observation and to write them down. Clark, 1987

Children extend far beyond what teachers can do in helping each other establish their territories of information. Graves, 1983

about the interviewee's feelings and opinions. Secondly, interviews force writers to think about what kind of information is needed and to formulate questions that will elicit that specific information. As with observation, writers learn the importance of taking notes to capture and retain information. Our students conduct interviews in person or by telephone, video conference, e-mail, or letters.

Strategy for interviews.   Common interview techniques help students' gather information. For factual reports or for fictional background information, students first determine what information is needed, decide who can best provide that information through an interview, and set up an appointment with the expert. Prior to the interview, students write questions; they then take notes on the responses to the interview questions. Finally, they summarize the information and organize the ideas according to importance and interest to the audience.

For personal interest interviews, Clark (1987) believes that even if the questions are not profound, they are a springboard for the interviewee to elaborate on interesting stories or experience. For example, when one of our students interviewed a grandparent about what it was like in the "old days," the question elicited a story about Grandma's experience as a child in a one-room schoolhouse. D. L. Mabery's children's book *Tell Me About Yourself: How to Interview Anyone, from Your Friends to Famous People* offers suggestions that help young writers conduct successful interviews.

Journalistic Questions.   By helping to gather surface facts and information, this heuristic is a quick, efficient, structured linguistic aid for initiating a subject and getting at the essential objective information necessary to almost any kind of writing task—whether it be literary, referential or persuasive. Beginning writers find it especially helpful because of its straightforward structure. To expand their ideas, we simply ask writers to identify the basic journalistic questions "who, what, when, where, how, and why" and then seek either simple or elaborated answers to those questions.

Debate.   Young writers delve into the underlying facts and proofs of a multifaceted issue. Debate appeals to interpersonal, logical/mathematical, bodily-kinesthetic, and linguistic intelligences and is usually more successful with upper level students. Debate involves a combination of several other heuristics in developing persuasion. The audience requires specific facts and well-developed proofs. Writers practice making clear distinctions between fact and opinion and take definite positions. Students learn to deal with opposition, a necessity in writing persuasion. Students gain immediate feedback from the opposing team, making them aware of strengths and weaknesses in their arguments or in the presentation of their positions. Debate can be a time-consuming process, lasting several class periods.

Strategy for debate.   Successful debate requires selection of a task that is realistic for writers and based on a universal theme. Students agree on the issue to be debated and then thoroughly research both sides of the question. Students might defend one position one day and switch to the defense of the other side on the next day. At the end, students analyze and evaluate the success of the points presented and the reasons for their success.

Research. This tool involves a combination of several heuristics. Students search for information in the library; read literature and texts; explore the Internet; take field trips; listen to speakers; correspond with pen pals; work with other students who have similar interests; observe events, phenomena, and experiments; work with mentors; and interview experts. In all of these situations, writers find relevant data and information and record their findings accurately and honestly. See Chapter 12 for details on research and report writing. Figure 6–11 outlines the heuristics discussed in this section.

Writing Conventions

Focusing and finding relationships underlie the fluency of communication. Regardless of the genre, certain writing conventions make an author's task easier. In addition to using the heuristics previously discussed, authors employ techniques to focus on a theme, elaborate that theme, organize the material for clarity, and finally, put those ideas into the most effective sentences for interest and readability.

First, we encourage young writers to generate and gather many ideas using the various heuristics that they have learned. Next, writers look at the mass of information and narrow it to a main idea, supporting ideas, and details that elaborate. They then find relationships among ideas, arrange them logically, and add effective transitions for successful delivery of their messages to an audience.

Main Idea

Student writers need to create a focus . . . some guidance is necessary to avoid problems that result from a focus that is too general or inadequate. Carney, 1996

. . . writers who learn to choose topics well make the most significant growth in both information and skills at the point of best topic. With best topic the child exercises strongest control, establishes ownership, and with ownership, pride in the piece. Graves, 1983

To find relationships, writers first identify a main idea or a focus for the message. Focusing or limiting is perhaps the most difficult of all the writing tasks, even for mature writers. It means narrowing the concept so that it is brief enough to be interesting and manageable, yet broad enough to cover the subject well. Sometimes the main idea doesn't surface or become clear until the writer has worked for a while to develop the piece. However, the heuristics of looping, listing, and mapping aid in discerning the main focus for a piece of writing. Writers learn to look at their lists, maps, and loops to find recurring strands of information that lead them to create main idea statements. These statements become topic sentences and later thesis statements or controlling ideas for longer pieces of writing.

Students need practice recognizing topic sentences or controlling ideas for nonfiction. A literature-rich classroom provides many models. We use examples from a variety of books and articles and help students find the controlling ideas for the pieces of writing and for specific paragraphs. Adler's children's book *Lou Gehrig: The Luckiest Man* highlights not only the events in the life of the baseball player, but also conveys the personal qualities that made Lou Gehrig one of the greatest and most beloved players of all time. The paragraphs elaborate particular events and issues in Gehrig's life and demonstrate how controlling ideas guide the writing. Gibbons' book *The Puffins are Back!* provides another example of how "tightly" written paragraphs convey the main idea message. Each sentence supports the topic of the paragraph with pertinent information.

FIGURE 6–11 Heuristics Chart

HEURISTIC	FUNCTION	CHARACTERISTICS	GROUP	MULTIPLE INTELLIGENCE
Drawing	Generating ideas	Unstructured, free form; flexible time	Individual	Spatial, intrapersonal
Role play/ dramatization	Generating details; develop audience and situational awareness	Structured, time consuming	Small group	Bodily-kinesthetic, musical, interpersonal
Journal writing	Identifying personal knowledge and interests	Unstructured, free form, quick	Individual	Linguistic, intrapersonal
Personal histories, diaries, poems	Identifying personal interests, feelings and habits	Structured: histories — time consuming; diaries and poems— quick	Small group, individual	Intrapersonal, spatial
Brainstorm	Generating ideas, information, new perspectives; audience awareness	Unstructured, quick	Group	Interpersonal
Listing	Finding, generating, and limiting a subject	Semistructured, quick	Group or individual	Intrapersonal, interpersonal
Mapping	Finding a subject, grouping related ideas	Semistructured, quick	Group or individual	Intrapersonal, interpersonal
Pyramid outline	Finding focus, identifying missing information, relating and ordering ideas	Structured, linear, quick	Group or individual	Spatial, interpersonal, intrapersonal
Looping	Finding focus for a subject, main idea	Semistructured, abstract, time consuming	Individual	Linguistic, intrapersonal
Experiment and observation	Gathering information, description, problem solving, situational awareness	Flexible structure and time	Group or individual	Spatial, logical-mathematical, bodily kinesthetic, interpersonal, intrapersonal
Interview	Gathering information, questioning, audience awareness, different perspectives	Semistructured, flexible time	Group of 2 or more	Interpersonal
Journalistic questions	Gathering surface facts and information	Structured, quick	Group or individual	Linguistic, interpersonal, intrapersonal
Debate	Gathering proof, developing a position, audience awareness	Structured, time consuming; combines several heuristics	Group	Linguistic, logical-mathematical, bodily kinesthetic, interpersonal
Research	Gathering necessary outside information	Flexible structure, time consuming, combines several heuristics	Group or individual	All or any one

Adapted from Hughey et al., 1983.

Many open-education teachers, in their enthusiasm for process and for student input in the curriculum, seem to reject formal instruction entirely. Yet when students are deeply absorbed in their subject matter, formal instruction can bring students to new levels of understanding and teacher-intervention can lead them to probe, test, and learn. Calkins, 1986

We model for students by demonstrating how a topic sentence or main idea develops into a cohesive paragraph related to a theme. We often use the pyramid heuristic to analyze a professional piece of writing and demonstrate how it might have developed.

Organization

Within the structure of any prose piece is an organizational strategy that includes a beginning, a middle, and an end. This structure resembles a hamburger. The top bun is the introduction; the lettuce, tomato, and hamburger provide the specific details and dominant flavor in the body; and the bottom bun is the conclusion. The buns hold all the pieces together and create a unified whole.

The beginning, or introduction, catches the reader's attention and interest. The introduction immediately involves the readers in the writing. For nonfiction writing, the writer provides information regarding the breadth and depth of the topic. For fiction, the beginning piques the interest of the readers and entices them to read more. Introductory strategies include asking a question, making a surprise statement, telling a vignette, using a quotation, or stressing the importance of the topic. Our writers often find that the beginning is easier to write or change after they have developed the body and the conclusion.

The middle, or body of the paper, is the substance of the story or the paper. The middle is the heart of the message, the reason for the paper, and is therefore the most detailed and developed part of the paper. The middle further establishes the focus of the paper and provides the background to support that focus through elaboration with illustrations, examples, descriptions, facts, reasons, details, and definitions.

The ending, or conclusion, wraps everything up into a complete bundle of ideas. It brings the message to a close, stops the action, or concludes the piece of writing in a logical manner. The conclusion takes the form of a summary, an inference, a question, a call for action, or the resolution of a problem.

Introductions.   In storytelling, writers use a *lead-in* to the story to catch the readers' attention. The lead-in establishes the main character, the setting, the tone, or the mood for the story. Lead-ins are covered in greater detail in Chapter 8 on literary writing.

In informative and persuasive writing, writers create a main idea statement that includes the main supporting points that they will discuss in the rest of the piece of writing. They also use strategies to catch the reader's attention and make them want to read more.

In writers' workshop, we present different introductory strategies (see Figure 6–12 for examples) one at a time so students can try them out and play with their effectiveness within the context of what they are writing. After they have used each one, we then play with writing more than one introduction for each paper. Working in small groups or in pairs, writers discuss which of their introductions is most effective for the piece each is writing. Our writers find it is often more effective to write, or at least rewrite, the introductions after the content of the piece has been set.

The Body.   In the middle is the body, or the important development of ideas in the piece of writing. This is the place where writers are as specific and detailed as possible. The body needs elaboration—description, details, facts, examples, and reasons—to fill out

FIGURE 6–12
Strategies for
Introductions

- *Ask a question:* "Have you ever flown high above the earth in a balloon? I have. It is an exciting experience and this is how it works."
- *Tell a vignette (a brief narrative that relates to the topic):* "One Sunday afternoon, after a sudden and heavy hail storm had passed over our area, several of us began to look at some of the pieces of hail that had fallen in our yards. We were amazed at the structure of these golf ball sized pieces of ice that had fallen from the sky and began to explore exactly how they are formed."
- *Explain the importance or purpose of the subject:* "When over 60 percent of the population in a certain area is experiencing health problems from the smog and other pollution in the air, it is time to find out what is causing the problem and stop it."
- *Use a quotation:* John F. Kennedy once said, "Ask not what your country can do for you; ask what you can do for your country." At this time in our country, there is a need for people to . . .
- *Use a startling fact:* "A new galaxy that supports life has just been discovered by scientists at the Hubble Laboratory."

the main points that writers include in the introduction. This is the place to include information from the journalistic questions—Who? What? What kind? When? Where? How? How long? Why?—and information from other elaboration heuristics such as brainstorming, listing, mapping, interview, and debate.

Elaborate with description and detail.   Once the focus is established, writers fill in their papers with relevant information. At this point writers manipulate ideas by grouping them into "piles" of similar ideas. Each supporting idea contains new or interesting information about the main idea.

Again we ask students to use the pyramid outline to arrange their ideas into related groups of information. This strategy shows writers where they need to add detail for the further elaboration of a piece, where to delete superfluous information, and how to rearrange for effectiveness.

The detail or elaboration that fills out the supporting ideas comes in the form of description, factual details, comparisons, examples, definitions, reasons, or a series of specific events or opinions. These elaboration techniques become the "meat" of the hamburger when organized in supporting paragraphs. Examples of elaboration in Figure 6–13 are taken from fourth-grade students' writing.

We also demonstrate for students how to use these elaboration strategies to "show rather than tell" the ideas they write about. Students practice each of these techniques so that they can apply them in the process of writing. Writers move from flat reporting to more active description, as illustrated by the student example below.

The apple broke when he dropped it on the ground.
Splat! The apple burst into pieces as it hit the hot pavement.

FIGURE 6–13
Fourth-Grade
Students' Elabo-
ration samples

ELABORATION STRATEGY	EXAMPLES FROM STUDENT WRITING
Description Leyla	The curry comb is made out of rubber. It has lots of little bristles. The bristles look like a bunch of sharp pins, but they are actually not sharp at all.
Factual details Hallie	Many New Yorkers depend on subways to get to work and to places too far to walk. The subway in New York is one of the largest in the world.
Comparisons Vincent	Put the key into the keyhole in the power box located on the right hand side. This is like sticking a knife in a jelly jar to get the jelly out.
Examples Sean	The adult gorilla does not have many enemies, but the babies do. Some of these predators are hyenas, jackals, leopards, lions, and pythons.
Definitions Paula	The bottlenose dolphin has lots of blubber, or fat, under its skin to keep warm and to help it float a little bit better.
Supportive reasons Sean	Do not feed your dog human food on a daily basis because if you do, your dog will be spoiled and won't eat his dog food.
Series of events Becky	The plan was to stop being lazy and wash her clothes by herself. So, she got all of her clothes washed, dried, and ironed perfectly. When her mom came in, she said, "You matched all of your clothes, and you look beautiful!"
Opinions Chris	You should mow your lawn so you will not have any snakes or mosquitoes, and you will have a lot of people admire your lawn.

Related Ideas. After writers establish their main idea(s) and elaborate on them, we discuss and model how the elaboration that follows the main idea or theme is related to it. Therefore, it is crucial that the main idea be clear and well developed. Writers discover that to create successful communication, information in the body needs to be related to the ideas in the introduction and that these ideas also need to be related to each other. In writing groups, students check to make sure that there is enough information to develop each event, step, or major point and that the details follow a logical sequence throughout the body of the paper. For example, in an informative piece, Joan wrote about how hail is formed. All of the ideas related to "hail" and "how hail is formed." The roses in the garden that were ruined as a result of the hail storm were deemed not relevant to the information she decided to explore and share with her audience. We discuss relevance and what it means. We practice and share our writing to identify ideas that are related to each other and to help rid our writing of those ideas that would better serve another, different piece of writing.

Our students enjoy working with pyramid posters in the drafting stages of these papers. Pyramid posters allow the children to write out their ideas, cut them into strips, and move them around on the pyramid poster until they are satisfied with the order and the relationships of the ideas.

Computer writing is excellent for this activity because students can print out sentences to cut and arrange on the poster. In working with related ideas, they learn that in order to develop relevance in their writing, they also need a logical ordering or sequencing of those ideas.

Sequence.   Sequencing of ideas is critical to the fluency of a paper. Sequencing helps readers follow the writer's train of thought more easily. Again the pyramid poster allows children to play with the sequencing of ideas before they feel they have been set in stone in a final draft on a piece of paper. For example, when children are writing narratives, they find chronological sequencing of events is usually most effective; however, in writing in the how-to mode, they discover that relevance and logical sequence are more effectively presented in steps from first to last.

> Essays require a logical development very different from the chronology of a narrative. Atwell, 1998

After writers gather information and create the overall basic structure of the piece, they determine the most effective ordering of the ideas. Students learn that there are different ways to sequence ideas for different kinds of content as well as for different effects on the reader. Figure 6–14 summarizes sequencing strategies.

Transitions.   Relevance and logical sequencing call for transitions—both transitional words and phrases. Transition words are the glue that hold ideas together and give them greater meaning. They are the cues that lead readers smoothly from one idea to another. While younger writers work mostly with transitional words or phrases, middle school writers move into using transitional sentences and paragraphs. Figure 6–15 suggests some connecting and transitional words.

> When children become more aware of their thinking strategies, they can become more strategic, deliberate thinkers. Calkins, 1986

Transitions range from simple words such as *first, second, then, later,* and finally to phrases, sentences, or paragraphs that take readers smoothly from one point to the next. Writers practice conventional transition techniques that make the difference between an abrupt, rough, choppy message and a smooth, fluent, cohesive message. For example, Patricia C. McKissack uses effective transitions in her Caldecott Honor book *Mirandy and Brother Wind* to move the character from place to place and to carry the events of the story forward:

> Mirandy hurried home. Like the conjure spell said, she found a crock bottle . . . washed it in water from the rain barrel . . . and poured in a measure of cider. Then she made her way to the big willow down by the branch and set the bottle on the tree's north side. Nothing left to do but wait. 'Fore long Brother Wind come out the woods.

Although some transitional words are used in several different modes of writing, each mode has its own special set of transitional words, which we will discuss as we work our way through the following chapters. These signposts guide readers and take them smoothly through a piece of writing. They help readers follow the writer's meaning.

FIGURE 6–14
Strategies for
Sequencing

LOGICAL ORDER
• *Spatial order* moves the reader from one focal point in a logical progression to another, from front to back, side to side, right to left, or top to bottom. • *Chronological order* moves from one point in time forward to another such as early to late or first event to last event, past to present to future. More experienced writers often enjoy using flashback in time. • *Sequence of steps* instructs the progression of processes; ordering may be from first step to last step; from one stage to another. • *Familiar to unfamiliar* moves from known to unknown: Ordering begins with what is most familiar or best known to the audience and uses the familiar for making comparisons and analogies to explain the unfamiliar. • *General to specific or specific to general order* determines the attitude or effect that writers could have on an audience. Does the writer want readers to have the big picture or to be focused on specific details? • *Least important to most important or most important to least important* order determines emphasis on the content of the message. Often, a writer begins with the least important idea and builds thoughts so that readers are left with the most important idea last. However, if the writer believes that the readers' interest must be captured immediately with strong impact, the paper begins with the most important ideas first.

Paragraphs and Topic Sentences.   When we work with personal narrative and fictional stories, our writers learn to use paragraphs to indicate changes in action, topic, or dialogue. Then we reinforce the idea of paragraphing in informative and persuasive writing by showing writers how paragraphing indicates separate units of thought. Students think through the main idea and the two to three supporting ideas first. When they place them on the pyramid poster, supporting ideas become topic sentences and writers can *see* where they need to fill out each supporting idea with details. They see, graphically, the concept of paragraph development. The heuristic, spread-it-out, discussed on pages 179-180 is also quite effective with our students for practicing topic sentences and paragraphing. Once writers firmly grasp the idea of paragraphing and topic sentences, we show them that topic sentences do not always appear at the beginning of a paragraph. There are times when the topic sentence may be the second sentence or the last sentence of the paragraph. In fact, some writing includes no specific topic sentence. The topic is implied.

Conclusions.   Eventually, our students bring their writing to a close. As they do, they learn that the end of a piece of writing must relate to the beginning of the piece and draw a logical conclusion from the sequence of events or information in the body. The conclusion helps tie all the writer's ideas together. While many children end their writing

FIGURE 6–15
Connecting and
Transitional
Words

TO SHOW	USE WORDS SUCH AS
Additions	and, as well as, also, in addition, besides, moreover, furthermore, besides
Examples	that is, for example, for instance, such as, in other words, to illustrate
Emphasis	in fact, of course, again, indeed, to repeat, above all
Conclusion	finally, in conclusion, last, in short
Sequence: Time	first, second . . ., now, soon, after, next, then, now, previously, soon, immediately, in the meantime, meanwhile, eventually, before, during, after, afterward, while, when, yesterday, today, tomorrow, after a while, at last
Space	above, at the top, on top of, below, under, at the bottom, in front of, behind, in back of, at the side, beside, near, next to, nearby, over, opposite to, to the left/right, on the left/right, beyond
Importance	first, in the first place, second, third, next, after, most important, more important, last, finally
Relationships: Comparison	like, likewise, similar to, similarly, both _____ and _____ , as _____ as . . ., more, better, not only . . . but also . . ., in the same way, compared with, as if . . ., as though . . .,
Contrast	unlike, dissimilar, contrary to, opposite, different from, but, yet, however, although, worse, while, though, although, nevertheless, at the same time, on the other hand, conversely, rather than
Cause and effect	because, therefore, as a result, consequently, so, so that, in order to, in order that, since, thus, if, as, hence, due to

Adapted from Hughey et al. (1983, p. 126)

with "The End," conclusions are meant to end writing. The conclusion is the writer's last chance to help the reader understand the message and is probably what the reader will remember best. We encourage our writers to learn at an early stage how to use different kinds of endings, so they will replace their colorful and highly illustrated "The End" with something more effective. Figure 6–16 summarizes strategies for conclusions.

In writers' workshop, we practice writing different kinds of endings for single pieces of writing. As they did with beginnings, students confer with each other to determine which one of their endings they think fits the piece of writing best.

These basic structures combine to form a unified and whole piece of writing. Later chapters discuss techniques for developing effective beginnings, middles, and

FIGURE 6–16
Strategies for
Conclusions

- *Restate the main idea or theme.* From Patricia MacLachlan's *Sarah, Plain and Tall:* "There will be Sarah's sea, blue and gray and green, hanging on the wall. And songs, old ones and new."
- *Summarize the main points.* Directions for making a peanut butter and jelly sandwich: "Remember to follow the right order. Get together your utensils and ingredients, next assemble the sandwich, and then eat it."
- *Draw a conclusion from the information presented.* A science report on mosquitoes at school: "We can't continue to use the nature area until we solve the mosquito problem. The mosquitoes swarm around us attacking and sucking our blood. Mosquito bites itch and hurt, and besides mosquitoes carry some diseases."
- *Leave it open-ended.* From Madeleine L'Engle's *A Wrinkle in Time:* "But they never learned what it was that Mrs. Whatsit, Mrs. Who, and Mrs. Which had to do, for there was a gust of wind, and they were gone."
- *Recommend an action to be taken.* A science report on mosquitoes at school: "We must clear the nature area of mosquitoes. When we are in the nature area, we can empty water out of all containers; we can write to the city and ask for a water sprinkler in the pond so the water won't stagnate. We use the nature area, we must take care of it."
- *Express an opinion or pose a question.* From Cynthia Rylant's *Missing May:* " 'What is the true mission of spirit messages? To bring us consolation in the sorrows of life . . .' Ob and I smiled at each other. And then a big wind came and set everything free."
- *Lead to the main idea for the first time.* A third grader describing a performing bear: "The colors of the bear and the stage and the sounds of all the animals made a very exciting show."

endings for various genres of writing, but these common characteristics distinguish the framework for children's creativity in writing. We help students discover and examine these three features in different models of writing and discuss how the structure makes each piece effective, or perhaps not so effective.

Sentence Variety

A particularly effective convention for putting ideas into words is the skillful use of sentence variety. Writers delight in using sentences for effect when they learn the impact of this strategy. Short, strong sentences have a powerful effect. They bring the reader to attention. They make a point. Longer, more complex sentences tend to describe and explain. They carry the meaning of the message along with elaboration. The key is learning what effect the writer wants to have and being able to achieve it with the help of sentence variety that carries the description, detail, events, or facts of the message. These strategies are covered in greater detail in Chapter 4, "Grammar through Writing."

EMPHASIZING THE MULTIPLE INTELLIGENCES

Linguistic: Oral narration, looping, journalistic questions, and listing

Logical/mathematical: Formal outlining, debate, Venn diagrams, and research

Spatial: Drawing, mapping, pyramid outlines, and spread-it-out

Musical: Poetry

Bodily-kinesthetic: Drama and role play

Interpersonal: Brainstorming, interview, and debate

Intrapersonal: Journal writing and personal narrative

Naturalist: Experiment and observation

SUMMARY

Our children will write—if we let them. Murray, 1982

Finding topics and generating ideas for those topics is dependent on the purpose for writing, the audience, and the message that the author wants to convey. Heuristics are techniques that set the mind in motion, stimulate thinking, stir memory, coax imagination, and solve problems. Common heuristics used by authors to generate ideas for writing include drawing and oral narration, role play and dramatization, personal and learning journals, personal narrative, poetry, brainstorming, listing, mapping, pyramid outlines, looping, experiment and observation, interviewing, journalistic questions, debate, and research.

Teachers need to immerse themselves in similar experiences: to build, to analyze, to solve, to cooperate—in short, to try out the kinds of activities they might extend to their students. Smith, 1995

Focusing on topics and finding relationships among pieces of information in a piece of writing requires structuring of ideas to make sense to readers. Authors identify the main ideas and organize the ideas for clarity by establishing a beginning, a middle, and an ending. Within the middle or body of the writing, authors sequence events and information to facilitate understanding. Elaboration adds interest and detail to the piece and can be accomplished using a variety of strategies. Transitions allow the reader to move smoothly from one concept or event to another. Variety in sentence structure adds interest and appeal to any piece of writing.

These are the key strategies in developing prose writing and will surface again and again in the ensuing chapters of this book. As a developing teacher of writing, practice and practice these strategies yourselves and share the results with each other.

Theory into Practice

1. Interview children of various ages about the kind of writing they do and their perceived audiences. Compare results with others who conduct the same interviews.

2. Keep a daily journal for a period of time. Examine entries for "kernels" that might be developed into pieces of writing to be shared with others.

3. Write the poem titled *My Favorite Place* and share it with classmates.

4. Participate in a class brainstorming activity as a prelude to writing on a particular topic.

5. Use the listing heuristic to develop ideas for a compare/contrast writing assignment. Use a Venn diagram to arrange and organize the lists.

6. Map ideas related to a fictional story or to a nonfiction report.

7. Create a pyramid outline to organize information generated from a brainstorming activity.

8. Use the looping heuristic to develop a theme.

9. Conduct a science experiment and take detailed notes on the methods used and the observations made. Compare notes with classmates.

10. Prepare interview questions and practice interviewing techniques with classmates. Discuss effective and ineffective questions and techniques.

11. Create a set of guidelines for children on how to conduct successful interviews.

12. Attend a sporting event, musical, movie, or other event or performance. Gather information on the event based on the journalistic questions "who, what, when, where, how, and why."

13. Pick a topic related to a current issue in education. Conduct a class debate on the issue and then discuss the strengths of each position.

14. Read several pieces of writing and analyze the basic purpose, modes of development, intended audience, and form.

15. Identify the main idea of a children's story. Read the introduction or first few paragraphs to identify the lead-in sentences.

16. Identify the main idea of a nonfiction piece of writing. Identify the main idea and topic sentences for several paragraphs. List the supporting information for the topic sentences.

17. Analyze several children's books for effective beginnings, middles, and conclusions.

18. Find examples from children's literature that use each of the following sequencing strategies: spatial order, chronological order, general to specific, specific to general, least important to most important, most important to least important.

19. Find examples from children's literature to illustrate effective use of each of the following kinds of elaboration: description, details, comparisons, similes, metaphors, examples, definitions, supportive reasons, series of events, and opinions.

20. Find examples from children's literature to illustrate effective use of transitions.

21. Find examples from children's literature to illustrate effective use of varied sentence structure.

CHILDREN'S LITERATURE

Adler, David A. 1997. *Lou Gehrig: The luckiest man.* San Diego: Gulliver Books.

Gibbons, Gail. 1991. *The puffins are back!* New York: HarperCollins.

Grimm, Jacob Ludwig Carl and Wilhelm Grimm. 1986. *Little Red Riding Hood.* New York: Holiday House.

L'Engle, Madeleine. 1994. *A wrinkle in time.* New York: Demco Media.

Mabery, D. L. 1985. *Tell me about yourself: How to interview anyone, from your friends to famous people.* Minneapolis, MN: Lerner Publications.

MacLachlan, Patricia. 1985. *Sarah, plain and tall.* New York: Harper Collins.

McKissack, Patricia C. 1988. *Mirandy and brother wind.* New York: Randon House.

Moss, Marissa. 1998. *Amelia takes a trip.* Berkeley, CA: Tricycle Press.

Moss, Marissa. 1994. *Amelia's notebook.* Berkeley, CA: Tricycle Press.

Moss, Marissa. 1996. *Amelia writes again.* Berkeley, CA: Tricycle Press

Viorst, Judith. 1972. Alexander and the terrible, horrible, no good, very bad day. New York: Atheneum.

Young, Ed. 1989. *Lon Po Po.* New York : Philomel Books.

BIBLIOGRAPHY

Atwell, Nancie. 1998. *In the middle,* 2nd ed. Portsmouth, NH: Heinemann.

Berke, Jacqueline. 1976. *Twenty questions for the writer: A rhetoric with readings.* New York: Harcourt Brace Jovanovich.

Buzan, Tony. 1976. *Use both sides of your brain.* New York: E. P. Dutton.

Calkins, Lucy. 1986. *The art of teaching writing.* Portsmouth, NH: Heinemann.

Carney, Barbara. 1996. Process writing and the secondary school reality: A compromise. *English Journal, 85,* 28–35.

Clark, Roy Peter. 1987. *Free to write.* Portsmouth, NH: Heinemann.

Elbow, Peter. 1981. *Writing with power.* New York: Oxford University Press.

Flack, Jerry. 1999. *Your story, my story.* Writing Teacher, 12 (March), pp. 14–19.

Graves, Donald H. 1983. *Writing: Teachers and children at work.* Portsmouth, NH: Heinemann.

Hillerich, Robert L. 1985. *Teaching children to write, K–8.* Englewood Cliffs, NJ: Prentice Hall.

Hughey, Jane B., Deanna R. Wormuth, V. Faye Hartfiel, and Holly L. Jacobs. 1983. *Teaching ESL composition: Principles and techniques.* Rowley, MA: Newbury House Publishers, Inc.

Kinneavy, J. L. 1971. *A theory of discourse.* Englewood Cliffs, NJ: Prentice Hall.

Koch, Carl, and James M. Brazil, 1978. *Strategies for teaching the composition process.* Urbana, IL: National Council of Teachers of English.

Lauer, Janice M. 1979. Toward a metatheory of heuristic procedures. *College Composition and Communication, 30* (October), 268.

McDonald, Daniel. 1975. *The language of argument,* 2nd ed. New York: Harper & Row.

Murray, Donald M. 1982. The teaching craft: Telling, listening, revealing. *English Education 14* (Feb), 56–60.

Murray, Donald. 1968. *A writer teaches writing: A practical method of teaching composition.* Boston: Houghton Mifflin.

Rodriguez, Milane, Cecilia. 1996. Where narrative autobiography, color, and feminism converge. *English in Texas, 27* (Winter) pp. 17–27.

Rosen, Harold. 1983. Speech, Ontario CTE.

Smith, F. 1982. *Writing and the writer.* Hollsdale, NJ: Lawrence Erlbaum Associates.

Smith, M. A. 1995. The national writing project after twenty years. *Phi Delta Kappan, 77,* 690.

Expressive Writing

*Using expressive language allows writers to explore ideas and
feelings and formulate hypotheses, predictions, and questions
as they record their developing meanings on paper.*

Wollman-Bonilla, 1989

Chapter Outline

Expressing one's self in writing plays a crucial role in fostering cognition in young school children, and it benefits people through all stages of life. According to Elias et al. (1997), cognition is basic to human functioning and essential in lifelong learning. Cognition is nurtured through understanding one's feelings, labeling and expressing those feelings, reflecting, identifying goals, and considering alternatives in problem solving and their consequences. Expressive writing is a natural and effective support for these thought processes. The heuristics discussed in chapter 6 indicate that expressive writing through journals, diaries, letters, and personal histories leads to identification of personal knowledge, interests, feelings, and habits. In this chapter, we will discuss expressive writing in the forms of (1) journals for personal reflection and engaging students in meaningful connections in learning, (2) personal narratives and autobiographies, and (3) letter writing.

Even the youngest school children benefit from expressive writing. In "Learning to Read and Write: Developmentally Appropriate Practices for Young Children," the joint position statement of the International Reading Association and the National Association for the Education of Young Children adopted in 1998, authors stress the need for teachers to provide daily opportunities for children to write, beginning in kindergarten. First graders should write about topics that are personally meaningful, with gradually more complex writing competencies expected at each grade level. Expressive writing is a natural and effective method of providing these essential writing experiences.

Expressive writing appeals to the intrapersonal, logical, mathematical, and linguistic multiple intelligences and is characterized in journal keeping by an unstructured approach that can stimulate inventiveness and problem solving. While pencil and paper journals have been the norm for many years, technological advances also make computer journals a viable alternative for many students. E-mail communication, for example, enhances teacher and student responses to interactive journal activities. All of the suggestions and activities in this chapter easily lend themselves to technology adaptations.

> Part of becoming a writer does not involve technique or process at all. It concerns developing the personal strength, resources, and habits that make undertaking the process possible. Clark, 1987

> We pay so little attention to the fact that creation starts in the formless. Holzer, 1994

Journals

Teaching Guidelines: Personal Journals

In the writing workshop, we adopt many different methods to accommodate a personal journal writing routine. The method of introducing journal writing in the workshop dictates the future success of the process. Helping writers understand these guidelines has been important to our success with journal writing.

> Like shooting baskets in your driveway, writing requires no audience beyond yourself to be considered worthwhile or enjoyable. Wilcox, 1999

Writer as Audience.   Writers need to understand the purpose of their personal journals. Before they write, they need to know that they are their own primary audience, and they need to know how the journals will help them grow as learners. A personal journal is a written record of one person's ideas, feelings, interests, events, descriptions, experiences, memories, and reactions. As in a diary, the writer records ideas with the "self" as the audience. A personal journal is not a finished, "published" piece of writing but rather an unstructured record of one's thoughts. Often a diary and a personal journal may be thought

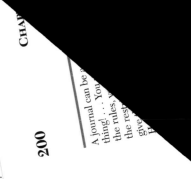

of as one and the same. *The Diary of Anne Frank*, for e̶ the self as the audience. When it was taken from the f̶ narrative, it became a literary classic, and its publication tions and atrocities of World War II. These written conv̶ reflection and problem solving as the writer clarifies issu̶ cused and organized in recurrent themes and reactions. A̶ you write a journal, you go for a stroll, without purpose̶ plan. . . . What you have is a record of your awareness" (p.̶

Personal Sounding Board. Journal writing holds the pr̶ ̶ ̶ ̶ ̶ to young writers. A journal is a writer's notebook and acts as a ̶ ̶ ̶ sounding board to the writer. In the classroom, journals function in several roles: helping a student find his or her voice, encouraging risk taking in writing, establishing rapport with teachers, incubating ideas, and refining those ideas into written communication. "Whether we keep personal journals, subject-related or introspective, reactive journals, whether we use three-ring or spiral notebooks, old-fashioned paper or new-fangled word processors, the act of recording our reactions, thought, ideas, fears, doubts, dreams, convictions, goals and observations is one of the most fulfilling and meaningful educational activities we can experience" (Woodward, 1994, p. 5).

Safe Writing. In the writing workshop, personal journals offer the ultimate opportunity for children to write in a nonthreatening environment. The clear knowledge that a journal is an unconditional, accepting friend elevates the journal to a position of importance and prized ownership. Students feel safe knowing that mistakes won't be counted "wrong." Clark (1987) observes, "The secret of journal writing is that no one expects entries to be particularly well written. They are, after all written in haste, often without careful regard for mechanics. . . . If it contains the seed of a good idea, the writer can expand it, improve it, and correct it in a different context" (p. 98).

Therapeutic Qualities. Dealing with one's feelings through personal journals is naturally therapeutic for children and adults alike. Adams (1997) says that personal journals enhance the ability to evaluate feelings and abilities and to accept criticism. Journals reduce stress by allowing the writer to express hurt or anger that might otherwise build up by holding feelings inside. By putting anger on paper, it is less likely to erupt later in an irrational outburst.

Student-Teacher Relationship. Journals create a bridge between student and teacher. When students and teachers share journals in an interactive writing environment, they establish closer personal relationships and a greater understanding of ideas and writing needs. Student ideas and experiences are validated, thus encouraging a sense of confidence. Marva Collins emphasizes building trust and caring relationships with children, so that real learning can take place. She says, "We find that once we take care of the basic child, teaching then becomes an easier endeavor (1992, p. 109). Journals play an important role in helping to build those relationships.

Control of Topic. Another benefit of writing journals according to Farr and Daniels (1986), is "the opportunity to write for real, personally significant purposes" (p. 53). Journals offer the promise and delight of choice. Journal writing time is the one time of

---

Journal writing is valuable and meaningful for us—whether or not anyone reads it. Wilcox, 1999

When we write our deepest feelings, we are better for having forced ourselves to face, organize, and express them. Wilcox, 1999

Journals provide a unique opportunity for students to express their ideas and for the teacher to recognize each one's thinking. Wollman-Bonilla and Werchadlo, 1995

A journal is a perfect place to think, feel, discover, expand, remember, and dream. Wilcox, 1999

The act of writing permits the student to deal with his own fears, accomplishments, feelings, and experiences. Clark, 1987

the day when students have total control over what they do. Indeed, Ferrara's (1990) finding that most students prefer to self-select writing topics supports this idea.

Familiar Images and Ideas. Perhaps the greatest value of journals is the opportunity to explore words and how they create coherent thought. As in any discipline, practice improves performance. Journal writing enhances fluency and style in writing, allowing students to play in private with the effects of words. As children strive to communicate their thoughts in words, even to themselves, they become increasingly proficient and develop a sense of confidence in their writing abilities.

Simons (1978) notes, "Journal keeping is probably as ancient as writing, and is perhaps one of the reasons for its development . . ." (p. 1). Just as artists keep sketch pads of images and ideas, writers keep journals of images and ideas. We advise young writers to write about things that are familiar to them: themselves, their feelings and reactions, their surroundings, and the events that happen to and around them. When children are encouraged to write about what is uppermost in their minds and lives and what is of greatest interest to them, no matter what the content, they are much more likely to produce a body of raw material that they can use later for communicating with others. A memorable event recorded in a daily journal may be just what a writer needs as the inspiration for his adventure story.

Expectations for Journal Writing. Some teachers establish specific times for daily journal writing. Some establish minimum entries, perhaps, two or more lines per day. Some teachers read and respond to journals daily, while other teachers respond weekly or biweekly depending on the numbers of students they have. The parameters are not so important as establishing the journal writing routine.

We reserve the first 10 minutes of each school day for journal writing in wide-ruled spiral notebooks. When computers are available, they too are an effective medium for journal writing. Students know that each day begins with reflections in their journals. They know that we teachers are ready to read and respond to their journals at least once each week. But they also know they will never be forced to share their journals with anyone, not even with the teacher. If special circumstances arise, such as a new baby in the home, writers know they can share their journal entries with the class, if they want to. They know they might select some journal entries to be the subjects of later full-length papers. They know their journals will never be graded. We find it helpful to post the expectations in the classroom to facilitate journal-writing activities (see Figure 7–1).

Journal Prompts. We begin with a brainstormed list of journal ideas that the students enter on the first page of their journals. Each student lists a personal set of potential journal topics. The general categories often include immediate family members or other relatives, pets, friends, school subjects or activities, teachers, vacations, church, free time activities (sports, movies, books, foods, toys, animals, TV shows), collections, routines (getting up, going to bed, cleaning house), career interests, holidays and other special events, lessons (music, language, sports), happy or sad things, and things that cause anger or excitement. When students are truly stuck for something to write in their personal journals, it is fair and acceptable to provide starters for them such as these:

Anything . . . make . . . you make . . . rictions, you . . . the permissions. Holzer, 1994

Journals invite children to use expressive language that is addressed to oneself or a trusted reader and is informal and conversational in tone. Wollman-Bonilla and Werchadlo, 1995

Most of the daily writing of students does not concern matters of life and death, but describes the normal anxieties and problems of being in the fifth grade. . . . Through these stories students hear the sound of their own voices on the page and learn the value of their feelings and experiences. Clark, 1987.

Within the sanctum of your diary, you can be yourself—honestly; gay or miserable, noble or petty, soul-searching or superficial. . . . Nor must you apologize for leaving a blank space for a blah day. Simons, 1978

FIGURE 7–1
Expectations for
Personal Journal
Writing

- Date each entry.
- Write about anything you choose. Check your topic list for ideas.
- Write for 10 minutes, unless you really want to continue.
- Write something every day.
- Illustrate an occasional entry if desired.
- Write for yourself, even if you share it with your teacher.
- Do not expect your journal to be graded. However, your teacher may respond to your message.

> They want to create, but they know nothing of their own creative process. Journal writing can provide fine insights into that process. Holzer, 1994

> In a journal situation in which both students and teachers write, responding to each other's entries—appropriate questions and reactions of the teacher gradually move the student to structure and amplify statements. This, in turn, makes them more understandable to a less personal audience. Hillerich, 1985

> In an age when children are vulnerable, the student writer can communicate problems to nurturing teachers. Clark, 1987

One of my scariest experiences was . . .
One of the things I most love to do on Saturday is . . .
If I could have a wish come true it would be . . . because . . .
If I could be an animal, I would choose . . . because . . .

The magazine *r•w•t: the magazine for reading•writing•thinking* has daily writing warm-ups in each issue that make excellent topics for journal entries. Many books on the market contain journal starter ideas. We keep a box of laminated, illustrated journal starters in the classroom so children with "writer's block" can go to the box for ideas. However, we encourage writers to choose their own topics as often as possible. One of the overriding rules with personal journals is that each student must have control over what he or she chooses to write about.

Modeling Journal Entries.   To get things started, we share some of our own everyday experiences to demonstrate how we record them as journal entries. This activity begins the interactive nature of the journal as the students listen to teachers share their lives. We stick to simple activities, everyday routines and concerns in these demonstrations so as not to overwhelm students who may think their lives are not as memorable. Students find reassurance in realizing that ordinary activities in their lives are significant material for writing. And, they enjoy hearing about the personal lives of their teachers and friends. This writing encourages the development of trust and understanding between students and teachers. One of our teachers shared the following journal entry with fourth graders as an introduction to journal writing:

> My mother called last night. She's 83 and lives by herself in Ohio. She said they had 5 inches of snow on the ground. I worry about her driving on slick and snowy roads. She rents the upstairs of her house to a young man who shoveled the walk and carried out the trash for her. But Mother is very independent and often does things she really shouldn't try. I worry about how long she can live by herself. She has no relatives in Ohio, but she has many friends there. She doesn't want to move to Texas near me because she wouldn't know anyone else.

Marisa Suhm, another experienced writing teacher, shared her journals about her son at age 3 and again at age 4 with her students.

THE SCARLET LETTER

Parents are frequently reminded of their own behaviors by the way their children act and react in certain occasions. The young ones present this untainted mirror of the, at times, absurd things we do. For example, I had not realized that whenever I get bills or junk mail, I react in a strong, negative way, and that my disgust is evident and vocal as if I were arguing with the sender. Morgan—my 3-year-old—was perfectly aware, however.

Last week, when we went to the post office, I let Morgan—as usual—pick up the correspondence. This time in anticipation of my reaction, he said as he was handing me the mail:

"Mommy, here . . . talk to the letter!" (Suhm, 1994)

EVERY SPILL HAS A SILVER LINING

Morgan, my four-year-old son, has a wonderful knack for seeing the positive side of life. In the past few months he has also developed a knack for knocking cups down, and spilling liquids all over. We have discussed this at length, and lately, I have been loosing my temper at his spilling episodes.

Today, while having his lunch—a sandwich and a drink, he again spilled a blood red Kool Aid all over my university papers. . . I had had just about enough. I screamed at him: "Morgan! You spilled the drink again!"

Morgan replied in a calm and sweet voice: "Mommy, but I din't spill the sanwich."

How could I be mad after that? (Suhm, 1995)

Writing provides a venue for young readers' reflections about their reading, reflections that help them clarify and deepen their understandings of what they have read. Dahl and Farnan, 1998

Literature as a Springboard. We often have great success introducing journals by reading some of Marisa Moss's children's books *Amelia's Notebook, Amelia Writes Again,* and *Amelia Takes a Trip.* Each book is designed as handwritten pages from a personal journal. Moss writes from the eyes of a child who keeps a personal journal by recording the mundane and whimsical interests of a saucy 10-year-old. Students quickly identify with Amelia who deals with such issues as moving to a new town, her annoying sister, tentative new friendships, and throwing sticky marshmallows on the ceiling. The books illustrate how ordinary children's lives are full of topics for writing and how writing about those topics fosters growth in understanding and relationships. Perhaps most important of all, the books convey the sheer joy in keeping a personal journal.

For older students, books in the award-winning *Dear America* series by Scholastic Books are powerful motivators for journal writing. These books by noted authors bring America's history alive through diary entries of characters who lived during various times in our nation's past. *The Journal of James Edmond Pease: A Civil War Union Solder* by Jim Murphy; *Across the Wide and Lonesome Prairie: The Oregon Trail Diary of Hattie Campbell* by Kristiana Gregory; and *I Thought My Soul Would Rise and Fly, The Diary of Patsy, a Freed Girl* by Joyce Hansen are but a few in the series. After reading the diary entries, students see how the seemingly small events of daily lives have value and meaning. They see that their own daily routines and activities are valid journal topics.

Early Reading and Writing Skills. Journal writing is at the heart of *interactive writing*, a research-based teaching method that immerses the youngest children in an integrated approach to reading and writing literacy (Button, Johnson, & Furgerson, 1996). After reading aloud, shared reading, guided reading, and independent reading, young children begin by composing messages and stories that they dictate to us. We use the dictated ideas as the basis for teaching writing skills such as right-left orientation, letter formations, conventions, sound/letter connections, and how words work. In writers' workshop, we guide students in their early attempts at using print to communicate ideas. Students then apply their learning to independent writing activities in self-selected topics—that is, to their own journal entries.

Illustrating Ideas. For very young children, illustrations are an integral part of the journal activity. Drawing helps children determine what they want to say and spurs ideas for writing. Most young children want to share their illustrations and journal entries. The sharing process provides mottivation for writing and encourages reading since children love to be "stars" while they read their journal entries. Figures 7–2 A, B, and C illustrate kindergarten journals.

Teaching Guidelines: Responding to Journals

Grade-Free Writing. The criteria for content and quality of journal writing remain with the writer, and, as such, personal journal entries are not evaluated or analyzed by another reader. A trusted teacher or friend may have permission to read journal entries and respond to the writer, but care should be taken to avoid comment regarding form or quality. The way teachers respond to students' journals and share with them either encourages or discourages continued efforts. A major factor in the relationship is trust. Students must trust their teachers to respect their privacy so they can express themselves without reservation, free from fear of being laughed at, ridiculed, or corrected for what they record. Students must know that what they write is received with respect and genuine interest by the teacher.

FIGURE 7–2A
Kindergarten
Journal

FIGURE 7–2B
Kindergarten
Journal

FIGURE 7–2C
Kindergarten
Journal

Respect for Privacy.   Students need the option of asking teachers not to read specific entries at times. One method of assuring privacy is a folded or stapled or taped page that signifies to the teacher, "Don't read this."

Importance of Response.   In the Writing Buddy groups that our university preservice teachers conduct at a local elementary school, preservice teachers and the five or six children assigned to them write extensively during journal writing time, often not wanting to stop when the time is up. Occasionally, there are children who don't think they have anything to write about; those who are stumped for ideas are given prompts or leads to help them get started. By writing with the students and responding to their journals, the preservice teachers encourage children to write during this journal time. The children are eager to have their journals returned to see how the preservice teachers have responded to them. Even in our college classes, we note the preservice writing teachers' eager anticipation to know how we, their writing professors, have responded to them.

Student entry: Every Sunday afternoon we go to Aunt Sallie's and Uncle Bur's house for dinner. All of our family come too. The kids eat at one table and the grown-ups at another one. They sit around for hours while we all go out to play "Kick the Can." Last week, my cousin Jim won every single time. I wish I could have won at least once.

Teacher response: It sounds like you have a great family. We always played "Kick the Can" when I was growing up, too.

Student entry: I want to be an astronaut when I grow up because I think it's the bravest job in the world and space is interesting. Imagine being on the moon with no gravity hopping around. Also, looking out the window of your space shuttle at earth with swirling clouds, green shapes of land, with blue sparkling water all around them. Earth looks just like a giant blueberry from space.

Teacher response: I agree that space is very interesting. I look forward to hearing about you in the future when you make your first space flight!

Brief but Genuine Comments.   We respond to the students' observations, thoughts, and ideas on a regular basis, but we don't always respond to each and every entry. We usually collect journals once a week and use the margin space to respond to a particularly interesting entry with comments or questions that indicate our genuine interest in the student and what he or she has to say. The use of sticky notes for responses is an option that preserves the integrity of the journal for the student. Students have the option of removing the teacher's sticky note responses later. Occasional brief, but genuine, responses are better than responses to every entry. A "Wow! What a great idea," "I agree with you on this point," or "I'd like to know more about your thoughts on this subject" show that you are attending to what the writer is saying. We are careful that our responses are not so long that they minimize what the student has written. The key is to keep responses brief, honest, and direct so as to build trust.

Credit.   Journals offer an excellent opportunity to give the writing efforts of all students encouragement and individualized attention. Although we never grade journals, we do give credit to those who write regularly. The credit is for the writing itself, not for the content or the correctness.

Problematic Journals.   What do we do with problematic journals? When presented with confidential or distressing information, wise judgement and professionalism are crucial. On rare occasions, we have found the need to refer extreme situations of abuse, violence, or hints of suicide to a school counselor, letting the student know we are making the referral. We also find that shocking content and gibberish usually lessen or disappear when ignored. A simple statement such as, "I don't understand what you are trying to say," is a direct and honest reaction to nonsense writing.

FIGURE 7–3
Responding to
Journals

- Keep the student's agenda and needs at the forefront of responses.
- Avoid "teacherness" by responding directly to the students' writing without a hidden educational agenda of correction or denial of the importance of the subject.
- Make responses unique to each student rather than resorting to the same general comments to all students.
- Be scrupulously honest in responses and suggestions, which may mean avoiding comments that everything will turn out fine in the end.
- Don't talk down to students. Treat journals with respect and write serious, reflective comments.
- Be prepared to share personal experiences in ways that are appropriate and helpful even if those experiences might not be part of usual classroom conversations. Students need to see teachers as persons rather than as institutional figureheads.
- Be careful to use experience, but not power, in written responses.

Adapted from: *Writing back: The teacher as respondent in interactive writing* from *Language Arts* (January, 1997). Reprinted with permission.

The weakest students are the ones who most desperately need to discover the value of their own voices in their writing. Clark, 1987

Responding will not come easily at first for most readers. After many years of 'indoctrinating' the idea that the purpose of reading is to accumulate information, few students immediately accept the fact that there is no right or wrong response. Perkins and Weissinger, 1995

Hall, Crawford, and Robinson (1997) investigated the teacher's role as a respondent to student's personal journals. Because of differences in age, power, and often class, teachers must take steps to build and maintain student trust. We use their recommended strategies, outlined in Figure 7–3.

Teaching Guidelines: Shared Journals

While personal journals with the self as the only audience are invaluable, the journal audience can expand to include the teacher and perhaps peers. The resulting interactive journal experiences build strong bonds between teacher and student and support the student's cognitive abilities.

Expanded Audience.   While journals are effective as records of personal thoughts, they can also be broadened in scope by expanding the audience beyond one's self. Much of the history of our country was recorded in journals by pioneers such as Lewis and Clark, who explored the great lands west of the Mississippi River. In their journals, they kept careful descriptions of plants and animals they had never seen before, knowing that others "back home" would read and pore over their findings. Their reactions to the Native Americans they encountered and the accounts of how they dealt with survival on their long journey were instructive and important to those who later followed similar paths. Lewis and Clark's journals were the basis for another important book in our history, Stephen E. Ambrose's (1996) *Undaunted Courage.* Many others—explorers, artists, scientists, and pioneers—throughout history have recorded their thoughts to make sense of their experiences and feelings. The journals of great personalities from all walks of life provide glimpses into their thought processes and hints to the seeds of their greatness. Christa McAuliffe, the first "teacher in space" on the ill-fated Challenger mission in 1986, won the nationwide contest for a place in the spacecraft by proposing to write a personal journal of her experiences to share with the nation's school children. The thoughts and reactions that our students and we record in journals today are just as important as our predecessors' were in their days.

Sharing experiences helped the students build bridges between their lives and the lives of others. Appelsies and Fairbanks, 1997

Teaching Guidelines: Dialectic Journals

Dialectic journals are thought provokers. Their purpose is to pose ideas, concepts, and situations for private debate. In dialectic journals, writers perform two tasks. They identify an issue or a concept, and then they respond to it. For example, preservice teachers often use the concept of "multiple intelligences in the classroom." They then briefly debate on paper what their thoughts are with regard to this concept. While these journals are personal, they are designed to elicit a reaction to or an opinion about a specific event, activity, concept, or issue. The sophistication of a dialectic journal depends on the age and maturity of the writer, the learning goal, and the mutual objectives of the teacher and the writers.

Because of the two-part nature of dialectic journals, they have a physical structure with an issue, event, or concept written in a brief sentence or a few words in a column on the left side of the page. The response to that thought is then written in a column on the right side of the page. See the sample that follows.

| The butterfly garden | The butterfly garden is right next to the cafeteria. We can see it through the big windows. A door from the cafeteria to the garden makes it easy for a class of kids to have lunch in the garden any time they want. |

As with personal journals, we use the same guidelines in responding to journal entries. In the classroom, the issue or concept for the dialectic journal entries can come from the children or the teacher, thus serving as a platform for airing ideas and reactions to classroom events, problems, or learning activities and fostering higher level thinking. For example, in our cafeteria, we had a problem with inappropriate behavior. One of the students asked that we discuss the problem in our journals. Below is an example of an entry.

| Cafeteria behavior | I really don't like eating in the cafeteria. T. R. is always playing with his food and it's disgusting. Today he sucked his Jell-O through his straw and blew it out on top of his macaroni and cheese. Everybody laughed and he thought it was funny but it made me not want to eat my lunch. |

After reading the journals, we saw a pattern of general unhappiness among the children regarding T.R.'s behavior. We then asked the students to recommend solutions to the problem.

| Solutions to cafeteria problems | I think T. R. should have to write 100 times "I will not play with my food." Or he should sit by himself for a few days. Or he should miss recess every time he plays with his food. |

Although dialectic journal entries remain personal, sometimes they are shared. When they are shared, we gain insights to the thinking processes of the students. This use of the journal carries out the democratic classroom concept from chapter 1 through dialectic journals. Students take responsibility for their classroom by identifying issues and being part of the solution through written dialogue.

Other dialectic journal topics can relate to classroom activities or lesson topics. Second graders presented a "living museum" to family and friends by dressing as famous characters from biography studies. The teacher asked the students to discuss their feelings about the museum before the event and then again after.

| The Living Museum. (before the event): | I'm scared to talk in front of anybody. My mom is coming. And my sister. I might forget my lines. Kids might make me laugh. My costume isn't ready. |

| The Living Museum. (after the event): | It was fun. My mom and sister came. People liked me. I forgot my lines sometimes. My hat fell off. People thought I was John Glenn but I was Neil Armstrong. I got tired of standing. Teacher response: *"I'm glad you enjoyed it. I thought you did a fine job."* |

Dialectic Journals in the College Setting.   Dialectic journals are a particularly effective device for the preservice teachers taking this class or for any teacher who is using this book as a reference to teaching writing. It is a way to explore reactions to ideas or concepts presented in this book or to put some of the ideas into practice. Dialectic journals via computers offer obvious benefits to college students and professors in the speed of communications and responses as well.

In our Writing Buddy program, university preservice teachers work with elementary children in a writing workshop each week. By sharing experiences, problems, and successes through a dialectic journal system, we maintain communication among cooperating classroom teachers, preservice teachers, and the university professor (Hughey, 1997). It is an ideal vehicle for preservice teachers to keep track of daily field experiences, and it serves as a forum where preservice teachers can ask for help from cooperating teachers and from the university professor. Further, it provides a mechanism for teachers and professors to monitor the problems, successes, and growth of preservice teachers.

Mentoring through Journals.   The preservice teachers, in turn, keep interactive personal journals with their elementary student writers. The journal keeping results in a multitiered mentoring situation among several groups: (1) preservice teachers and children, writing and responding to each other; (2) classroom teachers and preservice teachers, writing and responding to each other; and (3) university instructor and preservice teachers, writing and responding to each other. Everyone learns from everyone else. What's more, everyone writes often and freely. An example of a dialectic journal entries between a preservice teacher and the university professor follows.

| Brainstorming | This heuristic worked pretty well today in writing workshop with all of the children except one. J. C. really didn't want to participate. He continued to disrupt the group by changing the subject from dinosaurs to turtles. I'm not sure how to handle this problem with him if it happens again.
Instructor: Perhaps you could try giving him the important job of investigating for the group how, for example, turtles are similar to dinos OR why they survived when dinos didn't. |

Sometimes it seems as if one thing has nothing to do with another thing, but it does. The trick is to write it down. Not to figure it out. To write it down, one vision at a time. Holzer, 1994

Dialectic journals between preservice teachers and university professors also enhance one-on-one communication and provide insight as to course strengths and needs. When professors ask preservice teachers to write about certain concepts or guest speakers or field experiences, the preservice teachers have the opportunity to reflect and reaffirm their learning experiences and at the same time give feedback to the university professor regarding their progress, understandings, and growth.

Response-to-Literature Journals

Accepted practices in classroom reading instruction today include student-written responses to literature. Written responses to literature take the journal concept a step further, combining personal written response with learning outcomes. The success and popularity of this teaching method attest to the recognized role that writing plays in cognition. The parameters for setting up the routine for a literature response journal in the classroom comes from legions of practical application. While there are many adaptations of the written response to literature concept, most are characterized by the strategies in Figure 7–4.

For the students, responding provides opportunities to make themselves a part of the literature. They begin as mere observers, peering through windows of the text, and then they become members of the cast of players living in the story. Perkins and Weissinger, 1995

Shared Responses. In an elementary writing program where our preservice teachers are field-based for a semester at a time, the preservice teachers first observe, then participate in a response-to-literature journal writing activity with the children. Teachers and children together read stories after which both teachers and children write their reactions to the story, characters, or events in the story, or an experience of their own that is somehow triggered by some part of the story. Voluntarily, children and teachers share what they have written. The rest of the group gives positive feedback to the sharing writer. For example, the book *Where Butterflies Grow* by Joanne Ryder elicited from some writers an expression of wonder at the transformation from larvae to creeping caterpillar to scruffy cocoon to fragile, colorful butterfly. For others, reading the book evoked memories of chasing butterflies in grandmother's garden on a

FIGURE 7–4
Response-to-
Literature
Strategies

- After reading a book or a passage, students write personal responses to the literature in their journals. They may relate similar personal experiences or reactions as to their likes and dislikes of the piece or some memory that it triggers. They may choose to write their responses in the form of letters to teachers or peers. Teachers also write their responses to the piece to share with the class.
- Students' journal responses may be kept private, between teacher and student, or they may become the basis for discussions in literature circles where students share their responses.
- Teachers sometimes expect students to write thoughtful responses about such topics as author's style, characterization, predictions, and connections to their other books.
- Teachers model sample response-to-literature journal passages so that students understand the concept.
- Expectations for form, content, length, and deadlines are clearly stated to students, although free form is also often an option (such as response to a story with a poem).
- Teachers respond to students' literature journals on a regular basis and adapt their comments to meet the individual needs of each student.

sunny summer afternoon. Literary pieces give children and teachers the images and vocabulary that serve as a springboard, a stimulus, a starting place for expressing their own ideas, likes, dislikes, and other reactions.

E-mail Responses.   Sullivan (1998) established a successful interactive response to a literature journal program involving preservice teachers and fifth- and sixth-grade special needs students using computer e-mail as the medium for exchange. The computer component added interest and immediacy to the correspondences while eliminating the logistics of face-to-face meetings for the college students and the elementary students to exchange journals.

Atwell (1998) establishes literature response journals because she believes (1) that writing enhances reflection about reading and (2) that she can further extend and enrich students' reflections through teacher-student correspondence. Student growth in learning comes from Atwell's extensive, individualized responses to the students' letters.

Dialectic Responses.   Robb (1996) encourages children to use a response-to-literature journal that is similar to a dialectic personal journal. In it, the reader-writer notes a character, event, setting, or other feature of the literature in the left-hand column of the page and then records a response in terms of personal reaction, like, or dislike in the right-hand column. These responses form the basis for discussion in smaller groups or whole class sessions later. From Chicken Sunday (Polacco, 1992) one student responded to Miss Emma.

Literature response journals can help children become actively involved, engaged readers. Wollman-Bonilla and Werchadlo, 1995

While children may focus upon their feelings about particular characters or events when journaling about a fictional trade book, they may respond to the people, places, or things that form the topic of information trade books. Moss, Leone, and Dipillo, 1997

Miss Emma | She seems kind and comfortable because of the way she treats the children. I like the way her voice sounds like "slow thunder."

Letters.   Wollman-Bonilla (1989) based her literature response journal activities on the widely held belief that writing is a tool for thinking and learning. Rather than asking students to write answers to her predetermined questions, she moved control of the writing to the students by asking them to write letters to her about their reading. The following adapted list of suggestions that she and her students developed to guide journal responses can be used in some form in most classrooms.

Because it encourages personal engagement in reading, journal writing helps children refine their understanding of texts and their control of the reading process. Wollman-Bonilla, 1989

- Focus on ideas rather than neatness or spelling.
- Include such ideas as likes, dislikes, feelings, predictions, comments about how you read, character qualities, connections to other stories, and questions about the book.
- Refer to the text as you write.
- Don't retell the plot, but rather express personal reactions to the book. (Adapted from Wollman-Bonilla, 1989)

Like Atwell, Wollman-Bonilla responds to student letters individually, thereby taking advantage of the unique opportunity to assess and meet the needs of each student at his or her current level of understanding.

Children's written responses also served as a valuable springboard for discussion, which further revealed their text comprehension and thinking. Wollman-Bonilla and Werchadlo, 1995

Even first graders found success with literature response journals in a study by Wollman-Bonilla and Werchadlo (1995). The researchers began by reading aloud to children and modeling written responses for the whole class. Then they moved on to ask students to write and illustrate personal responses to the read-aloud selections. Later, they asked students to write personal responses to books they had read individually. The authors were struck by the interdependence of reading, writing, discussion, and thinking; consequently, they suggest that teachers include oral discussion as an integral component of the literature response routine.

Second-grader Shannon responds to her favorite book:

Poinsettia and the Firefighters is my favorite story! I liked the story so much because interesting words are in the story and it has good illustrations. I also like the colors. My mom and I love this story so much my mom bought me the book. Now I read the book every night and day.

Eighth grader Michelle responds to Edgar Allan Poe's *The Pit and the Pendulum:*

The character used good judgement, like when he realized that he had doubled the dimensions of the dungeon. He was also very astute when he rubbed the ropes with the meat smell. When the pendulum is slowly falling, you wonder if he'll die

Poinsettia and the Firefighters is my favorite story! I like the story so much because interesting words are in the story and it has good illustrations I also like the colors. My Mom and I love this story so much my mom brought me the book. Now I read the book every night and day. My sister got her book of Poinsettia and the firefighters for her birthday.

(and have Poe let this be a dark tragedy) or if he'll escape the blade and win freedom. The suspense was also very intense when the walls started closing in on him, and he was pushed to the pit's point.

Additional examples appear in Figure 7–5.

FIGURE 7–5
Eighth grade reading journal entry from *The Wave* by Todd Strasser

Excerpt from book:
"All his life he had been befuddled by machinery-film projectors, cars, even the self-service pump at the local gas station drove him bananas."

Katie's personal response:
I really don't understand why Ben Ross has such a difficult time with machinery. In my opinion, I think machines are very easy to handle. I don't think it is difficult at all to pump gas into your car or load a simple film projector. Ben Ross probably has such a problem with machinery because he never took the time or patience to learn about them. It sounds like he didn't read the instructions!

Excerpt from book:
"We're supposed to be a team. We're supposed to support each other. The reason we've been so bad is because all we've been doing is fighting all the time."

Katie's personal response:
This passage in the book reminds me about what happened to my basketball team. We weren't working as a team to win. Instead, every person on the team was competing against one another about how many points they could make. This leads to fights about how one person scored more points than another, and then they said they were the best player on the team. We were acting like five separate teams instead of working as one.

Excerpt from book:
"Because ever since we've become friends all I've ever done is try to compete with you and keep up with you."

Katie's personal response:
It seems like in almost all friendships there is a follower and a leader. One makes all the decisions and the other just goes along with it. Usually, the person who is the follower will want to be better than the leader because they are somewhat jealous of them. This creates competition between them. The follower will try to do the same things as the leader and try to keep up with them because they feel like they are being left in the dust.

Teaching Guidelines: Learning Journals

One area in which writing seems particularly to have potential for promoting learning is mathematics. When students write about their problem solving, they are making their thought processes explicit—for themselves as well as their teacher. Dahl and Farnan, 1998

One of the objectives of writing is to aid learning and thinking in language arts or in other subject areas. Learning journals, or learning logs as they are also called, are very similar to literature response journals but go beyond literature to encompass math, science, art, music, physical education, history, and any other discipline. The learning journal is not meant to replace, but rather to enhance, the various traditional methods of developing language and learning: reading books; writing papers, reports, or letters; carrying on class discussions; and being tested. It is a place to react, to question, to analyze, to organize, to synthesize—in short, it is a place to think. Hillerich (1985) notes that writing in content areas increases learning by helping students organize thinking and focus on important information. Such writing ultimately aids in developing and retaining understanding over a long period of time.

Teaching Strategies: Learning Journals

Summary Journals.   A writer-based summary, contrary to a reader-based summary, is written to help the writer understand a concept, a new idea, or a part of a text. When students use this kind of summarization in a learning journal, teachers can monitor comprehension or ensure understanding of content in any number of subjects. Anderson and Hidi (1988/89) note that "by following several simple precepts, teachers can help their students learn to select important ideas and condense text" (p. 26). When summarizing and reacting to text, students should first use reading material that they readily understand, with the text available. Later they can move away from dependence on the text and summarize and react from memory to what they have learned in a given area. Of great importance for journal writers in this area is identifying what is important and relating it to their own lives. They also learn to question what is not clear.

Dialectic Journals.   Moss, Leone, and Dipillo (1997) describe how young children can combine illustrations with their written responses to informational texts. Older students benefit from writing responses in a narrative form similar to a personal journal or in a two-column format much like the dialectic journals described above. The teacher or the student can determine topics or questions to be noted on the left column, and the right column is reserved for students' responses to that particular issue. Such responses solidify learning and let the teacher note student progress in understanding.

Response Journals.   Hillerich (1985) recommends using the last part of each content area lesson for students to write responses in learning journals. Whether a daily or a weekly routine is established for writing in response journals, growth in writing and understanding of the subject matter comes with practice. After students have practice with some of the suggestions in Figure 7–6, ask students to select their own ideas for response. This self-selection gives students a feeling of independence and control that results in greater motivation to respond thoughtfully. Some of the ideas that we have used to help students get started with their learning journals include those listed in Figure 7–6. Figure 7–7 includes examples from learning journals.

FIGURE 7–6
Strategies for
Learning Journals

- What did you learn during today's (music, social studies) class? Write the main ideas.
- Select an idea, a word, a phrase, or an experience from class and tell about it. Include your thoughts on why you think you chose this particular issue.
- Record your feelings about the subject. Do you like it? Why or why not?
- Describe in detail an activity from class (perhaps an experiment, hands-on activity, role-play, math manipulatives).
- Explain why you think your teacher chose this lesson (or set of lessons) for the class.
- How does what you learned in this class relate to your everyday life?
- Write about things or concepts that you didn't understand. What questions do you still have?
- What have you learned that you would like to find out more about?
- What questions do you have about what you have learned? Are you missing some information?
- What would you like to learn next in this subject?
- Compare what you have learned in this subject to something that you have learned in another one.
- Compare this subject to another subject.
- Explain how you would teach this subject.

FIGURE 7–7A
Sample Learning Journal

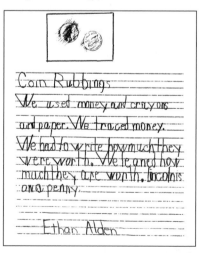

Coin Rubbings
We used money and crayons
and paper. We traced money.
We had to write how much they
were worth. We learned how
much they are worth. Lincolns
and a penny.

Ethan Alden

FIGURE 7–7B
Sample Learning Journal

my Favorite part of Science
In Second grade was when
We Studied aBout Weather
We Learnd aBoutH Clouds,
The names of The Clouds are
Cumulus, nimBus, STratos, and
Cirrls, When We Learnd Things
We Sang Weather Songs,

FIGURE 7–7C
Sample Learning Journal

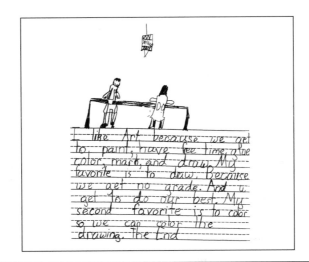

... like Art because we get
to paint, have free time, glue
color, mach, and draw. My
favorite is to draw. Because
we get no grade. And u
get to do our best. My
second favorite is to color
so we can color the
drawing. The End

FIGURE 7–7D
Sample Learning
Journal

Math

At Rock Prairie we did lots of problem solving. There were steps of how to solve it.

First, we would read and highlight the question. Our teacher, Mrs. Barker said that "if you read the questions first, you will have a clear idea of what it wants to do. The question usually gives you a clue of what operation you should use.

Now, read the problem. It contains information that allows you to solve it. It is a good idea to underline important information that you will need to solve the problem.

Last, find the key words in the question and pick the numbers you need from the story. Decide which operation you should use. Then work the problem. It might be helpful to work the problem on a seperate sheet of paper. Then you won't miss the problem easily.

These were the steps for problem solving. Some people think it's hard for them while other people think it's easy.

Parent-School Journals.   Parents can join the learning journal concept by participating in a journal activity with the teacher and the child. Joyce, et. al. (1997) describe a school where teachers and parents routinely share thoughts about children's progress in reading and writing. The parents write about what their children have read and their reactions to the books, and the teacher writes back about what is happening in the classroom.

Personal Narrative

Circles of Writing

It is often through my journal that I return to my other writing. It prepares me, warms up my fingers, and my words.
Holzer, 1994

Personal journal writing can be a means of validating each child, of saying to each child that what goes on in your life is important, that what you think and feel is relevant, and that everyday events are the things writers write about. Routman, 1994

At the center of the ever-widening concentric circles of writing, journals serve as the bridge to the more structured form of personal narrative. Rather than writing personal actions and reactions in an unstructured format without any seeming purpose as we often do in journals, now we move into the next concentric circle (Figure 7–8). In this circle students can use some of the raw material they have generated in their journals to write with form and the intent to communicate a specific message to someone else. We mentioned in chapter 6 that many children like to write about what they know best—themselves. Therefore, to generate enthusiasm for writing, we encourage children to employ their own experiences and perceptions in their writing.

Developmental Stages.   Early elementary school students enjoy creating personal autobiographies or memoirs. Kindergartners and first graders can illustrate significant events in their lives and then write or dictate sentences that tell about the events. Second, third, and fourth graders enjoy using story paper with lines at the bottom and space for illustrations at the top to write about some topics, using a new page for each topic. By the third or fourth grade, writers have grappled with problems, joys, disappointments, and surprises. By middle school, most have had a wide variety of experiences. Personal narrative takes the raw material of journals and other sources and prepares it for a broader

FIGURE 7–8
Concentric Circles in Expressive Writing

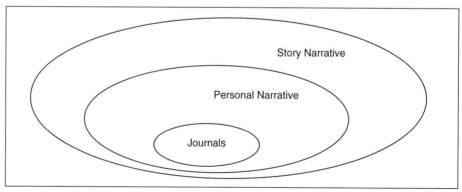

audience. When children realize that we believe their experiences and thoughts have value, they gain confidence in using them. Franza (1983) tells his students to write from experience, trusting your sensory data and having confidence in what you really know.

Teaching Guidelines: Personal Narrative

Essential Elements.　In personal narrative, we help students develop audience awareness, recognize intent, and understand form and structure. Many of these elements apply equally to literary writing and are discussed in detail in chapter 8.

Children must learn that in written language, unlike oral dialogue, they have to anticipate audience needs and independently elaborate on their ideas sufficiently to communicate clearly. Wollman-Bonilla and Werchadlo, 1995

Audience awareness.　Audience awareness requires students to consider the readers of their work. Will the audience be teachers, friends, classmates, family, or community? At this point in the writing workshop, the audience is close to the writer—peers, teacher, and family. Our students learn to ask, "What does the audience already know about me or what I have to say? What will they be interested in? How much detail and description do I need to use so they will understand my story?"

Intent.　Personal narrative is written to make a point, express a feeling or belief, describe the importance of an event or situation, or to help others understand who we are or why we act and feel as we do. We help students determine the intent of their writing and explore ways to communicate that intent. Students may ask, "Do I want my audience to understand what happened, or do I want them to be entertained and laugh?"

Form and Structure.　Like all prose in the English language, a personal narrative is organized with a beginning, a middle, and an end. We help students write clear introductions or lead-ins to their narratives, followed by a logical sequence of events or ideas. They work on conclusions that bring closure to the pertinent ideas for the reader.

Students then embellish with details—the who, what, when, where, why, and how—using the raw material from their journals as a springboard. Richness of description with adjectives, adverbs, verbs, similes, metaphors, alliteration, and onomatopoeia rounds out the expression. We show students how to include color, size, shape, texture, sound, smell, and taste along with comparison and contrast to "show" rather than tell the story.

Teaching Strategies: Personal Narrative

Several strategies, or heuristics, that have worked well for our students in writing about their lives include life graphs, memoirs, and autobiographical feature stories.

We can celebrate and validate home culture and family concerns and aspirations. McCaleb, 1994

Life Graphs.　In a nationwide project called "Write for Your Life," university faculty members and classroom teachers collaborated to help middle school children construct life narratives, generate questions about their narratives, and conduct investigations to learn about their experiences (Appelsies and Fairbanks, 1997). In this project, students made life graphs, visual representations of important events in their lives. A sample life graph is depicted in Figure 7–9.

Identity Boxes.　Next, students chose an event from the graph to expand into a narrative, developing the details and background of the event to share with peers. They simultaneously

FIGURE 7–9
Life Graph

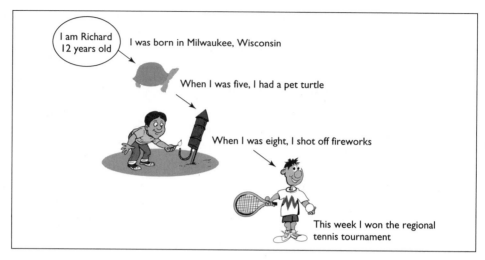

FIGURE 7–10
Identity Box

Memoir is how writers look for the past and make sense of it. We figure out who we are, who we have become, and what it means to us and to the lives of others: a memoir puts the events of life in perspective for the writer and for those who read it. Atwell, 1998

developed "identity boxes" (see Figure 7–10) of objects, poems, pictures, and illustrations from their lives, and then conducted research on relevant questions related to their personal experiences.

Topics ranged from drug abuse and gangs to divorce and illnesses. Because the topics were self-selected and deeply personal in nature, student interest and motivation for the project was strong.

Memoirs.   The term *memoir* appropriately describes these autobiographical writings. Memoirs take the everyday occurrences of personal journals and find meaning from them through thoughtful reflection. Roorbach (1998) defines memoirs as "a true story, a work of narrative built directly from the memory of the writer" (p. 9). He believes that memoirs need not focus on accurate history, but rather on the writer's expression of that history. Roorbach suggests the following characteristics of quality memoirs:

- Use the first person "I."
- Create vivid scenes that show the setting of the memoir.
- Develop complete, believable characters.
- Create action that the reader can "see" happening.
- Create details that support the topic even if they were not part of the original memory.
- Use realistic dialogue if it helps support the characters and the memory.

Memoir recognizes and explores moments on the way to growing up and becoming oneself, the good moments and the bad ones. Atwell, 1998

We encourage students, regardless of their age, to be "memoirists" by writing extensively about events from their lives, embellishing the actual facts with their feelings, reactions, reflections, emotions, changes, and lessons learned from the experience.

Autobiographical Feature Articles.   At an inner-city middle school where we conduct writer workshops, our students read from their favorite magazines about people who are being featured for something they have accomplished. We discuss the kind of information that is included in each of the articles. Usually, the features include some family history, school background, personal preferences, accomplishments, and future plans or dreams. The students then write their own autobiographies as if they were being interviewed for and featured in an article for their favorite magazines. Their pictures are scanned and placed on a facsimile of the magazine's cover. Again we model the kinds of information that such an article would contain by mapping on the blackboard our own histories for the workshop writers. We interview each other to stimulate answers to questions such as "When and where were you born? What is your family like and where are you in the family order? Where do you go to school? What are your favorite activities? What do you consider yourself good at or well known for? What are your future hopes and dreams?" These autobiographies also include personal relationships, character development (even for real people), time, experiences, and events.

Because autobiographical stories derive their meaning from both the individual and the social group, students can connect their cultural backgrounds, their own individual ideas and values, and those of the mainstream society. Allison, 1995

Writers use autobiographical mapping (see Figure 7–11) to capture their ideas, draft their personal narratives, read for each other to ask further questions in order to identify missing information, and then revise for publication in the magazine of their choice. Autobiographies of the class are compiled in an anthology for all the workshop writers to read.

FIGURE 7–11
Autobiographical
Mapping

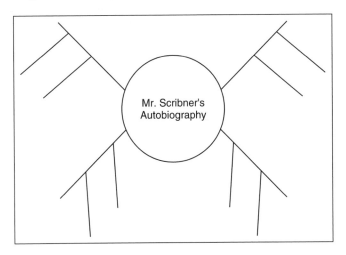

Mr. Scribner's
Autobiography

As an introduction to writing about life with younger students, Ross (1994) also used memory boxes similar to those in the "Write for your Life" project along with Mem Fox's book *Wilfred Gordon McDonald Partridge*. She felt that the personal objects spurred students to write more vividly and expressively. Personal journals become excellent resources for topics for these autobiographies. The illustrations become an integral part of the writing process by helping students clarify the important aspects of their memories and developing sufficient details to communicate the events. The resulting booklets become treasures for both the students and their families.

Darien's autobiographical entry touches the heart:

It was a Friday afternoon after school when I fell asleep right in the middle of my piano lessons. My mom and dad took me to the doctor. My doctor said I was very ill. She told us to go to the hospital to see what was wrong. We rushed to the hospital and the doctors said that I had liver cancer. Two days later they removed $\frac{3}{4}$ of my liver. They had to give me chemo so that I wouldn't have any more cancer in my body. I spent my 8th birthday in the hospital. My hair fell out little by little. Being bald was hard for me because whenever I walked up to a kid I didn't know they would tease me because I looked like a bald boy with earrings.

Stacey remembers getting her cat:

My dad, my mom, my sister Lauren and I were singing songs in my dad's truck. We were coming up on the barn when we heard a faint meow. My sister yelled, "Stop!" My dad pressed on the brakes and the truck lurched to a stop. My sister jumped out. She pointed to a sad, helpless skinny kitten. "Can we keep her?" my sister yelled. My dad answered, "No!" in a very harsh tone and my sister started crying. My dad picked up my sister and they climbed in the truck. My mom slipped a sandwich to the starving cat. And tears fell down my cheek as we drove away. We came back after fishing and the cat was still there. We begged and begged to our dad to let us keep her and finally he said, "Yes." We took her home and now we have had her for six years. She is now a sweet, loving pet for us all.

Alex remembers a humorous incident:

When I was about 8 years old I was at my grandparents' farm and I had to use the restroom. I went behind the barn and I saw him, the huge bull. I was afraid but not enough to keep me from doing my business. I was snapping up my jeans when I saw him beginning to run. I ran and tripped. He was right behind me. The gate was about 20 posts down the fence and the bull around 10. I thought I saw a piece of wire about 2 feet off the ground. I started towards it. I tumbled down and rolled off to the side right under the fence. Ha, ha, ha I heard everybody laugh. I didn't think it was one bit funny to get chased by an ill-tempered bull. The next time I used the bathroom I picked a better place.

When parents share childhood memories with their own children, they are creating the possibility for increased closeness in the relationship. McCaleb, 1994

Many students have personal histories that are strong impediments to learning, emotional health, and maturity. . . . The great moments for teachers of writing come when students turn personal tragedy into triumphant stories that enlighten the mind and lift the spirit. Clark, 1987

Writing as a way of defining self can be supported through personal narrative and through correspondence with people outside the classroom. Dahl and Farnan, 1998

Family Narratives. We have also had great success using family narrative approaches from the following authors. Different from the other personal narratives, the family narratives require interaction and participation by other family members in some way.

Childhood memories. Buchoff (1995) carries the concept of life stories to include the students' families. She begins by reading family stories in children's literature such as *Knots on a Counting Rope* by Bill Martin and John Archambault, *Grandfather's Journey* by Allen Say, *Skylark* by Patricia MacLachlan, and *My Great Aunt Arizona* by Gloria Houston. Students interview parents or other relatives with specific questions designed to elicit tales of times past and then translate those interviews into family stories. Kyle (1996) has students think back on their own childhood memories, both pleasant and unpleasant. In the classroom, they share their memories and categorize them. Then each student chooses a childhood memory to write about. They explore story angles to find the technique that works best with the particular memory that each chooses to write about.

As students develop their story lines, they work together in pairs, triads, or foursomes and review their ideas for sufficiency of detail, believability of character, and readability. Then they give each other suggestions for improvement. When final drafts are finished, the stories are sent to be read to a lower grade levels at a local school.

Parent-Child Collaboration. McCaleb (1994), too, uses the theme "Telling Our Stories." She uses the child's family as a resource in helping to build educational bridges between home and school, especially for at-risk, bilingual, or English-as-a-second-language children. Students, parents, and teacher all work together to build a community of learners by sharing family history and experiences. Themes such as "childhood friendships," "families building together," or "families as problem solvers through struggle and change," (p. 98) are established with input from parents and children. The child and his or her family then talk together about the ideas within the theme they have chosen to build their family narratives. The results, as McCaleb puts it, may become a "moment of truth for the teacher as she begins to see the necessity of building a learning community based on the reality of the student and family's life" (p. 97).

Teaching Strategies

NARRATIVE TECHNIQUES

- Focus on a *moral* or lesson to be taught.
- Write a story with specific pictures or photographs.
- Answer a question in the story.
- Write a story that will help the reader with an uncomfortable situation.

- Describe the beginning and the end of the situation first, then describe what happens in the middle.
- Create specific characters and then write around them.
- Decide how to begin and conclude.

FIGURE 7–12
Topics for Personal
Narratives

- My house
- My room
- My favorites: food, color, animal, book, sports, movie, television show
- My hobbies, collections
- Life in _____ grade (current or previous grades in school)
- What I want to be when I grow up
- Vacations
- What I look like
- Subjects in school
- A special place
- Special talents (such as music, sports)
- If I had a day to do anything I wanted, I would . . .

Adapted from Slack, Charlotte. 2000. *Foundations for writing*. San Antonio: ECS Learning Systems, Inc.

Story prompts.   While writers' journals provide an excellent source of ideas and topics for personal narratives, occasionally students need and want a little prompting. Even as we prompt, we are mindful not to encourage our students to become dependent on furnished topics for their narratives. For younger students, the topics for personal narrative can range from family to pets to friends. Slack (2000) suggests as additional topics those listed in Figure 7–12.

To help middle school and junior high school students develop topics for personal narratives, Atwell (1998) suggests the following questions:

- What are your earliest memories?
- What have you seen that you can't forget?
- What do you have strong opinions about?
- What problems need solving in your life or the world you live in?
- What might have solutions?
- What do you know about?
- What would you like to know more about?
- What are your tastes and preferences?
- What's a kind of writing you'd like to try?
- Who could you write for that you haven't yet?

Friendly Letters

Expressive Letter Writing

The Importance of Letter Writing.   Personal letters are also a form of expressive writing. A natural extension of writing life stories is to expand the audience through writing letters. Some consider letter writing a lost art. Throughout the history of our country, letter writing kept friends and relatives in touch. Because transportation was difficult, time consuming, and expensive, letters were a treasured means of communication. *The Boys' War* by Jim Murphy, a book for middle and junior high students, is based largely on the letters and diary entries of young men who fought in the Civil War. As Murphy noted, "Almost every soldier sent letters home . . ." They wrote about "the long marches, the people they met along the way, the fighting, the practical jokes they played on one another. Even the making of bread was an event worth noting." Andrew Carroll's *Letters of a Nation: A Collection of Extraordinary American Letters* is a treasure of American letters that touch the pulse of our history by allowing the reader to experience intimate feelings expressed through written correspondence. Carroll comments, "Letters are sacred. Love, rage, mundane things—it's all there. A letter is tangible; you can hold it in your hand. Some of them still have flecks of mud."

When improved transportation and the telephone connected friends and loved ones more easily than letters, fewer and fewer people picked up the pen to write. However, the intimacy of a letter, the permanence of the written word, and the joy of finding a hand-written message in the mailbox still place letter writing on a level of marked significance.

Computers in Letter Writing.   The advent of the computer ushered letter writing back into vogue by replacing the telephone with electronic messages. While email messages are typically direct and not prone to long discourse of emotional consequence, their widespread use for both pleasure and business emphasize once again the importance of effective letter writing. A sizable list of books on the market on how to write a variety of letters attests to the enduring interest in writing letters.

Models for Letter Writing.   A charming group of children's books introduce the concept of letter writing and set the stage for students to learn how to write letters of their own. Ezra Jack Keats' *A Letter to Amy* demonstrates the importance of a letter in the life of a little boy. *The Jolly Postman* and *The Jolly Pocket Postman* by Janet and Allan Ahlberg narrate the adventures of delivering mail to such characters as the three little pigs, Cinderella, and Alice in Wonderland. Real envelopes with letters inside provide beginning models of letters. In *Dear Mr. Blueberry* by Simon James, a child writes letters to Mr. Blueberry to convince him there is a whale in the back yard. Vera B. Williams' book *Stringbean's Trip to the Shining Sea* chronicles the daily adventures of a boy, his older brother, and his dog as they travel across the country to see the ocean. The book is a collection of the daily postcards that the boy writes back home to his family.

For older students, Beverly Cleary's award winning *Dear Mr. Henshaw* demonstrates how letters help a boy grow to maturity and face the pain of his parents' divorce. In *Sarah, Plain and Tall* by Patricia MacLachlan, letters play a prominent role in the budding relationship of a mail-order bride and the children of the man she will marry. *Letter from a Concentration Camp* by Yoshiko Uchida tells the viewpoint of a boy of Japanese ancestry who writes a letter about his family's imprisonment during World War II. *The Boys' War* mentioned above makes a fascinating introduction to letter writing. A list of other books related to letter writing can be found at the end of this chapter.

The United States Postal Service sponsors "Wee Deliver," a letter-writing unit for young students with extensive hands-on, practical activities to supplement letter writing experiences. The "Wee Deliver" school-wide mail delivery system heightens interest in letter writing and emphasizes the importance of correct addresses.

The Format of Social Letters.   Like other forms of prose, letter writing has a beginning, a middle and an end. The standard structure of a personal letter includes six parts: a heading, recipient's name, salutation (followed by a comma), body of the letter, closing, and signature. In the personal or social letter, the recipient's name and address may be eliminated and the recipient's name referred to only in the salutation. This letter is often handwritten, although it can be typed or written on a computer. For example,

> (optional) 1404 South 17th
> Shaw, KY 82543
> March 20, 2000

Dear Skip,

> (body of letter)

> Your friend,
> Joe Brown

Loreen Leedy's book *Messages in the Mailbox: How to Write a Letter* is an inviting, amusing book in cartoon format for students in kindergarten through grade four on how to write a variety of letters. In addition, the accepted format for business and friendly letters and envelopes is found in numerous sources, including English textbooks for all grade levels. Hundreds of trade books give instructions and hints on writing every kind of letter imaginable.

Personal Letters.   The technicalities of proper form have intrinsic meaning for students when letters relate to real world activities. Therefore, find authentic occasions to write letters. For example, at one of the elementary schools where our preservice teachers are located, the teachers and students have set up a mail delivery system for friendly letters in the classroom. Students write letters to classmates and mail them through classroom mailboxes after approval by the teacher. Teachers also encourage students to write "real" letters to relatives, friends, and former teachers. Many students, when availability of equipment permits, use the Internet to e-mail "pen pals" from other schools, states, or countries. In our own classrooms, we find frequent occasions to write letters of thanks to school personnel and volunteers. Secretaries, custodial staff, cafeteria staff, special teachers, the principal, and parent and community volunteers sincerely appreciated receiving letters of thanks. We also set aside time after holidays for students to send thank-you letters to friends and relatives who gave the writers gifts.

Following are excerpts from elementary students' letters written to Columbine High School students in Littleton, Colorado after the April, 1999 tragedy:

April 27, 1999

Dear Columbine High School Students,

I am very sad and very sorry about the shooting that happened at your school last week. It sounded like it was very scary and it looked like you had a tough time trying to get over this sad time. If you had your best friend or someone you really cared about that died, I am sorry that they died. I hope that nothing so bad like what happened will never happen to you or anyone else.

Sincerely,

Ali

April 27, 1999

Dear Students at Columbine High School,

All over the TV and newspaper we have heard reports about the shooting. We are really sorry that that happened. We know some of your friends died or were seriously wounded. It must be really hard for all of the people of your community to even imagine why those boys would do something like that.

Sincerely,

Stacey

April 27, 1999

Dear Students at Columbine High School,

I bet you had a really rough time last week. I feel really bad for those that lost friends. It's almost like losing a family member. Life is not perfect. The world is not perfect and neither are the people in it. I know a way that you could maybe help you think of the good times in your lives. Maybe you could take some photos and tape them on something you carry with you a lot. Maybe you could even make them into pins or buttons. You could tape pictures in your room or on your binder.

Sincerely,

Amanda

EMPHASIZING THE MULTIPLE INTELLIGENCES

Linguistic: Daily private writing in a journal.

Logical/mathematical: Problem-solving in a personal or learning journal.

Spatial: Draw a life graph, sequencing highlights for an autobiography.

Bodily-kinesthetic: Interview a relative about family traditions for a narrative. Create a real identity box, using objects that are important to you.

Musical: Find and play music that fits one of your journal entries or personal narratives. Keep a learning journal for chorus or choir.

Interpersonal: Share a dialectic journal about a situation at school with a classmate. Share a response-to-literature journal with your group.

Intrapersonal: Write a journal entry to fold over and keep just for yourself.

Naturalist: Find the best outdoor spot to observe nature and write a science learning journal.

SUMMARY

Expressive writing fosters cognition through putting writers in touch with their feelings, goals, and reflections about themselves and life around them. It gives them opportunities for personal problem-solving and a look at consequences and alternatives.

Journals are one of the primary outlets for expressive writing. They provide writers with a multitude of benefits beginning with a daily routine of recording thoughts and feelings, experiences, and observations. They give writers a personal sounding board and a place to incubate ideas. Journals are a safe place to start writing, without grades but with supportive and interested comments from the teacher. In addition, journals are a testing ground for topics, and students are encouraged to make topic choices for themselves. Finally, journals serve as a bridge between teacher and student, providing opportunities for mentoring and mutual trust.

Personal journals are an unstructured stroll through one's thoughts, where the primary audience is self. Teachers model and share their own journals with writers in the workshop to show them that even the smallest and most familiar images and ideas are important in journal writing. Young children illustrate their thoughts with picture journals, while older writers use a variety of journal formats. What students write and how they write is not so important as the fact that they develop the writing habit. When writers need occasional prompting, teachers assist them by using literature as a springboard or by suggesting journal prompts. Teachers respond daily, weekly, or biweekly to writers' journals, depending on the size of their classes. Responses are not corrective; they are brief but genuine comments.

Shared journals are for an expanded audience, usually including the writer's peers, teacher, or family. Writers read literature to discover how other writers' journals are often shared with a wider audience through published works. Dialectic journals help students identify concepts and issues, the value of which they debate with themselves in writing. When these journals are shared, they become vehicles for mentoring between teacher and students and for understanding between peers. Response-to-literature is another journal, frequently shared with teacher and peers, which helps students develop higher thinking skills through reading and analyzing ideas and concepts. Such responses often take the form of dialectic journals, e-mails, and letters.

Learning journals aid learning and thinking across the curriculum. These journals encourage writers to question, analyze, organize, and synthesize information in the content areas. Summary journals help writers learn to condense information to its essence, while parent-school journals serve to open lines of communication between home and school.

Personal narratives take the raw materials of journals to a wider audience. Now writers consider how they intend to present information about themselves to that audience. With personal narrative, children add form and structure to their writing, learning how to organize information and expand it with description and detail. They think about beginning and endings. A number of strategies such as life graphs, identity boxes, and autobiographical mapping help writers develop and organize their material for narrative.

Family narratives expand the idea of personal narratives to include writers' childhood memories of others who influenced or affected them. In many cases, family narratives create collaborative writing efforts that involve students and parents.

Theory into Practice

1. Keep a personal journal for a week or a month. Each day record your thoughts about your life experiences.

2. Keep a dialectic journal of the concepts taught in this course. Ask your instructor about questions that come to mind.

3. Consider Holzer's quotation, "They want to create, but they know nothing of their own creative process. Journal writing can provide fine insights into that process." Do you agree with this quotation? Why or why not?

4. Develop a buddy journal with a child. Encourage the child to reflect on his/her own experiences; practice responding using the suggestions from this chapter.

5. Read one of Marissa Moss's books about Amelia. Create a children's book from your own experiences, using some of the same design techniques.

6. Read a book from the Scholastic's *Dear America* series. If possible, select a title that relates to a classroom unit of study. Write a review of the book and suggest how it could be used to stimulate interest in keeping a journal.

7. Keep a response-to-literature journal while reading a book from the *Dear America* series.

8. Select a topic of interest or concern from this course. Create a dialectic journal to respond to the issue. Share responses with classmates.

9. Write summaries of sections from this textbook. Use the writer-based summary technique described in this chapter.

10. Keep a learning journal for this course by writing about the key concept for each class that most interested you.

(continued)

11. Think of a particularly memorable event and write a personal narrative about the experience. Share it with classmates.

12. Write a lesson plan, using a children's book suggested in this chapter as an introduction to writing memoirs or autobiographies.

13. Create an identity box to share with your classmates.

14. Interview family members about their earliest memories. Create a family story based on one or more of those memories. Include pictures or objects that reflect personal attributes. Share it with classmates.

15. Write friendly letters to friends or family about an event or project you are involved in at school.

CHILDREN'S LITERATURE

Ahlberg, Janet, and Allan Ahlberg. 1995. *The jolly pocket postman*. Boston: Little, Brown and Company.

Ahlberg, Janet, and Allan Ahlberg. 1986. *The jolly postman or other people's letters*. Boston: Little, Brown and Company.

Bond, Felicia. 1984. *Poinsettia and the firefighters*. New York: HarperCollins.

Houston, Gloria. 1992. *My great Aunt Arizona*. New York: HarperCollins.

James, Simon. 1991. *Dear Mr. Blueberry*. New York: Margaret K. McElderry Books.

Keats, Ezra Jack. 1968. *Letter to Amy*. New York: Harper & Row.

Leedy, Loreen. 1994. *Messages in the mailbox: How to write a letter*. New York: Holiday House.

MacLachlan, Patricia. 1985. *Sarah, plain and tall*. New York: HarperCollins.

MacLachlan, Patricia. 1994. *Skylark*. New York: HarperCollins.

Martin, Bill, and John Archambault. 1987. *Knots on a counting rope*. New York: Henry Holt.

Moss, Marissa. 1994. *Amelia's notebook*. Berkeley, CA: Tricycle Press.

Moss, Marissa. 1998. *Amelia takes a trip*. Berkeley, CA: Tricycle Press.

Moss, Marissa. 1996. *Amelia writes again*. Berkeley, CA: Tricycle Press.

Polacco, Patricia. 1992. *Chicken Sunday*. New York: Philomel Books.

Ryder, Joanne. 1996. *Where butterflies grow*. New York: Puffin Books.

Say, Allan. 1993. *Grandfather's journey*. New York: Houghton Mifflin.

Williams, Vera B. 1988. *Stringbean's trip to the shining sea*. New York: Greenwillow Books.

BOOKS FOR OLDER STUDENTS

Carroll, Andrew, ed. 1999. *Letters of a nation: A collection of extraordinary American letters*. New York: Broadway Books.

Cleary, Beverly. 1983. *Dear Mr. Henshaw*. New York: Morrow.

Frank, Anne. 1993. *Anne Frank: The diary of a young girl*. New York: Bantam Books.

Gregory, Kristiana. 1997. *Across the wide and lonesome prairie: The Oregon Trail diary of Hattie Campbell, 1847 (Dear America)*. New York: Scholastic.

Hansen, Joyce. 1997. *I thought my soul would rise and fly: The diary of Patsy, a freed girl (Dear America)*. New York: Scholastic.

Murphy, Jim. 1991. *The boys' war*. New York: Scholastic.

Murphy, Jim. 1998. *The journal of James Edmond Pease: A Civil War Union soldier (Dear America)*. New York: Scholastic.

Poe, Edgar A. 1999. *The pit and the pendulum and other stories*. New York: Viking Children's Books.

Strasser, Todd. 1999. *The wave*. New York: Econo-Clad Books.

Uchida, Yoskiko. 1990. Letter from a concentration camp, in *The big book for peace*, Ann Durrell and Marilyn Sachs (Eds.). New York: Dutton Children's Books.

BIBLIOGRAPHY

Adams, Kathleen. 1997. Journal-keeping. *Bottom Line* (July), 13.

Allison, Libby. 1995. Autobiography in multicultural classrooms: Bridging expressivism and social constructivism. *English in Texas, 26*(3), 37–41.

Ambrose, Stephen E. 1996. *Undaunted courage*. New York: A Touchstone Book.

Anderson, Valerie, and Suzanne Hidi. 1988/1989. Teaching students to summarize. *Educational Leadership* (December/January), 26–28

Appelsies, Audrey, and Colleen M. Fairbanks. 1997. Write for your life. *Educational Leadership, 54* (May), 70–72.

Atwell, Nancie. 1998. *In the middle*, 2nd ed. Portsmouth, NH: Heinemann.

Buchoff, Rita. 1995. Family stories. *Reading Teacher, 49* (November), 230–233.

Button, Kathryn, Margaret J. Johnson, and Paige Furgerson. 1996. Interactive writing in a primary classroom. *Reading Teacher, 49* (March), 446–454.

Clark, Roy Peter. 1987. *Free to write*. Portsmouth, NH: Heinemann.

Collins, Marva. 1992. *Ordinary children, extraordinary teachers*. Charlottesville, VA: Hampton Roads Publishing.

Dahl, Karin L., and Nancy Farnan. 1998. *Children's writing: Perspectives from research*. Literature Studies Series. Newark, DE: International Reading Association, and Chicago, IL: National Reading Conference.

Elias, Maurice J., Joseph E. Zins, Roger P. Weissberg, Karin S. Frey, Mark T. Greenberg, Norris M. Haynes, Rachael Kessler, Mary E. Schwab-Stone, and Timothy P. Shriver. 1997. *Promoting social and emotional learning: Guidelines for educators*. Alexandria, VA: Association for Supervision and Curriculum Development.

Farr, Marcia, and Harvey Daniels. 1986. *Language diversity and writing instruction.* Urbana, IL: National Council of Teachers of English.

Ferrara, Judith M. 1990. What I did on my summer vacation. *Writing Teacher, 6* (September), 17–22.

Franza, August. 1983. *Write as you are.* Portland, ME: J. Weston Walsh Publisher.

Hall, Nigel, Leslie Crawford, and Anne Robinson. 1997. Writing back: The teacher as a respondent in interactive writing. *Language Arts, 74* (January), 18–25.

Hillerich, Robert L. 1985. *Teaching children to write, K–8.* Englewood Cliffs, NJ: Prentice Hall.

Holzer, Burghild N. 1994. *A walk between heaven and earth: A personal journal on writing and the creative writing process.* New York: Bell Tower.

Hughey, Jane B. 1997. Creating a circle of many: Mentoring and the preservice teacher, in *Breaking the circle of one: Redefining mentorship in the lives and writings of educators,* C. A. Mullen, M. D. Cox, C. K. Boettcher, and D. S. Adoue (Eds.). New York: Peter Lang.

International Reading Association and National Association for the Education of Young Children. 1998. Learning to read and write: Developmentally appropriate practices for young children. *Reading Teacher, 52* (October), 193-196.

Joyce, Bruce, Emily Calhoun, Marcia Puckey, and David Hopkins. 1997. Inquiring and collaborating at an exemplary school. *Educational Leadership, 54* (May), 63–66.

Kyle, Kathryn. 1996. Writing a children's book based on your own childhood. *Notes Plus.* Urbana, IL: National Council of Teachers of English, (October), 4–5.

McCaleb, Sudia P. 1994. *Building communities of learners.* New York: St. Martin's Press.

Moss, Barbara, Susan Leone, and Mary Lou Dipillo. 1997. Exploring the literature of fact: Linking reading and writing through information trade books. *Language Arts, 74* (October), 418–429.

Perkins, Terry, and Lynne Weissinger. 1995. Exploring the 3 R's: Reading, 'riting, and responding. *The State of Reading: Journal of the Texas State Reading Association, 2* (Fall), 17–26.

Robb, Laura. 1996. *Whole language, whole learners.* New York: William Morrow.

Roorbach, Bill. 1998. *Writing life stories.* Cincinnati, OH: Story Press.

Ross, Kris. 1994. Writing creative memoirs. *Writing Teacher, 8* (March), 18–20.

Routman, Regie. 1994. *Invitations: Changing as teachers and learners K–12.* Portsmouth, NH: Heinemann.

Simons, George F. 1978. *Keeping your personal journal,* out-of-print.

Slack, Charlotte. 2000. *Foundations for writing.* San Antonio, TX: ECS Learning Systems.

Suhm, Marisa E. (1995). Unpublished journal.

Sullivan, Jane. 1998. The electronic journal: Combining literacy and technology. *Reading Teacher 52* (September), 90–93.

Wilcox, Brad. 1999. The reading and writing connection: Basic as ABC. *Writing Teacher, 12* (May), 6.

Wollman-Bonilla, Julie E. 1989. Reading journals: Invitations to participate in literature. *Reading Teacher, 43* (November), 112–120.

Wollman-Bonilla, Julie E., and Barbara Werchadlo. 1995. Literature response journals in a first-grade classroom. *Language Arts, 72* (December), 562–570.

Woodward, Patricia. 1994. *Journal jumpstarts.* Fort Collins, CO: Cottonwood Press.

Literary Writing

There is no writing separate from life . . . each person is at
once a single novel and a thousand stories.

Johnson, 1999

Chapter Outline

Children love to tell stories. Award-winning author Marion Dane Bauer says, "Human beings are storytelling animals" (1992, p. ix). Storytelling allows children to share their creativity by relating real-life experiences or soaring to the world of make-believe. Like all other writing skills, some students have a "knack" for telling stories and need little direction in pulling together a delightful story. Writing stories is particularly enjoyable and easy for students with a strong linguistic intelligence. However, all students can learn to write effective stories by building on their strong intelligences and using organizational scaffolding strategies and elaboration techniques to create vivid images. Bauer (1992) believes, "The creation of stories involves both craft and inspiration. About 90 percent craft and 10 percent inspiration" (p. 127). As teachers, we provide the essentials of the writing craft, and the children come up with the creative inspiration.

Strategies and techniques for writing stories abound. Hundreds of books for adults and children share the how-to of writing. While it is not necessary to teach children every strategy, it is important to give young writers a variety of tools with which to begin. Tobias (1993) believes that, "What all writers have in common is a method. There's a method for each of us. . . . The writer must know how he works *and* thinks in order to discover which method works best" (p. 31). The old adage "writers learn to write by writing" is only partially true. Trial and error are sometimes valid learning experiences, but much time, frustration, and discouragement can be alleviated by teaching students some basic skills in the writing craft. As they practice and grow as writers, students learn the particular strategies and techniques suited to their ideas, and they build repertoires of skills to apply to various genres of writing. As teachers and guides, we provide opportunities for writers to discover which methods work best.

This chapter presents the craft of writing stories in two basic parts: elaboration techniques and organizational strategies. This approach follows the accepted practice in many disciplines whereby students are taught basic skills to apply to a larger project. Basketball players learn to dribble, shoot, guard, follow rules, and execute plays before they face opponents. Pianists practice scales to develop skill and technique. Writers, too, need practice with writing basics and audiences so that creativity can flow and develop more easily.

Elaborate with Description

To a writer, elaboration can mean several things. It can mean expanding ideas with description. It can also mean adding detailed information to flesh out content. To show young writers how to expand with description, we often begin with similes and metaphors.

Teaching Guidelines: Description

Similes.   Similes enchant young children and adults as well. Similes use *like* or *as* to compare and connect concepts to prior knowledge and evoke powerful images for the reader's understanding and enjoyment.

A good writer is wasteful. He saws and shapes and cuts away, discarding wood ends, shavings, saw dust, bent nails—whatever doesn't fit and doesn't work. The writer cannot build a good strong piece of writing unless he has gathered an abundance of fine raw materials. Murray, 1968

Literary models.   Children delight in the images conjured up by similes such as those in Audrey Wood's *Quick as a Cricket*. Wood writes, "I'm as sad as a basset, I'm as happy as a lark, I'm as nice as a bunny, I'm as mean as a shark." In *Apple Tree,* Peter Parnall writes, "Just rotten stumps remain, looking like skeletons against the sky." In *Poinsettia and Her Family,* Felicia Bond writes, "If the sun was coming in the window just right, it would spread like warm butter across the pages of her book."

For older students, in *The Outsiders,* S. E. Hinton writes, "memory comes rushing over you like a wave"; Kathryn Paterson, in *Jacob I Have Loved,* describes Rass as "lying low as a terrapin back on the faded olive water of the Chesapeake"; Madeline L'Engle's *Wrinkle in Time* evokes a "sigh almost as noisy as the wind"; and Natalie Babbitt's *Tuck Everlasting* begins as "the first week of August hangs at the top of summer . . . like the highest seat of a Ferris wheel." Norman Juster's book *A Surfeit of Similes* also serves as a reference for similes such as, "As solemn as llamas. As useless as foyers. As cautious as lawyers. Contagious as yawning. As welcome as cousins. As useless as warts."

Along with developing awareness of similes through reading, in workshop we begin to discuss how similes help the authors create scenes, pictures, moods, and feelings for the reader. Our writers begin a classroom collection of similes that they discover in their reading and begin to use them in their own writing.

Practice.   In addition, we develop a list of common similes to familiarize students with these common expressions and to further develop the concept of how to form similes. We find that student similes are typically more creative and interesting than the often trite similes common to our language. Therefore, we encourage students to write and illustrate their own creative similes. We help them get started using the strategies in the accompanying box.

Teaching Strategies

SIMILES

- Similes compare two things.
- Comparisons are made using linking words such as *like* or *as . . . as.*
- The two things being compared have something in common. For example: *The train's engine whistled like a boiling tea kettle.* Or, *the tugboat's whistle was as shrill as a peacock's scream.* The two things being compared are the sound of the whistle and the sound of the tea kettle or the sound of the peacock' scream.

- One of the items in the simile is a familiar item and the other may be unfamiliar. This is a good way for writers to give added meaning to familiar words or expressions. "His heart beat quickly" takes on new meaning when the author writes, "He was so frightened that his heart pounded like a warrior's tom-tom."

Students practice creating similes from words we provide and then from their own. Students tap their strong interests for fresh similes. For example, third graders wrote, "The computer monitor screen is as smooth as laminated paper," and "The rug looks like brown tree bark." Students study objects such as crayons or rubber bands and practice writing as many similes as they can about the objects. They consider qualities such as size, shape, texture, color, sound, smell, feel, taste, or behavior in their similes. A class of students might easily write as many as 15 similes about a simple rubber band! Together, we discuss what qualities make the similes effective and ineffective. Students often delight in illustrating the similes they use in their writing.

Metaphors.   Metaphors, like similes, also add elaboration to writing. Once our writers have practiced with similes, in the same way, we introduce metaphors as an aid to elaboration.

Teaching Strategies

METAPHORS

- Metaphors are also made up of two things that share a common characteristic.
- The difference is that metaphors *do not* use *like* and *as.*
- Instead they give the characteristic directly to the object being compared. For example:

"The whistle was a screaming peacock." Whistle and peacock share the characteristic of screaming. "The garden was a rainbow of color." Garden and rainbow share the characteristic of color.

Onomatopoeia.   Onomatopoeia further enhances descriptive elaboration by bringing actions alive in writing. It is a way of giving words writers use the actual sounds that readers would hear if they read them aloud. To learn how to use onomatopoeia, our writers practice the sounds that different people, animals, machines, and elements make. "Whoosh," the cold wind swept out of the north. The "hum" of the fan lulled her to sleep. Brittle ice "cracked" at the center of the pond.

Strong Verbs.   Sports writers are masters at using action words. Because their reports relate primarily to "win-lose" situations, they find clever ways to say the same thing again and again. Instead of writing, "National Won, Country Lost," we find headlines blazing with, "National Storms Past Country" or "National Jolts Country" or "National Blanks Country" or "National Stuns Country." Lively words that create vivid pictures for the reader dramatically increase the quality of writing.

There is a lot of rewriting, but because it takes place throughout the process—each day I go back and rewrite the previous day's work—it is difficult to tell how many rewrites I do. Lowry, 1991

If you were a writer, you wouldn't *tell* about what happened in a story. You'd think of words that *show* what is happening. You'd use words that let people see what you see. The characters in your stories wouldn't just walk. They might stomp or stamp. Nixon, 1991

Thesaurus. Most professional writers list a thesaurus as an essential tool for their work, and we teach children the skills for using a thesaurus beginning in the second grade. Several quality student thesauri are listed in the children's literature bibliography at the end of this book and are a part of any well-equipped writing workshop.

Literary models. In addition to practicing with these techniques, we read books by authors who regularly incorporate lively and interesting words in their writing such as Jane Yolen and Arnold Lobel. Verbs are particularly effective when chosen carefully to elicit the exact action needed for a sentence. For example, Beverly Allinson writes in *Effie*, " . . . the beetle flipped in fright. He spun in a dizzy circle, snapped to his feet, and scurried away." Students watch for examples of effective verbs in their reading.

Practice. By experimenting with multiple drafts of writing, students practice writing sentences that replace words such as *went* for more interesting choices such as *scurried, lumbered, sauntered, ambled, marched, pedaled, biked, skipped, raced,* or *trudged,* or the word *said* for *growled, whined, whispered, murmured, coaxed, teased, added, gasped, thundered, squeaked, roared, sputtered,* or *cackled.* In other words, our writers practice the concept of "show, don't tell." Along with a thesaurus, the Hang Ten heuristic mentioned in Chapter 6 is helpful for expanding word choices.

Adverbs. Carefully selected adverbs become another tool of effective writing. We instruct students to check the verbs in their writing and tell "how" or "when" the verb happened. For example, "The duck swam *lazily* across the pond," or "The child slept *fitfully.*"

Literary models. Returning to literature once again, we find in *A Wrinkle in Time,* Madeline L'Engle wrote, "Behind the trees, clouds scudded frantically across the sky." In *Hank the Cowdog,* John Erickson wrote, "I had waited patiently. My nose was really pounding by this time, but I didn't complain."

Practice. When we are working with adverbs, our students enjoy playing a game that is called *Tom Swifties* (see accompanying box). This word game creates an awareness of adverbs in our writers that they may not have had before.

Teaching Strategies

ADVERBS

To create a *Tom Swift,* students write a sentence that contains an adverb relating to the main idea of the sentence, for example:

"*Chocolate cake is my favorite dessert,*" Tom hinted sweetly.

"*What a party!*" Tom shouted wildly.

"*Janette is still sleeping,*" Tom whispered softly.

We often use cooperative groups based on interests or multiple intelligences to stimulate discussion and broaden ideas among beginning authors. After our writers have experimented with new possibilities for words, they examine their word choices more carefully and consider options that express exact meanings and convey precise images.

Sensory Adjectives.   Since learning depends on sensory stimuli, we help writers tap their senses so they can create vivid pictures in their writing. Children's literature abounds with imagery based on the senses.

Literary models.   Margaret Wise Brown's *The Important Book* uses sensory adjectives to describe the essential characteristics of such items as a spoon, an apple, and a daisy. David Schwartz's *The Hidden Life of the Pond* paints pictures for the senses with such descriptions as, "Colored a dull, speckly brown, the female mallard is leading her newly hatched brood of downy ducklings." He describes a tadpole "Swimming with its long flattened tail, a spring peeper tadpole used gills to breathe and a small rasplike tongue to scrape tiny plants off the rocks." Older students benefit from the vivid descriptions in Cynthia Rylant's *Missing May* when she writes, "Your mind would see some lovely person in a yellow-flowered hat snipping soft pink roses, little robins landing on her shoulders." Natalie Babbitt's *Tuck Everlasting* touches readers with descriptions such as "He was still asleep, and the melancholy creases that folded his daytime face were smoothed and slack."

Practice.   Students brainstorm words that relate to the five senses. We find that providing students—even the preservice teachers training for the classroom—with food items such as crackers, popcorn, dry cereal, and peanuts is particularly effective in eliciting descriptive sensory words. This activity is especially helpful to students with strong bodily-kinesthetic (taste, smell, or feel the items), logical/mathematical (describe patterns in the food), visual (find shapes and images in the food), and musical intelligences (drop the food on a desk, a book, or a glass to note differing sounds). For example, crackers might be described in the sensory categories listed in Figure 8–1.

For students with a strong naturalist intelligence, sets of pebbles, leaves, flowers, insects, feathers, or other items from nature are effective. A child in one of our classes sprayed a spider's web with red paint and then gently pressed the web on a white paper to create a dramatic display. Such activities motivate students to develop unique description. Collaborative groups that encourage discussion and experimentation with new words and concepts are particularly helpful for young writers. In small groups, students describe a variety of sensory objects and then share their ideas with the larger group.

FIGURE 8–1
Sensory Adjectives for Food

SIGHT	TEXTURE	SMELL	SOUND	TASTE
square, flat	bumpy, crumbly	toasty, savory	crunchy, crispy	delicious, stale

Elaborate with Detail

Teaching Strategies: Detail

Sentence Expansion. With newfound skills in writing similes, metaphors, and onomatopoeia; selecting interesting verbs and adverbs; and creating sensory adjectives, students are better prepared to write expanded sentences. A precursor to sentence combining, expanding sentences is a simple yet highly effective technique that leads students to elaborate and develop a higher level of sophistication in their writing. At first, writers tend to overdo the description, but as they gain confidence in the power of their expression, they find authentic voices.

Journalistic questions. We pose the journalistic questions—*who, what, where, when, how,* and *why*—with our students, beginning with the sentence level. We also include questions such as *how many* and *what kind.* When our students answer these questions, they find that they include more information and detail. Our younger students begin with simple sentences from their own writing such as, "The cat ran."

Sentence-Level Models. First we model expansion of a simple sentence on the blackboard. Then we help students expand their own sentences with words that more distinctly express ideas by answering the journalistic questions. Using a step-by-step process, students gradually expand their sentences and build more vivid pictures.

> The scrawny gray cat ran. (*what kind*)
> The scrawny gray cat raced. (*what*)
> The scrawny gray cat raced like lightning. (*how*)
> The scrawny gray cat raced like lightning to the barn. (*where*)
> The scrawny gray cat raced like lightning to the rickety, weathered barn. (*what kind*)
> Yesterday, the scrawny gray cat raced like lightning to the rickety, weathered barn. (*when*)
> Because it was chasing a plump, juicy field mouse, the scrawny gray cat raced like lightning to the rickety, weathered barn yesterday. (*why*)

As students practice including a wealth of information to one sentence, they also learn that sentence variety is as powerful as a sentence loaded with an abundance of information. Information on effective sentence structures and sentence variety is included in chapter 4.

Paragraph Expansion. When our older students use the journalistic questions for their stories, it is often at the paragraph level. At this level, they practice laying out the overall plan of the story by mapping out and identifying *who, what, when, where, how,* and *why* for the whole story. We encourage them to create an abundance of raw material for their stories, and then they decide what to keep and what to throw out. They map specific, detailed information such as,

---

If you were a writer, you would let ideas bounce in your brain while you watched them grow, and turned them over to see the other sides, and poked them and pushed them and pinched off parts of them, and made them go the way you wanted them to go. Nixon, 1991

Rewriting is not only polishing sentences; it is also a process of searching for new things to improve your story. Waber, 1991

I think the classroom method for helping students learn to qualify thought and elaborate sentence structures should be essentially the same method by which children spontaneously learn to do these things out of school. Moffett, 1983

Students should write about what matters to them. Just as teachers urge them to find their own voice, so too should we urge them to find their own subjects. Rubenstein, 1995

. . . plot is—or must sooner or later become—the focus of every good writer's plan. Plotting then . . . must be the first and foremost concern of the writer. Gardner, 1985

Who? Who are the characters in my story? How are they related to each other? What are they like? How do they behave?

What? What actions do the characters take? What events do they participate in? What happens to them?

When? When does the story take place? What period of time does the story cover?

Where? Where does the story take place? In what specific location(s) does the story take place? Does it move from one place to another? If so, why?

How? How do the events occur? How does the problem get solved? How does the story end?

Advice to writers: Invent stories by beginning with a situation and asking, What's next? The answer you come up with is the story you should be writing. Yolen, 1991

Why? Why was there a problem? Why did the characters act as they did? Why did specific events in the story happen in the order that they did? Why does the story end the way it does?

I may know at the beginning how I want it to end. But the whole middle part of getting there I work through as I go. MacLachlan, 1991

Inquiry.   The heuristics that work for putting ideas on paper and for revising are used throughout these chapters. One of the strategies that our students love best for developing detail in their writing is the Green Martian "inquiry" strategy suggested by Hillocks (1986). After reading an abbreviated story that contains only a main character, the barest description of what happened to him and a sentence of conclusion, our writers work in small groups to brainstorm content. An example of this strategy appears in chapter 5. Even adults have fun practicing with this technique. Even though students map out a plan for their stories, they know that as they write, the story may change and take a different direction. That's OK. Having an initial plan helps them get started and helps them elaborate with specific detail.

Organize Story Structures

. . . there is nothing negative about using a formula to understand and control the structure of your story. Such stories can be as creative (or as uncreative) as those plotted by any other method. Bauer, 1992

In every story, an organizational structure leads the reader along a recognizable path. But in every story, that structure is different so that no two stories follow the exact same path. Recognizing this variety and complexity makes teaching students how to write stories difficult. Yet, we guide our students down some of the tried and true paths that many published authors use. Tobias (1993, p. 8) says that " . . . each plot is different, but each has its roots in pattern." We share some of the patterns for storytelling that have proven successful, and thereby empower our students to organize their thoughts. Wray and Lewis (1996) suggest that these scaffolding structures are especially helpful to struggling writers who otherwise may not understand how to organize thoughts on paper. For gifted writers, the structures become a launch pad for their creative approaches. While this section suggests some common approaches to storytelling, it should not be considered an exhaustive discussion of how to write stories.

FIGURE 8–2
Story Patterns

> - Relate the events of a day as in Michele Benoit Slawson's *Apple Picking Time*.
> - Show personal relationships as in S.E. Hinton's *The Outsiders* or Judy Blume's *Tales of a Fourth Grade Nothing*.
> - Teach a moral or a lesson as in *Cinderella*.
> - Tell how something happened as in Rudyard Kipling's *Just So Stories*.
> - Create historical fiction as in Laurie Lawlor's *The Real Johnny Appleseed*.
> - Convey a series of events as in Avi's *The True Confessions of Charlotte Doyle* or Mark Twain's *The Adventures of Tom Sawyer*.
> - Relate an adventure as in Hemingway's *The Old Man and the Sea*.
> - Solve a problem as in Patricia MacLachlan's *Sarah, Plain and Tall*.

I do a lot of my writing in my head first, just thinking the story through. dePaola, 1991

Teaching Guidelines: Story Patterns

Story patterns include a wide variety of formats. They are represented in genre such as fairy tales, fables, myths, tall tales, historical stories, and more. They may be designed in some of the ways described in Figure 8–2.

Shaping ideas is a constant process for most writers. They don't have everything mapped out absolutely before they begin writing. Tobias, 1993

Since it would be impossible to cover the development of all types of storytelling here, we have chosen to present several that our students have particularly enjoyed. The best teacher for other types of storytelling is reading, reading, reading in the different genre. Our writers learn to recognize patterns in the other genre that they can use as models for their future story writing. How close the relationship between reading and writing!

Teaching Strategies: Very Young Writers

Story patterns that are most accessible to our very young writers include alphabet and counting books, predictable patterns books, and problem-solving stories.

Some of us have found that having students create a visual plan before they begin to write works particularly well. Routman, 1994

Alphabet and Counting Books. Some of the simplest story structures involve ever popular alphabet and counting books. Young children not only delight in hearing these books read to them, but they easily understand the structure and enjoy creating their own alphabet and counting books.

Literary models. Some especially attractive alphabet books for very young children include *Alligators All Around* by Maurice Sendak, *The Alphabet Tree* by Leo Lionni, *C is for Curious: An ABC of Feelings* by Woodleigh Hubbard, *The Graphic Alphabet* by David Pelletier, and *A-Zenith of Creatures* by Angie Raiff, Greg Chinlund, and Liz Raiff. Particularly good counting books for very young children include *Arthur Counts!* by Marc Tolen Brown, *Ten Little Dinosaurs* by Pattie L. Schnetzler, *Clifford Counts 1 2 3* by Norman Bridwell, *The Twelve Circus Rings* by Seymour Chwast, and *One, Two Three to the Zoo* by Eric Carle.

Alphabet and counting books are not reserved only for the very young, however. Many fine books of this genre take students to a higher level by expanding the structure to include more complex concepts and story lines. In *Fire Truck* by Peter Sis, a child's fascination with fire trucks takes him on a counting adventure when he turns into a fire truck himself. Max Grover's *The Accidental Zucchini: An Unexpected Alphabet* piques the imagination of children to create their own depictions of their everyday lives. *Miss Mabel's Table* by Deborah Chandra relates the rhyming adventures of the main character as she bustles about her daily activities while assembling ingredients for strawberry pancakes. *When You're Not Looking . . . A Storytime Counting Book* by Maggie Kneen begs children to tell their own stories about the illustrated objects. *The King's Commissioners* by Aileen Friedman weaves a counting problem into the engaging tale. *Ashanti to Zulu: African Traditions* by Margaret W. Musgrove and *Children from Australia to Zimbabwe: A Photographic Journal Around the World* by Maya Ajmera, Anna Rhesa Versola, and Marian Wright Edelman introduces charming cultural information within the context of the alphabetic pattern.

Practice.   When using alphabet and counting books in the classroom, we read and reread particularly attractive and interesting books. We discuss the authors' word choices and literary techniques on a level appropriate to the children and write some alphabet and counting pages together as a class, following the patterns presented in the books. Then students create their own alphabet and counting books. Classroom alphabet or counting books developed to complement thematic units offer unique ways to connect content through writing.

Predictable Pattern Stories.   In addition to alphabet and counting books, predictable pattern books provide a structure for young children not only to learn to read but to tell stories.

Literary models.   *Brown Bear, Brown Bear, What Do You See?* by Bill Martin, Jr., *My Friends* by Taro Gomi, *I Went Walking* by Sue Williams, and *Alexander and the Terrible, Horrible, No Good, Very Bad Day* by Judith Viorst build stories on predictable sequences and familiar themes. The "If you give a . . . " series by Laura Joffe Numeroff takes pattern books a step further by introducing cause and effect into the story line. *If You Give a Mouse a Cookie, If You Give a Moose a Muffin,* and *If You Give a Pig a Pancake* all offer charming stories that students love to use as a structure for their own writing.

Practice.   After reading these and similar books, children practice writing their own variations of the patterns. Several books for teachers include detailed lesson plans for using predictable books in language arts instruction, such as Michael F. Opitz's *Getting the Most from Predictable Books: Strategies and Activities for Teaching with More Than 75 Favorite Children's Books* (1996).

Teaching Strategies: Emergent Writers

Picture Cues.   Beginning writers and readers often rely heavily on picture cues. We often use the fascination with pictures and actual objects to stimulate interest in the written word. Each day of class, beginning writers either create or focus on a picture or an object and generate oral sentences about it. Pictures or objects can be teacher-selected and full of rich details, or they can be student-created pictures or objects from home. Whatever the visual stimulus, teacher modeling is important for success.

Picture Drafting. Fox (1996) suggests picture drafting for beginning stories. Picture drafting consists of planning a piece of writing around a set of three pictures: a central picture that illustrates the climax or something exciting in the story, a picture that happens "before," and a picture that happens "after." Then the child writes sentences about each picture. The pictures provide the organizational strategy and planning of ideas for the words and sentences that build their stories. As children progress, they expand the complexity of the story.

Write Aloud. We often use the "write aloud" strategy suggested by Routman (1994) to demonstrate how to write sentences and fully explain orally the thought processes used to decide content, word choices, letter formation, and mechanics. Students record the sentences the class generates each day. We often begin with a simple sentence each day and gradually increase the length and number of sentences. In time, students create their own stories to share with the class.

Collaborative Writing. Collaborative writing is another valuable tool for emerging writers. Pairs of students work together on a story, taking turns to write the text on paper. Although collaboration is a more time consuming activity in the classroom, it involves the writing partners in the process, in active writing, and in revision. Both students are participating with the support of a friend, thus generating confidence for later independent writing.

Teaching Strategies: Young Writers and Adolescents

Problem-Solving Stories. A structure that appeals to younger writers and their older counterparts as well is that of the problem-solving story. For younger children, this familiar story structure involves a main character who tries to solve a problem by visiting several friends or strangers during a quest.

Literary models. Among the many books organized in this manner are *Who Took the Farmer's Hat?* by Joan Nodset, *Are You My Mother?* by P. D. Eastman, and *Henny Penny* by Paul Galdone.

For adolescents, a similar pattern applies to problem-solving stories. However, in adolescent literature, the main characters may be more like the writer, may have a problem or find themselves in difficult situations, and may seek the help of a wise counselor or a friend such as in Theodore Taylor's *The Cay* or Avi's *Captain Grey*.

Practice. After reading and discussing selected books organized on this structure, students brainstorm a problem for the main character, a hero or a heroine to solve the problem, and list some characters who might offer help or solutions. Students expand their ideas with a variety of elaboration techniques.

First I do little thumbnails right on the margin of the manuscript whenever there is a picture that comes to me. I just scribble. . . . It's just a record of images that are in my head. There are things that pictures can do that words never can. Young, 1991

Illustrators: When we sit down and start throwing ideas back and forth, one inspires the other and triggers new thoughts, new directions. That process brings about a type of thinking [we] could not achieve if we were working separately. Dillon and Dillon, 1991

I like to begin my story knowing my characters. I know what they are going to do and how the story will end. I don't always know how to get from A to B, but my characters often show me. Konigsburg, 1991

Teaching Strategies: Story Development

Literary Models.   For more intricate story patterns, again we use familiar literature to guide organizational strategies. We read and analyze authors' styles. When teachers analyze literature with students, the students learn to demystify storytelling so that it becomes a manageable task. Even for older students, children's picture books are excellent models of storytelling strategies that can be applied to their own writing. We develop organizational outlines for the literature and study the various authors' techniques. We note the setting, dialogue, patterns, character development, description, plot, and action. With older students, we also work together to develop tone and mood.

The following strategies help students consider and become familiar with various aspects of storytelling. However, the order is strictly optional. At times, a character is the first component to be developed. At other times, a unique setting guides and solidifies the entire story.

Perhaps a compelling problem is the first issue to be established, and all other components develop in relation to that problem.

Establish a Problem.   A common organizational structure centers on a main character with a problem to solve. As the story progresses, the character makes several attempts to solve the problem, eventually finding a solution that works. We encourage students to use the heuristics in chapter 6 to create possible story problems. The problem must be important to the main character so there is motive for action and a reason for the story, and the character must be willing and able to work on solutions by struggling with real difficulties.

Difficulty.   Class discussion of reasonable story problems opens possibilities and eliminates difficult topics before the writing begins. Problems might involve bothersome siblings, earning money, schoolwork, making friends, doing chores, being late, broken possessions, moving to a new school, being tall (or short or freckled), or biting fingernails. Difficult topics for very young children include problems involving fights, "getting mad," being lost, or getting chased. While they may initially find these topics attractive, they typically find the problem to be shallow, with satisfactory solutions difficult to develop. Older students may more easily tackle personal or societal problems such as grades, popularity, divorce, drugs, natural disasters, or team participation.

Personal interests.   Again we encourage students to tap their stronger multiple intelligences for story problems so they can build on their interests and sustain attention through the project. For example, a student with a strong musical intelligence might develop a story about a child who wants to play in the school band but has no money for an instrument or lessons. Problems the students have experienced themselves usually make the best topics because students have the depth of knowledge, feelings, and experience to bring validity to the story.

Background.   After establishing the problem, it is essential to let the reader know the background of the problem. How long has it been a problem? How did it begin? Did it start small and grow or was it a sudden occurrence? Were there hints about the problem

---

Adolescents are passionate and plain-spoken; their emotions are raw and real, and the stories they tell about empty homes, lost love, found friendships are the stuff of good writing. Rubenstein, 1995

In *Harriet the Spy*, the character of Harriet, her relationship to her parents, and her family life were partly drawn from Louise's own childhood. Fitzhugh, 1991

I always tell would-be writers to search their own memories for a time when they experienced a strong emotion: fear, anger, joy, sorrow, guilt. How . . . did they change? There is where the story lies. Lowry, 1991

Keep an honest, un-publishable journal that you don't show to anybody, because what you write down you tend not to forget. By writing in a journal, you're keeping track of your life. And you're having a say in your own life story. L'Engle, 1991

I always scribble down ideas when I get them. I find that so many ideas come to me that if I don't write them down, they're gone. Yolen, 1991

Good stories stand or fall on good charac-ters. Every fiction writer needs to learn to create characters who will live in their readers' hearts. Bauer, 1992

One interesting se-ries of action writing is based on the idea of observing . . . someone at work. This is a good oppor-tunity for using stu-dents' own experi-ence. Willis, 1984

that the main character chose to ignore? How does the main character react to the prob-lem? How do family, friends, and perhaps teachers see the problem? What would hap-pen if the problem were not solved? What are the long-term consequences of solving or not solving the problem?

Character Development. We find that young writers typically find success with few characters in a story, letting one central character dominate the story line.

Personality traits. Character development begins by describing the personality traits and, less importantly, the appearance of the hero or heroine—unless appearance is part of the problem, of course. Our students begin a folder or journal about the main charac-ter: his or her likes and dislikes, typical routines, interests, hobbies, and relationships with family or friends. Readers want realistic characters with whom they can identify. And real characters are not always "perfect." While the main character may be usually kind and helpful around the house, she might also forget to do certain chores or have a terrible time getting up in the morning. He may be a star on the dance floor but have a hard time figuring out how experiments work in science class. Perhaps she loves to play soccer but gets furious when the coach won't put her in the game. The story problem itself may re-flect a flaw in the character that needs to be resolved. All through the story, the charac-ter's personality continues to develop through his behavior and reactions to the central problem and his attempts to solve it.

For example, in John Erickson's hilarious *Hank the Cowdog,* the main character Hank relates his first-hand opinion of himself, expounding on his many talents, intelligence, and other outstanding traits. However, the reader learns from Hank's behavior in the face of problems that he isn't too smart. He is not the dog he paints himself to be. His attempts to use fancy words only highlight his ignorance. But Hank's bravery, loyalty, and love of a good time make him a character children love.

People watching. With older students, in addition to reading, we take time out to people watch. By focusing on the specific characteristics of a variety of people, writers become keenly aware of differences in manner of speaking, walking, standing, sitting, behaving, and reacting. Sometimes taking an hour out of workshop to sit at the front of the school building, we watch people come and go. Outside of school, students may take an hour at the mall, the swimming pool, or a basketball game to people watch and take descriptive notes. During a creative writing workshop at the Gulf Coast, we spent an af-ternoon on the Strand people watching and taking notes in a search for character de-scriptions for our stories. Back in the classroom, we painted word pictures of our char-acters for each other and made decisions about what we could use for our current stories and what we might save in our writers' notebooks for a later story.

Setting. Settings, like character development, help establish the storyline.

Literary models. We carefully select books with well-developed settings to read in workshop. Many times we only read the passages that describe settings so well that we can see them or draw them from the reading. Students begin to look for settings in other books.

Think of a place you know very well and like very much. Choose one sense: seeing, hearing, feeling, or smelling. Then use it to "explore" and write a description of that special place. White, 1991

The passage from *Miss Tizzy* referred to on page 252 in this chapter is a good example of setting, as is the setting in Jane Yolen's *Owl Moon:*

> It was late one winter night, long past my bedtime, when Pa and I went owling. There was no wind. The trees stood still as giant statues. And the moon was so bright the sky seemed to shine.

We discuss the authors' strategies for developing setting and the effect the setting has on the story line. We talk about our own locations for stories and how helpful it is to use specific places and details.

Observation in real settings.   In addition to being specific about where the story is taking place, our writers—younger and older—take time to observe, talk about, and illustrate real and present spaces and places for their stories.

Effective fiction employs, in a coherent and logical manner, the elements—the strings of related moments—that make up life. Johnson, 1999

To make our settings more realistic, again we take time out to play the part of observant reporters. If writers' stories take place at school, they take workshop time to go to that spot in the school and observe and take notes about the details of the setting. With this activity, ideas for the story expand as details of the setting stimulate information for the action or events. When stories take place in other parts of the community, we encourage writers to visit the location of the story and spend some time absorbing it and noting details that they can use in their settings—from sounds and smells to sizes and textures. In the Gulf Coast creative writing workshop, our writers researched information for their stories from the history of the city of Galveston. They visited with old timers, toured old homes and the old market area, wandered through the cemetery, and sat at the edge of the water on both the Gulf and the Bay. They listened; they smelled; they noted colors and textures; they observed wind, water, birds, fish and people. In short, they experienced the settings they were going to use in their stories. Our writers' settings came to life, and they became more involved in their stories. The very activity of exploration added interest for students, and all of their multiple intelligences were brought into play. Another bonus our writers experienced was that reading and observing characters and settings helped them come up with more and more inventive, yet realistic, solutions for their story problems.

When you get an idea for a story—a pig that yearns to fly, a girl obsessed with doing cartwheels, a grumpy grandfather—write it down. Cleary, 1991

Solutions.   Before writing a story, we encourage our students to do preliminary planning that will establish the character, the setting, the problem, and various solutions to the problem. The final solution often determines how to organize the unsuccessful solutions and how to force the character to face the ultimate requirements for reaching that final solution. Interest and tension build through the story as the main character repeatedly attempts to solve the problem, only to be disappointed.

Three attempted solutions.   A story based on three attempts to solve a problem is usually a successful structure, as evidenced throughout literature. This structure also allows for sufficient treatment of the problem and solutions without overwhelming the writer with a seemingly endless plot. The first two attempts to solve the problem are futile. The third attempt, perhaps requiring extraordinary skill, effort, or a change on the part of the main character, is ultimately successful.

Again, using the cowdog Hank as an example, we find Hank faced with a major problem: who ate the hen in the henhouse? In his initial attempt to solve the problem, he ends up implicating himself as the prime suspect. In despair, he gives up and runs away to join a pack of wild coyotes. He soon discovers these coyotes are the real culprits, but he is afraid to confront them. Finally Hank finds the courage to fight off the coyotes when he comes face to face with his old sidekick Drover who reminds him of the meaning of honor and duty.

Real action.   We encourage students to require the main character to solve the problem through struggle and sacrifice using action that the reader can visualize. We caution children to avoid solving the problem by introducing magic or new characters who show up at the last minute to "save the day" or adults who come to the rescue.

Dialogue.   Dialogue is a highly effective way to enhance character development. We learn about the thoughts and relationships among characters by how they talk to each other. We learn what is important to the characters and what priorities dominate their thinking. Dialogue makes the characters seem to come alive, giving the reader an immediate connection with the story. Dialogue also plays a role in breaking up the text by interjecting voices in an otherwise descriptive narrative. (See dialogue activity in chapter 6.)

> Dialogue is the major means of developing thought and language. Moffett, 1983

Speaker identification.   While dialogue is a natural and interesting part of most stories, children often have a difficult time handling conversations successfully. Some children write conversations that dominate the story to the exclusion of action, but convey little meaning. The author knows who is talking but is unable to make it clear to readers.

Importance to the story.   Other children add unimportant dialogue that interferes with the flow of the story as in this example of a telephone conversation. Often the superfluous conversation is written in a continuous flow of sentences:

> Hello? Hi, this is Mary. How are you? Fine. How are you? Fine. Can you come play? Let me ask my mother. OK. OK. Just a minute. OK. Mom, can I go to Judy's house to play? Yes, you can go. OK, I can come. What time do you want me to come?

Models.   Teacher modeling and finding good literary examples of appropriate dialogue are perhaps the best ways to help children who are having trouble. Emphasize that dialogue should say something very important and that it should say it better than a narrative sentence would say it. Dialogue should connect directly with readers by making them feel part of the story. For example, in Patricia C. McKissack's *Mirandy and Brother Wind*, the author could have stated that Mirandy hoped to dance with the wind at the cakewalk. But the author's dialogue lets the reader jump inside Mirandy's mind and "hear" her talk: " 'Sure wish Brother Wind could be my partner at the junior cakewalk tomorrow night,' says Mirandy, her face pressed against the cool cabin window. 'Then I'd be sure to win.' " We learn a lot about Mirandy's feelings and motivations from the dialogue, and we learn it in a more personal way than simple statements could convey.

> The human world runs on conversation. . . . We chat and argue, curse and cajole; everything happens to the tune of human conversation. Willis, 1984

Illustration.   An effective strategy that our students use to develop dialogue in the workshop comes from drawings they have created, or photographs or magazine pictures that they have collected to illustrate their stories. When the illustrations include people,

FIGURE 8–3
Sample Student
Dialogue

writers can develop dialogue for these characters that fits into the story. The visual, and the action shown in the visual, help add context to the dialogue.

Introductions.   Introductions or lead-ins to stories should grab readers and throw them into the middle of the action or entice them to keep reading. Great stories are useless if readers aren't interested enough to continue past the beginning. Therefore, it pays to give considerable thought to lead-ins that keep the reader involved.

Teaching Strategies: Lead-ins

Literary models.   Lead-ins often establish the scene: the site, the time, and some action by the main character. In addition, they often embellish the scene by describing the kind of day. To model how many writers use these devices to begin their stories, we keep sets of books that illustrate effective lead-ins. Students work together in small groups to analyze the lead-ins in three or four books, charting what they find in a table like the one in Figure 8–4. For example, Beverly Cleary's book *Ramona and Her Father* begins with, " 'Ye-e-ep!' sang Ramona Quimby one warm September afternoon, as she knelt on a chair at the kitchen table to make out her Christmas list." Immediately, the reader imagines a scene that beckons further reading. Appealing to the spatial intelligence, this activity clearly sets out the four elements in this introduction.

Adolescent writers also find this approach to analyzing story leads effective when they read the first few sentences of teenager S. E. Hinton's *The Outsiders* or Madeleine L'Engle's *A Wrinkle in Time:*

> It was a dark and stormy night. In her attic bedroom Margaret Murry, wrapped in an old patchwork quilt, sat on the foot of her bed and watched the trees tossing in the frenzied lashing of the wind.

The beginning of your story has one primary job: to capture your readers' attention so they will want to go on reading. Bauer, 1992

Unless you hold them from the first page, they're going to wander away and . . . do something else. Dahl, 1991

First lines are very important. From a writer's perspective, the first lines are a window to the entire work, and they can be to the reader as well. Graves, 1989

FIGURE 8–4
Components of
Lead-ins

KIND OF DAY	TIME	SITE	ACTION
foggy, humid, breezy, balmy, hazy, rainy, stormy, cloudy, sunny, frigid, brisk	last year, last month, birthday, Christmas (or any holiday), weekend, summer	playground, back porch, restaurant, mall, vacation sites, kitchen, front yard	lumbered, sauntered, ambled, scurried, crashed, danced, hopped, biked, hiked

Adapted with permission from Slack, Charlotte. 2000. *Foundations for Writing.* ECS
Learning Systems, Inc., P.O. Box 791437, San Antonio, Texas 78279-1437.

Equally as effective are books by Jean Graighead George such as *My Side of the Mountain,* or *On the Far Side of the Mountain* in which she opens with,

> This June morning is hot and humid with a haze so dense I can barely see the huge hemlock tree in which I live. . . . I lean back in the lounging chair I constructed from bent saplings . . . and enjoy the primitive forest.

A wealth of other lead-ins can be found for students to analyze and use as models; however, it is important to choose books that illustrate these strategies well. We keep a list of those books that contain effective passages so that we are ready at the teachable moment to draw on the literature for examples.

Practice.   Slack (2000) recommends having students brainstorm lists of words for the four categories of time, kind of day, site, and action. Later, students who are stumped for a lead-in can review the lists for fresh ideas. While examples abound, Figure 8–4 lists some possible words for four categories.

Kind of day.   The kind of day writers choose usually sets the tone for their stories. Weather reports are helpful in discovering words that describe the kind of day. Students study the weather map in their particular vicinity for ranges in temperature to descriptive words. Another kind of day might be an *ordinary, exceptional,* or *lazy* one. The kind of day fits into or determines action in the story.

Time.   The timing of a story is important in setting the stage. Writers plan the action for their stories to determine the time frame. Does the story take place at one particular time of day, on one day, or over a period of time? Young writers use past time more than other time frames since they usually relate events that have already happened. While we discourage younger writers from using the future because it becomes difficult and awkward for them, we find it often works well for older writers.

Site.   We also find that a choice of site is more successful when it is a place the writer has actually experienced. Otherwise, the richness of descriptive detail, plot, and actions

Leads usually refer to the opening paragraphs of a story or book. Leads, like opening lines, set the stage and tone for the entire piece. Graves, 1989

I cannot write about a place I've never been and don't know. I am so grounded, I have to know what the land looks like, the color of the sky, in each of my stories. MacLachlan, 1991

become stilted. The more specific the site, the more vividly the writer can paint the picture. For example, *school* is a common site, while *playground, classroom, principal's office,* or *library* make better sites because they are more specific.

Action.   What is the story about? The answers to this question determine the action for each writer. Since actions often relate directly to the site, the action list may need to be generic in nature, perhaps listing what generally happens at that site or ways to move from one specific site to another. Ultimately, writers brainstorm their own action lists based on the story line they have chosen.

Young children who need help launching stories find it very helpful to review these brainstormed lists and select a word or words from each category to create their lead-ins. Even second graders can create a story beginning like this if they have a collection of ideas from which to draw: *One warm, humid day last summer, I biked to the library to find a book on flying saucers.* Writer's block often disappears when those first words make their way to the paper with the help of the categories of choices. The introduction then seems to propel the writer into the remainder of the story.

Teaching Strategies: Conclusions

Circular pattern.   While there are many ways to conclude a story, a familiar strategy in children's books is a circular pattern. The main character begins the story in a particular setting or activity, and in the conclusion, the character is back in the same place doing the same thing. For example, *Andy and the Lion* by James Daugherty begins with a trip to the library to check out a book. After a wild adventure, the book ends with Andy returning the book to the library. *Barn Dance!* by Bill Martin Jr. and John Archambault begins with a hound dog waking up to sounds from the barn. After a night of dancing in the barn with assorted farm animals, the dog returns to his bed and falls to sleep. In *Ghost-Eye Tree* by the same authors, two children begin a journey to town to buy a bucket of milk. After some scary events along the way, the story ends as they return home with the milk. In *Two of a Kind* by Beatriz Doumerc et al., a cat has just returned from a night on the prowl. As he settles down to sleep, some strangers appear with outlandish tales that comprise the plot of the story. The story ends as the cat prepares for another night on the prowl.

Repetition of theme.   Other conclusions include repetition of a theme that has run throughout the story. In *Sarah, Plain and Tall* by Patricia MacLachlan, the theme of singing and songs runs throughout the story and is the element that both begins and concludes the story.

Unanswered questions.   In Madeleine L'Engle's *A Wrinkle in Time,* however, the conclusion is open-ended, leaving the reader with a question about what was going to happen next. Jules Verne's classic *Twenty Thousand Leagues Under the Sea* also leaves us with unanswered questions, yet to be resolved.

A problem solved.   A conclusion showing that the problem is clearly solved is evident in *The Legend of the Bluebonnet* by Tomie dePaola when the drought is broken and in

FIGURE 8–5
Components of
Conclusions

> A satisfying and effective conclusion usually contains the following elements:
> - The action stops.
> - The reader knows how the character feels.
> - The character has learned some lessons.
> - The character thinks about the future or future events.
> - The problem is resolved or is skillfully left as a question for the readers to ponder.

Sylvester and the Magic Pebble by William Steig when Sylvester is restored to his natural form and reunited with his parents. Figure 8–5 sets out some of the important component of effective conclusions.

As our writers progress and mature in their storytelling, we find that they are ready for new challenges. Many have been so busy developing their story lines that they have not noticed some of the subtleties in the books they have been using as models, subtleties such as point of view, tone, and mood. Again, going to the literature with our students helps demystify the jargon of writing. Looking at how authors of different books create the effects they do makes it easier for our own writers to use the same techniques.

A writing activity from Katherine Paterson: Try to write a story from an unlikable character's point of view. Example: The Great Gilly Hopkins, written by Agnes Stokes looking at Gilly rather than Gilly looking at Agnes. Paterson, 1991

Point of View. Whose voice is going to tell the story? It most likely will be the main character. But our writers must decide: Will "I" the writer be the main character and tell the story from the first person view, or will I tell the story through a third person's eyes? Will I tell the story as the main character, or will I tell the story about Jesse as the main character.

First or third person? Bauer (1992) maintains that there are advantages and disadvantages to using either point of view. While the third person is more traditional, it presents challenges, especially to the beginning writer. It is more difficult for young writers to get inside the character and to keep from skipping around from character to character. However, Bauer points out that there are "no limits on your language in third person. . . . You don't have to make your story sound as though someone other than you is telling it" (p. 66). She strongly recommends, and we agree, that beginning writers should tell their stories through the main character, even in third person. Of course, writers will determine the point of view or voice based on the kind of stories they are writing.

Literary models. Going to the literature once again, students can focus their reading to discover how voice sounds and feels to them. In Natalie Babbitt's *Tuck Everlasting*, they get a feel for third person voice as the author introduces the main character. "And so, at dawn, that day in the first week of August, Mae Tuck woke up and lay for a while beaming at the cobwebs on the ceiling. At last, she said aloud, 'The boys'll be home tomorrow!' " In John R. Erickson's *The Further Adventures of Hank the Cowdog*, writers can get a feel for first person as Hank the Cowdog relates his story in first person. "I suppose I was dreaming about Beulah again. . . . I don't let women distract me during working hours, but sometimes I lose control when I'm asleep."

My approach to working with children and fiction is one of experimentation. "Let's try this and see what happens." Graves, 1989

The conflict can be caused by an antagonist—a rival, opponent, or sworn enemy. This person stands directly opposite to your main character. Stanek, 1994

Real-life conversation is primary discourse—spontaneous, ongoing, unpondered, and uncomposed. . . . It is generated of the moment and moves in time, governed by setting and circumstances as well as by the wills of the speakers. Moffett, 1983

When they are ready for such experimentation, we encourage our writers to try the story out in both voices to see which one is best for what they are writing.

The Antagonist.   Writers create their characters, decide what they do, and control their destinies. They create brave and fearless heroes, good and thoughtful friends, embarrassed or frightened kids, and mean and grumpy foes. A main character's personality or behavior alone can create a problem to be solved; but as writers mature, they enjoy expanding their repertoire to include more complex problems. Enter the antagonist! While younger writers are more successful developing one main character, writers in our upper elementary and middle school workshops are intrigued with creating in detail both protagonists, the good guys, and antagonists, the characters who cause the problem or tension in the story. As writers build the problems in their stories, they build the personalities of the characters on both sides of the problem. They think about what motivates each character. What is the character's family background? What are his or her experiences and how have they affected the character's behavior? What makes the protagonist the *good* person or the hero? What makes the antagonist mean and ugly? As Stanek (1994) suggests, "A worthy antagonist has to be good at her meanness" (p. 71). Writers take time to think through what motivates this character's weaknesses, jealousies, and strange behaviors. As writers develop characters, the characters, in turn, develop the story line.

Tone and Mood.   Some writers are natural writers. They are the ones for whom tone and mood automatically creep into their stories. But, like the rest of writing, these elements can be learned.

Tone.   Different from voice yet related to it, tone conveys the way writers feel about their material. Tone shows the writer's attitude toward the content of the writing. In a story, the writer may show his displeasure with the way a character in the story behaves or his delight in what another character does or says. Tone is usually communicated through the words of the characters. The tone in this brief passage from *Sarah, Plain and Tall* implies impatience toward Caleb: "Did Mama sing every day?" asked Caleb. . . . "Every single day," I told him for the second time this week. For the twentieth time this month. The hundredth time this year? And the past few years?" Verbs, adverbs, repetition, sentence structure all contribute to the tone of a story. Groups of writers who are ready to play with tone can experiment and collaborate to develop tone in their story creations.

Mood.   Mood, like tone, is a feeling that the writer develops in the story. Rather than being an attitude toward a story event or a character; however, mood is a feeling created for the reader. Writers delight in creating moods through setting, situation, or description or a combination of all of these elements. They especially delight in creating moods that are scary or suspenseful at the beginning. Using our literary resources, we analyze words that authors use to make us feel a certain way as we read. With our younger students, we read together books such as *Miss Tizzy* by Libba Moore Gray to identify the happy whimsical mood of the story through character and setting.

Miss Tizzy wore a purple hat with a white flower in it and high-top green tennis shoes. The neighbors thought her peculiar. But the children loved her. Miss Tizzy's house was pink and sat like a fat blossom in the middle of the street.

With Robert D. San Souci's *Feathertop*, we explore a mood of power and magic. "While Dickson, her cat, watched, Mother Rigby crooked her little finger. Immediately, an old broomstick flew across the room and hovered in the air in front of her." With our upper elementary or middle school writers, we sometimes use Edgar Allen Poe's *The Fall of the House of Usher* to illustrate the somber mood in the setting of the story:

> One dark autumn day, when the clouds hung low in the sky, I rode on horseback through the dreary countryside. By evening, I could see the melancholy House of Usher. With the first glimpse of that bleak and lonely building, a sense of gloom overcame me.

With each of these strategies for storytelling, we read with our writers, model, and encourage them to explore and experiment with the techniques.

Teaching Strategies: Story Structures

Our students find several of the common organizational structures from literature helpful as they develop their own ideas. We remind writers, however, that the outlines or mapping heuristics do not have to be complete in every detail before the writing begins. Like adult writers, some young writers need to have extensive plans in mind before they begin, while others use a skeleton of ideas that becomes fully developed during the writing process. Writers usually have some basic ideas in mind when they begin a story, but they let the problem, plot, and characters shape the form of the story as it progresses.

Sequence of Events. In some stories, writers need to relate an event that was extremely important to them or a series of events that culminated in one exciting episode. When this is the case, the story structure shifts slightly to allow for tension to build as the story reaches its climax. Writers plan the sequence of events and relate each one to the next until they reach a peak. The events build in importance as the story builds to its climax. It is graphically described as an upward slope of major events that culminate in the peak or climax, followed by resolution. Figure 8–6 illustrates the sequence of events in *Apple Picking Time* by Slawson.

We and the students found that taking the time to plan out the characters and story encouraged more thoughtful, better organized, and more interesting story writing. Routman, 1994

Think of a real-life story that you would like to tell your friends. Instead of talking about it, write it down. dePaola, 1991

The story mapping was an important step because it forced students to think through the main problem in the story, the main happenings, and how the story might conclude. Routman, 1994

FIGURE 8–6
Sequence of Events in
Apple Picking Time

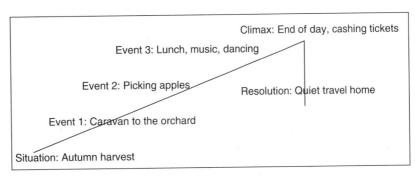

Katie's story illustrates use of the sequence of events story format.

THE BIGGEST SINK EVER
by Katie

My parents make me drink a significant amount of milk. They think it will advance my growth. I used to pour my milk down the drain. I will never do that again and here is why.

One bright and boiling morning I went downstairs to have a snack. When I got into the kitchen, the sink was growing instead of me! No Fair!! That night I poured more milk down the drain, and the next morning it looked a little bit bigger, but would my parents notice? No, they weren't very observant. That night I poured more milk down the drain. The next day it was immense! It jolted me awake. I screeched, "Mom, Dad!"

They said, "Be quiet or you will wake the dead!"

I said, "No, you've got to see this!"

When my mom saw it, she fainted and my dad yelled, "What's wrong? What happened to the sink?"

I did not want to admit what I did with my milk, so I said, "Beats me."

Then my mom came in and said, "It's time to go to school."

"Wait till I tell my teacher!" I shouted. "She won't believe it! She will think it's absurd!"

I raced to school without getting my friends. They hustled after me yelling, "Katie, your kitchen sink is monumental, and it's soaring up to the sky!"

Later I got to school and told my teacher and all the kids all of the weird news. They all went outside to see if it was true. My mom ran over the her friend's house with my pets Tipper, Misty and Kippy. Just in time, too, because the house exploded!

My teacher said, "Now you've really got something to write about!" And I did.

Problem-Solution. Figure 8–7 provides spatial organizers for students planning a problem-solving story. Because some writers find one pattern easier to use than another, we have included several styles and arrangements.

FIGURE 8–7A
Problem-Solving
Graphic Planner

BEGINNING	MIDDLE	END
Scene	Try to solve problem	Character feelings
Characters	Try to solve problem	Lesson learned
Problem	Solve problem	

CHARACTERS	SETTING	PROBLEM	COMPLICATION	RESOLUTION

FIGURE 8–7B   Graphic Organizer

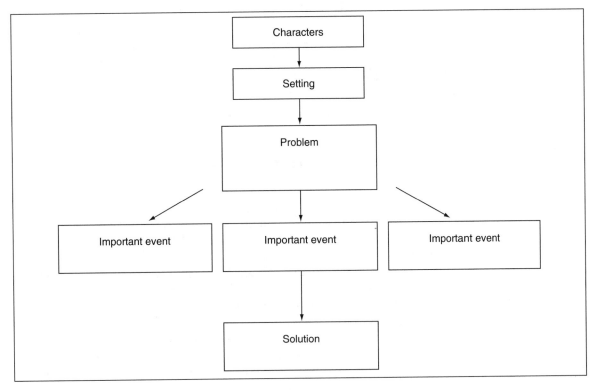

FIGURE 8–7C   Graphic Organizer

FIGURE 8–7D
Mapping Plan

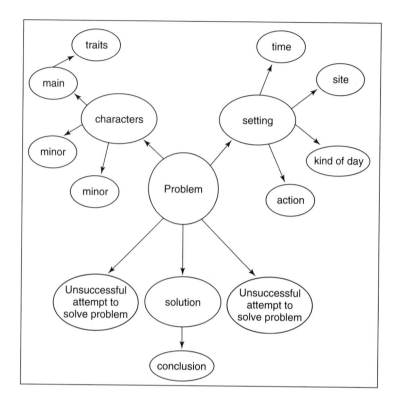

The following writing sample by Alex illustrates the problem-solving story structure.

HOMEWORK PROBLEMS
by Alex

"That's the 56th time you've forgotten!" chided John's teacher Mrs. Lotsofhomework. Before John was dismissed to go home, Mrs. Lotsofhomework called him to her desk because he had forgotten for the 56th time his science homework.

John was an intelligent, forgetful, kind and bold kid. He was as forgetful as an old man and was caring. He liked his teacher a lot, even when she got him in trouble. Because he forgot his homework so much, he hardly went out to recess.

The problem was that John kept forgetting to complete homework his teacher gave him. Every time his teacher assigned the class work, it was untouched in John's binder. The problem happened because he had such a rigid schedule. For example, he had student council at 3:10, soccer at 4:00, karate at 5:05 ... well, you get the idea.

Anyway, because John craved to solve the problem, he thought of an answer. He decided to try writing a reminder note on a small piece of paper. But, he forgot about the note after the student council meeting. The next morning, when John's mom was doing the laundry, John sat down to breakfast. That's when John's mother questioned him about the note about homework she found in his pocket.

"Oh, no!" thought John as he choked on his chocolaty cereal. As John tore through the hall to his room to check on his homework, he thought of what his teacher would say. He flung open the door and ripped his binder open. There were eight pages of math problems and each page had 90 problems. "So, there are only . . . 720 multiplication and division problems to do!" thought John groaning. He tried to finish but ended up completing only 70 problems. "Oh, man, my teacher's going to kill me!" mumbled John nervously as he walked to school. And he was right.

"That's the 57th!" signed his teacher. This idea didn't work because he forgot about the note.

John tried to solve the problem again by doing the homework at school. When he went to study hall that day, he got so distracted by watching the children playing outside that he never even wrote one letter for his oral report on toads for science. When he got home, he forgot for the 58th time that he had homework.

The next day, John sat up in bed. He thought of homework. There was no way he could finish his report in forty minutes. He jumped out of bed. As he was walking to school, he was thinking of excuses. "Mrs. Lotsofhomework, I left my note on the table but my cat ate it. No, no, Mrs. Lotsofhomework, an alien beamed up my homework and notes! Yeah, that's it!"

When John arrived at school, he told her his excuse he had composed during his walk to school. "Very funny! I am not that gullible! Now, get busy on your work!" bellowed Mrs. Lotsofhomework.

"Drat!" thought John. The problem was finally solved when John had an idea. "I could loosen up my schedule so I can have time for homework!" thought John. That day, John quit soccer and karate to make room for homework. He finished math and sighed with relief. His plan had worked.

The next day, John skipped to school not worrying about his math. Mrs. Lotsofhomework congratulated him. John felt very proud that he had finally solved his dilemma. In the future, he will probably go to recess more and get better grades on his report card.

Final Notes

If writing a story were as simple as following an outline or using a particular organizational scheme, everyone would be a published author. Clearly the intricacies, nuances, complexities, and forces that combine to create good fiction involve far more than following an outline or a set of rules. The suggestions in this chapter are merely beginning ideas of the craft and have proved successful in the classroom, particularly with young writers who need starting points. As in any writing effort in the writing workshop, writers are encouraged to share and publish their stories for all to enjoy.

EMPHASIZING THE MULTIPLE INTELLIGENCES

Linguistic: Read and discuss models for story components.

Logical/Mathematical: Brainstorm problems and solutions for stories.

Spatial: Graphically plan and illustrate stories.

Bodily-Kinesthetic: Assign characters from students' stories and dramatize for an audience.

Musical: Orally tell stories for an audience.

Interpersonal: Try out description and detail in small group sessions.

Intrapersonal: Personally observe real people for character development.

Naturalist: Observe natural settings, weather, and time of day to determine their effects on story development.

SUMMARY

Throughout time, human beings have been storytellers. Much of our culture and history is transmitted through the stories we tell. While some writers are natural storytellers, a myriad of strategies and techniques are available to help other writers learn the craft of storytelling. One of the strategies for developing the raw material for stories is elaboration through description and detail. Another is organization according to the conventions of story structures.

Elaboration with description involves helping writers learn how to use the language effectively. Writers practice with similes, metaphors, onomatopoeia, strong verbs, adverbs, and sensory adjectives. They reinforce their reading and writing skills by studying literary models and then practicing the craft through their own writing efforts.

Writers learn how to elaborate further by using detail for expansion of their ideas. They use the journalistic questions to expand at both sentence and paragraph levels. Inquiry into the characters, settings, and plots they are developing also aid elaboration.

Through reading models of a wide variety of story patterns, writers develop an appreciation for the many ways they can create story pictures in their readers' minds—from the youngest writers' accomplishments with creating their own alphabet or counting books and predictable pattern books to the older students' creation of more complex problem-solving stories. Writers collaborate and they also work individually to develop the story components of plot, character, dialogue, setting, tone, and mood. They experiment with introductions, conclusions, and story structures to find just the right combination for their stories.

Theory into Practice

1. In collaborative groups, discuss the methods for writing stories you were taught during your elementary school years. What common elements do you find? What differences?

2. Find a small object and write as many similes as possible about the object. Make them original.

3. Write a lesson plan that teaches students how to use a thesaurus.

4. In collaborative groups, develop lists of sensory adjectives for an interesting food item or object.

5. Use journalistic questions, similes, sensory adjectives, and strong verbs to expand this sentence: *The bird flew.*

6. Create an alphabet or counting book that relates to a unit of study in another subject.

7. Create a lesson plan to teach children how to write a predictable book, a fable, or a problem story.

8. Using several favorite children's books, analyze the authors' story patterns.

9. Analyze the introductions to three or four stories by listing their characteristics; then create your own introduction for a story using the four elements: time, site, kind of day, action.

10. Using a short story that you have already written, write the story again in another voice. If you used third person, now use first person and vice versa. Get feedback from your small group as to which one sounds most effective. Discuss your choice.

11. Write about one of the characters in your story so that the readers in your writing group will know what your attitude toward that character is.

12. Rewrite a scene from your story to set a mood for the story. Then write the scene again changing the words to give it a different mood.

13. Create a problem that could be the focus of a story. Give details of the problem: how it began, why it is important, how the main character feels about it, what will happen if it isn't solved, and what the long-term consequences are of solving or not solving the problem. Then create plausible solutions.

14. Create a main character for a story. Include character traits that would become evident through the story. Write some dialogue that reveals the character's traits.

15. Determine what story plans described in this chapter are most appropriate to various age groups.

CHILDREN'S LITERATURE

Ajmera, Maya, Anna R. Versole, and Marian W. Edelman. 1997. *Children from Australia to Zimbabwe.* Waltham, MA: Charlesbridge Publishing.

Allinson, Beverley. 1990. *Effie.* New York: Scholastic.

Avi. 1990. *The true confessions of Charlotte Doyle.* New York: Avon Flare Book.

———. 1993. *Captain Grey.* New York: Beech Tree Books.

Babbitt, Natalie. 1986. *Tuck everlasting.* New York: Farrar Straus & Giroux.

Blume, Judy. 1991. *Tales of a fourth grade nothing.* New York: Demco Media.

Bond, Felicia. 1981. *Poinsettia and her family.* New York: Harper Collins.

Bridwell, Norman. 1998. *Clifford counts 1 2 3.* New York: Cartwheel Books.

Brown, Marc Tolon. 1998. *Arthur counts!* New York: Random House.

Brown, Margaret Wise. 1977. *The important book.* New York: Harper Collins.

Carle, Eric. 1982. *One, two, three to the zoo.* New York: Philomel.

Chandra, Deborah. 1994. *Miss Mabel's table.* New York: Harcourt.

Chwast, Seymour. 1993. *The twelve circus rings.* New York: Harcourt Brace.

Cleary, Beverly. 1977. *Ramona and her father.* New York: Avon.

Daugherty, James. 1989. *Andy and the lion.* New York: Viking Press.

dePaola, Tomie. 1986. *The legend of the bluebonnet.* New York: G. P. Putnam's Sons.

Doumerc, Beatriz, Ricardo Alcantata, Laura M. Perez, and Kathry Corbett. 1994. *Two of a kind.* Louisville, KY: Amer Printing House for Blind.

Eastman, Phillip D. 1988. *Are you my mother?* New York: Random House.

Erickson, John R. 1988. *Hank the cowdog.* Houston: Gulf Publishing.

Friedman, Aileen. 1995. The king's commissioners. New York: Scholastic.

Galdone, Paul. 1999. *Henny penny.* Topeka, KS: Econo-clad Books.

George, Jean Craighead. 1991. *On the far side of the mountain.* New York: Puffin.

———. 1991. *My side of the mountain.* New York: Puffin.

Gomi, Taro. 1995. *My friends.* New York: Chronicle Books.

Gray, Libba Moore. 1993. *Miss Tizzy.* New York: Simon & Schuster.

Grover, Max. 1993. *The accidental zucchini: An unexpected alphabet.* San Diego, CA: Browndeer Press.

Hemingway, Ernest. 1995. *The old man and the sea.* New York: Scribner.

Hinton, S. E. 1997. *The outsiders.* New York: Puffin.

Hubbard, Woodleigh. 1995. *C is for curious: An ABC of feelings.* New York: Chronicle Books.

Juster, Norman. 1989. *A surfeit of similes.* New York: Morrow.

Kipling, Rudyard. 1990. *Just so stories.* New York: Penguin.

Kneen, Maggie. 1996. *When you're not looking: A storytime counting book.* New York: Simon & Schuster.

L'Engle, Madeleine. 1994. *A wrinkle in time.* New York: Demco Media.

Lawlor, Laurie. 1995. *The real Johnny Appleseed.* New York: Albert Whitman & Co.

Lionni, Leo. 1990. *The alphabet tree.* New York: Knopf.

MacLachlan, Patricia. 1985. *Sarah, plain and tall.* New York: HarperCollins.

Martin, Bill, Jr. 1983. *Brown bear, brown bear, what do you see?* New York: Holt, Rinehart and Winston.

Martin, Bill, Jr., and John Archambault. 1986. *Barn dance.* New York: Henry Holt.

———. 1988. *Ghost-eye tree.* New York: Henry Holt.

McKissack, Patricia C. 1988. *Mirandy and Brother Wind.* New York: Random House.

Musgrove, Margaret. 1977. *Ashanti to Zulu: African traditions.* New York: Dial Books for Young Readers.

Nixon, Joan Lowery. 1995. *If you were a writer.* Oklahoma City, OK: Aladdin Paperbacks.

Nodset, Joan. 1987. *Who took the farmer's hat?* New York: HarperCollins.

Numeroff, Laura J. 1985. *If you give a mouse a cookie.* New York: HarperCollins.

Numeroff, Laura J. 1991. *If you give a mouse a muffin.* New York: HarperCollins.

Numeroff, Laura J. 1998. *If you give a pig a pancake.* New York: HarperCollins.

Parnall, Peter. 1987. *Apple tree.* New York: Macmillan.

Paterson, Katherine. 1980. *Jacob have I loved.* New York.: HarperCollins.

Pelletier, David. 1996. *The graphic alphabet.* New York: Orchard Books.

Perrault, Charles. 1999. *Cinderella.* New York: North-South Books.

Poe, Edgar Allan. 1809–1849. *The fall of the house of Usher.* Mahwah, NJ: Troll.

Raif, Angie, Greg Chinlund, and Liz Raif. 1997. *A-zenith of creatures.* Forest Lake, MN: Bear Lake Publishing.

Rylant, Cynthia. 1992. *Missing May.* New York: Dell.

San Souci, Robert D. 1992. *Feathertop.* New York: Doubleday Books.

Schnetzler, Pattie L. 1996. *Ten little dinosaurs.* Denver: Accord Publishing.

Schwartz, David M. 1988. *The hidden life of the pond.* New York: Crown Publishers.

Sendak, Maurice. 1991. *Alligators all around: An alphabet.* New York: HarperTrophy.

Sis, Peter. 1998. *Fire truck.* New York: Greenwillow Books.

Slawson, Michele Benoit. 1998. *Apple picking time.* New York: Dragonfly.

Steig, William. 1969. *Sylvester and the magic pebble.* New York: Simon & Schuster.

Taylor, Theodore. 1995. *The cay.* New York: Camelot.

Twain, Mark. 1987. *The adventures of Tom Sawyer.* New York: Viking Press.

Verne, Jules. 1985. *Twenty thousand leagues under the sea.* New York: Bantam Books.

Viorst, Judith. 1972. *Alexander and the terrible, horrible, no good, very bad day.* New York: Atheneum.

Williams, Sue. 1996. *I went walking.* New York: Red Wagon.

Wood, Audrey. 1982. *Quick as a cricket.* Clarkston, MN: Child's Play.

BIBLIOGRAPHY

Bauer, Marion Dane. 1992. *What's your story? A young person's guide to writing fiction.* New York: Clarion Books.

Blume, Judy. 1991 In *Meet the authors and illustrators,* Vol. 1, Deborah Kovacs and James Preller (Eds.). New York: Scholastic.

Bruner, Jerome. 1966. *Learning about learning, a conference report.* Washington, D.C.: Office of Education.

Calkins, Lucy. 1986. *The art of teaching writing.* Portsmouth, NH: Heinemann.

Carle, Eric. 1991. In *Meet the authors and illustrators,* Vol. 1, Deborah Kovacs and James Preller (Eds.). New York: Scholastic.

Cleary, Beverly. 1991. In *Meet the authors and illustrators,* Vol. 1, Deborah Kovacs and James Preller (Eds.). New York: Scholastic.

Dahl, Roald. 1991. In *Meet the authors and illustrators,* Vol. 1, Deborah Kovacs and James Preller (Eds.). New York: Scholastic.

dePaola, Tomie. 1991. In *Meet the authors and illustrators,* Vol. 1, Deborah Kovacs and James Preller (Eds.). New York: Scholastic.

Dillon, Diane, and Leo Dillon. 1991. In *Meet the authors and illustrators,* Vol. 1, Deborah Kovacs and James Preller (Eds.). New York: Scholastic, Inc. 30–31.

Fitzhugh, Louise. 1991. In *Meet the authors and illustrators,* Vol. 1, Deborah Kovacs and James Preller (Eds.). New York: Scholastic.

Fox, Richard. 1996. The struggling writer: Strategies for teaching. *Reading, 30* (July), 13–19.

Gardner, John. 1985. *The art of fiction: Notes on craft for young writers.* New York: Vintage Books.

Geisel, Theodor Seuss. 1991. In *Meet the authors and illustrators,* Vol. 1, Deborah Kovacs and James Preller (Eds.). New York: Scholastic.

Graves, Donald H. 1989. *Experiment with fiction.* Portsmouth, NH: Heinemann.

Hillocks, George, Jr. 1986. *Research on written composition.* Urbana, IL: National Council of Teachers of English.

Johnson, Randy. 1999. A picture worth a thousand words. *Teacher Magazine,* (January), 56–57.

Konigsburg, E. L. 1991. In *Meet the authors and illustrators,* Vol. 1, Deborah Kovacs and James Preller (Eds.). New York: Scholastic.

L'Engle, Madeleine. 1991. In *Meet the authors and illustrators,* Vol. 1, Deborah Kovacs and James Preller (Eds.). New York: Scholastic.

Lowry, Lois. 1991. In *Meet the authors and illustrators,* Vol. 1, Deborah Kovacs and James Preller (Eds.). New York: Scholastic.

MacLachlan, Patricia. 1991. In *Meet the authors and illustrators,* Vol. 1, Deborah Kovacs and James Preller (Eds.). New York: Scholastic.

Moffett, James. 1983. *Teaching the universe of discourse.* Portsmouth, NH: Heinemann.

Murray, Donald. 1968. *A writer teaches writing: A practical method for teaching composition.* Boston: Houghton Mifflin.

Opitz, Michael. 1996. *Getting the most from predictable books: Strategies and activities for teaching with more than 75 favorite children's books.* New York: Scholastic Trade.

Paterson, Kathryn. 1991. In *Meet the authors and illustrators,* Vol. 1, Deborah Kovacs and James Preller (Eds.). New York: Scholastic.

Raphael, Taffy. 1999. Reading-writing connection. *Writing Teacher, 12* (May), 4–5.

Routman, Regie. 1994. *Invitations: Changing as teachers and learners K–12.* Portsmouth, NH: Heinemann.

Rubenstein, Suzanne. 1995. Going public. *Teacher Magazine* (February), 45–46.

Ruenzel, David. 1995. Write to the point. *Teacher Magazine* (May/June), 26–31.

Slack, Charlotte. 2000. *Foundations for writing.* San Antonio: ECS Learning Systems.

Stanek, Lou Willett. 1994. *Thinking like a writer.* New York: Random House.

Tobias, Ronald B. 1993. *Twenty master plots (and how to build them).* Cincinnati, OH: Writer's Digest Books.

Waber, Bernard. 1991. In *Meet the authors and illustrators,* Vol. 1, Deborah Kovacs and James Preller (Eds.). New York: Scholastic.

White, E. B. 1991. In *Meet the authors and illustrators,* Vol. 1, Deborah Kovacs and James Preller (Eds.). New York: Scholastic.

Wilcox, Brad. 1999. Basic as ABC. *Writing Teacher, 12* (May), 6.

Willis, Meredith Sue. 1984. *Personal fiction writing.* New York: Teachers & Writers Collaborative.

Wray, David, and Maureen Lewis. 1996. An approach to writing non-fiction. *Reading, 30* (July), 7–13.

Yolen, Jane. 1991. In *Meet the authors and illustrators,* Vol. 1, Deborah Kovacs and James Preller (Eds.). New York: Scholastic.

Young, Ed. 1991. In *Meet the authors and illustrators,* Vol. 1, Deborah Kovacs and James Preller (Eds.). New York: Scholastic.

chapter
9
Poetry

Pat-a-cake, pat-a-cake,
Baker's man.
Bake me a cake
As fast as you can.

Chapter Outline

The little poem, Pat-a-cake, pat-a cake, is often one of the earliest shared language experiences between parents and their children. It includes rhyme, rhythm, and physical activity. Poetry grows from the sounds of childhood songs, nursery rhymes, and playground chants. Children love rhyme and rhythm and find poetry a delightful experience. Building on early and positive connections fosters students' delight in writing their own poetry and even performing it. Perfect (1999) says that reluctant readers and writers find poetry particularly attractive because of its predictable pattern and shorter length compared to other forms of literature.

Teaching Guidelines: Introducing Poetry

Definition.   Let's begin with a definition of poetry. Interestingly enough, other forms of literature rarely need definition because they are so widely and universally recognized in form and function. But most references and discussions of poetry begin with definition. Jerome (1980) laments the fact that a definition of poetry is elusive because of a fear that parameters might stifle the creative component of the genre. Even though many experts have their own concepts and carefully chosen words to define poetry, most agree on several attributes that students can understand after they have experienced a wide variety of poems:

1. Poems have a sense of rhythm.
2. Poems create selected images.
3. Poems are composed of lines that have a visual effect on the page.
4. Poems have both a written form and a topic of content.

As with other types of writing, these attributes of poetry can be taught, experienced, and enjoyed by students of all ages.

Literary Models.   In the writing workshop, we make poetry a natural part of the daily routine. By sharing our own reactions to and appreciation for poetry, we also help our students feel the emotions, see the images, and understand the poet's intent. Our students laugh and chant with the funny, sometimes silly, lines and words of such poets as Shel Silverstein, Jack Prelutzky, John Ciardi, and Carol Diggery Shields. Who can resist the hilarious, timeless verse of Dr. Seuss? We read the poetry of Byrd Baylor, Jane Yolen, Eve Merriam, Myra Cohn Livingston, Valerie Worth, Lee Bennett Hopkins, Langston Hughes, Robert Frost, Robert Louis Stevenson, and countless others. Such experiences help students learn that poems have many forms. They learn that poets are masters at carefully selecting words. Each word holds an important place and can't be removed without disturbing the essence of the poem.

Teaching Strategies: Establish a Routine

Read Aloud.   We engage in frequent poetry reading to help writers understand and appreciate the various poetic patterns. Ellermeyer and Hechtman (1999) agree that ". . . read-aloud poems are a surefire way to delight and instruct young children" (p. 4). We read poetry aloud every day. Glover (1999) observes, "As teachers of young poets, we

---

Sidebar quotes:

The playfulness or poignancy of words, the ability of language to hold us almost captive in its intensity, beauty, or genius, is particularly apparent in poetry. Perfect, 1999

The very foundation of many poems rests on the fact that words can perform more than one function at the same time. Stevens, 1994

Poetry helps us make order out of our lives. Glover, 1999

I've discovered that many excellent teachers don't teach poetry because they're afraid of it. They remember the antiquated, rhyming "masterpieces" they were forced to dissect in high school, and they think that's all poetry is about. Sweeney, 1993

Nothing deadens a work quicker than weak feelings. Strong feelings, on the other hand, enhance a work, even if we were to read it in a foreign tongue. Tsujimoto, 1988

If poetry is alive in your classroom; if the children are hearing the poetic language of a wide variety of writers; if you, the teachers, are sharing some of your favorite poems; if poems appear on the bulletin boards and in classroom newsletters—the children will naturally begin to use this style of expression. Reuter, 1995

Poems that are reread for pleasure provide a way for students to build reading fluency and confidence as well as develop an appreciation of poetry. Routman, 1994

can't do it alone. We need the voices of other poets to help us find our way. We need to hear possibilities so we can make choices in the kinds of poems we want to write" (p. 34). We believe that poetry begs to be read aloud, thus providing the model of oral expression that becomes a spark for children to share in the love of poetry.

We practice the poems before we read them to the class so that we present the poems at their best. Poems read slowly with careful expression encourage students to notice the words, build vivid mental and sensory images, and deepen feelings and connections with the poems. Usually, students want to hear poems again, if not several times, and we are happy to oblige. The rereading of poems helps students discern the meaning, pattern, and subtle nuances and deepen their sheer enjoyment of the verse. We make copies of favorite poems for students to keep in their poetry collections or to practice for performances.

As we work with poetry, we avoid extensive over-interpretation that can "kill" the love of poetry for children. We believe that responses to poetry are highly personal. We may talk about the author's purpose and possible hidden meanings to help students build deeper understandings, but we do not consider interpretations "right" or "wrong."

Selection. Sometimes we select our own favorite poems, and sometimes we concentrate on a particular author's poems for a period of days. Or we select poems related to our thematic units of study. We invite students to share favorite poems they have found in their reading such as the following poems on poetry. The easiest and most natural

Poems on Poetry

To introduce the tradition of writing poems about poems, poetry, and the poet, Tsujimoto's (1988, p. 9) seventh- and eighth-grade students wrote poems about writing poetry.

Vulture in a Poet
The poet sits and waits for an idea
    like a vulture in a dead tree
    waiting for a fair chance
His gripped hands nervously tapping the desk
    like a vulture pacing the sky
At last an idea strikes as he grasps
    his paper
Like a vulture diving for his feast
    his mouth opened wide

                Brandy Spoehr

And the following poem:

The Poem in the River
As a river flows
so flows a poem
into every
crack and crevice
rearranging soil
inventing a new geography
it changes the
face of the Earth

                Kale Braden

starting point for teaching poetry comes from the students themselves. In the daily reading of poetry, we watch for individual poems or authors that seem to strike a positive chord in the classroom.

Models.   Regardless of the students' ages, we capitalize on that chord by rereading poems as often as the students want to hear them. Then, we develop lessons that elicit understanding about how the author developed a particular poem. Together we study the poem for the traits of words, images, lines, rhythms, repetitions, onomatopoeia, rhymes, alliterations, metaphors, and other poetic devices. This in-depth, systematic study of certain poems matches our procedure in analyzing other types of literature to discover the author's technique and style. We study the poems to suit our needs for writing, but we do not labor so long on an individual poem, author, or structure that students tire and lose interest.

We also show how the poem fits on the page, since line breaks and structure are essential to appreciating poetry. Charts and posters of poems decorate the room. Books of poetry are readily accessible to the students for browsing and independent reading. It seems less important to select the "right" poem than to make poetry a daily part of the writing classroom.

Group Writing.   We write poems together as a whole class using the favorite selections as patterns for our work. We revise our poems; we talk together about our choices and corrections. We write poems with partners or in small groups. We encourage talk among the students as they try out phrases, words, and images with each other. We encourage "play" with words in lively, often noisy discussions during the writing phase. Indeed, Grainger (1999) found these interactive, often playful, discussions while writing poetry to be essential in trying out possibilities and building on the words and ideas of others in the classroom.

Teaching Guidelines: Poetic Structures

Approaches to Teaching.   Establishing a routine for poetry in the classroom is only the beginning. Exposure to poetry, too, is only the beginning. Although some students will select poetry as the genre of choice for their written expression, to learn to write poems, most students need direct instruction. So, as with other kinds of writing, we design lessons with the goal of teaching children how to write poetry. They need skills and techniques to create poems that allow their creativity to soar.

Content.   There are a number of approaches to teaching poetry. Armour (1994), for example, cautions against teaching students external rules for poetry, believing that such constraints inhibit authentic poems. She concentrates first on free-form verse for young poets, helping them select the exact words and design placement on the page to convey thoughts and images in a satisfying way. Later, she teaches basic poetic forms, keeping the focus on content. This order of teaching is most helpful in convincing students that the rules of poetic structure are flexible. Heard (1995) considers the poetic forms one of many tools that students can use to express themselves, and she also believes that the forms should not dictate the poems. She offers a wide variety of poetic tools, including structures, to her students so they can select the tools best suited to their particular needs.

Writing a poem gives you a way to say something that just doesn't want to be said any other way. Stevens, 1994

Form.   Luce-Kapler (1999), on the other hand, believes that learning the structure of poetry is essential to successful composition and teaches students the "constraints" of poetic structure as a springboard for creativity. She feels the structure limits choices while providing the freedom to use language in new, creative ways. Without the structure, there is no poetry.

It doesn't take long for students to be captivated by the allure of poetry once it begins to weave its magic in the classroom. Perfect, 1999

Form and content.   We take a middle ground. Our writers "find" their own poems through constant exposure to poetry, followed by opportunities to express their thoughts in poetic words and structures. Acceptance and encouragement are key to individual successes and students' feelings of confidence as poets. Especially with very young writers, the emphasis is on content and word choice rather than a stylized pattern.

We also teach structure, using models of children's best-loved poems and basic poetic forms. The models are analyzed for form and content. Jerome (1994) believes that content and form must be combined in the writing of poetry. The predetermined forms or structures require the poet to "pick and choose, polish, twist, to manage these contortions with grace. It is the tug-of-war between form and content that makes the art of the poem" (Jerome, 1986, unpaged). Wray and Lewis (1996) believe that providing scaffolding structures for writing is important for beginning authors. While the initial uses of structures may decrease the quality of writing, these structures quickly become a helpful part of the students' repertoire of writing tools. Particularly for our older students, we believe that teaching poetry is no exception to this idea.

To Rhyme or Not to Rhyme.   One of the essential traits of nursery rhymes and chants, the earliest exposures children have with poetry, is the feature of rhyming words in poetry. Many children build on that love of rhyme to the extent that they often believe that poems *must* rhyme. Luce-Kapler (1999) says some children become obsessed with rhyming at the expense of the content and the tempo of the lines.

We believe that frequent reading of nonrhyming poems is one way to help students broaden their definitions and concepts of poetry. And we agree with Armour (1994) that beginning poetry instruction should focus on free verse to allow freedom from rhymes. This approach allows introduction of rhymes later as another, but not exclusive, component of poetry. Certainly we do not shy away from delightful rhymed poetry for fear it might narrow students' ideas about poetic form.

Teaching Strategy: Heuristics

Science and poetry are really wedded together. One of the scientists' biggest tools is observation and wondering, questioning and naming the world. Poets go through the same process. Heard, 1995

Poetry in Science.   The connection between poetry and science may at first seem odd but, on further investigation, is quite logical. Both the scientist and the poet look at items, issues, and ideas in depth, collecting as much raw data as possible to make predictions, consider new possibilities, and make connections. Chatton and Collins (1995) use a three-column journal such as the one below to help students organize their scientific-poetic thoughts and observations. The first column includes notes and drawings of actual scientific observations. The second column is for questions that may arise from the observations. The third column is for emotional reactions to the observations. They emphasize, however, that poems can arise from any of the three columns.

Notes	Questions	Reactions
The jelly eggs stick together. The tiny black dots in the clear, jelly-covered eggs begin to wiggle.	How can something so tiny grow into a frog? Why is the jelly substance clear? I wonder how many will live?	I feel like I'm spying on the tadpole's life. I feel sad when one dies.

Observation of a butterfly bush prompted the poem below:

> The butterfly bush
> Looks like dazzling purple corn cobs.
> Mother nature's microphone
> Calls
> Calls
> Calls for butterflies.
> Feels like a purple silk dress,
> Mother Nature's dress,
> Swishes when the wind blows.
> The butterfly bush.
>
> *Trevor*

Poetic Triggering Sheet. Denman (1995) uses the "poetic triggering sheet" in Figure 9–1 to help older students collect ideas for poems. In the center circle, students write their main ideas or triggering experiences. In the outer circles, students write images to support the center ideas. In the column on the right, students are encouraged to write personal associations with the topic or connections with another experience that the topic evokes. The sheet acts as a prewriting activity by encouraging students to gather ideas, play with words and images, and develop connections before they begin writing. After this initial prewriting activity, Denman then asks the students to simply begin writing as though storytelling or recreating the experience for the reader. He believes this strategy helps students get to the "heart" of the poem before they deal with form during the revision process. Figure 9–1 illustrates how this heuristic works.

Denotation–Connotation. Stevens (1994) likewise believes that extensive prewriting activities are essential in helping students create the ideas, feelings, and images they want to communicate. Later, authors manipulate carefully selected words within structures that best convey their thoughts. For example, Stevens teaches middle school writers the meaning of denotation and connotation by having them work in pairs to write the denotative and connotative meanings of words such as *night, sun, storm, mother,* and *heart.* Then each student selects an object that has strong meaning for him or her, such as an item from a collection, a souvenir, or a photograph, and writes a detailed list of the denotative qualities such as size, shape, color, and origin. A second column of connotative qualities such

FIGURE 9–1
Poetic Trigger Pattern

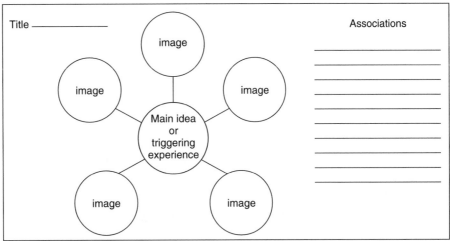

Adapted from Denman, Gregory A. 1995. Beating the write silence: Strategies from student poets. *Writing Teacher, 8* (May), pp. 11–15. With permission from ECS Learning Systems, Inc., P.O. Box 791437, San Antonio, TX 78279-1437.

Poetry writing is a way to sort out what is hard to know, an attempt to put words to something that is difficult or takes a long time to understand. Glover, 1999

as feelings and special meanings are added next. The final poem begins by creating a line from either column. The poem continues by combining and alternating words and phrases from both lists to convey the important ideas and qualities of the object. Extensive revision shapes the final poem or free verse or other appropriate structure.

After reading Byrd Baylor's *One Small Blue Bead,* third graders responded with the following poems.

A small blue bead
Lay there in the sand.
A helpless little bead,
Who cares?
But you might not know,
You might not understand,
That this bead,
Helpless as it is,
Was a boy's,
Who passed this path
Long ago,
And held it in his hand.

Keegan

One blue bead,
Very hard to see,
One small bead,
Could it lead
To friendship,

Between you and me?
Just a small blue bead,
Could it be
The beginning of an excavation,
Maybe...
Maybe...
Just a small blue bead.

D.J.

Teaching Strategies: Types of Poetry

At a time when the complexities of the world grow ever more confusing and even more frightening, poetry not only can grant us a place of beauty and temporary escape, but can also give us the language and imagery to make sense of our reality. Perfect, 1999

In addition to the heuristics presented previously, our writers love experimenting with a variety of poetry forms, including lists, acrostics and alphabet poems, shape and sensory poems, haiku, and cinquains. We begin with unrhymed verse and let the students' interests dictate the kinds of poem patterns and related techniques that we teach.

Lists.   A list poem consists of a brainstormed collection of nouns or words related to a particular topic. The list easily involves the whole class as students contribute words that are written vertically on a chart or chalkboard. The list becomes a poem in itself, or, after analyzing the words for common elements or images, becomes a springboard for other forms of poetry. This approach is particularly suited to topics from thematic units as students submit words related to concepts learned in the content of the unit. Graves (1994) finds success teaching beginning poetry to students of all ages with list poems. Below is a list that was satisfying as a final poem for its fourth-grade author.

No subject is too obscure for scrutiny in a poem, nor has any scientific, historic, or cultural event in any society passed without poetic commentary from multiple points of view. Sweeney, 1993

A Fish
Slimy
Slippery
Scared of movement
Thin fins
Small black eyes
Covered with scales
Makes me feel dry
Makes me feel bumpy
Makes me want to jump in the water.

Georgie

Good poems often spring from careful observation. You can learn a great deal about a person, place, or thing by observing that subject over a period of time. Stevens, 1994

Acrostics.   This form is another favorite for beginning poets because of its simplicity. After brainstorming a list of words related to a topic or thematic unit, each student selects a favorite word and writes it vertically on a paper. The letter at the beginning of the line becomes the beginning of the first word of the poem. Each line contains one or more words that relate to the vertical word. We often use acrostics at the beginning of the year and ask students to write poems using the letters of their names. They often decorate their writing folders with acrostics about themselves as a beginning piece of writing. The poems become a way for students to introduce themselves to the class.

Prancing
Outrageously fun
Noble
Independent
Elegantly moving
Suitable for children.

Amie

Alphabet Poems.   These poems often lead to delightful, silly laughter in the classroom. Again, the pattern is simple. Select any set of consecutive letters in the alphabet as the first letter of each line in a poem. Lines are aligned on the left margin or diagonally on the page. Topics are open ended or related to a particular theme.

All
    Boys
        Can
            Design
                Electric
                    Footballs and
                        Green slime.

Zach

One-Line Starters.   By establishing a beginning line or opening words, even reluctant writers conquer that initial fear of, "How do I begin?" Graves (1994) thinks that this form is most successful with students at least nine years of age, but we find that much younger students benefit from beginning lines as well. As with all poetry writing, lively chatter among the students is an essential part of the writing process as they try out their ideas and build on each other's suggestions. Some beginning line poetry also works well as "sandwich poems" by making the first and last lines alike. Some beginning lines follow, but others can come from favorite poems or memorable lines in a story the students read.

This is a day for. . .
My favorite food (sport, person, pet, place) is. . .
What I like most about. . .
Remember me. . .
I am the person who. . .
A good thing happened. . .
One good thing. . .
A _____ is an animal to see.
You ought to meet. . .
Have you ever seen. . .
Once when I went walking. . .
If I were in charge of the world. . .

Using the beginning line "I know . . ." a student composed this sandwich poem.

I know a bike shop.
Kids looking for bigger bikes.
The bell of the cash register goes "tinngg!"
The smell of tar from the tires.

I know a bike shop.
People crowding around the most expensive
        but coolest bike.
Two-year-olds screaming
        because they don't get their tricycles.
The smell of fresh new bikes.
"Mommy, can I have that one?" a little kid asks.
        I know a bike shop.

Leandra

Poems teach us to listen quietly to the voices of others by making us aware of language: its friendship and freedom, its precision, its power to shift meanings with the choice and placement of words. Sweeney, 1993

In a fifth-grade class, students used objects in their rooms at home to tell stories about themselves. The beginning line makes a simple statement about the author from the viewpoint of an object in the room and carries that pattern throughout the poem. One student transformed her ideas to include a rhyming quality.

She was an artist, say the drawings on the wall,
Created from crayons and markers bought at the mall.
And she liked bright colors, says the rainbow bedspread,
Sewn tightly together with blue and yellow thread.
She had good taste for music, says the huge stereo,
Looking at the CDs in Spanish from Mexico.
And she liked playing board games, says the Battleship piece,
Admiring one certain puzzle of different colored geese.
A woman came in daily, say the high heels on the floor,
Sometimes with some cookies for the little girl to adore.
And a dog did lots of tricks in here, said a soggy tiny bone,
Glancing at a pretend toy that seemed to be a cone.
The girl did homework every day, said the worn out pen,
Proudly looking at a paper with a grade of ten times ten.
And the girl was praised for her good grades, said the piggy bank
Holding the savings of dollars and pennies tightly like a tank.
But no one knew whose room it was, said the dirty sock
Not the dolls, not the games, not even the round clock.
It was somehow mysterious, said the bed,
But not quiet, now even while the girl read.
The joy of the girl was endless, shouted out the walls,
Looking at the now-grown girl dribble basketballs.
I wonder if we'll ever know whose room this really was.
Oh, now I see. I think it was Rebeca's.

Rebeca

Shape Poems.   When students use shape poems without being overly concerned about exactness of the shape, they find the results satisfying if not notable in quality. Simple triangle or circle shapes make good beginnings for this type of poem. More complicated shapes challenge writers to use more specific words and images. For example, Valerie Worth's poem, "Giraffe" opens possibilities for students to create their own shape poems. Here is a shape poem created for a leaf (note: a line drawing of a leaf will be drawn around the words):

shade in summer heat

resting so still to savor the sun's warmth

fluttering in spring breezes, bracing

against the storm's fury

making homes for squirrels, turning colors to signal fall

withered in winter, waiting, waiting

for new life

Diamante.   This is a version of the shape poem, but with more restrictive requirements. The pattern is simple, with each word centered on the page:

Line 1 - one word

Line 2 - two words

Line 3 - three words

Line 4 - four words

Line 5 - three words

Line 6 - two words

Line 7 - one word

Form requirements can be more restrictive depending on the age and interest of the child:

One noun

Two adjectives

Three participles

Four nouns

Three participles

Two adjectives

One noun (a synonym for the first noun)

Some diamante poetry gradually changes to opposites from beginning to end, such as the following poem by a fifth-grade writer.

Night

Shadowy, chilly

Snoozing, dozing, soothing, easing

Comets, moonshine, sunlight, clouds,

Charming, playing, fishing

Dazzling, cozy,

Day

Jud

Sensory Poems.   Fisk (1996) uses sensory poems to help students make connections between feelings and the senses. After brainstorming a list of emotions, students use the following form to connect the emotions to the senses. For an example of a sensory poem, see *My Favorite Place* in the section on heuristics in Chapter 6.

Line 1: name a place or an emotion or feeling, and finish the line with a color word.

Line 2: tell what it sounds like.

Line 3: tell what it smells like.

Line 4: tell what it tastes like.

Line 5: tell what it looks like.

Line 6: tell what it feels like.

Luce-Kapler (1999) likewise appeals to the senses in writing poems. She begins poetry writing activities by supplying students colorful suckers along with a large circle divided into five sections. Each section is labeled with one of the senses. Working in pairs, the children use the circle to write as many words and phrases about the suckers for each sense as they can. She encourages them to connect their familiar understanding of the sucker to other concepts through metaphors, such as "dragon's eyes to petrified Kool-Aid" (p. 300). Then she asks them to write five-line poems expressing the connections. Older students can then move to more sophisticated tools of poetry by applying the five-line poem to familiar chants drawn from movies, cartoons, and childhood poems. This step pushes students to juxtapose their words with the beat, thereby deepening the understanding of the role of rhythm in poetry.

Sweeney (1993) also uses senses to help students explore their thoughts for powerful images and connections. During prewriting, she models a "like what" image list for students to encourage a wide variety of poetic possibilities:

Hot like. . .

Cold like. . .

Color like. . .

Sounds like. . .

Tastes like. . .

Smells like. . .

Looks like. . . (shape, size)

Texture like. . .

Moves like. . .

Couplets.   The couplet is perhaps the most recognizable form of poetry, and certainly makes up a large number of famous children's poems. Children find this kind of poetry delightfully fun. In its simplest form, two lines of verse end in rhyming words, as shown in the following nursery rhyme:

One, two,

Buckle my shoe.

Three, four,

Close the door.

Five, six,

Pick up sticks.

Seven, eight,

Lay them straight.

Nine, ten,

Do it again.

The following couplet was written by a fourth-grade student.

MAGIC

Turning queens into aces,
All the people have smiling faces.
Turning rabbits into doves,
With a magic wand and gloves.

Joshua

> I think good poetry, at any level, offers a smorgasbord of ideas, feelings, and experience. Put a variety of good poetry on the table before children and they'll eat what they like and be nourished by it. Sweeney, 1993

Haiku. This form of poetry comes to us from Japan with a deceptively simple form: three unrhymed lines that use a 5-7-5 syllabic pattern. A fifth-grader's experience with haiku follows.

Clouds ever changing,
In the air, up above us,
Flying in the sky.

Sarah

Haiku seems so simple, in fact, that Cleland et al. (1995) fear that haiku is trivialized in many language arts curricula. Below is an adaptation of the steps they recommend in teaching students this poetic form.

- Analyze many examples and non-examples of haiku to help students learn the essential characteristics of the form.
- Topics for haiku usually come from nature. Therefore, use outdoor settings to help students capture words, phrases, and observations.
- Write haiku as a whole-class demonstration.
- Have students write individual haiku, with encouragement to avoid "flowery" words in favor of words that help the reader recreate the experience. Publish the final products, perhaps with illustrations.

Cinquain. This is a structured poem with five unrhymed lines of verse. This first form of cinquain is more flexible for young writers:

Line 1 - noun

Line 2 - two adjectives describing the noun

Line 3 - three verbs showing action of the noun

Line 4 - a four-word statement about the noun

Line 5 - repeat the noun or a synonym for it

> Dad
> Loving, sweet
> Helps, shares, cares
> He bakes our dinner
> Dad

Lindsay

The following cinquain structure counts syllables for each line:

Line 1 - two syllables

Line 2 - four syllables

Line 3 - six syllables

Line 4 - eight syllables

Line 5 - two syllables

Rap.   The pop culture phenomenon of rap is basically poetry mixed with small pieces of music or a strong beat played repetitively. Some credit Langston Hughes as the original rap artist because of his close connection to jazz and blues, sometimes performing his memorable poetry to rhythmic music beginning in the 1920s. As a recognizable poetic form originating in the mid-1970s, rap began to achieve popularity in the 1980s and remains a strong music force.

Although popular rap recording stars often focus on violence or illegal activities, the basic concept of rap as a poetry form for children is valid. The mesmerizing, easy-to-follow rhythm of rap appeals to the musical and kinesthetic multiple intelligences in particular. When rap poetry is adapted to content areas, it becomes a powerful tool for learning. A wide variety of teaching materials include rap as a memory technique to help students make connections to content. Catchy rap helps students learn information such as lists of states, presidents, grammar, health and safety rules, the solar system, and math facts. Special raps for some popular children's books build bridges to meaningful learning. Music teachers have resources related to rap such as *The Little Shekere* by the recording group Sweet Honey in the Rock. Barb Feuring publishes a complete eight-week unit available for purchase on the Internet called "Power of Rap" with accompanying percussion for middle school students on writing and performing raps.

Performance Poetry.   Presenting poems to an audience is a marvelous way to continue interest in this art form. The sheer joy of performance for some may be offset by the stage fright of others, but the benefits for both kinds of students are worth the effort. Students can present published poems or their own original works of poetry. By practicing for performance, poems become more ingrained and meaningful. Armour (1994) believes these memorized poems eventually find their way to later poems the students write, either in content or in structure.

The images these poems create for the inner eye are vivid, but it is when the words gain voice that we hear the music hiding in them. Armour, 1994

In writing workshop, we encourage students to select a favorite published poem along with one of their own poems for performance. We usually include some whole group performances of rap or choral chants as part of the program as well. Students practice the poems so thoroughly that they usually memorize them, although it isn't required. Even when they have memorized their poems, writers like to hold a copy of the poem during their presentation. For these presentations, we make small, stiff, black posterboard folders (8 by 16 inches folded to an 8-inch square). Inside each one, we place an enlarged copy of the writer's poem so he or she can easily glance at the folder to find the place. These folders present a professional appearance.

At the end-of-the-year authors' party, writers show off their talents for parents, classmates, and friends. Other audiences that we often use for performances of their poetry are children in lower grade levels, nursing home residents, and parent-teacher organizations.

Teaching Guidelines: Evaluation of Poetry

A middle school teacher questioned Tsujimoto (1988) "How much does the teacher advise, suggest to the poet. . . . In short, how much does the teacher tamper with the poems through pointed questions?" (p. 25). He responds that poets—like ballerinas, pianists, painters, or architects—are artists with a craft to be mastered and, as such, they must practice, correct, and refine. Evaluation is a fact of life. We find that the key is the writer's personal growth. When we evaluate poetry, then, we avoid general comments about the work and focus instead on specific word, lines, or stanzas. We encourage our student poets to see for themselves what kind of progress they have made through comparison of present work with what they have created previously. Like Tsujimoto, we advise: suggest changes, compression, or expansion and offer alternatives. We share our knowledge and expertise with our students, being careful all the while not to assume control or authorship of their work. Primarily, we work to bring our students to a level of expertise that allows for peer interaction and self-assessment.

EMPHASIZING THE MULTIPLE INTELLIGENCES

Linguistic: Use word play and sensory images.

Logical/mathematical: Develop predictable sequencing and numbered patterns.

Spatial: Create a shape poem and illustrate its shape.

Bodily-kinesthetic: Dramatize a poem or perform one with hand movements.

Musical: Write and perform a rap or a song.

Interpersonal: Perform for a real audience; read a poem to someone else.

Intrapersonal: Write a poem describing yourself or your feelings.

Naturalist: Observe a spot in nature and describe it in free-form verse.

SUMMARY

Since poetry is part of children's earliest experiences with language, they seem to have a natural love of poetry. Teachers build on this connection to help students grow as writers of poetry. Teachers introduce poetry through making numerous poetry books readily available in the workshop. Poetry becomes a part of the daily routine in each classroom, and the models of the children's favorite poetry become the basis of instruction.

By first introducing unrhymed verse, students seem more likely to accept the concept that poetry does not need to rhyme. However, a balance of both unrhymed and rhymed is desirable. A variety of poetic forms helps students learn how precise thoughts and images are conveyed through poetic structures. Heuristics that focus on observation and imaging help students make connections between poetry and other subject areas such as math and science.

The introduction of different types of poetry helps writers find a style or voice with which they identify. From simple list poems and acrostics to sensory and shape poems and rap, most writers find a rhythm that appeals to them and that they enjoy writing and performing.

Theory into Practice

1. Begin a collection of favorite poems that could be part of a "poem a day" routine in the classroom. Use a binder for the poems so that the collection can grow over time.

2. Select a set of favorite poems. Practice and present them to the class.

3. Become familiar with at least two of the anthologies listed at the end of the chapter. Compare and contrast the anthologies.

4. Become familiar with at least two authors of children's poems using some suggestions from the list at the end of the chapter. Compare and contrast the authors' styles and comment on the qualities that make the authors' work applicable to the classroom.

5. Write a poem using each of the forms discussed in the chapter: list, acrostic, alphabet, a one-line starter, shape, diamante, sensory, couplet, haiku, and cinquain.

6. Write a lesson plan for teaching poetry to a particular grade level.

CHILDREN'S LITERATURE

Baylor, Byrd. 1983. *The best town in the world.* New York: Charles Scribner's Sons.

———. 1974. *Everybody needs a rock.* New York: Charles Scribner's Sons.

———. 1977. *Guess who my favorite person is.* New York: Aladdin Books.

———. 1986. *Hawk, I'm your brother.* New York: Aladdin Paperbacks.

———. 1982. *Moon song.* New York: Charles Scribner's Sons.

———. 1992. *One small blue bead.* New York: Charles Scribner's Sons.

———. 1987. *When clay sings.* New York: Aladdin Paperbacks.

Baylor, Byrd, and Parnall, Peter. 1978. *The other way to listen.* New York: Charles Scribner's Sons.

Bruchac, Joseph. 1992. *Thirteen moons on turtle's back.* New York: Philomel Books.

Ciardi, John. 1992. *Doodle soup.* New York: Houghton Mifflin.

———. 1992. *The hopeful trout and other limericks.* New York: Houghton Mifflin.

———. 1991. *The monster den: Or look what happened at my house—and to it.* Honesdale, PA: Boyds Mills Press.

———. 1993. *Someone could win a polar bear.* Honesdale, PA: Boyds Mills Press.

———. 1991. *You know who.* Honesdale, PA: Boyds Mills Press.

———. 1987. *You read to me, I'll read to you.* New York: HarperTrophy.

Cole, Joanna, ed. 1984. *A new treasury of children's poetry.* New York: Doubleday.

Cole, William, ed. 1981. *Poem stew.* New York: J. P. Lippincott.

de Regniers, Beatrice Schenk. 1986. *A week in the life of best friends.* New York: Atheneum.

de Regniers, Beatrice Schenk, ed. 1988. *Sing a song of popcorn: Every child's book of poems.* New York: Scholastic Trade.

Evans, Dilys. 1992. *Monster soup and other spooky poems.* New York: Scholastic.

Fleischman, Paul. 1990. *Joyful noise: Poems for two voices.* New York: HarperCollins Children's Books.

Florian, Douglas. 1994. *Beast feast.* New York: Harcourt Brace.

Frost, Robert. 1979. *Poetry of Robert Frost: The collected poems, complete and unabridged.* New York: Henry Holt.

Giesel, Theodore Seuss. 1989. *And to think that I saw it on Mulberry Street.* New York: Random House.

———. 1987. *The cat in the hat.* New York: Random Library.

———. 1994. *If I ran the circus.* New York: Random Library.

———. 1971. *The lorax.* New York: Random House.

———. 1981. *One fish two fish red fish blue fish.* New York: Random House.

Hall, Donald, ed. 1985. *The Oxford book of children's verse in America.* New York: Oxford University Press.

Heard, Georgia. 1989. *For the good of the earth and sun.* Portsmouth, NH: Heinemann.

Hopkins, Lee Bennett, ed. 1993. *Extra innings: Baseball poems.* New York: Harcourt Brace.

Hopkins, Lee Bennett, ed. 1990. *Good books, good times.* New York: HarperCollins Children's Books.

Hopkins, Lee Bennett, ed. 1994. *Hand in hand: An American history through poetry.* New York: Simon & Schuster.

Hopkins, Lee Bennett, ed. 1999. *Lives: Poems about famous Americans.* New York: HarperCollins Juvenile Books.

Hopkins, Lee Bennett, ed. 1996. *School supplies: A book of poems.* New York: Simon & Schuster.

Hughes, Langston, 1994. *The dream keeper and other poems.* New York: Alfred A. Knopf.

———. 1990. *Selected poems of Langston Hughes.* New York: Vintage Books.

Livingston, Myra Cohn. 1987. *Cat poems.* New York: Holiday House.

———. 1986. *Earth poems.* New York: Holiday House.

———. 1984. *Sky songs.* New York: Holiday House.

Merriman, Eve. 1986. *Fresh paint.* New York: Macmillan Child Group.

———. 1981. *A word or two with you.* New York: Atheneum.

Prelutsky, Jack. 1995. *My parents think I'm sleeping.* New York: Mulberry Books.

———. 1984. *The new kid on the block.* New York: Greenwillow.

Prelutsky, Jack, ed. 1986. *Read-aloud poems for the very young.* New York: Alfred A. Knopf.

Prelutsky, Jack. 1990. *Something big has been here.* New York: William Morrow.

Rosenberg, Liz, ed. 1996. *The invisible ladder: An anthology of contemporary American poems for young readers.* New York: Henry Holt.

Sandburg, Carl. 1999. *Poems for children nowhere near old enough to vote.* New York: Knopf.

Schertle, Alice. 1995. *Advice for a frog.* New York: Lothrop, Lee and Shepard Books.

Shields, Carol Diggory. 1995. *Lunch money and other poems about school.* New York: Dutton Books.

———. 1998. *Month by month a year goes round.* New York: Dutton Books.

———. 1997. *Saturday night at the dinosaur stomp.* New York: Candlewick Press.

Silverstein, Shel. 1981. *A light in the attic.* New York: HarperCollins Juvenile Books.

———. 1974. *Where the sidewalk ends.* New York: Harper & Row.

Worth, Valerie. 1987. *All the small poems.* New York: Farrar, Straus & Giroux.

———. 1976. *More small poems.* New York: Farrar, Straus & Giroux.

Yolen, Jane. 1990. *Dinosaur dances.* New York: G. P. Putnam's Sons.

———. 1977. *An Invitation to the butterfly ball: A counting rhyme.* Honesdale, PA: Boyds Mills Press.

Yolen, Jane, ed. 1997. *Once upon ice and other frozen poems.* Honesdale, PA: Boyds Mills Press.

Yolen, Jane, ed. 1982. *Street rhymes around the world.* Honesdale, PA: Boyds Mills Press.

BIBLIOGRAPHY

Armour, Maureen W. 1994. *Poetry, the magic language: Children learn to read and write it.* Englewood, CO: Teacher Ideas Press.

Atwell, Nancie. 1998. *In the middle.* 2nd ed. Portsmouth, NH: Heinemann Educational Books, Inc.

Chatton, Barbara, and Norma Decker Collins. 1995. Always wondering. *Writing Teacher* 8 (May): 18–22.

Cleland, Jo, Peter Rillero, Karen Conzelman, and Brooke Carlson. 1998. Haiku: Poetic zoom lens for nature observations. *Writing Teacher* 11 (March): 38–39.

Denman, Gregory A. 1995. Beating the write silence: Strategies for student poets. *Writing Teacher* 8 (May): 11–15.

Ellermeyer, Deborah, and Judi Hechtman. 1999. *Perfect poems for teaching phonics.* New York: Scholastic Professional Books.

Fisk, Sally. 1996. *Poetry plus.* Grand Rapids, MI: Instructional Fair, T.S. Denison.

Glover, Mary Kenner. 1999. *A garden of poets.* Urbana, IL: National Council of Teachers of English.

Grainger, Teresa. 1999. Conversations in the classroom: Poetic voices at play. *Language Arts* 76 (March): 292–297.

Graves, Donald H. 1994. *A fresh look at writing.* Portsmouth, NH: Heinemann.

Heard, Georgia. 1995. Writing poetry: An interview with Georgia Heard. *Writing Teacher* 8 (March): 3–7.

Jerome, Judson. 1986. *The poet's handbook.* Cincinnati, OH: Writer's Digest Books.

Luce-Kapler, Rebecca. 1999. White chickens, wild swings, and winter nights. *Language Arts* 76 (March): 298–304.

Perfect, Kathy A. 1999. Rhyme and reason: Poetry for the heart and head. *Reading Teacher* 52 (April): 728–736.

Reuter, Janet R. 1995. Rx for poetry-dead classrooms. *Writing Teacher* 8 (May): 33–35.

Routman, Regie. 1994. *Invitations: Changing as teachers and learners K–12.* Portsmouth, NH: Heinemann.

Stevens, Clark. 1994. *As blue as a rainy day without a friend.* Portland, ME: J. Weston Walch.

Sweeney, Jacqueline. 1993. *Teaching poetry.* New York: Scholastic, Inc.

Tsujimoto, Joseph I. 1988. *Teaching poetry writing to adolescents.* Urbana, IL.: National Council of Teachers of English.

Wray, David, and Maureen Lewis. 1996. An approach to writing non-fiction. *Reading* 30 (July): 7–13.

Informative Writing

*Because different contexts for writing incorporate different
genres, we need to provide a variety of contexts for writing
so that children's repertoires of genres can expand.*

Chapman, 1995

Chapter Outline

PROCESS NARRATIVE
Teaching Guidelines: Process
  Literary models
Teaching Strategies: Conventions
  of Process Narratives
  Common characteristics
  Topics
  Teacher modeling
  Introductions
  Organizational patterns
  Transitional words
Teaching Strategies: Elaboration
  Detailed description
  Location
  Definitions
  Reasons
  Negative directions
  Examples or comparisons
  Illustrations
  Conclusions
Whole Class Writing
Small Group Writing

COMPARISON AND CONTRAST
Teaching Guidelines: Comparison
  Definition
  Teacher modeling
  Literary models
  Comparison in fiction
  Comparison in nonfiction
  Real purposes
Teaching Strategies: Topic Selection
  Personal decisions
  Inform others
  Thematic units
  Advantages and disadvantages

Teaching Strategies: Conventions
  of Comparison
  Introductions
  Organizational pattern
  Methods of comparison
  Transitional words
Teaching Strategies: Elaboration
  Audience
  Purpose
  Issues
Whole Class Writing

CAUSE AND EFFECT
Teaching Guidelines: Cause and Effect
  Thematic units
  Literary models
  Gathering data
Teaching Strategies: Conventions of Cause
  and Effect
  Introductions
  Organizational patterns
  Transitional words
Teaching Strategies: Elaboration
  Primary and secondary results
  Natural sequence
  Special conditions
  Speculation or prediction
  Intentional action
  Modeling
  Conclusions

BUSINESS LETTERS
Emphasizing the Multiple Intelligences

SUMMARY
Theory into Practice

Expressive writing is rooted in self-exploration; literary writing in the entertainment of others. Informative writing is just that, to inform, to explain, to teach others about a variety of things. The centerpiece is the information itself. Accuracy replaces the imagination of fiction, and writers translate the techniques they have learned for stimulating their readers' interest into making information interesting. In the concentric circles of writing, the writer moves farther away from the self and closer to the subject matter.

The motivational key to informative, or expository writing, for our young writers is its connection to real-world situations. It is the kind of writing that we use most often to tell how something happened or how to perform a task. We use it to compare two ideas, objects, or situations in order to make a choice or an evaluation. We use it to analyze issues and events, to discover how they developed, what effects they have, and how we might use or adapt them. When students choose expository topics that match their interests and strong intelligences, they are more likely to become highly motivated and involved in the subject matter. For example, students with strong musical intelligence might select topics such as how to play a particular instrument, how some instruments are alike and some are different, or how an orchestra program has a positive effect on a school. Students with strong bodily kinesthetic intelligence, on the other hand, might write about how to perform a specific dance step, how to be a team player, or how to build a go-cart.

Whether writing fiction or nonfiction, the basic components of writing remain much the same. There is an obvious need for a beginning, a middle, an ending, transitional elements, audience awareness, and elaboration. However, specific techniques, strategies, and guidelines help young authors write nonfiction effectively. They are the conventions readers expect when they read expository writing.

This chapter presents writing strategies for three modes of informative writing: (1) process narrative for giving directions or explaining how something happens, (2) comparison and contrast for making judgments and evaluations, and (3) cause and effect for reasoning and analysis. In real-world writing, these modes often blend in one piece of writing, yet the emphasis is on one of them. Initially then, we teach the modes one at a time to help writers distinguish the importance and the effect produced by each one and to help them practice effective presentation of their ideas.

Process Narrative

Teaching Guidelines: Process

We begin our writing with process narrative, or how-to writing, by showing students how relevant this mode of writing is to their everyday lives. We explore examples such as cookbook recipes; directions for Monopoly, Scrabble, Clue, or similar games; appliance directions; craft and hobby books and magazines; car instruction manuals; and teaching manuals for various subjects. Students quickly learn that how-to writing is not only essential to our lives but is also much more common than they realized. We ask students to list the similarities from the materials we have examined together, so they can use those similarities to structure their own guidelines for how-to writing. Because process narrative requires logical mapping of explanatory steps and often physical activity, it holds appeal for writers stronger in the logical/mathematical, spatial, and bodily-kinesthetic intelligences. It also appeals to the commonsense learner who wants to know how things work.

Literary Models. We read children's books of directions such as *How a Book is Made* by Aliki, *Fifty Nifty Origami Crafts* by Andrea Urton, *Apple Picking Time* by Michele Benoit Slawson, *Ant Cities* and *A Tree is Growing* by Arthur Dorros, *Adventures in Art: Arts and Crafts Experiences for 8- to 13-Year-Olds* by Susan Milord, and *Hair Wraps* by Anne Akers Johnson. Author Gail Gibbons has many especially appropriate titles including *The Pottery Place, The Milk Makers, Deadline: From News to Newspaper, Catch the Wind: All About Kites, How a House is Built,* and *Click: A Book About Cameras and Taking Pictures.* We talk about the techniques used by the various authors to organize and present their ideas.

> A good how-to essay is more than a list of directions; it is a piece of communication from one person to other people. . . . Readers like to hear a "voice" behind the words. Cowan and Cowan, 1980

Teaching Strategies: Conventions of Process Narrative

Common Characteristics. The following list includes some of the common characteristics of how-to writing that the students notice when they analyze written pieces:

- An introduction designed to elicit interest
- A sequential process, usually in recognizable steps, that follows a logical order
- Full explanation of each step, with details and examples
- Reasons for various steps, including negative directions
- Illustrations accompanying the text
- A conclusion that summarizes an outcome

Topics. When our writers have become familiar with the basic structure, they are ready to discuss topics for their papers. As with other genres of writing, we encourage students to select topics that they know about or have experienced.

Personal experience. Without personal experience on a topic, we find that students are unable to provide the depth of detail, description, and reasoning essential to this mode of writing. Personal hobbies and interests, along with routine tasks around the home, provide reliable topics. School experiences with hands-on cooking projects, art projects, science experiments, and social studies models also lend themselves to effective topics for direction giving. Younger writers happily write about "how to brush their teeth" or "how to set the table." As writers become proficient in writing about simple processes, they take on more complex challenges such as how to play a game or how a clock works. We often use our thematic units as the basis for how-to writing with a science experiment, a cooking project, or a craft activity. More mature writers find that they can move on to processes such as how hail is formed, how our bodies make blood, or how a mountain range comes into being. Some of these topics grow into excellent choices for writing research reports, discussed in Chapter 12.

> The "spiral" principle [is that] the same general types of assignments can be given to students in successive grades, if the particular subject matter or work in the higher grades is more complex and demanding than that in the lower grades. Larson, 1981

Teacher Modeling.   Sometimes, we take our students on a tour of the teachers' work-room to show them some of the machines used in preparing classroom materials. While the students watch and take notes on the processes, we demonstrate how to use one of the machines such as the transparency maker, the bookbinder, the letterpress, or the copy machine.

Back in the classroom, we brainstorm a list of the steps required to use the equipment that was demonstrated. Together we arrange the steps in sequential order, checking to be sure that all of the important steps are included. We practice introductions, effective organizational patterns, elaboration, and conclusions specifically suited to process narrative or how-to writing.

Introductions.   Introductions use many of the basic strategies discussed in Chapter 6. First we work to catch the readers' attention. Then we identify the other elements that comprise an effective introduction for giving directions: for example, a list of the necessary materials, the topic of the paper and why the reader needs to know how to do it, why it happens, why it is important to the reader, and what result to expect. In other words, writers give their readers a reason to keep reading.

Interest catchers.   Students work with the introductory strategies listed in Figure 10-1 to make readers want to find out more. Younger students use these abbreviated introductions as stylistic models.

Materials.   An introduction for how-to also includes a description of the basic materials, equipment, and supplies needed to complete the task. To demonstrate the importance of this information, we ask our students to list everything they need to complete a simple project. In class, we demonstrate processes such as conducting science experiments, making

---

It seems to make sense to use explicit teaching to focus young students on the prototypical features of genres and to teach those features, not as rule-bound necessities, but as "default" instances among a range of choices. As students gain experience and acquire the prototypes, they can learn how to create texts that range beyond the prototypical. Williams and Colombo, 1993

Modeling is a form of teaching in which the instructor demonstrates a desired outcome and encourages the learner to internalize and imitate it. . . . *Inquiring minds beget inquiring minds.* Manzo and Manzo, 1997

FIGURE 10-1
Teaching Strategy: Interest Catchers

- Ask a question: *Did you know that with just a few easy steps, you can build a model airplane?*
- Tell a vignette (a brief story that relates to the topic): *Last week when I got home from school, I discovered that my dog had spent the day digging holes in the back yard. He was covered in mud and dirt from head to tail. I had no choice but to give him a bath. When it is time to give your dog a bath, these simple steps will make the job a breeze!*
- Explain the importance or purpose of the subject: *Some people think table manners are a list of rules to make everyone uncomfortable. However, table manners are simple ways of showing care and respect for other people. If you learn the basics of table manners, you will never be embarrassed while eating with your friends.*
- Present a startling fact: *Children in this school use approximately 1,100 sheets of printed paper per day. Read on to find out how teachers prepare those papers for their classroom.*

crafts, brushing teeth, squeezing orange juice, making popcorn, baking cookies, and making peanut butter and jelly sandwiches. When we make sandwiches, most students quickly suggest as materials the three basic ingredients for peanut butter and jelly sandwiches: peanut butter, jelly, and bread. But they often forget a plate, a spoon for the jelly, and a knife for spreading. They also tend to forget additional supplies such as water and paper towels to clean up after the task is finished.

Organizational Patterns. We work with the concepts of time and sequence in developing how-to writing. We show writers that the underlying organizational pattern explains how something happened in chronological order. Writers learn to describe how something moves, or has moved, through time using step-by-step progression; a combination of past, present, and future; or flashbacks.

first	→	last	
past	→	present	→ future
present	→	past (flashback)	→ present

Sentences excerpted from Sarah's composition on preparing a fish tank show the first-to-last progression through time:

> The first thing you need to do is buy an aquarium at a pet store and buy the equipment you need such as gravel, an air pump, air tubes, and a water filter. . . .
>
> Next, you need to wash out your aquarium. . . .
>
> Then you need to rinse the gravel thoroughly to remove all dirt and dust. . . .
>
> Now you should install the water filtration system. . . .
>
> At this point, it is time to put the gravel in the aquarium. . . .
>
> With your tank ready, you may add the water. . . .
>
> Finally, you're ready for fish. . . .
>
> Your aquarium is finished and you can sit and enjoy watching the fish swim. . . .

Transitional Words. Students learn that sequencing of steps or chronological events is a strong structural component for this mode of writing. As illustrated in the fish tank example, transitions in the form of sequencing words are signposts that guide readers and tell them the order of the steps in the process. Common sequence words for describing a process include *next, then, before, after, finally, last, in conclusion,* and ordinal numbers such as *first, second, third.* Because children sometimes overuse *next* and *then* in particular, we spend time brainstorming a list of sequence words that might be used in how-to writing. Then we encourage students to try using a variety of sequence words in their writing. A complete chart of transitional words appears in Chapter 6.

Teaching Strategies: Elaboration

The writer realizes that words have to do all the teaching in a how-to essay. These words must be as clear and sharp in detail as possible. Cowan and Cowan, 1980

By applying the elaboration strategies that they have used in other kinds of writing, writers make their directions clear. Observation, note taking, and group sharing are especially helpful heuristics for writing process narrative.

Detailed Description.   Detailed description is often a cornerstone of writing directions. Sizes, shapes, colors, and textures help the reader communicate the written directions more clearly and offer valuable background information. For example, *The smooth round plastic binders are 11″ in length and come in sizes ranging from $\frac{1}{4}$″ to 1″ in diameter.* This kind of description should not detract from the directions for carrying out the process but rather contribute information necessary to carrying out the process. In this example, the information is necessary for carrying out the instructions and for distinguishing which binders we refer to in the process.

Location.   Location of supplies or certain parts of the process is another essential element of directions. For example, the button that stretches open the bindings on a bookbinding machine must be located to complete the step, "open the bindings." Helpful location indicators include *on the right, in the center, above, below, beside, under, next to,* or *opposite to.*

Definitions.   Definitions of specialized terms often help the reader understand the text: *Plastic spirals are distinguished from other book bindings by their ability to stretch open and then snap closed for a secure, permanent, professional-looking way to fasten sets of pages together.*

Reasons.   Reasons for doing a step are sometimes very important to directions. Readers tend to skip some steps if they do not have a clear understanding of why the step is essential: *On a bookbinding machine, the binders must be placed carefully between the tines so that the tines can properly engage and stretch open the bindings.*

Negative Directions.   Negatives or cautions about what not to do and why can also be especially important in process writing. For example, *to prevent accidental breakage, the plastic bindings should not be stretched too tightly. When this happens, they snap off and fly through the air.*

Examples or Comparisons.   Examples or comparisons to common activities provide connections to the readers' experiences: *Placing the spiral binding on the vertical tines is like placing your fingers in the correct fingers of a glove.*

Illustrations.   Illustrations connected to the visual senses help the reader more fully understand the process. Illustrations also allow the writer to use spatial, bodily-kinesthetic, and interpersonal intelligences to communicate the message.

Conclusions.   Conclusions to directions are usually brief and direct, often simply stating that the process is finished and perhaps offering ways to apply the information to new situations: *The next time you want to publish a finished piece of your writing, you will find a bookbinding machine a cinch to operate.*

Whole Class Writing

As a whole class, we create a how-to paper on the overhead projector by writing paragraphs for each step of the activity demonstrated for the class. We begin each paragraph with a topic sentence, or a sentence that tells what the paragraph is about, and model for the students how to write those topic sentences (see Chapter 6). We use sequence words throughout the paper so readers will be able to follow along easily. We elicit ideas from the students about how to elaborate each paragraph with supporting details. When we have completed our draft, students test the effectiveness of the directions by giving them to someone else to follow. The trial audience provides feedback to the writer about what was not clear or questions that arose. With this feedback, students revise and edit to clarify and fill in the gaps.

Small Group Writing

Keep content at the center of the writing process. . . . Students first need to know a subject well and then must be committed to presenting their thoughts clearly to an audience. Tchudi and Huerta, 1983

After we have worked through a how-to paper together, students work together to develop their own papers. They try out introductions in small groups, with peers checking for the inclusion of forgotten materials in equipment lists. They also practice following each other's directions to ensure that the process is complete, with adequate details to accomplish the task.

Third-grader Leyla wrote the following directions on "how to tack a horse."

I'm here to tell you how to tack up a horse. Tacking a horse means to groom, bridle, and saddle up a horse. You need to know these things if you have a horse. If you don't, then you can't ride a horse.

First comes the curry comb. The curry comb is usually made out of rubber but can also be made out of metal. The curry comb has lots of little bristles. They look like a bunch of sharp pins, but they're actually not sharp at all. The reason this step is done is to loosen the dirt, mud, and hair from the horse's body. You use the curry comb by rubbing it in a circular motion.

Next, you get a hard brush. This brush is also called a dandy brush. The hard brush is well named because it will get most of the mud and hair out, but not all of it. That's done with the soft brush. The soft brush is as soft as velveteen. This brush is used for getting the rest of the dirt and hair that the dandy brush didn't get out.

After that, get an old comb and gently brush the mane and tail. You don't have to do this procedure but you should. You should never pull on a tangle too hard. If you do, the horse might kick you!

Get a hoof pick and clean out the horse's hooves. The hoof pick has a straight handle with a metal scraper. The reason you must do this is so that all the rocks and hardened mud will come out. It's not good for a horse's feet to have rocks in them, especially if they aren't shod, because if they aren't shod, the hoof might crack. If that happens, you probably never will be able to ride that horse ever again.

Now, get a saddle pad and lay it over the horse's withers and back. The saddle pad is like a blanket that is about as big as a pillow. The saddle pad can be any color from blue, green, red, and white. The saddle pad is needed because if there was only a saddle, the horse's back would become hurt. Get a saddle and lay it on the horse's back and withers. You use the saddle for balance, because you wouldn't want to fall off your horse.

Next, get a girth and buckle it up to the left side of the saddle. Now, go to the right side of the horse and tighten the girth almost as much as you can.

Finally, put a bridle on. The way you do this is to hold the ear piece and with the other hand hold the bit and push it into the horse's mouth. Make sure you are not too forceful. Buckle the nose band tightly but not too tightly. Next, buckle the throat latch loosely. Never make the throat latch too tight.

And now you will always know how to tack up a horse. You will need to learn this if your future has anything to do with horses.

Comparison and Contrast

Compare-contrast composition is more difficult for students . . . to generate than sequence, enumeration, and description text structures. Englert and Thomas, 1987

Life is a constant stream of decisions for adults and children as well. Children compare to make choices about what to eat for lunch, when to do homework, what game to play at recess, what clothes to wear to school, which movie to see, which book to read, or which extracurricular activities to join. Two students might have a conversation that goes like this:

Preliminary research provides evidence that instruction in compare-contrast composition benefits students with and without learning disabilities. Dickson, 1994

"Hey, Joe, which movie did you see last Saturday?"

"We went to see *Star Wars*."

"Really, why did you choose that one?"

"It started early, and we wanted to see something exciting."

To make a decision, Joe considered the merits of more than one movie. Obviously, his criteria included the time that the movie was showing and the exciting content. Thus, we also become aware that comparisons require specific criteria for decision making and evaluation.

Teaching Guidelines: Comparison

Definition.   When we consider many alternatives, we classify. When we look at the characteristics of two alternatives, we compare. The word *comparison* is often used to include both comparison and contrast. It may take the form of explaining similarities and differences between two objects, actions, ideas, concepts, or situations. It may also take the form of presenting advantages and disadvantages of one of these elements. Writing that compares and contrasts leads to more thoughtful and informed decision making. This form of writing also hones students' observational, evaluative, and synthesizing skills. And it requires that the writer establish a set of criteria by which the comparisons are made. By learning to use comparison effectively, writers advance developmentally, in terms of Bloom's (1984) Taxonomy, from comprehension and understanding to evaluation and synthesis.

Teacher Modeling.   With our younger students, we define the words *compare* and *contrast.* Slack (2000) appeals to writers spatial intelligence by defining comparison with one black and one white sheet of construction paper along with one black and one white crayon. To explain the meaning of *compare,* she draws a line on the white paper with the white crayon and a line on the black paper with the black crayon. The colors blend so that it is hard to distinguish them. This illustrates the meaning of *compare* or how things are alike or closely related. Then she draws a black line on the white sheet and a white line on the black sheet to demonstrate how the bold differences cause a *contrast,* or how things are different.

Literary Models.   In our approach to introducing written comparison, we move from a definition of the concept to reading literature that illustrates the concepts. We choose literature that depicts clear comparisons and contrasts and books that show how good decision-making skills lead to positive endings.

Comparison in Fiction.   While children's literature, especially fiction, is not usually written in the format of compare/contrast, many authors use compare/contrast thought processes to bring their characters to life and to make particular choices in the plots of their stories. For example, Betsy Byars' *The Midnight Fox* presents a character who has to make difficult decisions throughout the book. Tom is forced to think through his actions in saving the fox. In *Lionel at Large* by Stephen Krensky, Lionel makes decisions that could lead to some sad consequences. D.W. gives many explanations about why it's bad to go to the beach in *D.W. All Wet* by Marc Brown. In classic tales such as *The Hole in the Dike,* Norma Green recounts the decisions faced by a little boy in his efforts to save a town. In *Animal Farm* by George Orwell, the pigs must make decisions with regard to how they will be governed; and in *The Pearl* by John Steinbeck, Kino's decision about the pearl affects his family.

We also use literature to develop comparisons when students read two versions of the same story such as the classic *Cinderella, Mufaro's Beautiful Daughters* by John Steptoe, or *The Egyptian Cinderella* by Shirley Climo. The classic *Little Red Riding Hood* and *Lon Po Po* by Ed Young also work well for this kind of comparison. Writers can also compare the style and content of two books by the same author such as Tomie dePaola's *The Legend of the Poinsettia* and *The Art Lesson.*

Comparison in Nonfiction.   In the area of nonfiction, students compare two different news accounts of the same incident. They also read literature that makes comparisons between two similar animals such as alligators and crocodiles or that shows similarities and differences between natural phenomena such as tornadoes and hurricanes as found in *The Book of Natural Disasters.*

A very common way to help your reader "see" what you mean is to compare it to something else, showing how the two things are alike, or to contrast it with something else, showing how your idea is different from something else. Cowan and Cowan, 1980

Because writing involves multiple skills, instruction in compare-contrast composition integrates varying combinations of components including instruction in text structure, writing process, and integrated reading and writing. . . . These instructional components mutually support each other. Dickson, 1999

Students preparing to teach writing in public school or college should understand important conceptual underpinnings of composition and the teaching of writing and should test them out in practice. Gebhardt, 1981

Compositional categories such as analysis, classification, comparison and contrast, besides being principles of thought, are categories that suggest questions that can be used in exploring ideas for writing. D'Angelo, 1975

The teacher [must] know at what point his students are starting. . . . must know what new "increments of complexity," what techniques of thinking or organizing or expressing that students have not previously practiced—are demanded by the assignment. . . . [The teacher] must see that these new techniques of thought or writing are thoroughly understood by his students before they write. If he does not take care to teach new procedures as they are demanded. . . . the students will flounder and their papers will fail. Larson, 1981

We also use events and objects, or even people, to show similarities and differences. Often when students compare and contrast common objects or ideas, they develop new understandings and relationships about their worlds. We find that an isolated activity, such as the one that follows, often helps students gain a better understanding of the comparison concept. For example, when comparing simple topics or items that are related but different, students often discover surprising relationships:

pencil-pen	desk-chair	cracker-cookie
photograph-illustration	dog-cat	boots-shoes
carrot-celery	toothpaste-toothbrush	spoon-fork
sea shell-corral	sand-clay	Mac-PC

Real Purposes.   We compare for a purpose not just for the sake of comparison alone. Comparison is the basis of evaluation, judgment, and decision making. To compare two things, writers must establish a set of criteria, a specific audience, and an organizational pattern. Even our preservice teachers, as they review the concepts of comparison, enjoy practicing concrete and abstract applications of comparison and contrast. They find it helpful, for example, to compare two lovable, but very different looking, stuffed teddy bears that they pass around the room. Their task is to create a complete description of each one based on criteria that include price, size, and the specific details of each bear's character and appearance. The object is to evaluate which bear would make the best gift for a favorite niece, nephew, or friend's upcoming birthday. By actually experiencing the kinds of activities they will use in their own classrooms, preservice teachers better understand the concepts, and strategies for communicating them, when they are ready to share them with young writers. When students are writing for a specific audience and to accomplish a specific purpose, their comparisons are couched in a meaningful context.

Teaching Strategies: Topic Selection

In writing workshop, we also explore comparing the advantages and disadvantages of an issue or a thing when making choices among options. We brainstorm and list the many times during the day that decisions, both simple and complex, require us to compare and contrast choices. When students see the relevance of these decisions to their everyday lives, they become more highly motivated to use this mode for communication.

Personal Decisions.   While becoming comfortable with the comparison mode, students may relate the comparison strategies to personal decisions. However, it is important that they also see how they can use the mode to focus on the subject matter and use it to inform others about that subject. For personal use, students might ask:

Should I do my homework first, or should I watch television and then do my homework?

Should I ride my bike to school or should I walk?

Should I bring my lunch from home or should I buy a lunch at school?

Inform Others. However, for informing others, the questions take a different form, with the focus on informing or advising an external audience:

For most students, what are the benefits of doing homework before or after watching television?

For a new student, which would you recommend—riding a bike to school or walking?

For someone on a diet, what are advantages of bringing a lunch from home or buying it at school?

Thematic Units. Topics for comparison and contrast, like those for process narrative, often evolve from thematic units or personal interests. Older students sometimes write about leaders of the Civil War, immigrants of the early 20th century, or in-depth looks at different ecosystems. Younger students often use information from units to write about planets, clouds, community workers, or seeds. As with other types of writing, topics that are meaningful to the student are more motivating and interesting.

Advantages and Disadvantages. Decision making or evaluation often requires determining the advantages and disadvantages of such everyday activities as the ones in the following list.

Writing in first (or third) person

Creating a particular science experiment for the science convention

Playing the viola (or the violin) for the orchestra

Shortening the school day

Being required to participate in sports

Having homework every day

Being the oldest (or youngest or only) child in the family

We find that it is generally easier for younger writers to use advantages and disadvantages with a single issue rather than a choice between two issues. For example, most of our younger students are more successful addressing the single task of writing about the advantages and disadvantages of a longer recess than they are trying to discuss the multiple tasks of writing about the advantages and disadvantages of playing soccer *and* of playing baseball. As they master the concept of using comparison, they are more successful in the more complex multiple tasks.

Teaching Strategies: Conventions of Comparison

Introductions. Many of the same interest-catching introductory techniques described in Chapter 6 work equally well for comparisons. Introductions also specify the reasons why the writer is making the comparison and the criteria on which the judgment or evaluation will be made.

Establish the criteria.   The introduction establishes the *criteria* so that the reader understands how the author prioritizes the information. For example, in comparing a dog and a cat for the purpose of choosing a pet, the author establishes that certain criteria are important in making the decision: size, weight, color, cost, hair length, intelligence, friendliness, age, behavior, and gender. If the writer is using advantages and disadvantages for the decision-making process—should we buy a dog or a cat—then the criteria may include such factors as time, behavior, companionship, cost, and care. A criteria statement in the introduction might read something like this:

> Do you really want to invest your time and money in a pet? For any of you who are trying to decide whether to buy a dog or a cat, these facts about the behavior, cost, and care of each may help you make up your mind.

Organizational Pattern.   The underlying organizational structure for comparison depends somewhat on the reason for writing, but points generally move from the least important points progressively to the most important points, or from the weaker points to the stronger points.

| Least important | → | Most important |
| Weaker points | → | Stronger points |

Methods of Comparison.   Appealing to their spatial, logical, and interpersonal intelligences, our students experiment in small groups with heuristics, or basic patterns of presentation, that help them see that they have developed complete comparisons. These heuristics also help writers make the comparison clear to the audience. They are block and point-by-point patterns.

Block pattern.   In a block pattern, writers discuss all of the criteria for one of the items and then discuss all the criteria for the second item. Usually, the criteria are presented in the same order in each of the blocks of information. Writers make an effort to present balanced information in each block or on each point. In comparing the traditional apples and oranges, the following strategy follows the block pattern:

Block pattern

Item 1:	Criteria 1: Taste
Oranges	Criteria 2: Texture
	Criteria 3: Size and shape
	Criteria 4: Color
Item 2:	Criteria 1: Taste
Apples	Criteria 2: Texture
	Criteria 3: Size and shape
	Criteria 4: Color

FIGURE 10-2
Venn Diagram

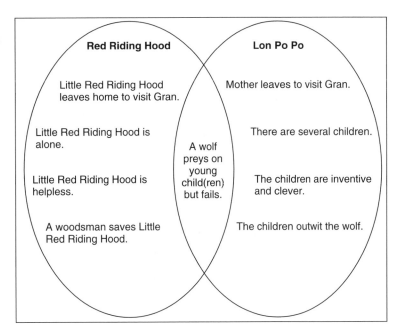

We also arrange characteristics in a Venn diagram so that we can see similarities, differences, and overlaps such as those in *Little Red Riding Hood* and *Lon Po Po* (Figure 10-2).

In the following excerpt, Amanda, one of our writing workshop students, illustrates the block arrangement of similarities and differences in the accounts of the Texas Revolution from the viewpoints of a Texas social studies book and a Mexican social studies book.

> Both of the versions tell about Santa Ana, although the Mexican version tells more about Santa Ana. Both of the versions talk about Santa Ana's surrender at San Jacinto, and they say the same thing about having boundary problems. The two versions also tell about the treaty of Guadalupe Hidelgo which ended the war on February 1, 1848.
>
> One difference is that Mexico didn't say much about the Alamo or Texas's very important people. And they certainly didn't say enough about Texas's history. Now Texas seemed to leave out some parts also. Texas left out the part about the Mexicans' defense of the Chapultepec Castle or about what the Treaty of Guadalupe said. The Texas book said zip about Mexico suffering an economic and political crisis after the war.

Writing about the advantages and disadvantages of a topic, the block pattern looks like something like the arrangement illustrated by Nick's paper on being the only child:

Advantages   Criteria 1: get attention
              Criteria 2: own room
              Criteria 3: no one gets you in trouble

Disadvantages	Criteria 1: get blamed
	Criteria 2: lonely
	Criteria 3: no one to help

Hi. I will tell you the advantages and disadvantages of being an only child. My first advantage is that you get all the attention. You get all the attention because you're the only kid there. Getting all the attention is like being the star of a show with millions of people watching you. For instance, if you win the science fair, everyone will congratulate you and not one other person.

My second advantage is that you get your own room. In your room, you could keep all your private things from people. Having your own room is just like having a top secret undercover fort. You won't have any pesky brothers or sisters rummaging through your closet. Your own room is like having a private paradise.

My last advantage is that no one can get you in trouble. No baby brother or sister can get you in trouble. For example, a baby brother or sister can sit next to your mom's favorite vase on a table and knock it over. Then your mom would call you and the baby can blame it on you.

Now I will tell you the disadvantages. My first disadvantage is that you get blamed for everything. You get blamed for everything because there is no one else to do anything. For example, if you accidentally throw your basketball on your bedroom door and hit something your dad will probably say you're grounded.

My second disadvantage is that you will be lonely. If you want to play a board game and on the side it says two to four players, you can't play because you're only one. Another example is that if you want to play a two-player game on Nintendo 64, you can but you will always win and that's boring.

Finally, my third disadvantage is that you have no one to help you when you need it. For example, if a bully told you to meet him at the playground at 4:00 you won't have anyone to tell you what to do. Being an only child is like being the President and all the Secret Service members who guard you are dead.

Now I have told you the advantages and disadvantages of being an only child.

She needs to practice writing all the time in order to begin to do it well. . . . We don't object to tennis players or skaters or jazz musicians or ballet dancers practicing incessantly, or to their knowing the technical names of the tools they use. Mead and Metraux, 1976

My experience has been that students will be more likely to attempt a project if they are encouraged to explore topics of genuine interest and to use direct experiential learning methods. Isenberg, 1997

Writers experiment with the block and point-by-point organizational patterns to determine which one fits their subject matter best and which one creates a smoother presentation. Our writers learn that their intended outcome determines which characteristics are presented first and which are presented last in the paper. The general rule we try to help our writers see is that it is more effective to finish with the points they most want to emphasize.

Point-by-point pattern.   The point-by-point organizational strategy, a more complex pattern, helps writers make specific distinctions between the two items as they present the material. In addition to a more complex rhetorical structure, point-by-point also requires complex syntactical structures with more compound and complex sentences. Writers usually have greater success with this pattern after they have mastered the simpler block patterns.

Point-by Point Pattern

Criteria 1: Taste	Apples	Oranges
Criteria 2: Texture	Apples	Oranges
Criteria 3: Shape and size	Apples	Oranges

Sixth-grader Mark illustrates the point-by-point comparison and contrast in a review of a book and a movie version of the same title:

Although the book and the movie *Congo* are very different, they share the same plot and some of the same characters. A few of the many differences are the overall personalities of the main characters, the number of characters, and the endings of the book and the movie *Congo*. They, however, share the gorilla Amy, the reasons for the journey into the Congo, and the problems of the expedition.

As I stated, the book and the movie share the cute female mountain gorilla, Amy. Amy was taken from the Congo as an infant and taken to the zoo where Dr. Peter Elliot trained her for research. Amy was taught how to use sign language to communicate with humans. Amy had been having nightmares which were expressed by finger paintings of the jungle. Also, the reason Dr. Karen Ross and Elliot go to the Congo is the same: Elliot, to release Amy into the wild, and Ross, to find the rare blue diamonds that were in the Congo.

Finally, the problems with Congo's government and the cannibals that lived in the Congo were the same in both the book and the movie. This caused the government to almost shut down the borders. This problem also caused the expedition's airplane to be shot down by the government's SAM missile batteries.

One of the differences between the book and the movie is the personalities of the characters. In the book *Congo,* Dr. Ross is a twenty-one-year-old prodigy that would do anything to get the diamonds, which in the movie she is going to the Congo to see if her ex-fiancé was killed by the grey gorillas.

Also in the book there are fewer characters than in the movie. The movie adds a crazy explorer who is searching for King Solomon's diamonds, which were believed to be in the lost city of Zinj. Another movie character is Elliot's friend who helped take care of Amy throughout the journey.

Finally, the book and the movie have completely different endings. In the book, they found the diamonds and set explosives to blow part of them off the wall. This sets off the volcano and sends the expedition members running for their lives with no diamonds at all. However, in the movie, the expedition members wander into the home of the grey gorillas and the diamonds. While being defended by the living expedition members, Ross finds her fiancé dead and holding a diamond that she puts into a laser. This laser can basically cut through anything; she then used it to fight their way to safety just as the volcano is erupting. In both stories, they find a crashed airplane with a hot air balloon with which they fly to safety.

So, as you can now see, this book/movie combo is very different, but still alike in the main story plot. You may prefer Hollywood's special effects, but, in my opinion, you should read the book before watching the movie *Congo*.

Transitional Words.   While we are in the process of composing, we spend time on transitional elements, using some of the following words to make distinctions between comparisons and contrasts. To make direct comparisons, our writers practice with words such as *likewise, akin, similar, similar to, better, similarly, in a similar manner, both . . . and, as . . . as, compared to, compared with, like, likewise, not only . . . but also, resemble, identical*, and *related*.

Using grammar through writing pointers such as those in chapter 4, students become aware of the distinction between using "compared to" when the items for comparison have more differences than similarities and using "compared with" when the items are more similar than different.

For direct contrasts, our writers practice with transitions such as *more . . . than, differences, different from, unlike, in contrast, on the contrary, contrary to, conversely, rather than, yet, but, while, however, on the other hand, at the same time, though, nevertheless*, and *dissimilar.* These transitions are available on wall charts for easy reference in chapter 6.

Other terminology that helps writers make distinctions between objects, situations, ideas, or concepts are words such as *consistent, inconsistent, superior, inferior, distinctive, diverse, appropriate, worthwhile, favorable, unfavorable, advisable, inadvisable, convenient, inconvenient, hindrance, help, detrimental, drawback, obstacle, hamper, annoying, encouraging*, and *disturbing.*

During revision, students often return to this list for transitional words to use in their writing.

Teaching Strategies: Elaboration

As a part of elaboration in comparison, writers consider specific issues in comparison and contrast papers. Note that we adapt the following material as needed for particular grade levels and ability levels of students.

Audience.   In a discussion of our audiences, we talk about how much information writers should include in their comparisons and what kinds of information to include. We ask the students to consider the following questions: *Who is the audience? What does the audience already know? What does the audience need or want to know?* If the audience has limited information about a subject, then the paper needs full details and explanations. If the purpose of the paper is to help the audience make a decision or to advise the audience, writers need to provide full information so the reader can make an informed decision.

Purpose.   To develop information for comparison and contrast writing, we begin by asking students to think about why they will use comparison as a writing tool. What does each writer hope to convey to his or her audience? Will the comparison be the basis for a decision, a recommendation, or a value judgment? Writers make main idea statements that they will support with the information they have generated for comparative purposes.

Issues.   Next students brainstorm how two items, ideas, or situations are alike and then how they are different. Or, depending on the topic, we brainstorm lists of advantages and disadvantages. We encourage students to create long lists of ideas, knowing that some

The students explore knowledge through exploring issues. . . . Students learn that knowledge is not an accumulation of textbook statements . . . but a multi-faceted ability to gather data, sift among the pertinent and the unnecessary, compare interpretations, establish one's own point of view, defend that perspective, and change it as one's data grow. Thaiss, 1986

may or may not be used in the final paper. This strategy helps students think deeply about their topics and develop more meaningful similarities and differences (or advantages and disadvantages) than a cursory, "top of the head" brainstorming activity. With long lists of ideas, students then have the option of selecting the most effective ones for use in the paper, those ideas that lend themselves to clear elaboration and explanation.

Whole Class Writing

As we do with how-to papers, the class creates together a comparison based on similarities and differences and another based on advantages and disadvantages so that students can see the structures that lead to effective decision making and evaluations. Some strategies that we work through together, before students work on their own, are particularly helpful for older students: clarifying ideas, reducing repetition, facilitating transitions, and adding sophistication to the comparison through attention to sentence structures.

Cause and Effect

The genres we emphasize in terms of quantity of experiences may become the genres children believe we value. Chapman, 1995

Cause and effect is a mode of writing that explains "why": why something exists the way it is, why it happens, or why it works the way it does. It is one of the primary modes used in problem solving, and it takes our writers yet another step higher on the ladder of Bloom's taxonomy.

Teaching Guidelines: Cause and Effect

A good informational essay will have these characteristics: 1) the information itself will be the center of attention in the essay; 2) presentation of information will be as lively and as interesting as possible; 3) new information will relate to something already familiar to the reader. The essay will be filled with specific details, colorful word pictures, familiar examples or references. Cowan and Cowan, 1980

To "tell why" pervades thinking, speaking, and writing, especially when we think of writing as a lifetime skill. Cause-and-effect writing is the basic tool for teaching almost everything. Children begin to ask why almost as soon as they learn to speak. Telling why is the basis for all learning because it involves curiosity and an examination of causes and effects. It appeals to our most analytic and logical learners. Understanding actions, facts, and ideas comes with knowing the situation—the why behind them (Hartfiel et al., 1985). For problem solving, it helps writers identify the problem and the causes of the problem, allowing them to discover possible solutions. When our writers can explain why in writing, they are close to the pinnacle of higher order thinking skills.

Thematic Units. Telling why provides ideal opportunities for thematic writing across the curriculum and for using all of the intelligences for information gathering about the causes and effects of all kinds of topics. Why do metal shavings cling to a magnet? Why does one area of the playground have more grass than another area? Why is the violin a better instrument for a certain piece of music than a French horn? Why did the North win the Civil War? Why can't we look directly at the sun for a long period of time? We develop writing that tells why with processes and comparison/contrast, but the mode most often used for overall development of *why* is the cause-and-effect mode. In math, science, social studies, history, art, and physical education, we create opportunities for our writers to observe phenomena and to try to explain what they have observed.

Literary Models. We begin with literature that illustrates the cause-and-effect mode. With younger writers we use books that illustrate a chain of cause and effect, for example, Verna Aardema's delightful and whimsical book *Why Mosquitoes Buzz in People's Ears,* Laura Joffe Numeroff's *If You Give a Mouse a Cookie,* William Steig's *Sylvester and the Magic Pebble,* and Elphinstone Dayrell's *Why the Sun and the Moon Live in the Sky.* The *Math Curse* by Jon Scieszka + Lane Smith is a delightful way to illustrate the application of cause and effect in mathematics. Melvin Berger's *If You Lived on Mars* takes older students on an exciting exploration of the effects of living on a faraway planet. *Mistakes that Worked* by Charlotte Foltz Jones takes readers on an odyssey of how accidents became inventions as a result of some fluke. *Surtsey* by Kathryn Lasky is an award-winning account of how a new island was formed in 1963 after a volcanic eruption near Iceland. Analyses of stories, books about natural phenomena, and articles from science magazines and newspapers help students develop the concepts and ideas they need for writing cause and effect.

Gathering Data. Any number of hands-on activities from classrooms across the curriculum adds knowledge and information to writers' repertoire for using the cause-and-effect mode. Experiments in math, science, music, art, or physical education provide first-hand experiences for writers. Research in social studies or history gives writers greater depth of knowledge and a basis for developing the reasoning for cause and effect. Along with the wealth of information that our writers need comes the necessity for organization of the material.

Teaching Strategies: Conventions of Cause and Effect

As in the other informational modes, there are special strategies that help writers present cause-and-effect material more effectively. Before writers begin to develop writing on their own, together we work through the conventions that readers expect. Like process narrative and comparison, cause and effect is a mode that helps communicate information and explanations using certain organizational formats.

Introductions. Introductions generally establish the situation or question to be explained or the problem to be solved. The main idea or primary thesis may accomplish one of the following objectives:

- question a result, such as "Why is the sky blue?"
- explain the effect of a disaster, such as "What are the effects of hurricanes or tornadoes?"
- require a chain of causes and effects, such as, "Why did the artist end up with a paint can on his head?"
- inquire into a problem, such as, "Why are children being plagued by mosquitoes on the playground?"

Do remember, though, that the introduction must contain, either explicitly or implicitly, the thesis of that writing. Readers must know or be able to sense your point and purpose. Be sure that they can. Cowan and Cowan, 1980

Perhaps the most important thing about nonfiction writing within the writing workshop is that it allows students to become teachers, claiming, developing, and sharing what they know. Calkins, 1986

Take time in your essay to explain to the reader the connections you see. Cowan and Cowan, 1980

Written verbal language requires the establishment of systematic connections and relationships. Clear writing by definition is that writing which signals without ambiguity the nature of conceptual relationships, whether they be coordinate, subordinate, superordinate, causal, or something other. Emig, 1983

Writers practice asking and answering *why* questions, stating clear relationships and playing cause-and-effect logic games to develop the main focus for writing. This period of prewriting helps students see where the logic of the cause and effect will take them.

As in other informational modes, they realize they need a real reason for using the cause-and-effect mode for explaining a real situation to someone else. Their reasons for writing sometimes include explaining or teaching a concept to their classmates, such as the principle of magnetism or the purpose for stretching before participating in physical activity.

As they map ideas for their papers, they practice writing two or three introductions that catch the readers' interest, choosing the one that fits the finished paper best. They clearly state the relationship they are explaining and the supporting causes and effects that will lead the reader through the explanation. They practice drawing logical conclusions and testing them out on their writing group.

Crossing over into the literary purpose for writing, eighth-grader Chris used a cause-and-effect strategy to explain events in this excerpt from his narrative story:

> Juliet ran as fast as she could down the compact and crowded New York streets. She was fifteen minutes late for her work as a clothes designer. She arrived at the back entrance of the building. She decided she shouldn't waste time and go around to the front of the building. As soon as she entered the back door, a loud, high-pitched horn went off and an incandescent light turned on right in her face. It was then that she realized she had walked in through an emergency exit door.
>
> When the siren rang, Juliet was scared stiff. She didn't know what to do. An employee turned off the siren and said, "Well, you know this means a trip to Ms. Freeman's office!"
>
> When Juliet closed the door in the boss's office, the boss immediately spoke up. "So! You went in an emergency exit door. Well, let's see. Punishment is immediate firing of worker and possible $5,000 fine."
>
> "Aahhhh . . . I didn't . . . " started Juliet.
>
> "Just hold on. I know what you are like. I know you meant to do no harm and that going into the door was purely accidental. I'm actually not going to fire you. I've seen your work, and I think the designs that you make are very wonderful and exquisite."
>
> "Thank you," replied Juliet.
>
> "Well, I know that you work very hard and are a little faster in creating designs. If you promise to at least be on time and not go in the back door, I'm going to make you lead of the avante-garde department!"
>
> "Really? You're going to do that for me?" asked Juliet.
>
> "Certainly! So I take it you will be on time?"
>
> "Yes, ma'am!"

Organizational Patterns.   Logical ordering of cause and effect often requires that information be arranged in a sequence of stages that show the interrelationship of the

FIGURE 10-3   Effect as the Major Premise: Multiple Causes Lead to this Effect

Effect	Primary Causes	Cause/Effect	Effect	Effect
	Fertilizer	Too much Too little	Lack of nutrients Acid soil	Starvation No growth
	Water Conditions	Too much Too little	Lack of oxygen Dry soil	Roots rot Roots wither
Unhealthy Plants	Light	Too much Too little	Plants burn No photosynthesis	No growth Can't grow
	Temperature	Too hot Too cold	Plants wilt Plants freeze	No growth No growth

Adapted from V. Faye Hartfiel, Jane B.Hughey, Deanna R. Wormuth, and Holly L. Jacobs. 1985. *Learning ESL Composition*. Rowley, MA: Newbury House Publishers, Inc.

Patterns [of arrangement] are not simply static conventional forms. They represent, rather, dynamic organizational processes.
D'Angelo, 1975

events or results of an action. The information might be arranged in order of the importance of the effects moving from general to specific or from specific to general.

First	→	Last
Specific	→	General
General	→	Specific

Primary premise.   Depending on whether the primary focus is on cause or on effect, writers use organizational heuristics such as those in Figures 10-3 and 10-4. The diagram in Figure 10-3 illustrates a primary focus on an effect—unhealthy plants—that has multiple causes.

Or, the pattern may stem from a primary cause—hurricanes—and their effects as illustrated by Figure 10-4.

FIGURE 10-4A Cause as the Major Premise: Multiple Effects Result from this Cause

Cause	Primary Effects	Effect/Cause	Effect
	Individual	Loss of home	Change in Lifestyle
		Injury	Loss of work
		Hunger	Dependent on others
	Health	Unsanitary conditions	Illness
		Shortages	Food Medicine Clothing
Hurricanes	**Emotions**	Fear	Need for counseling
		Grief	
		Despair	
	Environment	Power loss	Disruption of routine
		Property loss	Financial stress
		Destruction of nature	Loss of resources

Adapted from V. Faye Hartfiel, Jane B. Hughey, Deanna R. Wormuth, and Holly L. Jacobs. 1985. *Learning ESL Composition.* Rowley, MA: Newbury House.

Transitional Words. Writers rarely need to be shown the transitional words for cause and effect because they use them naturally in speech. Nevertheless, we review transitions that help writers connect their ideas in a cause-and-effect explanation, including such words as *because, as a result, thus, consequently, therefore, since, so that, in order that, in order to, as, as if, hence.*

Teaching Strategies: Elaboration

As children develop as writers, they would also benefit from other contexts of writing, including writing in different academic disciplines (such as science and social studies) and integrating writing into their play activities. Chapman, 1995

We use experimentation, observation, and note taking in the initial stages of writing. Much as in process narrative, students observe experiments that their classmates perform, only this time they are looking for causes or effects of the activity they are observing. They take notes and then compare and analyze their notes in small groups, discussing what they think they have observed. To emphasize the importance of accuracy and primacy of cause-and-effect relationships, they often write up the results as if they were going to teach the concept to someone else.

FIGURE 10-4B

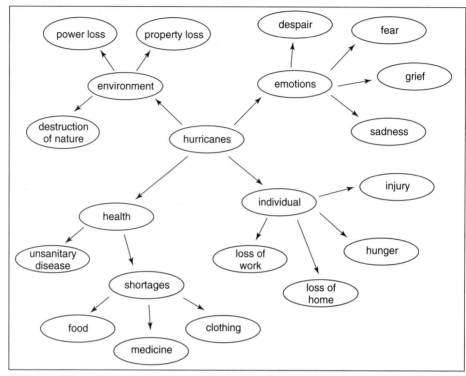

Adapted from Hughey, Jane B., Deanna R. Wormuth, V. Faye Hartfiel, and Holly L. Jacobs. 1983. *Teaching ESL Composition: Principles and Techniques*. Rowley, MA: Newbury House.

[Investigatory research] requires them to gather information from a variety of sources. . . . The information gathering involves interviewing informants and tracing primary sources. . . . [It] involves synthesizing information and making previously unmade connections. Finally, it involves presenting the newly organized information in a way that parsimoniously communicates what the student investigator has discovered.
Marazano, 1991

Primary and Secondary Results.   Together we brainstorm both immediate and long-term results and consequences, and we discuss which explanations and consequences are most important or relevant to the information we are seeking to explain. For example,

My tooth hurts (cause)

Immediate result: I'll put an ice pack on my jaw.

Long-term result: I'll go to the dentist.

Cause-and-effect writing focuses on associations and relationships. Some relationships are affected by a natural sequence of events, others by special conditions that affect the sequence, and still others by predictions about more uncertain conditions. We analyze the interactions in several ways.

Natural Sequence.   Natural sequences are causes and effects that are beyond our control. Seasonal weather changes cause birds to migrate, and plants, insects, and animals to change in form and behavior. For example, *since it is May, the bluebonnets and Indian paintbrush have already bloomed, and the summer flowers are beginning to show.* Students brainstorm other natural phenomena that are occurring as a result of the time of year.

Stacey's investigation of grizzly bears employed a natural sequence in cause-and-effect relationships:

> The massive animal can only be found in Wyoming, Idaho, Montana, Washington, Alaska, and Western Canada. They are found in those places because Grizzly Bears like high rolling hills, thickets, cool and shady places for cover and protection, and meadows and valleys where their prey is plentiful.

Special Conditions.   Volcanic eruptions change weather patterns and, as a result, the natural life sequence of plants, insects, and animals. For example, *unusually severe weather in the form of a half-mile-wide tornado in Oklahoma caused the deaths of 40 people and the destruction of people's homes, cars, and businesses.* With a report like this one in the news, students listen to and read reports of this unusual phenomenon, discussing as many of the causes and effects as they can.

Speculation or Prediction.   Why did the bluebonnets bloom in *The Legend of the Bluebonnet?* Was it because One Who Dearly Loved Her People sacrificed her doll, because she spread the ashes over the hillside, because the people did a rain dance, or because the rains came?

Intentional Action.   Second-grader Deepak wrote about the cause-and-effect relationship of one of his school experiences.

> On the first day of school, we did a name tic-tac-toe so we would know everyone's name.

In most situations, there are many causes and many effects, many explanations and many consequences. One of the key elements that we hope to achieve is to help writers distinguish primary causes from secondary ones and to distinguish immediate from long-term results. For example, when a mosquito bites you, the immediate effect is that you itch and are uncomfortable; however, the long-term effect could be an extensive illness or allergic reaction.

Modeling.   We introduce these concepts to our writers in many ways. For example, we take our students out to the creek that runs behind the school so they can explore and discover why mosquitoes bite them while they are on the school ground. Their exploration takes them from mosquito bites, to time of year, to weather conditions, to poor drainage, to overgrown weeds, to poor maintenance of the property. As they did with process narrative and comparison, students find that they must be keen observers, gather specific details, and question that the causes and effects are specifically related. Our writers learn that they must also be researchers to gather information about their topics. As they collect information, they take notes and discuss in small groups the causes and effects related to their inquiries. Students develop their higher order thinking skills through the writing process.

Conclusions.   Conclusions may emphasize a specific result, a long-term effect, a solution to a problem, or a summary of the importance of the explanation. Writers may raise an important question or state a moral that emerges from the explanation.

Causal networks involve events that result in a product or an effect. A causal network can be as simple as a single cause for a single effect. . . . More commonly though, effects have complex networks of causes; one event affects another event which combines with a third event to affect a fourth. Marzano, 1991

Investigatory research is the process of filling in missing information about specific events. Marzano, 1991

Even after you have isolated the cause of a situation in your mind, ask yourself, "Are there any other causes I should include?" Cowan and Cowan, 1980

Eighth-grader Greg wrote the following conclusion to a paper on the Third Reich.

The story of the Third Reich can be a lesson in life. Simply put, I believe that everyone is either part of the problem or part of the solution, and it is up to each of us to decide upon which side of the fence we belong.

Grady used numerous cause-and-effect relationships in the following informational paper about gray wolves:

Some scientists near Yellowstone National Park have released several packs of gray wolves in an attempt to restore the original population. For thousands of years the gray wolf was one of the most widespread mammals on earth up until the 1900s when the animal was trapped, hunted, and shot nearly to extinction.

There have been some problems arising, though, like when someone took this project [reintroduction of wolves in the park] to court, the judge declared it illegal. Another is that most ranchers and farmers shot wolves that trespassed on their property.

One strange problem is that the elk in Yellowstone haven't seen wolves since 1926. They still knew what to do, though, seeking shelter in numbers while the wolves searched for weaker members of the herd.

Sometimes the packs would hunt domestic animals, for instance a young calf named Minnie that they attacked and badly mauled. The poor little innocent, defenseless calf, torn apart by these savage creatures, had to be put down. This attack forced officials to shoot the local pack's alpha male. A similar attack later prompted the officials to shoot four more of the pack's members.

Now, after 70 years of near extinction, the gray wolf has emerged and hopefully can stay on top. I found it interesting that after all of that time of being close to extinction, the gray wolf can come back and survive. I'm sure this event will go down in the books as one of the greatest restorations of an endangered species in all time.

In a third-grade science writing project, "children do not conduct their research haphazardly. . . . Rather they work from lists of questions that they have generated. How tall was the Tyrannosaurus Rex? How many teeth did it have? Where on Earth did it live? For every question a child answers (all data are kept in a notebook), another . . . is added . . . to accommodate new data . . . or because another child, out of curiosity, asks it of the researcher. Thaiss, 1986

Business Letters

Writing in the content areas . . . can turn the traditional unit on the business letter in to a real exercise in communication when students write genuine letters to live people in an attempt to learn something for class. Tchudi and Huerta, 1983

Business letters take informative writing to the real world through authentic activities. Many business letters constitute simple requests for information, and numerous companies and organizations provide free materials and information in response to student letters of request. Most County Agricultural Extension Offices and Chambers of Commerce across the country respond to student requests for information about particular areas. Fan clubs for movie and recording stars, sports teams, and sporting stars are happy to send materials in response to letters. Special interest hobby clubs welcome inquiries. Colleges and universities respond to requests for information. Local, state, and national elected officials take pride in responding to constituent mail. Michael Levine's *The Kid's Address Book: Over 3,000 Addresses of Celebrities, Athletes, Entertainers, and*

More . . . Just for Kids has enough mailing addresses and email addresses to spark the interest of every writer in a class.

Other business letters may involve letters of complaint, reservations, goods and services, persuasion or specific detailed information. For example, when students write research reports as described in Chapter 12, letters to scientists, or experts on the topic yield interesting replies from primary sources.

The standard structure of a business letter includes a more formal format and additional information as compared to a personal or friendly letter: a heading with the writer's address; the date; a second heading that contains the recipient's name, title, and address; a salutation (followed by a colon); body of the letter; a formal closing; a signature; and a printed signature. The letter is usually typed, although it is not a requirement, and it is usually aligned with the left margin. For example:

2392 Clear Creek Circle
Buckingham, Idaho 43090

June 14, 2002

Ms. Malinda Masencona
Director of Marine Mammal Research
University of Florida
1311 Brussels Hall
Gainesville, Florida 02030

Dear Ms. Masencona:

My favorite food is shrimp, and I followed this personal interest in developing a research report for my English class. My title is "Farming for Shrimp—A Hope for the Future." After reading your recent article in the Journal of Marine Studies, I would like to ask for further information about your research in raising shrimp in captivity. I was not aware that successful shrimp farms existed. I would appreciate any other articles you might have or recommend on the subject of shrimp farming.

Sincerely,

Jeffrey Sorrelston

Business letters that have content regarding problems are best written without strong emotion. Clear, concise word choice and statements of fact about a situation, such as the letter that follows, are much more likely to receive attention than an inflammatory, accusatory tone.

1982 Wind Crossing
Wildwood Briar, Ohio 47908

August 29, 2002

Ms. Blanche Herontine, President
Spirit of Time Yogurt
100245 Innovation Avenue
New Winston, Illinois 32068

Dear Ms. Herontine:

As a big fan of Spirit of Time Yogurt, each day I take a carton to school for lunch. My favorite flavor is strawberry. Imagine my surprise today in the cafeteria when I peeled off the shiny silver lid to discover pure white yogurt inside. I dipped my spoon deep into the carton, pulled up from the bottom, and not one strawberry, or even a remnant of a strawberry, came into view. I ate the yogurt, because I was quite hungry, and found it tasted much like strawberries but without the real berries to add the color and texture that I like.

So, I am taking this opportunity to alert you to the fact that at least some of your cartons of Spirit of Time Yogurt were overlooked in your quality control system. I am not sure what happened. Perhaps your machines ran out of strawberries just as my carton was filled. I hope that I am not disappointed in the future when I open my carton of strawberry yogurt. I would hate to be forced to change brands.

I appreciate your attention to this matter.

Sincerely,

Aaron Weltoning

EMPHASIZING THE MULTIPLE INTELLIGENCES

Linguistic: Take notes on the style of two books and organize the information into a recommendation for one of them.

Logical/Mathematical: Create a step-by-step process narrative telling how to solve a mathematical word problem.

Spatial: Develop a graphic pattern, either block or point-by-point, for comparing two things.

Bodily-Kinesthetic: Conduct an experiment and explain its causes and effects.

Musical: Explain how to set words to music or play an instrument.

Interpersonal: In small groups, follow each other's written directions and give feedback to each other on the clarity of the process.

Intrapersonal: Decide which is the best mode for explaining something you know about.

Naturalist: Observe and explain in writing the causes and effects of a natural phenomenon.

SUMMARY

Informative writing does just that—it informs, explains, and teaches about a number of subjects. It is easily used for writing across the curriculum, from science class to playground activities. Its focus is on subject matter rather than on self or audience. The amount and kind of information imparted in informative writing depends on the writers' knowledge and experience and on what the audience needs to know about the subject. It is rooted in factual information. For all of the informational modes, we read, model, and relate our writing to real purposes and audiences.

Like other kinds of prose, the basic format requires introductions, elaboration, conclusions, and attention to the conventions of each particular mode: process narrative, comparison, and cause and effect. As with the other purposes for writing, students read literary models, teachers demonstrate the genre, and students collaborate to try out the effectiveness of their communication on each other.

In process narrative, also referred to as how-to writing, topics develop from writers' experiential base. Observation and note taking are key heuristics for developing this mode. Process narrative conventions call for factual, logical step-by-step accounts of how to do something or how a phenomenon occurs. Sequencing, order, reasons, and negative directions are important for clear communication in this mode.

Comparison calls for evaluation and decision-making. Writers identify similarities and differences between two things, or they debate the advantages and disadvantages of a situation or an issue. Writers observe the conventions of comparison that include block or point-by-point organizational strategies. While process deals with the how-to of things, comparison addresses which idea or object a writer may choose. Comparison, then, requires writers to establish a set of criteria on which to base an outcome. Real audiences and real reasons for comparison are essential to effective use of the mode.

The cause-and-effect mode takes writers to the peak of Bloom's Taxonomy because it requires the analysis and synthesis of information. It is the *why* mode. Writers use this mode to explain phenomenon and to solve problems. This mode requires clear reasoning and distinctions between primary and secondary causes and effects. Key heuristics for this mode include observation, experimentation, and note taking. Data gathering and synthesis of the data help writers reach logical conclusions. Cause and effect stem from natural sequences, special conditions, and speculation or prediction.

Theory into Practice

1. Read some of the suggested books for process narrative. Find examples of five nonfiction books that could be used for classroom examples of this writing.

2. Plan two sets of prewriting activities that give appropriate experiences to students for writing process narratives.

3. Write a process narrative or how-to paper following the suggestions provided in this chapter.

4. Write a set of lesson plans that teach process narrative concepts to a particular grade level.

5. Read two versions of the same story such as a fairy tale or folk tale. Develop a Venn diagram of the likenesses and differences between the two versions.

6. Write a comparison and contrast paper for a topic of your choice using the block organizational strategy. Write a second paper on the same topic using the point-by-point strategy.

7. Write a set of lesson plans that teach comparison and contrast strategies to a particular grade level.

8. Find five new examples of nonfiction articles or books that employ a cause-and-effect organizational strategy.

9. Create a web to develop a cause-and-effect topic.

10. Write a cause-and-effect paper using natural conditions, special conditions, or speculation.

11. Write a set of lesson plans that teach the cause-and-effect organizational strategy.

12. Write a business letter to a real company to express a concern or to ask for information.

13. Write a set of lesson plans to teach the proper form of business letters.

14. Write a letter of inquiry to a city council member or a congressional representative about a current issue.

CHILDREN'S LITERATURE

Aardema, Verna. 1975. *Why mosquitoes buzz in people's ears.* New York: PA Puffin Pied Piper Book.

Aliki. 1986. *How a book is made.* New York: Harper Trophy.

Berger, Melvin. 1989. *If you lived on Mars.* New York: E. P. Dutton.

The book of natural disasters. 1994. New York: Shooting Star Press.

Brown, Marc Tolon. 1988. *D.W. all wet.* Boston: Joy Street Books.

Byars, Betsy. 1996. *The midnight fox.* New York: Viking Press.

Climo, Shirley. 1989. *The Egyptian Cinderella.* New York: HarperCollins Publishers.

Dayrell, Elphinstone, 1968. *Why the sun and the moon live in the sky.* Boston: Houghton Mifflin.

dePaola, Tomie. 1989. *The art lesson.* New York: G. P. Putnam's Sons.

———. 1986. *The legend of the bluebonnet.* New York: G. P. Putnam's Sons.

Dorros, Arthur. 1987. *Ant cities.* New York: Crowell.

Foltz, Charlotte. 1991. *Mistakes that worked.* New York: A Doubleday Book for Young Readers.

Gibbons, Gail. 1997. *Click: A book about cameras and taking pictures.* New York: Little Brown.

———. 1987. *Deadline! From news to newspaper.* New York: Thomas W. Crowell.

———. 1991. *From seed to plant.* New York: Holiday House.

———. 1990. *How a house is built.* New York: Holiday House.

———. 1987. *The milk makers.* New York: Aladdin Paperbacks.

———. 1987. *The pottery place.* San Diego: Harcourt Brace Jovanovich.

Green, Norma. 1974. *The hole in the dike.* New York: HarperCollins.

Johnson, Anne Akers. 1998. *Hair wraps.* Palo Alto, CA: Klutz Press.

Krensky, Stephen. 1993. *Lionel at large.* New York: Puffin Books.

Laskey, Kathryn. 1992. *Surtsey: The newest place on earth.* New York: Hyperion Press.

Levine, Michael. 1999. *The Kid's Address Book.* New York: Perigee.

Milord, Susan. 1997. *Adventures in art: Arts and crafts experiences for 8- to 13-year-olds.* Charlotte, VT: Williamson Publishing.

Numeroff, Laura J. 1985. *If you give a mouse a cookie.* New York: HarperCollins Publishers.

Orwell, George. 1946. *Animal farm.* New York: A Signet Classic.

Scieszka, Jon, + Lane Smith. 1995. *Math curse.* New York: Viking.

Slawson, Michele Benoit. 1998. *Apple picking time.* New York: Dragonfly.

Steig, William. 1969. *Sylvester and the magic pebble.* New York: Simon & Schuster.

Steinbeck, John. 1974. *The pearl.* New York: Bantam.

Stepoe, John. 1987. *Mufaro's beautiful daughters.* New York: Lothrop, Lee & Shepard Books.

Urton, Andrea. 1993. *Fifty nifty origami crafts.* Los Angeles: Lowell House.

Young, Ed. 1989. *Lon Po Po.* New York: Philomel Books.

BIBLIOGRAPHY

Bloom, Benjamin S., and David R. Krathwohl. 1984. *Taxonomy of educational objectives, handbook 1: Cognitive domain.* New York: Addison-Wesley.

Calkins, Lucy. 1986. *The art of teaching writing.* Portsmouth, NH: Heinemann.

Chapman, Marilyn L. 1995. The sociocognitive construction of written genres in first grade. *Research in the Teaching of English, 29*(2) (May), 164–192

Cowan, Gregory, and Elizabeth Cowan. 1980. *Writing.* New York: John Wiley & Sons.

D'Angelo, Frank J. 1975. *A conceptual theory of rhetoric.* Cambridge, MA: Winthrop Publishers.

Dickson, Shirley. 1994. *An examination of the effects of an integrated reading and writing instructional approach on the ability of middle school students to produce and comprehend compare/contrast text structures.* Unpublished doctoral dissertation. Eugene: University of Oregon.

Dickson, Shirley. 1999. Teach compare-contrast text structure: A research-based methodology. *Reading & Writing Quarterly, 15*(1) (January-March), 49–79

Emig, Janet. *The web of meaning.* 1983. Upper Montclair, NJ: Boynton/Cook Publishers.

Englert, C. S., and C. C. Thomas. 1987. Sensitivity to text structure in reading and writing: A comparison between learning disabled and non-learning disabled students. *Learning Disability Quarterly, 10,* 93–105.

Gebhardt, Richard C. 1981. Balancing theory with practice in the training of writing teachers. In *The Writing Teachers Sourcebook,* Gary Tate and E. P. J. Corbett (Eds.). New York: Oxford University Press.

Hartfiel, V. Faye, Jane B. Hughey, Deanna R. Wormuth, and Holly L. Jacobs. 1985. *Learning ESL composition.* Rowley, MA: Newbury House Publishers.

Hughey, Jane B., Deanna R. Wormuth, V. Faye Hartfiel, and Holly L. Jacobs. 1983. *Teaching ESL composition: Principles and techniques.* Rowley, MA: Newbury House Publishers.

Isenberg, Richard. 1997. Walkabout in sixth grade. *Phi Delta Kappan,* (March), 513–516.

Larsen, R. L. 1971. A plan for teaching rhetorical invention. In *Classical rhetoric for the modern student,* E. P. J. Corbett (Ed.). New York: Oxford University Press.

Larson, Richard L. 1981. Teaching before we judge: Planning assignments in composition. In *The writing teacher's sourcebook,* Gary Tate and E. P. J. Corbett (Eds.). New York: Oxford University Press.

Manzo, Anthony V., and Ula Manzo. 1997. *Content area literacy: Interactive teaching for active learning,* 2nd ed. Upper Saddle River, NJ: Prentice-Hall.

Marzano, Robert J. 1991. *Cultivating thinking in English and the language arts.* Urbana, IL: National Council of Teachers of English.

Mead, Margaret, and Rhoda Metraux. 1976. *Redbook Magazine* (Nov), p. 674.

Ruszkiewicz, John J. 1985. *Well-bound words: A rhetoric.* Dallas, TX: Scott, Foresman.

Slack, Charlotte. 2000. *Foundations for writing.* San Antonio, TX: ECS Learning Systems.

Tchudi, Stephen N., and Margie C. Huerta. 1983. *Teaching writing in the content areas: Middle school/junior high.* Washington, DC: National Education Association.

Thaiss, Christopher. 1986. *Language across the curriculum in the elementary grades.* Urbana, IL: National Council of Teachers of English.

Williams, Joseph M., and Gregory G. Colombo. 1993. The case for explicit teaching: Why what you don't know won't help you. *Research in the Teaching of English, 27*(3) (October), 252–264.

Argument and Persuasion

The men from whom we inherited the classical system—Aristotle, Cicero, and Quintilian—firmly believed that some of the skills involved in the process of composition could be taught. Having studied the practice of successful speakers and writers, they brought together a set of precepts to aid their students in acquiring those skills, but they were sensible enough to recognize that one does not acquire a skill simply by studying rules; one must submit to the discipline provided by imitation and practice.

Corbett, 1971, p. xi

Chapter Outline

Teaching Guidelines: Argument and Persuasion
- *Definition*
- *A culmination*
- *Expectations*
- *Multiple intelligences*
- *Key elements*

Teaching Strategies: Elementary
- *Personal experience*
- *Public forums*

Whole Class Writing
- *Brainstorm issues*
- *Focus*
- *Organize*

Teaching Strategies: Upper Elementary and Middle School
- *Advertising*
- *Editorials*
- *Demonstration*

Teaching Strategies: Conventions of Persuasion
- *Establish a claim*
- *Focus*
- *Valid issues*
- *Identify the audience*
- *Present the evidence*
- *Fact versus opinion*
- *Answer counter arguments*
- *Organizational patterns*
- *Introduction*
- *Elaboration*
- *Conclusions*

Emphasizing the Multiple Intelligences

SUMMARY
Theory into Practice

The NAEP 1992 *Writing Framework* identifies three primary purposes for writing—informative, persuasive, and narrative. Applebee et al., 1994.

Indeed, of all the uses of language, persuasion may be the most frequent. Kinneavy, 1980

Writing that focuses on the reader with the purpose of changing opinions, modifying values, or encouraging action is persuasive. Ruszkiewicz, 1985

Argument and persuasion are so closely linked that they are almost always considered together. Connolly, 1953

Students simply have not had enough exposure to or instruction in strategies for persuasive writing. White, 1989

Persuasive student writing demonstrate(s) the following weaknesses: "inadequate content," "poor organization," and "stylistic inappropriateness." Crowhurst, 1991

Persuasion comes naturally to all children. From the time they begin to wheedle and cajole, "Ple-e-ease, let me have another cookie," or "If I clean up my room and take out the trash, I deserve a raise in my allowance," children learn the fine art of persuasion. Persuasion and argument are rooted in strong feeling and usually pertain to something deemed valuable or important. In persuasive writing, the author convinces the reader to agree with him about an issue and to take specific action.

Teaching Guidelines: Argument and Persuasion

Definition.   In this chapter, we use the terms *argument* and *persuasion*. Argument attempts to win agreement of the audience to the writer's belief or opinion, while persuasion uses arguments as motives for a proposed action. As simple as these definitions sound, Ferris (1994) points out that "persuasive/argumentative writing is an important and difficult mode of discourse for student writers" (p. 45). Applebee et al. (1994) also report in the *NAEP 1992 Writing Report Card* that "persuasive writing tasks in general posed more difficulty for students at all three grades [4, 8, 12] than did the informative writing tasks" (p. 47). Less than one-half of fourth graders and just over one-half of eighth graders provided responses to persuasive prompts that were minimally developed or better. Some of the students barely responded to the topics if they responded at all. Further, teacher responses to questions about classroom assignments indicated that they spent less time on persuasive writing than on informative or narrative writing. As a result, we find it is important to provide specific instruction in the discrete elements of formal argument.

A Culmination.   Persuasion is a culmination of all of the modes of prose writing. Argument is closely related to informative writing in that "it presents its evidence in a unified, coherent, and emphatic arrangement and in a clear, vigorous, and interesting style" (Connolly, 1953, p. 413). It may contain quantities of information, such as facts, details, examples, comparisons, statistics, or anecdotes, but its main purpose is to go beyond the presentation of knowledge in order to persuade others to take some action or bring about some change. It involves having a clear awareness of what arguments might be most effective in persuading the audience being addressed" (Applebee et al., 1992, p. 45).

Expectations.   Because persuasion is a genre that employs skills in a wide range of writing competencies, we find that our writers are more successful with persuasive writing when they have a sound foundation in the other purposes and modes for writing. For this reason, we usually begin in-depth instruction in persuasive writing after the foundation in other genre has been laid. Our third- and fourth-grade students mount simple arguments when they have personal interests in an issue and plenty of information about the problem. For example, a third-grade class wrote letters to the editor of the local newspaper pleading with the city to save a wonderful old tree that provided shade for the school ground and a home for squirrels and birds. The city was planning to cut the tree down to widen the street at that spot. The children's persuasive letters printed in the newspaper, such as the one in Figure 11–1, were instrumental in saving the tree. In the process, these writers learned how powerful written persuasion can be.

FIGURE 11-1

Persuasive Letter
The *Eagle* © 1985.
Bryan, TX.

Persuasive

LETTERS TO THE EDITOR

Children right about tree

I was very touched by the May 18 article on the removal of a beautiful pecan tree. I can understand why the students at St. Joseph Parochial School are so upset. The pecan tree is probably 100 years old or more, and a haven for small animals. What is more important, extra pavement or one of nature's finest art pieces?

I was surprised city official Ed Ilschner said, "I wish they were able to understand." I wish he could understand! These children have better values than he. More money may have to be spent to preserve this tree. But, no amount of money can compare with a tree, a true statue of life. God gave us this earth, let's do our best to take care of it, not destroy it.

JENNIFER WELLS
Bryan

Concerned student writes in

Dear Eagle Editors,
Can you please help us
save our tree?
How can they cut
down the state tree? They
want to cut our tree down
to make
the road by our school wider.
We love our tree and
don't want it cut down.
It gives us shade and
a place for the squirrels
to live. The road will
also take up part of our
playground. William S.

WILLIAM SCARMARDO
St. Joseph Parochial School

Later, by sixth, seventh, and eighth grades, students are capable of writing more complex persuasive papers.

As our students learn to develop argumentative and persuasive writing, we show them how these forms of communication bring all of the other kinds of writing together. (See appendix I.) As with other genres, we read and analyze clear models, use heuristics (brainstorm, list, map, interview, role play, debate, and organize) to develop and practice persuasive strategies, demonstrate the organizational patterns that create smooth presentations, practice arguments and persuasion in writing groups, and provide feedback for revision. We tackle real issues and write for real audiences by helping students identify situations in which their arguments might actually affect the outcome.

Multiple Intelligences.   Persuasive writing appeals to a wide range of multiple intelligences since it employs a wide spectrum of writing genres and competencies. Students with a strong linguistic intelligence enjoy the challenge of using words to persuade others to their way of thinking. Those with a strong logical/mathematical intelligence find the structured, commonsense approach of persuasive writing appealing. In fact, Lunsford and Connors (1995) report that ". . . supposedly abstract and seemingly objective subjects like mathematics depend to a large extent on successful argument: language whose whole purpose is to persuade." They observe that issues in medicine and other areas of science are settled through argument and data interpretation rather than reliance on straightforward facts (p. 78). Students with strong interpersonal skills are particularly adept at determining audience needs and appealing to those needs in developing their persuasive thoughts. Students with a strong intrapersonal intelligence find persuasive writing to be an outlet for expressing their confident, well-reasoned convictions. When students with strong bodily-kinesthetic, spatial, and naturalist intelligences are encouraged to select topics related to their interests, their motivation for persuasive writing is heightened.

Key Elements.   Like the other purposes for writing, persuasion carries with it a set of specific characteristics that readers expect: (1) the claim or assertion, (2) the point(s) at issue, (3) proof, and (4) refutation or answers to counter arguments.

Eisterhold and Carrel (1987) suggest teaching students persuasive writing strategies to address the following components:

- formulate an effective claim or state a position
- use data or proof to support that claim
- use justification to link the data to the claim
- anticipate and answer counter arguments, and
- introduce and model specific rhetorical tools such as rhetorical questions, inductive and deductive reasoning, and effective conclusions

When our writers learn how to use these elements effectively, they are more successful in persuading someone to see things their way or to act upon their words. In addition, Cowan and Cowan (1980) describe six characteristics of effective persuasive writing:

- Readers know what the writer wants them to do or believe.
- Writers indicate that they know the subject well.

- Writers appeal to the needs of the readers.
- Writers choose language in the appropriate tone.
- Writers concentrate on one area of change rather than momentous changes.
- Writers make clear what the readers should do.

In this chapter, we lay the beginning groundwork for argument and persuasion. Students develop their skills in this genre as they mature and progress as writers through school and throughout a lifetime.

Teaching Strategies: Elementary

Personal Experience.   For our third- and fourth-grade students who are learning persuasive writing techniques for the first time, we begin with lessons to connect persuasive writing with real life. We explain that persuasive writing is a powerful tool in convincing others to agree with our ideas and that they have been practicing persuasive techniques since they were very small. We ask students to think of times they tried to convince their parents to let them do something or buy something. We discuss as a class the success of their pleas and identify reasons why they were or were not successful.

To bring persuasion to a personal level, we discuss some high-interest persuasive topics such as: a classroom rule students would like to change, something they would like to buy, something special they would like to do, wearing school uniforms, getting an allowance (or a raise in allowance), taking a vacation to a particular place, year-round school, or adopting a pet.

We discuss how persuasive writing often takes the form of a letter written to a particular person who might be able to help with the change.

Public Forums.   We then share examples of persuasive writing such as magazine and newspaper advertisements and editorials. Most of our young writers are surprised that advertisements are a form of persuasion, and they take great interest in the persuasive techniques of advertising. We discuss various professions that use persuasive writing such as business owners, teachers, lawyers, scientists, and salespeople. We emphasize that persuasive thinking and writing techniques influence everyone each time they make a purchase or make a decision based on information supplied by other people. Our environment provides constant exposure to persuasion on radio and television commentary, sermons, political speeches, and advertising.

Whole Class Writing

Brainstorm Issues.   As with other genres, we write a class paper together to model persuasive strategies. After we select a topic and determine a position on an issue that most class members feel strongly about, we discuss the audience of the paper and what issues would be important to the audience. For example, if students want to persuade the principal to have a longer recess, we talk about the principal and the various responsibilities and priorities that the principal has. We brainstorm lists of reasons that the principal

---

Sidebar notes:

While there is no ideal or universally favored organizational framework for an argumentative essay, you may find it useful to try the classical system . . . followed by ancient Greek and Roman orators. The speaker began with an introduction . . . then gave the background information. Next came the . . . argument and . . . consideration of opposing arguments. A conclusion both summed up the argument and made a final appeal to the audience. Lunsford and Connors, 1995

In most informative writing, the thesis appears early on in the piece, often in the first paragraph. That can be the case with persuasive writing too, but writers will often delay the statement of their opinion until after they have explained and demolished opposing opinions. Ruszkiewicz, 1985

Teachers promote learning, first by making explicit their tacit knowledge or by modeling their strategies for students in authentic activity. Brown, Collins, and Duguid, 1989

might not agree with us and also lists that support our position or claim, reasons that we think the principal will be interested in hearing. We encourage students to avoid emotional arguments that rely on pleas or begging. After discussion, students discover that such emotional ideas are difficult to elaborate and support and that more substantive arguments are more effective.

Focus.   The brainstormed list is then narrowed to three reasons so as not to overwhelm our young writers and to encourage them to concentrate on the best persuasive arguments. We present the most compelling reason against our position with arguments to counteract it. We then rank the positive reasons in order of importance, saving the most important reason for last so the reader is left with the strongest argument in mind. Our young writers seem to understand the logic of this arrangement.

Organize.   Next, we offer students a simple organizational strategy for persuasive writing that mirrors the strategies they have used with other genres. The basic outline is as follows.

Introduction.   As we write the whole class persuasive paper, we use the same techniques we used in other genres to develop the introduction by using startling facts, quotes, or questions to catch the reader's attention. We state the opinion on the issue and encourage the reader to consider the ideas carefully.

Elaboration.   The body of the paper usually consists of several paragraphs, at least one for each of the reasons that support the persuasive position and one for the argument and counterargument in opposition to it. We encourage students to fully elaborate each paragraph with details, facts, explanations, comparisons and contrasts, examples, definitions, descriptions, and processes they have used in other genres.

Conclusion.   The conclusion of the persuasive paper is a restatement of the issue and the opinion and a request for the reader to agree or take a specific action.

This simple model for persuasive writing allows our third- and fourth-grade students to form strong arguments and express their ideas for specific audiences. While the papers lack the sophistication of more advanced students' papers, we find that persuasive writing for these students builds their thinking and expressive skills and builds the foundation for later attempts to persuade.

Third-grader Jessica wrote a persuasive paper using this organizational strategy:

Dear Ms. Noble,

Will you please stop giving my class homework? My sister and I have been talking and we think the homework is dull, and she is only in first grade! I hope you will listen to my letter before you make up your mind.

First, a reason why I think you shouldn't give my class homework is that the homework you give us is either too easy or too hard. For example, sometimes you just make us write five interesting words out of a book. Other times you make us finish a story.

Another reason why I think you should stop giving us homework is that children have after school activities like sports or other stuff and we don't have time for homework. My after school activity is gymnastics. It is 3 hours long. Gymnastics is from 6:00 to 9:00 most of the time. Besides, we already go to school for $7\frac{1}{2}$ hours.

My last reason why I think you shouldn't give us homework is that it wastes time. It wastes time because you could be reading or playing outside. You could even be playing with your little brother or sister.

Now I'm done telling you why I think you should stop giving us homework. Thank you for listening to my story. I hope you will consider my ideas.

Your friend,

Jessica

Fourth-grader Stephen uses persuasive writing to ask his parents for a pet snake.

Dear Mom and Dad,

I want to choose a pet of my choice which in this case is a snake.

First, one reason I want a snake is so that I have something to keep me company. When it's a rainy day and you have grounded me from almost everything in the house, I can play with my long snake. Snakes crawl all over your body and it sometimes tickles. If I play with my snake a lot, my brother might be interested in snakes also. Snakes are known for slithering their tongues, and I like when they do that. I can try teaching my snake some tricks like sticking his tail up when he is fulfilled and slithering slowly when he is mad.

Second, I really want a snake because I can learn things about them. If I learn things about them, I can do well on reports that are on snakes. If I get one soon, it will help me do well on an easy report that is due on Friday. Maybe you might learn something about snakes, too.

Finally, I want a snake because it will be a gigantic responsibility for me. I could add this to my list of jobs which are taking out the trash, vacuuming the carpet, sweeping the floor, and setting the table. Taking care of my snake will be as easy as hitting a golf ball 75 yards. Snakes are very easy to feed. You only need to feed them one dead and frozen rat a week and you don't have to feed them any water. Even though this responsibility is easy, it is going to be my hardest one yet.

After you have read my letter, does it convince you to let me have a snake? I hope it does. Please let me have a snake.

Your son,

Stephen

> Just as a picture can sometimes be worth a thousand words, so can a well-conceived example be extremely valuable in arguing a point. Lunsford and Connors, 1995

Teaching Strategies: Upper Elementary and Middle School

Advertising.   Persuasive models exist in many literary genres, but perhaps none are so abundant or have such an impact on our daily lives as advertisements. As with our younger students, we find that advertisements provide high-interest connections to the real-life genre of persuasion for our seventh- and eighth-grade students. We ask students

to search magazines, newspapers, and the Internet for products or services that interest them. With several ads for the same kind of product, we have a basis for comparison. Figures 11–2 and 11–3 show sample ads appropriate for classroom instruction.

In small groups, students analyze the ads to determine which one(s) are the most appealing to them and make notes as to the reasons why some ads were more persuasive than others. As a class, we use their notes to define terms and develop criteria for determining the ad's effectiveness. For example:

- Was the appeal emotional or factual?
- Did the layout of the ad have an effect in terms of text, print size and style, and photos?
- What facts supported the ad?
- For whom was the ad intended?

Because different contexts for writing incorporate different genres, we need to provide a variety of contexts for writing so that children's repertoires to genres can expand. Chapman, 1995

FIGURE 11–3
Sample Ad

Goes from zero to fun in two shakes of a rabbit's tail.

Introducing the Chevy™ Venture® Warner Bros. Edition,* a new minivan that took a left turn at Albuquerque and found its way into the hearts of parents everywhere. Only Chevy and Warner Bros. could design this kind of fun. With its amazing three-way audio controls, flip-down monitor and built-in video player, you can entertain a small army of kids for miles. And to keep the good times rolling there's VentureTainment!, a unique ownership package of ongoing benefits and special privileges from Chevrolet® and Warner Bros.

Since your child's safety is always a concern, the Warner Bros. Edition has a standard integral child safety seat† so you won't have to struggle with installing one. (According to the National SAFE KIDS Campaign, child safety seats are misused 85 percent of the time.**) Plus the flip-and-fold modular bucket seats give you over 200 ways to rearrange the interior, because you never know what the day will bring. All this fun, and more, is standard in the new Warner Bros. Edition. After all, it's a Chevy Venture, the most versatile minivan ever.

To find out more call 1-877-4FUN-VAN.

Chevy Venture   **L t's G !**

www.chevrolet.com

*Limited availability. Call 1-877-4FUN-VAN for ordering information. †See dealer for details regarding integral child safety seat usage. **Child Passengers at Risk in America Study, National SAFE KIDS Campaign, Feb. 1999. ©1999 GM Corp. Buckle up, America! LOONEY TUNES, characters, names and all related indicia are trademarks of Warner Bros. ©1999.

™ & ©2000 Warner Bros.

Modeling . . . does appear to be an effective method of teaching. Stolarek, 1994

Students found that although the ad for the Toyota Prius has only a few facts, it is based on an emotional, yet logical, appeal to intellectual conservationists. The appeal is created by the simple and sleek pictures of the car, one representing the car as a green leaf from nature, and the strong textual language (gas power, electric power, and brain power). Most of the facts presented appear in small type and require careful reading. The main messages are that the car represents a breakthrough in environmental technology, is affordable, and is built to last (today, tomorrow, Toyota).

Students found that the ad for the Chevy Venture contained both emotional and factual information. They liked it because of the action and the idea of entertainment and fun connected with the car. They found that the text contains more detailed information (3-way audio controls, flip down monitor, built-in video player, child safety seat), yet they noticed that it also included emotional language (hearts of parents everywhere, small army of kids, keep the good times rolling, and won't have to struggle). Another feature they noted with regard to the ads is that they both start with a clear claim. The ad for Chevy Venture claims "It's fun," gives evidence to support the claim, and calls for action at the end "Let's Go!" (call us or visit our web site). The Toyota Prius ad claims that the Prius is a smart idea. It, too, provides a phone number and web site. Each ad has its own unique features and each one appeals to specific and easily identifiable audiences.

Editorials.   When working with more complex issues such as those found in newspaper and magazine editorials, we use models to establish the criteria for an effective argument: identification of the audience, a strong claim, factual evidence, effective answers to counter arguments, and a strong appeal for action. We talk about and record the author's intention for writing. Then we analyze audience, evidence, and opposing views. We talk about and analyze fact versus opinion to determine how strong the evidence is, and we evaluate the overall effectiveness of the editorial. The *Time* magazine article and analysis in Figures 11–4 and 11–5 illustrate how we work through such an analysis.

Demonstration.   As we have done with other types of writing, we compose a persuasive piece together as a class. We establish a claim, identify an audience, generate proof or evidence, answer counter arguments, call for change or action, and arrange material. We typically write one paper *for* an issue and one paper *against* the issue to demonstrate to students the importance of clearly understanding all facets of the issue.

Teaching Strategies: Conventions of Persuasion

Establish a Claim.   Careful selection of the topic and, in turn, the subject for the argument or persuasion often determines how successfully a writer develops the argument. Establishing a claim or an assertion means identifying the problem or issue. We help students identify issues that are real, practical, potentially solvable, and controversial. We use the brainstorming heuristic to generate a number of controversial topics that are interesting to the group; then we record them on the board for students to consider. For example,

Recess	School dress code
Year-round school	Mandatory uniforms
Smaller schools	Computers replace teachers
14-year-old drivers	Boys/girls only soccer teams

Focus.   As a class, we narrow the topic to focus on a specific issue that is the basis for our claim or assertion. For example, students may narrow the topic *dress code* to a question about whether or not they want to have a dress code at our school. Then, they further define the issue to ask a specific rhetorical question such as *Should students at XYZ School wear uniforms?*

Valid Issues.   We point out that good persuasive writing assumes there are opposing opinions on an issue, and the author then takes a stand: "Do I agree or disagree?" with regard to the issue. For example, in the advertising claim, "Oatmeal Crisp is the

Sidebar (left margin):

It seems to make sense to use explicit teaching to focus young students on the prototypical features of genres and to teach those features, not as rule-bound necessities, but as "default" instances among a range of choices. As students gain experience and acquire the prototypes, they can learn how to create texts that range beyond the prototypical. Williams and Colombo, 1993

When topics are posed in the form of questions, . . . they work better for students as generating devices, perhaps because a question, by its very nature, stimulates a response. Larsen, 1971

FIGURE 11–4
Persuasive Writing
Sample

Christian, Nichole. Is
smaller perhaps bet-
ter? *Time.* May 31,
1999 p. 43.
Reprinted by
permission

IS SMALLER PERHAPS BETTER?

MARY PERRY DREAMED OF ATTENDING ONE OF CHICAGO'S BIG PUBLIC schools—a place like prestigious Whitney Young High, with its student body of 2,200. Instead she ended up at a tiny school with only 140 students and a funny name: Best Practices High. And now, to her surprise, she couldn't be happier. Few people in town know her school's name—but everyone at school knows hers. Once a shy student with low test scores, Perry, 16, has won admission to the National Honor Society. Her high school, she says, is "small, but it's like a big extended family."

Across the U.S., education reformers have begun promoting smaller schools as a remedy for the alienation that many students experience when they are tossed into one of the college-size, 2,000-to-4,000-student behemoths often found these days in major cities and their suburbs. Smaller schools not only allow students and teachers to know one another better; they also have less crowding and competition for membership in bands, student councils, sports teams and other extracurricular activities through which students express and define themselves.

At the big schools, hundreds of students compete for the relatively few spots on the élite teams and squads, which can make everyone else feel like nobodies. And that feeling, as events have shown, can contribute to private rage and public tragedy. "We want to make sure the kids feel they mean something, that they don't get lost," says David Pava, principal of James Logan High School, home to 4,180 students in Union City, Calif. "That's particularly difficult at a large school." (Columbine High in Littleton, Colo., has 1,965 students. Heritage High in Conyers, Ga., has 1,300.) Vice President Gore last week urged school districts to stop "herding all students ... into overcrowded, factory-style high schools [where] it becomes impossible to spot the early warning signs of violence, depression or academic failure."

FUNNY SCHOOL NAME: Mary Perry gets attention at Best Practices

The smaller-school movement is already well under way in Chicago, New York City and Los Angeles, which in recent years have opened high schools with student populations of 500 or fewer—in some cases splitting existing campuses into several "schools within a school." Studies show that students make better grades in smaller schools. They are less likely to be involved in fights or gangs because they know someone is always watching. They are less embarrassed to discuss problems with teachers. They have better attendance, lower dropout rates and more participation in extracurricular activities. "It doesn't matter what category you measure," says Kathleen Cotton, a researcher at the Northwest Regional Educational Laboratory in Portland, Ore. "Things are better in smaller environments. Shy kids, poor kids, the average athletes—they all are made to feel like they fit in."

Chicago's Best Practices High, which has been open just three years, has seen only two fights, in part because students report bad behavior to teachers. Last year when freshmen decorated lockers with graffiti, older students tattled before the paint could dry. When one student showed up with unkempt hair and satanic messages on his shirt, students reported him as well. Teachers saw his costume as a symptom of other problems, which they got him to discuss.

Smaller schools—if equipped with full facilities and sports teams—can cost more per student than larger schools. But there's also a human cost for the impersonal institutions in which so many adolescents are left adrift on their own. —*By Nichole Christian. With reporting by Maggie Sieger/Chicago*

You may define [the problem] by means of description, narration, classification, analogy, analysis, or cause and effect. Most probably, you will need a combination of some of these methods, perhaps all. Dunbar, Dunbar, and Rorabacher, 1997

best tasting cereal on the market," students could probably agree or disagree easily. But, we would probably have problems agreeing on the criteria and defining what we mean by *best tasting*. This topic would be difficult to support with strong, specific, credible proof.

On the other hand, consider the claim, "Babe Ruth was a better baseball player than Joe DiMaggio." Or phrased as a question, "Was Babe Ruth a better baseball player than Joe DiMaggio?" Could this claim be argued successfully? By agreeing on a criteria that defines *better*, such as number of home runs or runs batted in, number of games played, fielding record, and so on, this question is easily argued. Through reference materials, statistical data or evidence is available to build a credible case for one or the other of these players. We explain to students that arguments are stronger and more effective

FIGURE 11–5
Analysis of Persuasive Writing

Title	Is Smaller Perhaps Better?
Author	Nichole Christian
Source	*Time* magazine, May 31, 1999
Claim/assertion	Across the U.S., education reformers have begun promoting smaller schools as a remedy for the alienation many students experience in larger schools.
Audience	Parents, communities, general public
Evidence	
Reason #1	Smaller schools allow students and teachers to know one another better.
Reason #2	Less crowding and competition for membership in school activities.
Reason #3	Kids feel they mean something; they don't get lost.
Reason #4	Students make better grades, have fewer fights, better attendance, lower dropout rates, more participation in extracurricular activities.
Counter arguments	
Counter #1	Don't have enough facilities.
Answer	
Counter #2	Cost more per student than larger schools.
Answer	Human cost for impersonal institutions in which so many adolescents are left adrift on their own.
Conclusion	
Call for action, request for change	(implied change: more small schools)

Part of the difficulty in persuasive writing is developing the ability to recognize the perspective of the intended audience in order to maximize the chance that the writing will have the desired effect. Applebee et al. 1994

when they are supported with factual, concrete evidence than they are when they are supported with emotional appeals and personal opinions.

After determining the subject for our persuasive paper, we create a claims statement with description and explanation. The explanation may include how one process differs from or is better than another, a comparison between two things, or a series of causes and effects that lead to a conclusion about the superiority of one thing over another.

Identify the Audience.   Another important step is to determine who we want or need to convince about our issue and why. We discuss, "What will happen if they believe as we

FIGURE 11–6
Audience Checklist

- Who is the audience?
- What do I know about them (age, gender, occupation, socioeconomic, beliefs, residence, education)?
- What are their interests?
- What do they already know about the issue?
- How do they feel about it?
- What is my role in relation to them (student to student, student to principal, student to teacher, student to elected official, other)?
- What is the occasion for my writing?
- Will my writing be published? If so, where? Who will read it?
- How do I feel about my subject?
- Will the audience agree, disagree, or be unconcerned?
- What objections or counter arguments might they have?
- How can I interest them?
- What questions might they want to ask me?
- What do I want them to believe or do?

The nonfiction writer's rare privilege is to have the whole wonderful world of real people to write about. When you get people talking, therefore, handle what they say as you would handle a valuable gift. Zinsser, 1998

My students read historical fiction and nonfiction about World War II, the Korean War . . . or the Gulf War. The students interview a veteran from one of these wars. . . . The students use a primary resource for their research. What a difference this primary resource makes in their writing. Eggemeier, 1999

Give as much factual evidence as you can, such as statistics, historical background, newspaper reports, your own experience, your direct observations of the experience of others, and references to books and articles that present such observations. Dunbar, Dunbar, and Rorabacher, 1997

do? What is the power of the audience to help us effect a change?" We help writers learn as much as possible about the audience by answering the questions in Figure 11–6.

If the audience is accessible (family, friends, classmates, school personnel), writers interview them or take surveys on the issue. These preparatory activities allow students to coordinate their research and analyze different facts and opinions (Dickson, 1995). Figure 11–7 highlights interview techniques.

If the audience is not accessible (readers of magazines, newspapers, Internet), we ask students to find out as much as possible about them and role-play potential reactions to our claim. Figure 11–8 provides notes on using role play to develop persuasive arguments.

When we have established an issue and the audience, we begin gathering data and evidence to support our position on the issue. Gathering evidence also means understanding the other person's point of view and being able to argue effectively against it.

Present the Evidence. To guard against hasty generalizations or overall statements that cannot be supported with facts, examples, or data, our students work together in groups to analyze and identify the point(s) of the issue. If the point to be argued is *Should students at XYZ School wear uniforms?*, then reasons may include cost, accessibility, comfort, and personal freedom. Students collect credible evidence or proofs in support of each side of the issue such as those listed in Figure 11–9.

When our writers use authority to support a claim, such as Superintendent Jones or Mrs. Smith cited in Figure 11–9, they learn to use credible references. Using credible personal references means quoting someone who is an expert, a recognized and respected name, or someone in a position to make significant decisions. Weather statistics,

FIGURE 11–7
Interview
Technique

To discover alternate views on a subject, each student:

- analyzes the issue to determine what information is needed.
- decides whom to interview.
- develops a set of questions for the interview.
- contacts the interviewee(s) to set up an appointment.
- takes notes on the responses to the interview questions.
- decides what is valuable to use and what is not relevant to the question.

FIGURE 11–8
Role Play

With a small group of three or four—

- **Establish the situation clearly.** For example, you are going to meet the principal to ask for a longer lunch period.
- **Decide who will take each role.** Who will play the principal? Who will be the student or students making the request?
- **Emphasize the importance of staying in character, no matter how much you may disagree with their position.** Use the language of response that you think the person you are playing would use. Talk like your character!
- **Analyze the attitudes that surface during the role play.** The rest of the group takes notes on what is happening for discussion after the role play is completed. What positions developed?

Never go into an interview without doing whatever homework you can . . . Make a list of likely questions—it will save you the vast embarrassment of going dry in mid-interview. Zinsser, 1998.

Language intended to persuade us—to gain our assent (and often our souls, our bank accounts, and our votes)—surrounds us more than ever before. This language—in advertisements, news stories, textbooks, reports, and electronic media of all kinds—not only competes for our attention but argues for our agreement as well. Lunsford and Connors, 1995.

for example, come from the weather bureau, a reliable television or newspaper report, or a meteorology journal. Baseball facts come from a sports database. Information from the Internet needs to be carefully chosen from reliable sites that carry credibility rather than someone's chat room, for example. As students present evidence in writing workshop, peers quickly question sources that aren't clearly authoritative.

Fact versus Opinion.   An important element we review with our writers is the difference between fact and opinion. Many of our young writers think of argument or persuasion in terms of an emotional appeal or wanting something to happen just because they think it should or that it is right. Consequently, an important lesson for our writers to learn about this purpose for writing is how to support their positions with facts.

Facts.   Facts tell us with a high degree of probability that something *is* or *has actually happened.* Hartfiel et al. (1985) point out that "facts are truths, actual happenings, and findings based on concrete proof. They are truths for all people at all times" (p. 134). Because facts are objective and verifiable, statements about them are characterized by phrases such as "It happened . . .," "It is . . . ," or "I (or someone else) saw or observed or

	PRO POINTS	CON POINTS
Emotional:	Uniforms make everyone seem equal.	I don't like uniforms.
	Uniforms eliminate gang symbols in clothing.	Uniforms make me feel like I'm in the Army or in prison.
Ethical:	It is easier to decide what to wear.	Having to wear uniforms would take away my freedom of choice.
		Uniforms would stifle my personality.
Logical:	Uniforms are economical.	Some people can't afford to buy new clothes.
	Supt. Jones says the school will sponsor a clothes bank. (credible authority)	Not everyone can wear the same style of clothes comfortably.
	Mrs. Smith, manager of XYZ Store, has agreed to sell uniforms at a special low price during the month of August. (reliable source)	If I don't wear the uniform, then I will get in trouble with my teacher.

FIGURE 11–9 Pros and Cons

found . . ." Facts require accuracy, thoroughness, and truthfulness. Factual information often requires specific numbers, names, dates, times, statistics, percentages, and observable events. For example,

> More than 88,000 tickets were sold for the Women's World Cup soccer finals between China and the United States. Brokers were getting from $75.00 to $1000.00 a ticket.

Opinions. Opinions, on the other hand, state what we personally *think* or *believe* or *hope* to be true, while speculation theorizes about what we *guess* might be true. This kind of support often involves biased judgment or position taking and may or may not be supported by proof. To appeal to readers' senses, advertising often combines facts and opinion as it does in the Chevy Venture ad. For example,

> Plus the flip-and-fold modular bucket seats give you over 200 ways to rearrange the interior, because you never know what the day will bring. All this fun and more is standard in the new Warner Bros. Edition.

Speculation. Speculative statements are somewhat more biased because there is not a body of evidence to support speculation. When using speculative statements, since they are largely unsubstantiated, writers learn to qualify their statements with words such as *It seems . . ., probably. . ., and based on.* For example,

A one-sided argument convinces no one for long. Moreover, recognizing your opposition will show your fairmindedness and the thoroughness of your research. Dunbar, Dunbar, and Rorabacher, 1997

The student must know how to analyze these arguments and how to present arguments of his own. Connolly, 1953

A modified debate form named "Opinion/Commentary" . . . exposes the [sixth grade] children to reasonable criticism of their ideas. Commentators are admonished to be "specific and polite." Thaiss, 1986

The primary question in looking at student persuasive writing is what kinds of analytic models to use. Ferris, 1994.

Persuasion, in practice, is not committed to any order. Kinneavy, 1980

Knowledge of argument structure improved students' judgment regarding the content and organization needed to generate strong, logically connected arguments. Yeh, 1998

Although the final results are not in at this time, it seems likely that the game will be a sellout.

Clearly, the strongest arguments or persuasive pieces are usually supported with factual information.

Answer Counter Arguments. An argument without counter arguments or disagreement is not an argument. If no one disagrees, then there is no one to persuade or convince. In developing the claim, students identify opposing views; in developing audience awareness and evidence, they attempt to establish the specific pros and cons. Students benefit from seeing both sides of the issue so that they can better answer arguments against the issue. For example, on the issue of wearing uniforms at school, examples of potential arguments from our students are shown in the pros and cons in Figure 11–9.

It is important to address opposing views courteously, clearly, and with strong evidence to the contrary. Some writers discuss objections at the beginning of the argument, while others address them nearer the end of the argument, depending on what seems most effective for the particular argument.

When our writers recognize their opponent's view, they show how their position takes the opponent's point of view into consideration. Then they respond with a strong answer to their objections, providing evidence that the counter argument is wrong or illogical or does not directly address the issue.

Debate. For our older students, debate is a particularly effective heuristic for practicing the presentation of information students have gathered through their research, interviews, and surveys. It gives them a chance to present evidence, hear counter arguments from peer adversaries, and defend their positions to a live audience before they write. Debate stimulates creation of new arguments that writers hadn't yet thought of and prepares them for the unexpected reactions of other points of view.

For debate, we divide the class into two groups, with each taking one side of the issue. We often advise our students to debate the side of the issue that they actually oppose to gain a better understanding of the opposition's thinking. Debate also helps our writers clarify the most effective arrangement of their arguments. This process is also valuable training for developing critical thinking skills. Procedures for a workshop debate appear in Figure 11–10.

Organizational Patterns. Next we create links between the reasons we have stated and concrete logical proof for those reasons. To introduce novice writers to argumentation, we begin by using the pyramid model in Figure 11-11. It is a visual that allows writers to see the necessary connections between the reasons and the proofs that support the claim. It also helps them see where they need to strengthen their reasoning.

Levels of appeal. While classic rhetoricians categorize arguments according to types of claims, Yeh (1998) advocates using a bridging heuristics for direct instruction. Rather than proposals, Yeh asks students to consider arguments regarding facts, values,

FIGURE 11–10
Debate Procedures

- Establish the importance of the subject with the class.
- Be sure the subject is reasonably limited.
- Clarify the issue to be debated: XYZ school should/should not have a one-hour lunch period. Or, Students at ABC school should/should not wear uniforms.
- Research both sides of the question thoroughly.
- Set a time limit (e.g., 20–30 minutes for each side) and appoint a timekeeper.
- Suggest that classmates take notes on the points made in the debate.
- After the debate, analyze the success of the points presented and discuss the reasons why they were successful.

FIGURE 11–11
Pyramid Model

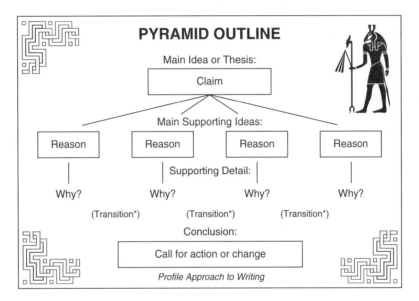

Hughey, Jane B., and V. Faye Hartfiel. 1989. *The profile guide.* College Station, TX: Writing Evaluation Systems. Illustration by Mario Saragosa.

and causes as heuristics for connecting reasons and claims. He teaches students to bridge each reason and opinion by writing facts, statements defending *values,* and *if then* statements spelling out causal reasoning. Yeh's bridging model helps writers see how they can use causal reasoning by arranging the support for their reasons in a visual like the one in Figure 11–12. Writers see how the argument supports the claim, and they see that it is important to connect reasons to their claims.

FIGURE 11–12
Bridging Model

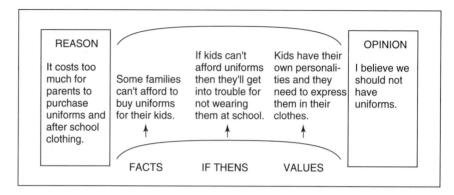

Yeh, Stephen S. 1998. Empowering Education: Teaching argumentative writing to cultural minority middle school students. *Research In the Teaching of English,* 33 (August): pp. 49–83. Copyright 1998 by the National Council of Teachers of English. Reprinted with permission.

Again, we emphasize the use of factual or logical evidence for purposes of developing the genre in our classrooms since, without this emphasis, most of our students tend to rely on emotional appeals and personal opinions.

Arrange material.   Toulmin (1958) believes that well-formed arguments have the same basic components. In addition to claim, proof, counter argument, and call for change or action, we interpret some of those components to be introduction, body, and conclusion. However, the presentation of the evidence in the body may vary according to the subject matter, the audience stance, and the kind of evidence that supports the claim. Our students practice with different arrangements to discover which one may be most effective for their specific piece of persuasion. We begin with the overall framework.

Introduction.   As with introductions for all genres of writing, arousing reader interest is the goal. Writers return to the strategies for introductions that we used in chapter 6 to find the ones that best suit their persuasive pieces: rhetorical questions, vignettes illustrating the stance of the writer, or startling statistics. While writers want to create reader interest, the tone of an argument is generally more formal, and "a straightforward introduction is probably the most effective" in persuasive pieces (McDonald, 1975, p. 266).

Qualifiers and explanations.   They also practice using qualifications or explanations preceding the claim or thesis statement. For example,

> *While some students think of uniforms as a restriction of their freedom of choice,* (qualification) *uniforms actually free us from costly wardrobes, decision-making demands on our time, and prejudice based on difference in appearance* (explanation). *School uniforms should be adopted at XYZ School* (claim or thesis statement).

Persuasion is an exercise in freedom and choice. When your aim is to persuade, you ordinarily do not have to search for a thesis. You start out with an idea to defend . . . a product to sell . . . a program to recommend.
Ruszkiewicz, 1985

The thesis statement takes a definite position in the introduction. The thesis statement clarifies the issue and states the writer's viewpoint at the beginning or at the end of introductory paragraph following the interest-catching device. A brief statement of the supporting reasons in the introduction, to be fully expanded in the body of the argument, sets the pattern of reasoning required to support the claim: facts from reliable sources, citing authority, examples, and so on.

Elaboration. While the introduction and conclusion set the framework for the argument, the paragraphs of evidence and support in the body are the argument.

Arrangement. Effective arrangement of information depends on subject matter and audience awareness. An overall pattern of presentation, one that readers expect in persuasion, begins with a statement of the issue with clarification or explanation of the issue, why it is an issue, and for whom it is an issue. Recognition of the opposing point of view with answers to their counter arguments precedes the writer's stated position. The writer's position is usually presented last so that it will have the strongest impact on the reader. This ordering of materials adheres to the idea that readers remember best what they read last. Figure 11–13 illustrates a heuristic that is a general pattern for argument and persuasion.

Our writers practice building on their readers' understanding of the issue. To help keep readers with them, they review the arrangement of material in patterns that best clarify the information. For example,

Least important	→	Most important
Known	→	Unknown
Concrete	→	Abstract
General	→	Specific

Inductive and deductive patterns. Organization of argument or persuasion follows one of two general patterns: inductive or deductive. With an inductive organizational scheme, writers build factual information from specific to general, known to unknown, or least to most important. With this approach, the writer presents the parts and then the whole. The evidence builds, piece by piece, to the logical outcome, which is the writer's claim (thesis statement), presented for the first time in the conclusion of the paper. This pattern is particularly effective if the writer believes the audience would read no further if the claim were presented at the beginning. Figure 11–14 illustrates the inductive pattern.

The following paragraph is an example of inductive arrangement:

> In April, the average rainfall is higher than it is in other months. It rains approximately 20 out of the 30 days of the month. Temperatures range from the high 60s to the high 70s. Since the temperatures in May are in the same range as those in April, but the rainfall is minimal, the committee recommends that the outdoor sports banquet be held in May.

Students learned the thesis-support style by talking about and participating in argumentation, but explicit instruction plus a variety of activities including peer response was more helpful in learning the genre than the same activities without explicit instruction. Yeh, 1998

Heuristics added structure to students' essays, but did so in a way that reinforced students' voices, providing a framework for sympathetic consideration of opposing viewpoints and inclusion of personal experiences and emotional appeals. Yeh, 1998

Traditionally, logical arguments are classified as using either inductive or deductive reasoning, both of which almost always work together. Lunsford and Connors, 1995

FIGURE 11–13
Argument/Persuasion
Heuristic

State the issue.

Define the issue clearly:

That is,

> In other words
>
> Although (opposition)

Give reasons for the origin of the issue:

> Because
>
> For example,
>
> As a result,
>
> At first . . . but now

Identify for whom this is a problem:

> Why is it a problem for (them, you)?

Show how the issue relates to your audience.

State alternative positions (counter arguments).

Present answers to the counter arguments.

State your position on the issue:

> Because
>
> Because
>
> Because

Demonstrate how your position will change the problem:

> For instance,
>
> First,
>
> If . . . then

Ask for action, a change of belief.

A deductive pattern, on the other hand, begins with a strong, clear statement of the writer's position and then proceeds to prove it with a body of evidence. With this pattern, a writer moves from the whole to its parts, with each part supporting the claim stated in the introduction. The author returns to the claim at the end of the argument, calling for some action or change. Figure 11–15 illustrates the deductive pattern.

The following paragraph is an example of a deductive arrangement of material:

The outdoor sports banquet should be planned for May rather than April (*claim*). The weather bureau reports that average rainfall is higher in April than in other months (*argument*). In fact, it rains approximately 20 out of the 30 days in the month (*proof*). Temperatures are approximately the same in April and May, ranging from

FIGURE 11–14
Inductive Organizational
Pattern

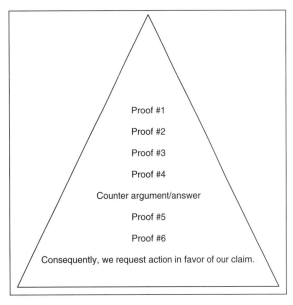

FIGURE 11–15
Deductive Organizational
Pattern

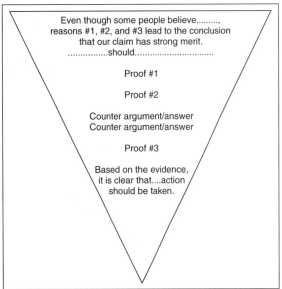

the high 60s to the high 70s (*argument/proof*). Some people on the committee disagree with having the banquet in May because it is too near the end of the school year (*counter argument*). However, this year the school term does not end until the first week in June (*answer*). Since the banquet is planned as an outdoor event and since there is plenty of time before the end of school, we should choose a date in May for the banquet (*call for action*).

Conner and Lauer (1988) have identified variables that are useful in predicting the overall quality of student persuasive writing:

- Cohesion and coherence
- Quality and types of persuasive appeals
- Argument superstructure
- Audience awareness
- Informal reasoning
- Syntactic factors

Conclusions.   The conclusion holds the writer's real, believable, and workable solution to the issue. As with other purposes for writing, the conclusion ties to or reemphasizes the introduction by restating what the writer has been trying to prove. It includes a call for action, well supported with the reasons why it is the best course of action or the right stance. We help our students build the body of the paper with such strength that the conclusion can be short and powerful.

Eighth-grader Whitney uses persuasive writing to convince her parents to buy her a car.

Dear Mom and Dad,

I think you should buy me a car for my sixteenth birthday. The five reasons are as follows: I can run errands for you, I'll be safe when you're not home since we live so far out, I'll be able to take the car to college with me, and I'm very responsible. In addition, we definitely need a third car because Dad takes his to work and Mom uses hers to run errands all day. Since I'm involved in so many activities, I will need a car to drive myself around.

My first reason, running errands for you, makes this a very reasonable request. I can take my brothers places when you are busy, making your life easier. Also, if you're home making something and you need an ingredient, I can drive to the store for you. Take for example the time we were about to go to the lake and you were making that dip and realized you got the wrong type of tomatoes. Mom even said, "Man, Whitney, I wish you could drive!"

Also, when you're out of town or doing something with both cars, I'll be able to leave if someone starts to break in. One time everyone was at my brother's game and I was doing homework, I heard noises outside. I went and got a baseball bat just so I was able to feel safe. I just kept thinking how much safer I would feel if I could just drive away. I like living in the country, but sometimes I would feel a lot safer if I could just drive into town and go to a friend's house. Also, I know you would feel better about leaving me home all day when you go to baseball tournaments. Sometimes I have things to do and have to give them up just because I can't stay home.

Third, I think you should buy me a car for my sixteenth birthday present because I'll take it to college with me. Since you will already be spending so much money on sending me to college, it would work better financially to buy the car first so you'll be able to save money during the two to three year period before I go to college. It could be a present for my sweet sixteen (it will really be sweet if you buy me a Mustang!). That way when I go to college it won't be just extra money being spent to buy me a car—it will be birthday money. Since I've been saving soooo long, I'll even pay half. You don't have to get me a really nice car (like that silvery-blue BMW with tan interior that I've always wanted!) but you could buy me a red, black interior Mustang. I've wanted one forever, and since I'll pay half, it will be less expensive. Also, maybe Uncle Mark could get us the extra luxuries at cost.

Furthermore, you've always said I'm very responsible, and if you buy me a nice, clean, dependable car, then I can take my friends places. Since I am so responsible, wouldn't you rather have me driving than my friends? I'll make sure they wear a seat belt, and I won't let food and drinks in if you buy me a nice car. I'll represent you well on the road. I will not lose my temper and promise not to say rude things or do bad signs to other drivers. I promise not to speed or be careless causing me to get in an accident making the insurance go up. If I don't get a car, my friends will get one. Then they would be driving me and might not be as careful as I am. I know you are big on safety, so I'll take my car in for regular check-ups; I'll also make sure it's in top condition. That's why you shouldn't give me Dad's car because I wouldn't care as much about his as I would my own. And then one day I'll be driving along and ... BAM! I'll break down because I forgot to get the oil changed. If it was my own car, I'd take it in for all the necessary check-up and keep it in tip-top shape. I'll even pay for gas with my own money because I'll have a part-time job ... because I'm responsible. And if I had a car, I'd be able to drive myself to work.

We will definitely need a third car before I leave for college. Dad's car is always at work, and Mom needs hers to run errands and take the boys places. Since most of the time both cars are being used, you will need to buy me one. That way if you are taking my brothers to practices or something, I'll be free to drive myself to the mall; I'll just do it when I don't have homework. I think the third car should be mine also because it will be easier on you. For instance, if I have a volleyball or basketball practice in the morning, I can drive myself to school so you won't have to get up at 5:15 a.m. three days a week. Or, if I have afternoon activities, you won't have to go out of your way to pick me up. It would also make my life easier because if something comes up, like a NJHS meeting, I can leave a message on the answering machine but won't have to worry as much about it if you got the message because I'll be driving myself home. Also, if my brothers have friends over and are being too loud, I can get into my car and drive away and do my homework in peace.

In conclusion, I think you should buy me a car for my sweet sixteen for all the excellent reasons I have addressed. I can run errands for you, I'll be safe at home in the country, and I'll take it to college with me. Also, I'm responsible and since I'm involved in so many activities, I need a car to drive myself around. Thank you for your time and consideration of my request.

Your loving daughter,
Whitney

EMPHASIZING THE MULTIPLE INTELLIGENCES

Linguistic: Write a letter to the editor; develop an advertisement.

Logical mathematical: Develop an argument and its counter argument.

Spatial: Map an issue deductively and inductively to determine which pattern best presents the argument or persuasion.

Bodily-kinesthetic: Plan and participate in a class debate.

Musical: Persuade the parents' organization at school to support your favorite musical interest (e.g., band trip, free instrument program, orchestra group).

Interpersonal: Choose an issue; interview people who hold strong views on each side of the issue.

Intrapersonal: Document your stand on an issue by keeping a personal journal of the information you find related to the issue.

Naturalist: Develop and write a position on an environmental issue of interest to you (e.g., save the whales, clean water or air, develop an arboretum).

SUMMARY

While persuasion comes naturally to children, younger children do not yet have the foundation to be able to write effective persuasive pieces. Therefore, teachers need to be sure they know where students are in their writing development, provide the writing foundation they need in other purposes for writing, and then offer careful instruction in persuasive writing.

Persuasion is a culmination of all forms of prose in that it may contain narration, facts, details, examples, comparisons, contrast, statistics, anecdotes, and processes in an effort to persuade an audience to agree with the writer or take a specific action. Because persuasion requires a sound foundation in other genres of writing, we teach in-depth persuasive techniques to middle school children.

Key elements in persuasive writing include establishing a claim, analyzing the audience, elaborating reasons to support the claim, refuting counter arguments, and concluding with a call to agree or take action.

Teaching strategies for third- through fifth-grade students include connection to real-life situations with high interest examples and topics. In lessons that model persuasive writing strategies, students select viable topics, establish a claim, brainstorm reasons for support of the claim, and then narrow their support to three strong reasons. The students learn to write an introduction, a body that fully supports the three reasons, and a conclusion that calls for action or agreement.

Upper elementary and middle school students study persuasive writing in depth. Students analyze persuasive models and select a topic that has opposing issues. Writers learn strategies to identify the audience, present strong evidence, and use authority to support a claim. Concepts of fact and opinion are explored as they relate to evidence presented in persuasive writing. Counter arguments become valuable tools for understanding all facets of the issue and for developing strong arguments.

Upper elementary students learn organizational strategies and patterns that enhance persuasive writing and apply appropriate heuristics to support their claims. Introductions arouse audience interest. The body is arranged to facilitate audience understanding of the issue and uses inductive reasoning patterns. Conclusions restate the claim and call for action or agreement with the writer.

Theory into Practice

1. Discuss in small groups the difference between argument and persuasion. How is the purpose of persuasive writing different from informative writing? How does persuasion use other modes of writing?

2. Analyze several persuasive pieces of writing to see how well they meet the criteria for effective persuasion.

3. Brainstorm and select an issue of interest to your group. Take a stand on the issue and gather evidence on the topic.

4. Conduct an interview and/or a survey to obtain information and to analyze attitudes toward your issue.

5. In small groups, create a pyramid and a bridging chart to develop arguments for a persuasive paper.

6. Identify the people who would support or oppose the issue. Using those people as the principal characters, role-play the pros and cons of the issue.

7. Debate the issue during a class session. Critique your debate to determine how you would adapt it to make the process effective for third- through eighth-grade students.

8. Write lesson plans for teaching persuasive writing skills to a particular grade level.

9. How many of the multiple intelligences can you tap in developing this purpose for writing? Specify how you would appeal to them in your teaching of persuasion.

10. Write a persuasive piece to your future principal to convince him/her that it is important to include writing as a regular part of the curricula.

BIBLIOGRAPHY

Applebee, Arthur N., Judith A. Langer, Ina V. S. Mullis, Andrew S. Latham, and Claudia A. Gentile. 1994. *NAEP 1992 writing report card.* Washington, DC: Office of Educational Research and Improvement, U.S. Department of Education.

Brown, J. S., A. Collins, and P. Duguid. 1989. Situated cognition and the culture of learning. *Educational Researcher, 18* (May), 7–10.

Carrel, Patricia L., and Joan C. Eisterhold. 1983. Schema theory and ESL reading pedagogy. *TESOL Quarterly 17.* (Dec.), 553–73.

Chapman, Marilyn L. 1995. The sociocognitive construction of written genres in first grade. *Research in the Teaching of English, 29* (2) (May), 164–192

Connolly, Francis. 1953. *A rhetoric casebook.* New York: Harcourt, Brace and Company.

Connor, Ula, and J. Lauer. 1988. Cross-cultural variation in persuasive student writing, in *Contrastive rhetoric,* A. C. Purves (Ed.). Newbury Park, CA: Sage.

Corbett, Edward P. J. 1971. *Classical rhetoric for the modern student.* New York: Oxford University Press.

Cowan, Gregory, and Elizabeth Cowan. 1980. *Writing.* New York: John Wiley & Sons.

Crowhurst, M. 1991. Interrelationships between reading and writing persuasive discourse. *Research in the Teaching of English, 4,* 314–335.

Dickson, Marcia. 1995. *It's not like that here: Teaching academic writing and reading to novice writers.* Portsmouth, NH: Boynton/Cook.

Dunbar, Clement, Georgia Dunbar, and Louise E. Rorabacher. 1997. *Assignments in exposition.* New York: Addison Wesley.

Eggemeier, Judith K. 1999. Developing the craft of writing in the sixth-grade classroom. *Primary Voices K–6, 7* (4) (April), 25–32.

Ferris, Dana R. 1994. Rhetorical strategies in student persuasive writing: Differences between native and non-native English speakers. *Research in the Teaching of English, 28* (February), 45–65.

Hartfiel, V. Faye, Jane B. Hughey, Deanna R. Wormuth, and Holly L. Jacobs. 1985. *Learning ESL composition.* Rowley, MA: Newbury House Publishers.

Kinneavy, J. L. 1980. *A theory of discourse.* New York: W.W. Norton & Company.

Larsen, Richard L. 1971. A plan for teaching rhetorical invention, in *Classical rhetoric for the modern student,* E. P. J. Corbett (Ed.). New York: Oxford University Press.

Lunsford, Andrea, and Robert Connors. 1995. *St. Martin's handbook.* New York: St. Martin's Press.

McDonald, Daniel. 1975. *The language of argument,* 2nd ed. New York: Harper & Row.

Ruszkiewicz, John J. 1985. *Well-bound words: A rhetoric.* Dallas, TX: Scott, Foresman.

Stolarek, Elizabeth A. 1994. Prose modeling and metacognition: The effect of modeling on developing a metacognitive stance toward writing. *Research in the Teaching of English, 28* (2) (May), 154–174.

Thaiss, Christopher. 1986. *Language across the curriculum in the elementary grades.* Urbana, IL: National Council of Teachers of English.

Toulmin, S. E. 1958. *The uses of argument.* New York: Cambridge University Press.

White, J. 1989. Children's argumentative writing: A reappraisal of difficulties, in *Writing in schools: Reader,* F. Christie (Ed.), (ECT 418). Geelong, Victoria: Deakin University Press.

Williams, Joseph M., and Gregory G. Colombo. 1993. The case for explicit teaching: Why what you don't know won't help you. *Research in the Teaching of English, 27* (3) (October), 252–264

Yeh, Stephen S. 1998. Empowering education: Teaching argumentative writing to cultural minority middle-school students. *Research in the Teaching of English, 33* (1) (August), 49–83.

Zinsser, William Knowlton. 1998. *On writing well: The classic guide to writing nonfiction.* New York: Harper Reference.

Report Writing

Nonfiction is the genre that will dominate most children's
school and vocational careers.

Graves, 1989

Chapter Outline

Research Reports

"Why does a leopard have spots? Why does it live in Africa?" Children have a natural curiosity about the world around them. They love to learn about new things, and that enthusiasm is nurtured and encouraged through research report writing. Research reports allow students to explore their interests and share those interests with others. The interdisciplinary/thematic approach to teaching described in chapter 2 lends itself well to teaching skills for research report writing. Whatever the theme, students select topics of interest within the theme and become self-made experts on those topics. The skills of such writing are lifelong skills that apply to a wide range of occupations and personal interests. For example, research skills needed for a job report or for buying a car are very similar. The major difference is the audience, but the skills and processes are the same.

Teaching Guidelines: Report Writing

A Variety of Skills.   Writing reports requires practice with varied writing skills over a period of time. Knowing and being able to use three broad areas—literature search, primary sources, and basic writing skills—are important to successful research reports. Some of those skills are set out in Figure 12–1.

A Starting Point.   We begin teaching research skills in early grades so that students can internalize and apply these varied and complex skills successfully in later grades and in their personal lives. Curriculum guides for the school, state guidelines, and graded textbook materials determine appropriate research skills for specific grade levels. We select research report objectives based on observations of students' writing experiences, academic needs, and appropriateness for the grade level. What is it that students need to learn? Note-taking skills? How to paraphrase information? How to cite references? Topic selection skills? How to use an index? How to use the library or search the Internet? How to synthesize information from different sources?

Many of the writing skills and strategies that we teach throughout the year also fit within the context of research reports. These essential skills apply to a broad range of student activities and content in addition to research reports. For example, in the early primary grades we teach students library organization, use of a table of contents, the main idea of a piece of information, and the difference between fiction and nonfiction. Older students have usually learned all of these skills, but we allow for ample review and practice of the skills before working on research report assignment.

The students' purposes and the perceived audience determine the shape of the final product. Not all practice of research report skills requires a full-fledged documented paper. Sometimes a simple assignment to answer a specific question provides essential practice in locating information in the library, within a text, or on the Internet. For example, during a discussion about Abraham Lincoln, a young child points out that Lincoln's picture is on the penny. Questions for research arise: "When did Lincoln's picture first appear on the penny?" or "Whose picture was on the penny before Lincoln's?" These

FIGURE 12–1
Research Report
Writing Skills

Literature searches require the ability to use the following tools:
  Alphabetic order
  Key words
  Table of contents
  Indices
  Dewey Decimal library system
  Library call numbers
  Library search systems
  Encyclopedias, almanacs, atlases
  Internet searches
Primary source searches require the ability to use the following skills:
  Conduct interviews and surveys
  Experiment and make observations
Writing the report requires the ability to recognize and use the following concepts:
  Understand fiction/nonfiction and fact/opinion
  Select a topic
  Stay on topic
  Take notes
  Categorize information
  Organize information into paragraphs
  Paraphrase
  Summarize
  Write introductions and conclusions
  Revise
  Edit
  Document sources and cite references

questions encourage practice in locating information and result in quick oral reports to the class or a sentence or two taken from an Internet entry or a book.

To select topics, we first generate a list of potential topics. From first grade on, students learn the importance of using nonfiction in a search process and categorizing books as fiction or nonfiction. To teach them how to find relevant information in a reference book or from a site on the Internet, we practice with a variety of texts and printed Internet information. During a library day in the workshop, students use the library search systems and then locate texts on the shelves related to a particular topic.

> It appears that how young learners interpret the task strongly affects how they approach the research and writing. Dahl and Farnan, 1998

Relevance. Before deciding the scope and scale of any research project, students discuss the relevance of the research report to their own interests and activities. When students understand why they are embarking on the project, motivation and attitude stay on target. Dahl and Farnan's (1998) review of research on writing reports suggests that students' understanding of the purpose for writing the reports is crucial to the quality of the final product. Students need to see the relevance of the research project and the clear expectations for completion. Students who believe that the writing task is to transform information are most successful in planning, searching, using sources, synthesizing, connecting content, writing, and revising for a specific audience.

Such findings suggest that teachers who promote ownership of the task, clearly state the objectives, teach necessary skills, provide support, and model the intended products are most successful in helping students learn the processes and skills of the research writing process.

The following sequence of research skills suggests a general outline of how research reports progress. Often the skills overlap and recur throughout the project. For example, preliminary library searches may show that a topic is too broad or that predetermined organizational strategies need adjustments.

Teaching Strategy: Topic Selection

Kerr, Makuluni, and Nieves (2000) define the beginning of a research process as ". . . identifying an issue, naming a problem, or asking a question" (p. 15). Further, in a study of parents, children, and teachers working together on research projects, Whitmore and Norton-Meier (2000) emphasize the importance of choice as an essential ingredient in developing research topics. We find that young children respond enthusiastically to research when they have the opportunity to find answers to their own questions.

Interest.   The first item, interest in the topic, is nearly guaranteed when students have a choice in their topics. Young children respond enthusiastically to research when they have the opportunity to find answers to their own questions. We use children's frequent questions as topics of research: "How does that work?" or "Why did that happen?" or "Who is that?" Rather than offer instant answers, instead we offer opportunities for children to find out for themselves. During these teachable moments, we introduce students to relevant books, indices, tables of contents, Internet searches, and experts on the topic.

For older students, since major research projects last over a period of time; maintaining student interest is important. Therefore, self-selection of topics becomes an even more essential element of long-term projects. We are careful about setting parameters that relate to the thematic unit, and we then encourage students to select topics within those parameters.

Multiple Intelligences.   Students who use their strong intelligences in selecting topics are more likely to sustain interest in a project. For example, topics related to art, architecture, or engineering appeal to the spatial intelligence. Topics related to natural phenomenon in the plant or animal world appeal to the naturalistic intelligence. Students brainstorm ideas related to personal interests and their strongest intelligence in order to develop potential lists of topics.

The list of "140 Things to Wonder About" in appendix J serves as a guide for developing thematic units, and it also serves as survey of student interests. It is a means of prompting students to think of ideas on related topics. Students limit topics to include specific information related to larger ideas, or they broaden the topic when they find limited resources and references. Small group discussions allow students time to "try out" their potential topics with each other and further expand or narrow the scope of the project.

Projects also help students succeed because they allow them to use all of their "intelligences," just as the "projects" of normal day-to-day living do. Wolk, 1995

When given an opportunity, students can, and do, take ownership of their learning. Checkley, 1995

The critically important guideline for choosing a topic is that the student wants to know about or could become highly invested in that topic. Whitehouse, 1994

Learning how to learn is one of the most essential skills. Polete, 1989

I take time for talk during the topic search because talking is something writers do. Atwell, 1998

Teaching Strategy: Develop Information

Children need to know something about the content of their first report subjects before they even begin. Graves, 1989

Intent. Information for a report depends on the intent of the report, the audience, and what the writer and the audience already know. For example, the intent of a school research report is often to share information with classmates about a topic of interest to the writer. Implicit in this intent is a desire to make the topic appealing to classmates. To determine what classmates already know about a given topic, the author asks classmates to list facts they know or questions they have on the topic. The writer begins the process by recording information already known about the topic and listing questions for further investigation.

I find that too many children are introduced to reports by trying to research something they know little about at the start. This approach usually guarantees that the child will see little sense in the function of the report other than to fulfill a school requirement. Graves, 1989

Models. Levine's books for children . . . *If Your Name Was Changed at Ellis Island* (1990) and . . . *If You Lived at the Time of Martin Luther King* (1993) demonstrate how to organize nonfiction reports in response to a series of questions. McGovern's books . . . *If You Grew Up with Abraham Lincoln* (1976) and . . . *If You Lived with the Sioux Indians* (1992) follow the same format. In the books, questions form chapter titles, and the text responds directly to the questions. The same strategy helps students determine what kinds of information to gather.

Category Questions. We demonstrate how defining categories of information about a topic helps to organize the search through references and to plan the final products. Category questions help lead writers to the information they need. For example, category questions for an animal report might include some of the following:

- What does it look like (distinguishing characteristics)?
- Where in the world does it live?
- What kind of home does it have?
- How does it care for its young?
- What does it eat?
- How does it catch or eat its prey?

We can help students become ready for writing by showing them that their task is to develop only a single aspect of their topic, to write about one corner of their information and to write for a particular audience. Calkins, 1986

We encourage students to design four or five basic questions related to the research topic. Figure 12–2 illustrates how a third-grade student mapped answers to his category questions. This process again narrows the scope of the research and allows students to concentrate on the specific information rather than trying to "cover" too large a topic.

Category questions for research topics are broad in scale with many possible answers. A question that has a single answer limits the quality and depth of the research. For example, a category question that asks, "How many eggs does a robin lay at a time?" generates a short answer insufficient to develop into a full section of a research paper. However, a category question that asks, "How do robins raise their young?" generates a wide variety of information including nest building, number and description of eggs laid, incubation time, behavior of new chicks and parents, growth rates, and fledgling activity.

Practice. To help younger students organize their search for information and organize their final papers, we ask them to write each category question at the top of a blank page much like the process described in the "spread it out" heuristic in chapter 6. Writers place the pages in a research folder or staple them together as a research booklet. We

FIGURE 12–2
Category mapping

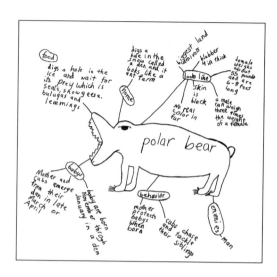

Perhaps the complex
nature of the research
paper is what over-
whelms young writ-
ers, and teachers can
relieve that anxiety by
emphasizing the sim-
plicity of each step.
Whitehouse, 1994

show the students that all information on a certain category belongs on the same page, even if the notes come from different sources. We demonstrate how to collect notes from several sources on the same sheet of paper and how to document the sources of the information. Older students, using note cards, label each note card with the category question and the source.

In addition to answering the established basic questions, we ask students to reflect on their personal attitudes, feelings, and interest in the topic in either an opening or a closing paragraph. During the process of a research project, students develop a personal response to the topic that is legitimately a part of the report. This personal response legitimizes the reasons for embarking on the search and strengthens student ownership throughout the project.

Teaching Strategy: The Research Process

Select Information.   The daunting task of tackling thick reference materials and extensive Internet sites clearly demonstrates to students the need for shortcuts. The use of tables of contents, indexes, key words, headings, and subheadings fill that need. With reference books or printed Internet reports, we demonstrate how the parts of books or articles streamline the search for information. We plan specific lessons that give students plenty of practice in using these organizational tools on a regular basis so that they are internalized and available when needed. When students are adept at these skills, the final research project becomes an authentic assessment of these skills.

Before students can
be successful in the
research process,
they need to be able
to take notes effec-
tively. Routman, 1994

Note Taking.   As Clark (1987) says, we must make students "efficient collectors of information." Note taking is an essential skill in the collection of information. Clark defines note taking as a lifelong educational skill, a "way of collecting, organizing, and synthesizing information." Routman (1994) says that note taking is "a lifelong skill that students need to have demonstrated over and over again throughout the school year."

FIGURE 12–3
Notes

trunk
40,000 muscles and tendons
strong, flexible
great control
pluck a flower
lift a log

We use copies of reference pages to demonstrate how to skim paragraphs and write specific notes related to needed information. This requires the ability to see the main idea of a paragraph or selection and glean the important information. For example, we show students the following paragraph from *Zoobooks*.

> There are 40,000 muscles and tendons in an elephant's trunk. This makes the trunk strong and very flexible. It also allows an elephant to control its trunk with great skill. It is possible for an elephant to delicately pluck a single flower—or lift up a huge log (Wexo, 1994, unpaged).

Then we demonstrate how to write notes about the pertinent information. Notes from this selection are depicted in Figure 12–3.

Students need much practice to become proficient in this important skill before they begin work on their projects. Therefore, we use classroom textbooks or other nonfiction references as demonstration and practice materials.

Teachers find that demonstrating note taking pays big dividends. The key to success is repeated demonstrations and reteaching throughout the year with various genres and contexts. Routman, 1994

Ballenger (1994) recommends a dual-purpose note-taking process that encourages students to react to and reflect on information as they take notes. Much like the dialectical learning journal discussed in Chapter 7, Ballenger's note-taking process is carried out by dividing papers or note cards in half vertically. On the left, students write the exact quotes or concept from sources. On the right, they record personal comments and reactions to that information. These personal reflections establish ownership and interest in the topic and help shape a personal approach to the final draft. We recommend taking that process one step further by dividing papers or note cards into three columns. After the sections of notes and personal comments, the third column includes reference information of author, book title, and page number. Figure 12–4 illustrates this technique.

Reference Materials.   Reference materials from the library, newspapers, and Internet all provide valuable information for research papers. In workshop, we design specific lesson plans that cover how to use library search programs and how to locate the references on the shelves. Students get ample practice conducting Internet searches and then printing hard copies of valuable sites for the purpose of taking notes. They handle Internet sources the same way they do other reference materials, by writing notes from the Internet information that relates to specific categories on their note cards or question sheets.

elephant's feet
walks on toes
large pad to
cushion foot
surefooted
walks quietly

Many animals
have padding in
feet! In the
wild, surefooted
animals would
not survive.

Wexo. *Zoobooks*
Elephants. p. 3

FIGURE 12-4   Dual-purpose Note Taking

Miss Peach

FIGURE 12-5   Miss Peach Cartoon
By permission of Mell Lazarus and Creators Syndicate

Original Information.   Students use heuristics to gather interesting, important new facts and data. See chapter 6 for heuristics that facilitate collection of original data. For example, *interviews* with experts or guest speakers are valuable sources of information, and many students consider interviewing a highly enjoyable part of collecting information. For the journalistic community, interviews are the essence of news and communication. We review interview skills along with listening and note-taking skills so students make the best use of these resources.

Note taking from a speaker requires intense listening skills and the ability to quickly sift through thousands of spoken words to write essential information in a highly accurate manner. Students practice this skill by taking notes from class lessons and from interviews with classmates.

Some topics lend themselves well to survey information. We teach students how to design, survey, and collect information, and then we demonstrate how to add it to the question categories. For example, a research topic on the role of color in food preferences leads to a survey of student reactions to such foods as green pizza or blue ice cream. A question category for classmates' reactions to odd colors in foods generates interesting, original data for the report and increased levels of interest in the audience.

Experiment and observation are also highly motivational heuristics that generate original information. For example, on the topic of color in food preferences, a student offers classmates a variety of different colored cookies and then records how many students selected each color of cookie. When authors incorporate this original information into their reports, they increase their credibility as research writers and their ability to intrigue the audience.

Teaching Strategy: Write the Report

Students need to learn the process of reporting on something they know about in order to learn how to organize information and to discover their own voice. Graves, 1989

Synthesis.   This step moves students from the knowledge level of Bloom's (1984) Taxonomy, which includes copying information to the level of synthesizing information to make sense of it for an audience. Teachers often bemoan the fact that "all my students do is copy from a book." With careful guidance, students move from copying to synthesizing. Many et. al. (1996) discovered that students able to transform information "engaged in extended and continuous planning as they searched for materials focusing on their intended direction, and they revised these plans as new possibilities emerged." In addition, they monitored the coverage of each category to assure balance, and they selected, organized, and connected the content. This sophisticated behavior requires the use of higher level thinking skills and ample practice with those skills.

Most writing requires the generation of main ideas and details and the careful planning of content and structure. Summarizing is based on material that has already been written. The summary writer must decide what to include, what to eliminate, how to reword or reorganize information. Anderson & Hidi, 1988/89

Arrange material.   Older students shuffle note cards to arrange information in a reasonable sequence. They group closely related information into a paragraph within one of the categories. Younger children number notes on each separate category question sheet in a logical order. Then, each category question sheet becomes a separate paragraph. We demonstrate how notes from different sources are combined in the same paragraph. Through demonstrations, we teach students how to write topic sentences for paragraphs and how to organize notes into logical connections between the paragraphs.

Regie Routman's (1994) method of "talking aloud" is an effective way to demonstrate the thinking process and decision making that combine to create the necessary synthesis of information from the notes. Students engage in discussion to explore the process. They practice synthesizing information before they apply these skills to the research project.

Just as a class of students cannot move uniformly along in rehearsal, drafting, revision, editing, and publication, so too, they cannot proceed uniformly through a sequence of research steps. Calkins, 1986

Revise, Edit, and Publish.   Revision and editing skills are as important to research papers as they are to other genres of writing. As with other kinds of writing, much of revision and editing is a recurring activity that students engage in as they write and as they revisit the work. The revision and editing techniques discussed in chapter 5—peer conferences, rubrics of specific criteria, or read-alouds—also apply to research projects. The class designs its own rubric after a study of research models. This rubric guides students in evaluation throughout the process and is used with the final product.

Cite References.   This information-age society requires clear reference documentation. We use student reference books with citations at the back (sometimes called "references" or "bibliography" or "works cited") to explain the importance of citations. As students record notes, they also keep separate lists of the sources. In planned lessons, students organize the references in alphabetical order and use standard formats. They list Internet and interview sources separately in the citations. Students use the citation formats most frequently used for the particular subject matter they have chosen, or they select any standard format from the several that are commonly used such as MLA, APA, or Chicago.

Teaching Strategy: Share the Report

After completion of research projects, students are experts on their topics. At this point in the process, students deserve the rewards of sharing their work. Sharing this new information with peers and other audiences provides a powerful motivation to continue writing. Those students with strong spatial intelligences are skillful at including posters, artifacts, models, and computer-generated drawings to supplement their presentations. See the list of visual aids that enhance presentations in appendix K. We often videotape the presentations and invite parents, other classes and visitors to hear the reports. Copies are available in the library, the foyer, the office, and other gathering spaces to further validate the students' work.

Self-Evaluation.   The sharing process also offers students a chance to evaluate their own work. Jensen (1998) discusses brain research indicating that self-evaluation is critical to learning. Self-evaluation strengthens meaning and has a strong impact on future endeavors. Much self-evaluation takes place during the revision and editing processes, but sharing final products should also be recognized as a major tool in learning and self-evaluation.

Teaching Guidelines: Develop Research Skills

While there is a place in the real world for full-blown written research reports, many alternative methods of teaching research skills accomplish the same objectives in smaller chunks or in other innovative products. Some of the following suggestions are ones we use effectively for skill development with different grade levels and for different kinds of final products.

Why . . . Because.   When children ask "why," we show them books that will answer their questions or direct them to an Internet search. They can share verbal reports of their answers with the class.

Literature as a Springboard.   During literature studies, we use student questions about sites, settings, plots, and characters to launch mini-searches for information to answer the questions. They write findings in short reports or share orally with the class.

We use a collection of nonfiction books by Gail Gibbons as models for young researchers. Such books as *From Seed to Plant, Whales, The Pottery Place,* and *Trucks* provide models and the basis of a genre study of research writing.

For young writers, we encourage "all about" books. A student writes and illustrates a book "All About Dogs" or "All About Butterflies" or other topics of interests. Students read nonfiction materials and state the information in their own words. They learn to elaborate and stay focused on the topic. We challenge creative students to write reports from a unique point of view. For example, a writer might report on snakes from the viewpoint of the snake.

Perhaps the most powerful thing about nonfiction writing within the writing workshop is that it allows students to become teachers, claiming, developing, and sharing what they know. Calkins, 1986

When you finish a topic, make sure that you allow learners to evaluate the pros and cons, discuss the relevance, and demonstrate their patterning with models, plays, and teachings. Jensen, 1998

Children of all ages need to experience informal reporting before attempting longer, more extensive formal reports. Graves, 1989

Statements into Questions.   We don't wait for a child to ask the perfect question. Nancy Polete (1989) suggests taking literal facts and turning them into questions. For example, *It is raining today* can be turned into a question, *Why is it raining today?* The simple question becomes the basis for lessons on such skills as using the table of contents in a book about clouds or reading a weather report in the newspaper. The final product is an illustrated booklet of information about rain.

For older students, consider the statement *The state of Georgia is known for growing great peaches.* Students learn to turn that statement into a question: *Why is Georgia known for growing great peaches?* Such questions send students on quests for specific answers, but they quickly learn that the answers are neither short nor simple.

Fact or Fiction.   We use Seymour Simon's (1979) book *Animal Fact, Animal Fable* as a model for "fact and fable" booklets about topics of interest. On one page, the writer makes a statement about a subject and asks whether it is fact or fable. On the next page, she answers the question with support from references. She devotes several illustrated "fact and fable" pages to topics such as frogs, bicycles, bears, tap dancing, or soccer. Students can use the same concept to make "fact or fiction" or "true or false" books, making statements on one page and on the next page verifying with research whether it is fact or fiction.

Important Book.   For young children, we use *The Important Book* by Margaret Wise Brown (1977) as a format for organizing information on a topic and for personal reflection about the important concepts about of the topic. A sample page from the book reads, "The important thing about a daisy is that it is white. It is yellow in the middle, it has long white petals, and bees sit on it, it has a ticklish smell, it grows in green fields, and there are always lots of daisies. But the important thing about a daisy is that it is white." We ask students to write a page for a new class "important book" using information they learn from investigation of various topics related to the thematic unit.

Related Information.   We show students a graph or list of information from a newspaper or other source and ask them to find information related to the list or graph and locate new information, perhaps creating a new list or graph. For example, a list of children's favorite books might be printed in a newspaper. Students investigate:

- How the list was compiled or who made the decisions as to what books were included on the list. Write a report on the fairness or accuracy of the list.
- Why authors are on the list. Find other books by the same authors and determine how they are similar to the book on the list, or do mini-author studies.
- How books are categorized. Graph the categories. Write a reflective report about the graph explaining why certain categories were large or small.
- Why certain books are favorites. Survey classmates about their favorite books. Create a list of class favorites. Write a report about common traits among the books.

Guest Speaker Presentations.   Students take notes from a guest speaker's presentation. They use the notes to create a report of the main ideas and include a list of further questions about the topic. Students write thank-you letters to the speaker and express the main ideas they learned from the talk.

Favorite Objects. Students bring favorite objects from home to class. As students share the objects with the class, classmates questions become the basis of a search for information. For example, a baseball stimulates the question: "How long has baseball been a sport in the United States?" or "What other countries have professional baseball teams?" or "How many professional baseball players are there in the United States?" or "What women's leagues play professional baseball?" We give students the opportunity to find the answers and then share the answers with the class.

Group Sharing. For young children, we assemble a collection of books and materials on a topic and allow small groups to read and share the materials among themselves. Each group shares information learned either in oral presentations or illustrated booklets.

Competition. Students love games and races. We give matched pairs of students separate topics and ask them to see who can quickly locate materials or Internet information. We design a game of Jeopardy on a bulletin board and use students' ages and expertise to develop general or explicit categories such as people, animals, sports, places, science, history, or plants. Categories related to the thematic unit encourage depth on the subject. We design questions for the categories and ask individuals or teams to research the answers. We narrow the game's focus to using a certain kind of reference material or to practicing a particular research skill and leave the game in place over a period of time for occasional review and maintenance of skills. Students love to offer their own statements for research.

Location of Information. Students pick random cities in different parts of the country. Either individually or in small groups they decide which would be the best place to move. Their answers must be based on documented information along with their opinions of what makes a place "best."

Teaching Strategy: Lesson Plan

As a teacher, you need to inspect each learning task or assignment to see how you can enhance its meaning. Hunter, 1998

A sample lesson plan for one research report objective follows.

Goal: Understanding the research paper concept.

Objective: Students will select a topic for a research report.

Materials: Small magnets, one for each student; examples of professional journals that include reports of research; a few reference books; "researcher at work" name tags.

Time: Approximately 40 minutes.

Motivation: Give each student a small magnet to stimulate a class discussion. After a few minutes of "play" with magnets, ask students if they have ever wondered how magnets work. While magnets are fascinating to children, few can fully explain how and why they work or explain the role of magnetic principles in our everyday lives. Tell students that a research report is a way of learning about a topic and sharing the information with others.

Display professional journals, showing that scientists often use research reports as a way to explain the experiments and the ideas they have developed. Research reporting skills are useful in the real world because they help us share important information in an efficient way.

Display reference books, explaining that some research skills make finding needed information in a big book easy. It isn't necessary to read an entire reference book to find information for a report. That makes research skills major time-savers.

Tell students that having knowledge about a subject leads to good decisions rather than guesses. Each student becomes an "expert" on a subject, someone who knows more about a topic than almost anyone else. Continually refer to students as experts on their subjects. They like that status, and they deserve it. Show students that what they will do in this lesson is only the first step in the much longer process of writing a research paper. A sample of that process appears in appendix L.

Procedure: The first step in the research paper process is to select a topic. To begin, discuss definitions of "broad" and "narrow," asking students to look up the words in the dictionary. Then relate broad and narrow to topic selection. Topics need to be:

- broad enough to have information (at least two books in the library). This eliminates such topics as a current blockbuster movie because there would be few, if any, references other than the Internet.
- narrow enough that the information search is not overwhelming because of an over-abundance of reference material.

For example, the topics of "animals" or "United States" are too broad because there are hundreds of books in the library to search. Depending on the age and writing experience of the students, the topics of "alligators' habitats" or "symbols of Ohio" are manageable choices, but "alligators' teeth" or "hummingbird's flight patterns" could be too narrow.

Next, distribute a copy of "140 Things to Wonder About" (appendix J). As the list is discussed, ask students to check those that seem interesting or that spark a related idea. Ask each student to list on paper three subjects they would like to research related to the thematic unit. Suggest that they should choose several topics because the topic may need to be changed later if there is an inadequate supply of reference materials. If someone else selects the same topic, the writer might want to research a different facet of the general subject.

Note: Asking each student in a class to select a different topic eliminates problems of sharing reference materials. Also, students find it hard to see themselves as "experts" if someone else in the class is also an "expert" on the same topic.

Third, ask each student to read his or her topic choice to the class. Discuss as a class the qualities of the topic. Is it broad enough and yet narrow enough? This discussion helps all students become comfortable with decisions regarding topic selection.

Fourth, explain that it may still be necessary to change topics after a library/Internet search and indeed even during the process of writing the report. After a search, students sometimes find that the topic is still too broad or narrow. In that case they change or refine their ideas based on the information.

At the initial stages of any learning task, wise teacher guidance will greatly increase the rate and degree of that learning. As a student gains proficiency with a particular learning, guidance should be withdrawn gradually so the student learns to depend on himself and is able to function without guidance. Hunter, 1998

Finally, make a classroom chart listing the topics for each student. They like knowing who is doing what topic, and they like seeing their names as the "experts" on the topics. **Closure:** Distribute name tags that say "researcher at work" to each student. Students can wear these name tags as they work on their projects. The name tags alert librarians and computer laboratory instructors that students have specific tasks to complete. Remind students of the role research skills play in their lives and share in their excitement about the projects. Review the steps of the overall project and explain how tomorrow's lesson will proceed.

This paper in Figure 12–6 shows fourth-grader Sean's first attempt at synthesizing information for his research paper about gorillas.

FIGURE 12–6
Gorilla Story

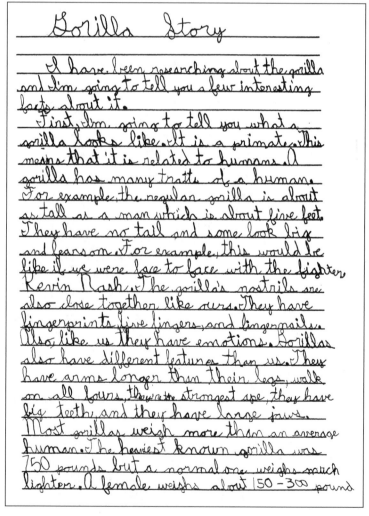

Journalism

An aura of reality and urgency take over when a student dons a reporter's cap, rests a pencil on the ear, and heads off for the fast-breaking story. In writer's workshop, we capitalize on our students' natural excitement about being real reporters by publishing a classroom or a campus-wide newspaper. To connect this genre with real-life examples, we begin by studying our local newspaper and *Time for Kids,* a weekly news magazine for students patterned after the adult version of *Time.*

Teaching Guidelines: News Reporting

Characteristics.   The unique nature of news reporting includes the characteristics shown in Figure 12–7.

Creation of a Venn diagram comparing news reporting to fiction writing helps students further develop clear understandings of how journalism relates to and is different from other kinds of writing. Figure 12–8 illustrates some of the similarities and differences between journalistic and other prose writing.

In addition, Gail Gibbons'(1987) book *Deadline! From News to Newspaper* helps writers learn how newspapers are written, and we often invite a local reporter to speak to our classes for a first-hand look at being a journalist. Field trips to the newspaper offices also add to the real-life connection.

News Sections.   For older students, we explore the different sections of a newspaper such as international, national, state, local, comics, opinions/editorials, weather, obituaries, advertisements, want ads, sports, food, entertainment, and business. We talk about

FIGURE 12–7
Characteristics of News Reporting

- News reporting requires quality writing each and every day. Whether the medium is newspapers, television, radio, news magazines, or the Internet, the news is first written.
- The common denominator for news reports is clear, concise, timely, interesting, and honest writing.
- Story topics are usually current events, and as such, may not have references to search for background information. Reporters must often collect information in other ways. They conduct interviews, attend meetings or other events, search public records, or participate in particular activities.
- News stories contain factual information rather than personal opinions, possibilities, creative approaches to situations, or slanted comments.
- News stories are interesting to wide numbers of people.
- Headlines give readers hints about the content of the article.
- Stories are often shorter than fiction pieces.
- Many news stories do not list the author.
- Advertisements often overshadow the news to help pay for the newspaper.

FIGURE 12–8
Venn Diagram: Journalistic Compared to Informational Prose Writing

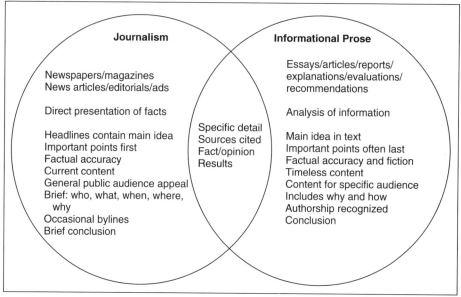

what makes information for each of those sections "newsworthy" for particular groups of people and determine what kinds of topics would be appropriate for a campus newspaper. For example, a snowstorm in a distant state would not make news for a campus newspaper, but a story about the principal's broken arm would be a high-interest topic.

Techniques.   By studying individual newspaper or magazine articles, we explore the writing techniques used by reporters. Because that is information readers want to know, we discover the long-standing importance of using the journalistic questions—who, when, where, why, and how—in the news articles. We discuss how the reporters probably gathered the information, how they introduced the topic, how they developed the ideas, and how the stories ended. We talk about word use and writing style, and characteristics that distinguish news reporting from other writing. The newspaper articles in Figure 12–9 illustrate features that we discuss in workshop. One article discusses the bare-bones facts of the endangered species stamp collection, while the second article carries a reporter's byline and descriptively reports the importance of light and shadow in photography.

The classroom itself provides the first circle of ideas. Students brainstorm to discover their own interests and experiences. Clark, 1987

Assignments.   After brainstorming a class list of possible topics for a campus or classroom newspaper, we evaluate each idea for its importance and appropriate place in the newspaper. We assign reporters for each topic and make plans for students or pairs of students to have equal chances at writing articles for various issues during the school year. For a workshop newspaper, we concentrate on articles that would be of interest to families of class members and perhaps other classes on the same grade level. We usually include short biographies of each student in the class so that all feel they are part of the experience. Students interview and write about each other for these articles. For a campus

FIGURE 12–9
Newspaper
Articles

UN group unveils stamps

By SYD KRONISH
Associated Press

Each year since 1993, the United Nations Postal Administration has issued a set of stamps dedicated to protecting and saving the world's endangered species.

The 2000 set of 12 stamps by the U.N.P.A. continues this theme by depicting various endangered species and fauna. The stamps are divided into three groups of four different species with denominations of 33 cents U.S. currency, 90 Swiss francs and S7/Euro 0.51 (Euro dollars).

The four 33-cent stamps show the brown bear, black-bellied bustard (crane family), Chinese crocodile lizard and the bonobo (pygmy chimpanzee).

The four 90 francs stamps illustrate the hippopotamus, coscoraba swan, the emerald monitor goanna (snake family) and the sea otter.

The S7/Euro stamps portray the leopard, white spoonbill, killer whale and the Chilean huemal (deer family).

Also released as part of the endangered species issuance is the 2000 Endangered Species Annual Collection Folder in a special album.

It contains all the stamps in the set with colorful photos related to the various species.

The mint stamps and the folder are available from the United Nations Postal Administration, P.O. Box 5900, Grand Central Station, New York, NY 10163-9992. Or you may phone 1-800-234-UNPA.

Kronish, Sid. UN group unveils stamps. *The Eagle*, Bryan, Texas. April 2, 2000, p. D4.

newspaper, we broaden the topics to include upcoming special events, school personnel, jokes, comics, musicals, special programs such as community service projects, neighborhood interests, the library, safety concerns, cafeteria lunches, and playground issues.

Qualities of a Good Story. We list information that supports the newspaper topics, the information they will look for as reporters, which essentially includes the basic questions who, what, where, when, why, and how. Blundell's (1988) requirements for writing good news stories guide our process:

- Determine the elements of the story that are intrinsically interesting.
- Look for action stories.
- Seize the attention of the audience.
- Tell the story to hold the readers' interest.
- "Nail" the story to the readers' memory.

> The main incentive journalism teachers can offer is the immediacy of the product—something is going to happen to the article—it is going to be *printed!*
> Melton, 1985

Teaching Strategies: Gather Information

We discuss how to gather information for the various topics. For some articles, students need to learn interview techniques. D.L. Mabery's (1985) children's book *Tell Me About Yourself: How to Interview Anyone from Your Friends to Famous People* is a good reference for these skills. For other topics, students might attend a performance or a meeting or participate in a particular activity. We discuss the importance of taking notes from these experiences and use the following tips adapted from Clark's (1987) suggestions:

> To improve students' writing, we must make them efficient collectors of information. This takes hard work. Students are used to being passive receivers of information. Clark, 1987

- Write quickly but clearly.
- Write key words.

FIGURE 12–9   Newspaper Articles

Shadows add to mystery

By RICK SAMMON
Associated Press

There's a popular saying among professional photographers who consider themselves artists: "Take away the mystery, and you take away the interest of the photograph."

But how does one create a sense of mystery on film? One method is to have an interesting subject or scene, one that causes the viewer to ask what's happening.

When there isn't enough going on to create that sense of mystery, photographers rely on lighting for impact. Specifically, they use shadows.

Think about those publicity shots of movie stars, especially the black-and-white photos from the '30s and '40s. In many of the studio portraits, half of the face is in a dark shadow, created by strong side lighting.

Think about some of the interesting landscape photographs you have seen. Most likely, your favorites are those taken in early morning or late afternoon—when long shadows, created by side lighting, hide some of the elements in the scene.

Remember the first *Godfather* movie? In some of the indoor shots, you couldn't look into the actors' eyes. The effective technique created by top lighting made viewers wonder what the characters were really thinking and feeling.

And have you seen any of the *National Geographic* photos of the remains of the Titanic? Photographer Emory Kristof used strong side and back lighting to make the viewer say, "I want to see more."

So, if there's a bit of an artist in you, you can add impact to your photographs by thinking shadows—for your indoor and outdoor pictures. Here are a few techniques to keep in mind:

Indoors: Position the subject by a window—shoulder toward the glass—and take the picture facing him or her. Strong side lighting from the window will create a shadow on one side of the face. When using a flash, use a synch cord and hold your flash off-camera to the left or right of the subject. This technique also will create a strong shadow on the face.

Outdoors: As mentioned, photographs taken in the early morning or late afternoon have strong shadows. Nighttime is also a good time to take dramatic pictures, because street lights create interesting shadows. When taking daytime portraits, use trees and buildings to cast shadows on and around your subject.

In summary, see the light and look for shadows, because they can make the difference between a great shot and a snapshot. And remember, only the shadows know what mystery lies within.

AP photo

A SENSE OF MYSTERY IS CREATED BY THE STRONG SHADOWS AROUND THIS JAGUAR.

Sammon, Rick. Shadows add to mystery. *The Eagle,* Bryan, Texas. April 2, 2000, p. D6.

- Create a personal shorthand; invent spellings.
- During an interview, if it is necessary to get full and accurate information, request that the person slow down.
- Read notes while the information is fresh and add as many details as possible.

Models.   As with other kinds of writing, we model how to write news articles. As a class, we select a topic to explore together. We discuss how to gather the information for the topic and how to organize it. We establish the purpose and focus of the story and measure all parts of the story in relation to that purpose. Leads or introductions get special emphasis as they hook the readers' interests. Without a good lead, the story won't be read. Cappon (1991) advises, "A good lead makes a clear statement of the essential news point and when possible includes a detail that distinguishes the story from others of its kind" (p. 29). We practice writing good leads and presenting the information in a clear manner, adhering to fact rather than opinion. We shy away from "flowery" language that may interfere with readers' understanding of the purpose.

Eighth-grader David used questions to lure readers into his review of O. Henry.

> Do you like stories with ironic endings? Do you like stories that don't gross you out but still are fun to read? Well, then, I think you should read some stories by O. Henry, who puts these qualities into his work.

Eighth-grader Seth used intrigue to interest readers in his article.

> The most dangerous and useful vessel in modern naval warfare is not the giant battle ships, not the aircraft housing carriers but the nuclear submarines that lurk under the Arctic ice cap.

We make sure we have answered all the questions that readers want to know. We use Cappon's (1991) checklist to evaluate our piece:

- Have I said what I meant to say?
- Have I put it as concisely as possible?
- Have I put things as simply as possible?

On the Beat.   Now it is time to send reporters out for their stories. We turn the classroom into a newsroom much as Clark (1987) does in Florida. Daily time in class allows students to gather information and prepare their reports. The classroom buzzes in collaborative effort as students work toward a common goal, a predetermined deadline when all copy must be submitted. Because there is a definite audience, students want their articles to be just right. They meet in organized or impromptu gatherings to help each other produce the best possible stories both in terms of content and presentation. The conventions of mechanics and spelling take on new importance in this real-life setting.

Third-grader Darien wrote this review of a class play. Although she is lacking some of the important details for a full report, she has put herself wholeheartedly into a reaction of the play for her readers.

> "Piggie Pie" was a great play! My favorite part was when Gritch couldn't get her broom to turn on. She made up some lines that weren't in the script, but that was okay because it was still funny and good. My other favorite part was when Melanie (the head of the cow) didn't have the drape all the way up over her shoulder and you could see the pink shirt that she had on under the drape. All of these mistakes made it a good comedy.

Publish.   Publication of the newspapers might take two forms, one paper and one computer. We discuss the advantages and disadvantages of ways to distribute the pa-

---

Sidebar (left margin):

The lead entices, cajoles, entertains, and informs the reader. It may offer a promise of things to come or illuminate the essence of the story.
Clark, 1987

Tack the main theme statement up where you can see it. Let it guide your work. . . . I consider the main theme statement the single most important bit of writing I do on any story.
Blundell, 1988

per: a computer-based newspaper compared to a hand-delivered paper version. Paper newspapers promise wide access to all students at school and an immediate yet lasting presence. Computers versions promise low cost for production and unlimited photo and graphic possibilities, but they require readers to have a computer available and motivation to locate the site of the particular newspaper. For the paper version, students type reports on the computer and then merge the articles for the final document. An editorial student group agrees on placement of stories, artwork, or graphics, and, of course, each student's name is included as a byline. Final copies are assembled and distributed free or sold during lunch in the cafeteria for a nominal charge. Free copies of the newspaper seem to lack importance and are often discarded by students in the school, whereas charging a small fee seems to add significance to the effort.

For computer versions, we use the school web site as our home base. Page layout still receives the same attention, but scanned pictures and computer graphics add a lively dimension to the process. Paper costs and color printing issues are eliminated by using the web site, and an unlimited number of articles can be included. In addition, families with computers can access the student project from home.

While publishing a newspaper is a challenge for busy teachers, it is also a high-interest motivator for reluctant students who enjoy the opportunity to do short bits of writing and see their names as published authors. We agree with Clark (1987) who says, "Students love the collaborative effort of producing a newspaper.

> The reporting process becomes a learning process, an active skill that places a burden of responsibility on the writer. The writer must acquire and communicate knowledge. Clark, 1987

They carry out the roles of reporters, editors, and artists. All their efforts at writing interesting stories about their world reach a crescendo when the stories are prepared for publication, typed, printed, stapled, and distributed" (p. 168).

Assessment.   A brief word about assessment in journalism. Grades are out, but feedback is in. Fellow writers give feedback to each other during the journalistic process, and rubrics are developed to establish standards and guidelines. The basic assessment, however, comes from the reading audience that the news article reaches. As Melton (1985) observes, "Whether good or bad or in-between, as soon as that newspaper is printed, it is seen by others and the writer gets immediate feedback."

EMPHASIZING THE MULTIPLE INTELLIGENCES

Linguistic: Write a feature article for a magazine or newspaper.

Logical/mathematical: Gather and analyze the facts for a research paper or an article.

Spatial: Create ad layouts; build charts to illustrate facts.

Bodily-kinesthetic: Experiment with materials for a research project.

Musical: Research the development of a musical genre.

Interpersonal: Conduct "on the beat" interviews or interviews for a research project.

Intrapersonal: Choose an area of personal interest for reporting.

Naturalist: Observe and take notes on phenomena in nature for a research project.

SUMMARY

Reporting comes in the form of research reports and journalism. While the two kinds of reports are quite different in format, both require attention to factual detail and accuracy. Both use "questioning" techniques to get at the information that is needed for a report. Both require that the writer search for truth and accuracy in reporting. Research reporting often requires long-term projects and experimentation, while journalistic reporting is done quickly. While research reporting gathers data from a number of sources and strives to synthesize that information into a more focused presentation that may evaluate, recommend, or simply report facts, journalistic reporting usually gives the simple who, what, when, where, and why of a situation or event. Research reporting more often deals with academic subject matter, while journalistic reporting is concerned with current events.

Research reports are an essential part of a writing curriculum as they provide young writers with an opportunity to explore personal interests and to share those interests with a variety of audiences. Research report writing provides practice on lifelong problem-solving skills that have real-world applications. A complete, documented research report involves a variety of integrated, complex skills that can be taught and practiced beginning in very early grades. Successful research questions must be relevant to the students' lives to maintain their interest and enthusiasm. Steps in developing a research project closely follow other genres of writing: select a topic, develop categories of information, locate reference materials, take notes, generate original information, write rough drafts, revise, edit, publish, document references, and share. A variety of materials and techniques can enhance novel approaches to acquiring research report skills.

Journalism, on the other hand, carries with it a sense of urgency. Journalistic pieces are short, and the content is general and addresses current topics that are of interest to a broad population. Headlines carry main ideas, with the body of a story filling in the details necessary to communicate the bare bones of the story. Often the why and the how of the story are missing from journalistic writing.

Theory into Practice

1. Think about your own personal experiences with research reports in school. Discuss in small groups how students tend to react to research reports and what steps can be taken to ensure a high level of student interest and enthusiasm.

2. Design a lesson plan for teaching a specific kind of documentation.

3. Design a lesson plan to teach students Internet search skills.

4. Develop a list of research topics that lend themselves to interviews as a part of the data gathering. Design a set of questions to use as prompts for the interviews.

(continued)

5. Develop a list of research topics that lend themselves to experiments or observations as part of the data gathering. Design an experiment that would result in original data for one of the research topics.

6. Synthesize information collected from three or four sets of resource materials.

7. Select a topic of interest and take notes on the topic using the three-column approach to note taking as described on page 351. Discuss with a group of classmates how this method leads to higher order thinking skills.

8. Design a game or hands-on activity that teaches a specific research skill.

9. Discuss in small groups the similarities and differences of journalistic and other kinds of prose.

10. Write a news story about a recent event on the school campus.

11. Create an advertisement that is directed to a specific audience for an everyday product.

12. Write a set of headlines for the front page of a school newspaper.

CHILDREN'S LITERATURE

Brown, Margaret Wise. 1977. *The important book.* New York: HarperCollins Publishers.

Gibbons, Gail. 1997. *Click: A book about cameras and taking pictures.* New York: Little Brown.

———. 1987. *Deadline! From news to newspaper.* New York: Thomas W. Crowell.

———. 1991. *From seed to plant.* New York: Holiday House.

———. 1987. *The pottery place.* San Diego: Harcourt Brace Jovanovich.

———. 1981. *Trucks.* New York: Crowell.

———. 1991. *Whales.* New York: Holiday House.

Levine, Ellen. 1990. . . . *If you lived at the time of Martin Luther King.* New York: Scholastic.

———. 1993. . . . *If your name was changed at Ellis Island.* New York: Scholastic.

Mabery, D. L. 1985. *Tell me about yourself: How to interview anyone, from your friends to famous people.* Minneapolis: Lerner Publications.

McGovern, Ann. 1976. . . . *If you grew up with Abraham Lincoln.* New York: Scholastic.

———. 1992. . . . *If you lived with the Sioux Indians.* New York: Scholastic.

Simon, Seymour. 1979. *Animal fact, animal fable.* New York: Crown Publishers.

BIBLIOGRAPHY

Anderson, Valerie, and Suzanne Hidi. 1988/1989. Teaching students to summarize. *Educational Leadership,* (December/January), 26–28.

Atwell, Nancie. 1998. *In the middle,* 2nd ed. Portsmouth, NH: Heinemann.

Ballenger, Bruce. 1994. Beyond note cards: Negotiating authority in freshman research papers. *English in Texas, 26* (Winter), 23–29.

Bloom, Benjamin S., and David R. Krathwohl. 1984. *Taxonomy of educational objectives, handbook 1: Cognitive domain.* New York: Addison-Wesley.

Blundell, William E. 1988. *The art and craft of feature writing.* New York: Penguin Books.

Calkins, Lucy. 1986. *The art of teaching writing.* Portsmouth, NH: Heinemann.

Cappon, Rene. J. 1991. *Associated Press guide to news writing.* New York: Macmillan.

Checkley, Kathy. 1995. Student-directed learning. *Education Update,* Association for Supervision and Curriculum Development, 37 (December), 1, 4, 5, 8.

Clark, Roy Peter. 1987. *Free to write.* Portsmouth, NH: Heinemann.

Dahl, Karin L., and Nancy Farnan. 1998. *Children's writing: Perspectives from research.* Literature Studies Series. Newark, DE: International Reading Association, and Chicago: National Reading Conference.

Graves, Donald H. 1989. *Investigating nonfiction.* Portsmouth, NH: Heinemann.

International Reading Association and National Association for the Education of Young Children. 1998. Learning to read and write: Developmentally appropriate practices for young children. *Reading Teacher, 52* (October), 193–214.

Hunter, Madeline. 1988. *Teach more—faster!* El Segundo, CA: TIP Publications.

Jensen, Eric. 1998. *Teaching with the brain in mind.* Alexandria, VA: Association for Supervision and Curriculum Development.

Kerr, Anita, Anita H. Makuluni, and Monica Nieves. 2000. The research process: Parents, kids, and teachers as ethnographers. *Primary Voices K–6, 8* (January), 14–23.

Many, Joyce E., Ronald Fyfe, Geoffrey Lewis, and Evelyn Mitchell. 1996. Traversing the topical landscape: Exploring students' self-directed reading-writing-research processes. *Reading Research Quarterly, 31* (January-February-March), 12–35.

Melton, David. 1985. *Written and illustrated by . . .* Kansas City, MO: Landmark Editions.

Polete, Nancy. 1989. Notes from workshop sponsored by Book-Lures, Inc., June 25–28. Lindenwood College, St. Charles, Missouri.

Routman, Regie. 1994. *Invitations: Changing as teachers and learners K–12.* Portsmouth, NH: Heinemann.

Wexo, John Bonnett. 1994. *Zoobooks: Elephants.* San Diego, CA: Wildlife Education, Ltd.

Whitehouse, Ann M. 1994. Research papers without fear: Seven simple steps for reluctant writers. *English in Texas, 26* (Fall), 4–6.

Whitmore, Kathryn F., and Lori A. Norton-Meier. 2000. Reflections. *Primary Voices K–6, 8* (January), 43–46.

Wilson, Jo-Anne R. 1990. Report writing. *Writing Teacher, 3* (February/March), 20–21.

Wolk, Steven, 1995. *Project-based learning: Pursuits with a purpose.* Creating the school of the future: The multiple intelligences series. Alexandria, VA: *Educational Leadership.*

MI Inventory for Adults

Check those statements that apply in each intelligence category. Space has been provided at the end of each intelligence for you to write additional information not specifically referred to in the inventory items.

Linguistic Intelligence

_____ Books are very important to me.
_____ I can hear words in my head before I read, speak, or write them down.
_____ I get more out of listening to the radio or a spoken-word cassette than I do from television or films.
_____ I enjoy word games such as Scrabble, Anagrams, or Password.
_____ I enjoy entertaining myself or others with tongue twisters, nonsense rhymes, or puns.
_____ Other people sometimes have to stop and ask me to explain the meaning of the words I use in my writing and speaking.
_____ English, social studies, and history were easier for me in school than math and science.
_____ When I drive down a freeway, I pay more attention to the words written on billboards than I do to the scenery.
_____ My conversation includes frequent references to things that I've read or heard.
_____ I've written something recently that I was particularly proud of or that earned me recognition from others.
Other linguistic strengths:

Source: "Multiple Intelligences Checklist," from *7 KINDS OF SMART* by Thomas Armstrong, copyright © 1993 by Thomas Armstrong. Used by permission of Plume, a division of Penguin Putnam Inc.

Logical-Mathematical Intelligence

_____ I can easily compute numbers in my head.

_____ Math and/or science were among my favorite subjects in school.

_____ I enjoy playing games or solving brainteasers that require logical thinking.

_____ I like to set up little "what if" experiments (for example, "What if I double the amount of water I give to my rosebush each week?")

_____ My mind searches for patterns, regularities, or logical sequences in things.

_____ I'm interested in new developments in science.

_____ I sometimes think in clear, abstract, wordless, imageless concepts.

_____ I like finding logical flaws in things that people say and do at home and work.

_____ I feel more comfortable when something has been measured, categorized, analyzed, or quantified in some way.

Other logical-mathematical strengths:

Spatial Intelligence

_____ I often see clear visual images when I close my eyes.

_____ I'm sensitive to color.

_____ I frequently use a camera or camcorder to record what I see around me.

_____ I enjoy doing jigsaw puzzles, mazes, and other visual puzzles.

_____ I have vivid dreams at night.

_____ I can generally find my way around unfamiliar territory.

_____ I like to draw or doodle.

_____ Geometry was easier for me than algebra in school.

_____ I can comfortably imagine how something might appear if it were looked down upon from directly above in a bird's-eye view.

_____ I prefer looking at reading material that is heavily illustrated.

Other spatial strengths:

Bodily-Kinesthetic Intelligence

_____ I engage in at least one sport or physical activity on a regular basis.

_____ I find it difficult to sit still for long periods of time.

_____ I like working with my hands at concrete activities such as sewing, weaving, carving, carpentry, or model building.

_____ My best ideas often come to me when I'm out for a long walk or a jog, or when I'm engaged in some other kind of physical activity.

_____ I often like to spend my free time outdoors.

_____ I frequently use hand gestures or other forms of body language when conversing with someone.

_____ I need to touch things in order to learn more about them.

_____ I enjoy daredevil amusement rides or similar thrilling physical experiences.

_____ I would describe myself as well coordinated.

_____ I need to practice a new skill rather than simply reading about it or seeing a video that describes it.

Other bodily-kinesthetic strengths:

Musical Intelligence

_____ I have a pleasant singing voice.

_____ I can tell when a musical note is off key.

_____ I frequently listen to music on radio, records, cassettes, or compact discs.

_____ I play a musical instrument.

_____ My life would be poorer if there were no music in it.

_____ I sometimes catch myself walking down the street with a television jingle or other tune running through my mind.

_____ I can easily keep time to a piece of music with a simple percussion instrument.

_____ I know the tunes to many different songs or musical pieces.

_____ If I hear a musical selection once or twice, I am usually able to sing it back fairly accurately.

_____ I often make tapping sounds or sing little melodies while working, studying, or learning something new.

Other musical strengths:

Interpersonal Intelligence

_____ I'm the sort of person that people come to for advice and counsel at work or in my neighborhood.

_____ I prefer group sports such as badminton, volleyball, or softball to solo sports such as swimming and jogging.

_____ When I have a problem, I'm more likely to seek out another person for help than attempt to work it out on my own.

_____ I have at least three close friends.

_____ I favor social pastimes such as Monopoly or bridge over individual recreations such as video games and solitaire.

_____ I enjoy the challenge of teaching another person, or groups of people, what I know how to do.

_____ I consider myself a leader (or others have called me that).

_____ I feel comfortable in the midst of a crowd.

_____ I like to get involved in social activities connected with my work, church, or community.

_____ I would rather spend my evenings at a lively party than stay at home alone.

Other interpersonal strengths:

Intrapersonal Intelligence

_____ I regularly spend time alone meditating, reflecting, or thinking about important life questions.

_____ I have attended counseling sessions or personal growth seminars to learn more about myself.

_____ I am able to respond to setbacks with resilience.

_____ I have a special hobby or interest that I keep pretty much to myself.

_____ I have some important goals for my life that I think about on a regular basis.

_____ I have a realistic view of my strengths and weaknesses (borne out by feedback from other sources).

_____ I would prefer to spend a weekend alone in a cabin in the woods rather than at a fancy resort with lots of people around.

_____ I consider myself to be strong willed or independent minded.

_____ I keep a personal diary or journal to record the events of my inner life.

_____ I am self-employed or have at least thought seriously about starting my own business.

Other intrapersonal strengths:

My MI strengths are _____

Checklist for Assessing Students' Multiple Intelligences

Keep in mind that this checklist, like the "MI Inventory for Adults" is not a test and should only be used in conjunction with other sources of assessment information when describing students' multiple intelligences.

Name of Student: _____

Linguistic Intelligence

_____ writes better than average for age
_____ spins tall tales or tells jokes and stories
_____ has a good memory for names, places, dates, or trivia
_____ enjoys word games
_____ enjoys reading books
_____ spells words accurately (or, if in preschool, does developmental spelling that is advanced for age.)
_____ appreciates nonsense rhymes, puns, tongue twisters, etc.
_____ enjoys listening to the spoken word (stories, commentary on the radio, talking, books, etc.)
_____ has a good vocabulary for age
_____ communicates to others in a highly verbal way
Other linguistic strengths:

Logical-Mathematical Intelligence

_____ asks a lot of questions about how things work

_____ computes arithmetic problems in his/her head quickly (or if in preschool, math concepts are advanced for age)

_____ enjoys math class (or if in preschool, enjoys counting and doing other things with numbers)

_____ finds math computer games interesting (or if no exposure to computers, enjoys other math or counting games)

_____ enjoys playing chess, checkers, or other strategy games (or if in preschool, board games requiring counting squares)

_____ enjoys working on logic puzzles or brain teasers (or if in preschool, enjoys hearing logical nonsense such as in _Alice's Adventures in Wonderland_)

_____ enjoys putting things in categories or hierarchies

_____ likes to experiment in a way that shows higher order cognitive thinking processes

_____ thinks on a more abstract or conceptual level than peers

_____ has a good sense of cause-effect for age

Other logical-mathematical strengths:

Spatial Intelligence

_____ reports clear visual images

_____ reads maps, charts, and diagrams more easily than text (or if in preschool, enjoys looking at more than text)

_____ daydreams more than peers

_____ enjoys art activities

_____ draws figures that are advanced for age

_____ likes to view movies, slides, or other visual presentations

_____ enjoys doing puzzles, mazes, "Where's Waldo?" or similar visual activities

_____ builds interesting three-dimensional constructions for age (e.g., LEGO buildings)

_____ gets more out of pictures than words while reading

_____ doodles on workbooks, worksheets, or other materials

Other spatial strengths:

Bodily-Kinesthetic Intelligence

_____ excels in one or more sports (or if in preschool, shows physical prowess advanced for age)

_____ moves, twitches, taps, or fidgets while seated for a long time in one spot

_____ cleverly mimics other people's gestures or mannerisms

_____ loves to take things apart and put them back together again

_____ puts his/her hands all over something he/she has just seen

_____ enjoys running, jumping, wrestling, or similar activities (or if older, will show these interests in a more "restrained" way—e.g., punching a friend, running to class, jumping over a chair)

_____ shows skill in a craft (e.g., woodworking, sewing, mechanics) or good fine-motor coordination in other ways

_____ has a dramatic way of expressing herself/himself

_____ reports different physical sensations while thinking or working

_____ enjoys working with clay or other tactile experiences (e.g., fingerpainting)

Other bodily-kinesthetic strengths:

Musical Intelligence

_____ tells you when music sounds off-key or disturbing in some other way

_____ remembers melodies of songs

_____ has a good singing voice

_____ plays a musical instrument or sings in a choir or other group (or if in preschool, enjoys playing percussion instruments and/or singing in a group)

_____ has a rhythmic way of speaking and/or moving

_____ unconsciously hums to himself/herself

_____ taps rhythmically on the table or desk as he/she works

_____ sensitive to environmental noises (e.g., rain on the roof)

_____ responds favorably when a piece of music is put on

_____ sings songs that he/she has learned outside of the classroom

Other musical strengths:

Interpersonal Intelligence

_____ enjoys socializing with peers
_____ seems to be a natural leader
_____ gives advice to friends who have problems
_____ seems to be street-smart
_____ belongs to clubs, committees, or other organizations (or if in preschool, seems to be part of a regular social group)
_____ enjoys informally teaching other kids
_____ likes to play games with other kids
_____ has two or more close friends
_____ others seek out his/her company

Other interpersonal strengths:

Intrapersonal Intelligence

_____ displays a sense of independence or a strong will
_____ has a realistic sense of his/her strengths and weaknesses
_____ does well when left alone to play or study
_____ marches to the beat of a different drummer in his/her style of living and learning
_____ has an interest or hobby that he/she doesn't talk about much
_____ has a good sense of self-direction
_____ prefers working alone to working with others
_____ accurately expresses how he/she is feeling
_____ is able to learn from his/her failures and successes in life
_____ has high self-esteem

Other intrapersonal strengths:

Naturalist Intelligence

_____ spends as much time as possible out-of-doors
_____ collects samples from nature such as rocks, leaves, insects, snakes
_____ has and cares for a pet; shows interest in different kinds of animals
_____ is interested in stars, planets, asteroids, etc.
_____ is able to identify species in nature such as types of trees, plants, shrubs
_____ prefers science class to other classes
_____ chooses subjects from nature for special reports
_____ likes to walk in the rain and squeeze mud between his/her toes
_____ volunteers readily for science projects
_____ chooses to work in the school's plant or butterfly garden

Other naturalist strengths:

_____(name) MI strengths are _____

Adapted from Thomas Armstrong, _Multiple Intelligences in the Classroom_, 1994, Association for Supervision and Curriculum Development, pp. 18–20. The eighth intelligence has been added by the authors to the original inventory.

Sensory Character Illustrations

Sizzling Sound

Fuzzy Feeler

Nose Tickler

Tongue Tingler

Kaleida-Color

Landmann, Rick–Illustrator, Teacher, South Knoll Elementary, College Station, TX.

Ways of Organizing Groups

1. Positioning of participants is important.
   a. Eye contact builds high interaction (e.g., 1 and 5, 2 and 4, or 3 and 6).
   b. Proximity (1 and 2, or 3 and 4) produces low interaction and is usually effective positioning for opponents.

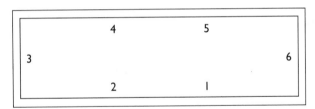

2. Effective positioning for Brainstorming: With groups of two, three, four, or more, positioning should be equal.

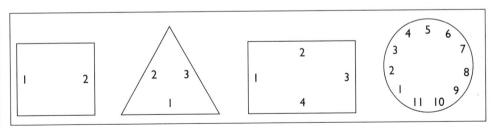

379

3. Positioning for control: The person who is seated in an unequal position is in the control seat.

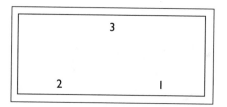

or for centralization—

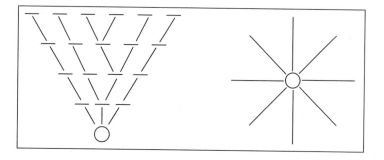

4. Positioning for independent work and for introducing beginning skills: Using cubicles or facing in the same direction so that there is little interaction among students.

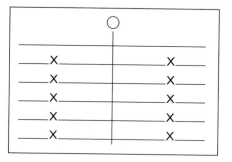

Positioning.   Look at the diagrams below and label them according to their effectiveness for centralization, decentralization, equal group work, or group control. Which person is in control? Which seating would you use to minimize problems between two students?

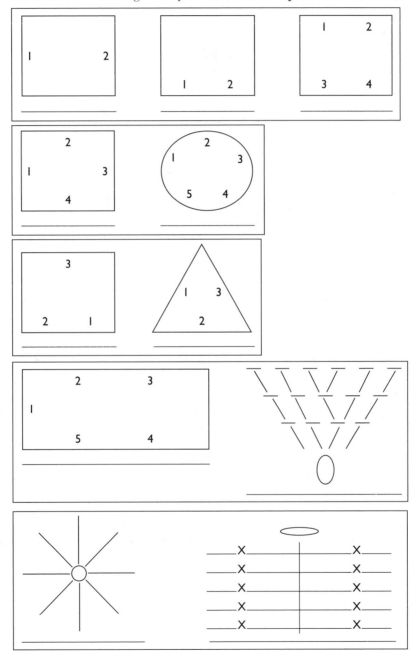

Hughey Class notes Reading 467 (1997)

Suggestions for Lesson Focus

Advertisement

Animal or insect

Art activity

Balloons

Board game

Brainstorming activity

Bulletin board

Cartoon book or strip

Chart

Choral reading

Clay sculpture

Collage

Collection

Computer program

Cooking utensil

Costume

Crossword puzzle

Demonstration

Diorama

Drawing

Dress as a literary character

Family tree

Field trip

Filmstrip

Food samples

Guest speaker

Hats

Hidden picture

Holiday-related activity

Internet site

Letter

Magazine

Magic trick

Magnet

Map

Mobile

Model

Musical instrument

Mystery bag or box

Nature walk

Newspaper article/picture

Painting

Personal experience story

Photograph

Poem

Puppet

Puppet show

Puzzle

Riddle

Role play

Samples of student work

Science experiment

Science specimen

Skit

Slide show

Song

Sporting equipment

Story read aloud

Toy

Treasure Hunt

Unique object

Video clip

Video game

Assessment Definitions

- Assessment: the process or instrument used to measure, quantify and/or describe those aspects of learning or performance related to the attributes.
- Performance Assessment: (1) the process of measuring or describing performance attributes of an individual or a group. (2) a measurement approach in which the individual displays behaviors or produces products that are judged by an assessor according to pre-specified standards or scoring rubrics.
- Criteria: an extended basis upon which performance (e.g., learning, acquisition of a skill) is rated or judged as successful or meritorious. Each criterion falls within a domain covered by the assessment or evaluation system and is defined by elements, indicators, and descriptors. The indicators and descriptors should be stated specifically and in measurable or observable terms. Satisfactory levels of performance on criteria are specified by standards.
- Criterion-referenced assessment uses an instrument developed to estimate how much of the content and how many of the skills covered have been acquired by the individual being assessed. Performance is judged against a set of criteria rather than in comparison to other individuals tested, as with norm-referenced assessment.
- Standard: the level of performance on the criterion being assessed that is considered satisfactory in terms of the purpose of the evaluation. There are three major categories of standards, related to various purposes.

    Developmental: improvement levels to be obtained.

    Minimum: designate the level below which performance is not acceptable.

    Desired Performance: accomplished learning or meritorious performance.
- Evaluation: the systematic process of determining or judging the merit, value, or worth of something (such as a product).
- Scoring Rubric: a set of rules, guidelines, or benchmarks at different levels of performance, or prescribed descriptors for use in quantifying measures or attributes and performance.
- Scoring Scale: a system of ordered values or points at fixed intervals that range from the lowest to the highest possible level of performance on an assessment.
- Consistency [Rater-reliability]: the degree to which a judge or different judges scoring the same test or assessment agree across test takers and/or over time.

- Prompt: (noun) a verbal statement or question that provides a cue, reminder, or inspiration, or that motivates the person being assessed into action. Examples include essay topic questions and follow-up interview questions.
- Portfolio: a purposeful collection of documents concerning an individual's performance (e.g., awards, assessment results) and of products produced by the person. The types of documents to be included may be specified, or the individuals may be free to choose what types of documents to include.

Sager's Writing Scale

Components of Excellence

Vocabulary.   The use of words to express a particular thought or idea

Elaboration.   An abundance of related ideas which flow smoothly from one idea to the next

Organization.   The arrangement of ideas in order

Structure.   The way in which language forms are used to convey meaning

Elaboration

RATE 3: A variety of related ideas help readers see, hear, and feel what the author intends
Details make people, places, and/or events come alive
Details make the reader feel what the characters feel
Details and ideas create an impression on the reader
All ideas are fully developed
Ideas that follow each other easily and naturally

RATE 2: Ideas are clear but fail to make an impression on the reader
Ideas follow each other easily and naturally but lack punch
Some details help readers use their feelings
Some ideas are fully developed
Some details are inadequate or overdone

RATE 1: Much more detail needed to help readers, see, hear, and feel what the author intends
Ideas are sometimes confusing and hard to follow
Details are often inadequate
Important questions are left unanswered
Ideas are jumbled and/or unconnected

Sager, Carol. 2000. Sager Scale: Components of Excellence. 21 Wallis Road, Chestnut Hill, MA.: Sager Educational Enterprises.

Vocabulary

RATE 3: A variety of new and interesting words and comparisons that create vivid impressions
Words help readers use their senses
Synonyms provide variety and interest
Exact words paint vivid pictures
Unusual expressions, word combinations, and comparisons add zest and color to the story

RATE 2: Words are adequately descriptive and exact, but fail to make an impression on the reader
Some words are descriptive and exact
Some use of new and interesting words
Some variety of word choice
Some vivid words and comparisons

RATE 1: A few interesting words, but little variety of word choice.
Vague, general words rather than exact words
Few descriptive or picture words or phrases
Mostly common, overworked words

Organization

RATE 3: Ideas are arranged in a way that is interesting and easy to follow
Events are told in logical order
A main idea ties all story parts together
A beginning that captures interest
A well-defined story problem or happening
Action that builds to a climax
A conclusion that sums up the story
No irrelevant details

RATE 2: A main idea but some story events are poorly arranged
Some events are told out of order
Events are not always arranged in a way that builds interest for what might happen next
A beginning and a conclusion
Action which rambles without reaching a high point
Some irrelevant details

RATE 1: A main idea but many irrelevant events
Many events are out of order
Weak beginning and/or ending
Jumbled arrangement of ideas leads to a sense of disorder

Structure

RATE 3: A variety of sentences that state ideas accurately, effectively, and fluently
Each sentence is complete
Sentences emphasize the author's meaning
A variety of sentences
The story reads aloud with ease

RATE 2: Sentences state ideas accurately, but not always effectively or fluently
Almost all sentences are complete
Some variety of sentences
Sentences sometimes emphasize author's meaning
Parts of the story sound stiff or uneven when read aloud

RATE 1: Ideas are sometimes difficult to understand
Some sentences are complete
Some run-on sentences, omissions, and sentence fragments
Little variety of sentences
Story is often difficult to read aloud

Composition Profile

LEVEL I	COMPOSITION PROFILE		
STUDENT		DATE	TOPIC
SCORE LEVEL CRITERIA			COMMENTS

	SCORE LEVEL	CRITERIA
CONTENT	30-27	EXCELLENT TO VERY GOOD: suits audience/purpose • one idea expressed • specific development • relevant to topic • creative
	26-22	GOOD TO AVERAGE: one idea expressed but some unnecessary information • some specific development • mostly relevant
	21-17	FAIR TO POOR: nonspecific statement • incomplete development • little relevance
	16-13	VERY POOR: not related • no development

Writer's Checklist for Content

_____ 1. Who is going to read your composition? _____

_____ 2. Have you written especially to that person? _____

_____ 3. What kind of writing are you going to do–such as a letter, a composition, or a story?

_____ 4. What topic are you going to tell your reader about? _____

_____ 5. Can you answer the following questions about your topic?

   Who (is it about)? _____

   What (is it about)? _____

   When (did it happen)? _____

   Where (did it happen)? _____

   Why (do you want to tell about it)? _____

   How (did it happen) or

   How (do you know about it)? _____

Hughey, Jane B. 1994

6. Is every sentence in your writing about the topic you named in question #4?

7. Have you included many specific details and examples to explain each part of your topic?

8. Did you use an unusual (or a funny or sad or exciting) way to tell your reader about this subject so that he or she would be interested in reading what you write?

LEVEL I   **COMPOSITION PROFILE**

STUDENT	DATE	TOPIC

SCORE LEVEL   CRITERIA   **COMMENTS**

ORGANIZATION

20-18   EXCELLENT TO VERY GOOD: effective lead/topic sentence • logical order (time-space-importance) • effective connecting/transitional words • conclusion

17-14   GOOD TO AVERAGE: adequate lead/topic sentence • logical but incomplete order • adequate connecting/transitional words • adequate conclusion

13-10   FAIR TO POOR: weak or no lead topic sentence • illogical order • lacks connecting/transitional words • weak or no conclusion

9-7   VERY POOR: no main idea • no organization • not enough to evaluate

---

Writer's Checklist for Organization

1. What idea did you use to begin your composition? _____

2. Does the beginning let your readers know what they will be reading about? _____

3. Is the beginning interesting or unusual? _____

4. What makes it interesting or unusual?

5. Are the ideas in your composition arranged in a logic order? Did you tell things in the order (sequence) that they happened? Did you tell things in the order that they should be done? Did you tell about least important things first and more important things last?

6. Did you use connecting words (such as and, but, or, so, if, because) to combine two or more ideas?

7. Did you use order words (such as first, second, next, last, after that, finally) to help your reader move from one idea to another?

8. If you are writing more than one paragraph, does each paragraph have a topic sentence or a sentence that identifies what the paragraph is about?

9. Did you write an ending to your composition to tell your reader why you wrote what you did (or) to summarize what you wrote? Which sentence(s) make up your conclusion?

LEVEL I	COMPOSITION PROFILE		
STUDENT	DATE		TOPIC

	SCORE LEVEL	CRITERIA	COMMENTS
VOCABULARY	20-18	EXCELLENT TO VERY GOOD: correct word forms • meaning clear • effective word choice/description/figurative language	
	17-14	GOOD TO AVERAGE: mostly correct word forms • meaning not hidden • adequate word choice • some description/figurative language	
	13-10	FAIR TO POOR: many incorrect word forms • slang • meaning unclear • limited word choice • little description/figurative language	
	9-7	VERY POOR: inadequate vocabulary • not enough to evaluate	

Writer's Checklist for Vocabulary

_____ 1. Are the words in your writing in the correct form (such as *there, their, they're*–or–Joe is the *happiest* person I know)?

_____ 2. Are your words clear enough that your reader knows exactly what you mean?

_____ 3. Are your words lively enough to help your reader see, hear, smell, taste, and feel what the subject is about? For example: *A rabbit ran across the road.*

or

A furry, brown jackrabbit bolted across the busy, four-lane highway.

_____ 4. If your writing requires lots of description, did you use similes, metaphors, or personification? For example–
That pillow that is *as fluffy as a cloud.*
Her face *shines like a new penny.*
The *sun walked* across the sky.

_____ 5. If your writing requires giving directions, did you make each direction as clear and understandable as possible? For example–which is clearer?
First, you plug it in.

or

First, plug the large end of the popcorn popper cord into the popper and the small end of the cord into the plug nearest to the kitchen counter.

LEVEL I		COMPOSITION PROFILE	
STUDENT		DATE	TOPIC
SCORE LEVEL	CRITERIA		COMMENTS

LANGUAGE USE

25-22	EXCELLENT TO VERY GOOD: sentence variety • complete sentences • correct verb tenses, word order, agreement (subj-pred, noun-pron), articles, negatives
21-18	GOOD TO AVERAGE: simple sentences • mostly complete sentences • several errors in verb tense (past-present-future), word order, agreement (subj-pred, noun-pron), articles, negatives, run-ons
17-11	FAIR TO POOR: few complete sentences • frequent errors in verb tense, word order, agreement, articles, negatives, run-ons
10-5	VERY POOR: unable to use sentence rules • many sentence errors in verb tense, word order, agreement, articles, negatives, run-ons

MECHANICS

5	EXCELLENT TO VERY GOOD: mastery of spelling, capital letters, punctuation • first sentence indented • neat
4	GOOD TO AVERAGE: occasional errors in spelling, capital letters, commas, periods, question marks, indention
3	FAIR TO POOR: frequent errors in spelling, capital letters, commas, periods, questions • difficult to read
2	VERY POOR: dominated by errors in spelling, capital letters, commas, periods, questions • illegible handwriting

Writer's Checklist for Language Use and Mechanics

_____ 1. Did you use several different kinds of sentences such as simple, compound, complex?

_____ 2. Does each sentence have a subject and a verb?

_____ 3. If the subject is singular, is the verb also singular; if the subject is plural, is the verb also plural?

_____ 4. Did you use the past tense to tell about things that have already happened, the present tense for what is happening now, and the future tense for what will happen later?

_____ 5. Do the *adjectives* come before the nouns or pronouns they describe (such as a *bright* sun or the *fuzzy, black and yellow* worm)?

_____ 6. Do the adverbs follow the verbs in your sentence (such as Juan jumped aside *quickly*. Time passed *slowly*. Sue spoke *smoothly*)?

_____ 7. Did you change the order of subjects and verbs for questions?

_____ 8. Do the pronouns, such as Mary (*she*), John (*he*), people (*they*), money (*it*) agree with the nouns they replace?

_____ 9. Did you use the pronouns (*I, she, he, we*) in the place of subject and predicate adjective words? For example:

      Subject: *Mary* is my choice./*She* is my choice.

      Predicate adjective: This is *Carl.*/ This is *he.*

Did you use the pronouns *me, her, him, us* in the place of object words? For example:

      Please elect *John.*/ Please elect *him.*

_____ 10. When you used negative words, did you use only one negative word in the sentence? For example:

      Frances does *not* have any paper.

_____ 11. Did you end each sentence with a period (.), a question mark (?), or an exclamation mark (!)?

_____ 12. Did you indent each paragraph?

_____ 13. Did you check spelling, punctuation, and capitalization?

_____ 14. Did you write your paper neatly enough that it is easy to read?

For the Preservice Teacher: A Checklist for Persuasive Writing

The following matrix from Ruszkiewicz (1985, p. 175) is adapted to show the modes of writing plotted against the types of appeal available in most persuasive situations. It clarifies the ways in which the other purposes for writing contribute to the building of persuasion. Each number represents one of the questions that follow.

	Description (analysis)	Narration (history)	Classification (theory)	Evaluation (criticism)
Logical appeal	1	2	3	4
Emotional appeal	5	6	7	8
Ethical (Personal) appeal	9	10	11	12

1. What are the facts, statistics, examples, and circumstances that support your case? Which ones might be used against you? How will you anticipate the opposing arguments? How much evidence must you present to clinch your case?
2. What historical circumstances or precedents support your argument? What are the causes of the current situation or problem? What will happen if the situation continues? How would your proposal(s) change the situation?
3. What familiar and accepted values or ideas does your position support? How is your proposal different from others? How is it similar? How are your definitions of key terms different from those of others?
4. How will your argument improve the current situation? How is your proposal superior to other arguments in its use of facts or evidence?
5. What emotions (fear? anger? goodwill?) do you want associated with your argument? What emotions will opponents' arguments stir? How can you look for or avoid these feelings?

393

6. What bad feelings or beliefs have been caused by the current situation? How would your proposal change the unfortunate effects of the current situation? What emotional, physical, social, or economic pains or problems does your proposal address? Who has been affected or hurt by the current situation? What has happened to them? How are your readers likely to feel about the current situation?

7. How would you compare and contrast the consequences of the present situation with the consequences of your proposal? What words, phrases, or concepts in the controversy that you are addressing have powerful meanings? How can you use those terms?

8. How will others benefit personally from your argument? How does it affect their self-interest? How will your proposal make their lives more secure, content, stable, happy, or predictable?

9. What characteristics or experiences can you claim that make it appropriate for you to address the issue? Education? Practical experience? Familiarity with the persons, places, things involved? The trust of all parties involved in the dispute? What proves that you are concerned with the issue? What can you reveal about yourself to suggest your reasonableness? Will your audience believe you?

10. How have you been affected by the current situation? What personal experiences or anecdotes explain your involvement in the dispute, argument, or issue?

11. What knowledge do you have of the current situation and of alternatives to it? What social, political, religious, recreational, or other associations do you have that make you especially fit to address the topic? What other authorities can you introduce who agree with you? How is your personal interest in the situation like or unlike that of your readers?

12. What limitations do you have in presenting the argument? What particular knowledge, skill, or authority do you possess that makes you among the most able to present a case? What authorities who oppose your argument or point of view can you discredit?

Synonyms

Informative = expository and referential

Claim = assertion and proposition

Proof = evidence, data

Refutation = answers to counter arguments; a direct and formal answer to specific objections

Counter arguments = arguments against the claim

Classification = comparison

Evaluation = cause and effect

Ruszkiewicz, John J. 1985. *Well-bound words: A rhetoric*. Dallas, TX: Scott, Foresman.

140 Things to Wonder About

Name _____

Circle the items you enjoy or would like to know more about.

Acting in plays	Camping	Deserts
Airplanes	Car races	Designing costumes
Animals such as _____	Cartoons	Diseases
Antiques	Castles	Doctors
Architecture	Cats	Dogs
Authors	Caves	Dolls
Baseball	Chemistry	Drawing
Basketball	Clouds	Ears
Beaches	Clowns	Endangered species
Bikes	Codes	Eyes
Birds	Coins	Exotic pets
Blood	Collecting dolls	Farms
Boating	Collecting things	Fashion
Body parts	Composers	Fish
Brain	Computers	Fishing
Building electrical things	Contests	Flags
Building models	Cooking	Flowers
Butterflies	Dance	Football

Forests
Gardening
Glass
Going on vacations
Gold
Golf
Government
Growing seeds
Gymnastics
Heart
Heredity
Hospitals
Indians
In-line skating
Insects
Inventions
Jets
Jump rope
Jungles
Keeping a diary
Lawyers
Listening to music
Magazines
Magnets
Making crafts
Maps
Math
Medicine
Model trains

Money
Moon
Mountains
Movies
Mummies
Musical instruments
National parks
Newspapers
Ocean animals
Other countries
Other languages
Painting
Pen pals
Photography
Planes
Planets
Plants
Playing tennis
Playing the piano
Playing the violin
Playing with friends
Pond life
Presidents
Pyramids
Radio
Reading books
Reading comics
Repairing broken things
Rockets

Rocks
Sea shells
Secret codes
Singing
Snakes
Snow skiing
Soccer
Sound
Spiders
Stamps
Stars
States
Sun
Swimming
Television
Tennis
Theme parks
Training animals
Trains
Travel by car
Trees
Veterinarians
Water pollution
Water skiing
Weaving
Writing letters
Writing poems
Writing stories
Zoos

Visual Aids for Research Reports

Illustration	Chart	Scrapbook
Diorama	Poster	Machine or gadget
Video	Photograph	Student-made book
Transparency illustration	Game	Collage
Clay model	Dress in costume	PowerPoint presentation
Mobile	Experiment	
Puppet show	Collection	

Research Paper Procedures

1. Explain the scope of the project, expectations, and the benefits students will receive from a research project. Post these objectives in the classroom.
   - Write compositions about topics using references such as books, magazines, the Internet, surveys, interviews, observation, and experiments.
   - Create computer illustrations using a computer drawing program.
   - Design posters, models, or other supplements regarding the selected topics.
   - Present reports to the class.
2. Give each student a pocketed folder to hold all research materials and define a specific location for the folders to be stored.
3. Display a chart or transparency of the skills they will be using in the research project. (Use the list on p. 347.) Explain that it is understood that they already know many of the skills, but they will practice and get better at them as they work.
4. Display and briefly discuss a list of the steps to complete the project so students know how the project is organized.
   - Select a topic.
   - Develop categories of information about the topic.
   - Do library/Internet search.
   - Collect references.
   - Find information using headings, subheadings, indexes, etc.
   - Conduct interviews, surveys, experiments, or observations if applicable.
   - Take notes from multiple sources.
   - Write introductions and conclusions.
   - Write paragraphs.
   - Revise and edit.
   - Cite references.
   - Publish.
   - Share.

Index